The Role of Data at the Semantics–Pragmatics Interface

Mouton Series in Pragmatics 9

Editor
Istvan Kecskes

De Gruyter Mouton

The Role of Data at the Semantics–Pragmatics Interface

edited by

Enikő Németh T.
Károly Bibok

De Gruyter Mouton

ISBN 978-3-11-024026-9
e-ISBN 978-3-11-024027-6
ISSN 1864-6409

Library of Congress Cataloging-in-Publication Data

The role of data at the semantics–pragmatics interface / ed. by Enikő Németh T., Károly Bibok.
p. cm. – (Mouton series in pragmatics; 9)
Includes bibliographical references and index.
ISBN 978-3-11-024026-9 (hardcover : alk. paper)
1. Pragmatics. 2. Semantics. 3. Data processing. I. Németh T., Enikő, 1964– II. Bibok, Károly.
P99.4.P72R65 2010
401'.43–dc22

2010034288

Bibliographic information published by the Deutsche Nationalbibliothek

The Deutsche Nationalbibliothek lists this publication in the Deutsche Nationalbibliografie; detailed bibliographic data are available in the Internet at http://dnb.d-nb.de.

Printing: Hubert & Co. GmbH & Co. KG, Göttingen
∞ Printed on acid-free paper

Printed in Germany

www.degruyter.com

Contents

Contributors

Károly Bibok is an Associate Professor in the Department of Russian Philology, University of Szeged, Hungary. He is the editor of *Dissertationes Slavicae: Sectio Linguistica* (University of Szeged, Hungary); co-editor of *Pragmatics and the Flexibility of Word Meaning* (Elsevier, 2001) and special issues on Hungarian pragmatics (*Acta Linguistica Hungarica* 2004, 2005). His special area of interest includes lexical pragmatics and the relationship between linguistics of the Russian language and theoretical linguistics.

Reinhard Blutner is a Lecturer in Artificial Intelligence and Cognitive Philosophy at the University of Amsterdam and a *Privatdozent* at the Humboldt-University in Berlin. His main research interests lie in the semantics and pragmatics of natural language, but he has contributed to other fields as well, including the psychology of language and reasoning, neural-symbolic integration, quantum cognition and personality psychology. He has numerous publications, including a monograph on *optimal communication.*

Richard Breheny is a Reader in Linguistics at University College London. His publications cover formal semantics, pragmatics, psycholinguistics and developmental science and can be found in journals such as *Cognition, Journal of Semantics* and *Mind and Language.*

Thorstein Fretheim is Professor Emeritus at Norwegian University of Science and Technology, Department of Language and Communication Studies. He has published widely on a range of topics within linguistic pragmatics, including applications of Relevance Theory. He takes a particular interest in the pragmatic interpretation of features of spoken language.

Michael Haugh is a Senior Lecturer in Linguistics and International English in the School of Languages and Linguistics at Griffith University, Brisbane, Australia. His research interests include face and politeness, intention and implicature, as well as mockery and humor. He is the co-editor of *Face, Communication and Social Interaction* (Equinox, 2009), as well as special issues for *Intercultural Pragmatics* (2008), *Australian Journal of Linguistics* (2009) and *Journal of Pragmatics* (2010).

Napoleon Katsos is a Senior Research Associate at the Research Centre for English and Applied Linguistics, University of Cambridge, England. Together with his colleagues he has published papers in the *Journal of Semantics, Cognition, Language and Cognitive Processes*, and other theoretical linguistic and cognitive science journals. He is interested in semantics and pragmatics from an interdisciplinary perspective, and his work focuses on conversational implicature, quantification and connectives.

Márta Maleczki is an Associate Professor in the Department of General Linguistics, University of Szeged, Hungary. She is the head of the department from 1994. Her main research areas are semantics–pragmatics interface and formal semantics, with special interest in theoretical problems of indefiniteness, as well as descriptive problems of Hungarian constructions with indefinite expressions.

Katalin Nagy C. has completed her coursework in PhD Program in Theoretical Linguistics at the University of Szeged, Hungary. She currently works for the *Research Group for Theoretical Linguistics of the Hungarian Academy of Sciences* and is an Assistant Professor in the Department of Hispanic Studies, University of Szeged, Hungary. She has recently published a paper on the pragmatics of grammaticalization in the *Journal of Historical Pragmatics* (2010).

Attila L. Nemesi received his PhD from the University of Szeged, Hungary in 2008 and teaches at the Institute of Communication and Media Studies, Pázmány Péter Catholic University, Hungary. His previous and current research has focused on pragmatics of figurative language, verbal strategies in impression management and some syntactic variables in present-day Hungarian. His book entitled *The issue of figurative language in pragmatics*, written in Hungarian, was published in 2009.

Enikő Németh T. is an Associate Professor in the Department of General Linguistics, University of Szeged, Hungary. She is the editor of *Pragmatics in 2000* and *Cognition in language use* (IPrA 2001); co-editor of *Pragmatics and the Flexibility of Word Meaning* (Elsevier, 2001) and special issues on Hungarian pragmatics (*Acta Linguistica Hungarica* 2004, 2005). Her interests include intentions in language use, interaction between grammar and pragmatics and implicit arguments in Hungarian.

Zoltán Vecsey is currently a Research Associate of the *Research Group for Theoretical Linguistics of the Hungarian Academy of Sciences.* He received his PhD in 2000 from the Institute of Germanistic Studies, University of Szeged, Hungary. His research interests include formal semantics, pragmatics and non-classical logics. His book, *Names and Objects: On the Semantics of Proper Names* (in Hungarian) has been published in 2007.

Introduction: The semantics–pragmatics interface from linguistic and metalinguistic perspectives

Enikő Németh T. and Károly Bibok

1. A general overview of the book

1.1. The data problem in linguistics

In recent years, several works have been published discussing the nature of linguistic data and evidence in different linguistic theories (cf. e.g. Lehmann 2004; Penke and Rosenbach 2004; Borsley 2005; Kepser and Reis 2005). These works raise the following questions:

(i) What constitutes data and evidence in linguistic theories?
(ii) What kind of relationship is there between data/evidence and hypotheses of linguistic theories?
(iii) What is the relationship between evidence and the rest of data in linguistic theories?

In a state-of-the-art study of the answers given to (i)–(iii), Kertész and Rákosi (2008a) characterize the current approaches through two kinds of duality. The first one is that the approaches, on the one hand, maintain methodological prejudices in connection with the structure and function of data and, on the other hand, attempt to shed fresh light on these methodological issues. The second is that they recognize the necessity for metascientific reflection but do not search for an alternative perspective instead of the untenable standard view of analytic philosophy. Such an emerging picture is confirmed in further papers by Kertész and Rákosi (2008b, c), discussing two more recent debates on (un)grammaticality and data in generative grammar, published in thematic journal issues edited by Stefanowitsch and Gries (2007) as well as Sternefeld (2007). These contributions have both conservative and innovative elements but even the latter are fragmentary and clearly require metatheoretical reflection. Therefore, one can state that the views in the literature could serve as points of departure to continue reflecting consciously on data use in particular object theoretical research, but we should also take it one step further to seek and apply highly new metatheoretical tools.

To join the recent debate on the data problem in linguistics, we propose a volume of 10 original contributions. The chapters of the book, relying on a large range of data sources from a number of languages (English, including its Australian variety, Dutch, German, Norwegian, medieval Spanish, medieval Catalan, French, Hungarian as well as even Hebrew, Amharic, Slave and Zazaki) and applying several current linguistic theories, attempt to address the above mentioned metatheoretical questions from new perspectives. They do this on the basis of various object theoretical investigations situated at the interface of semantics and pragmatics. They concern a broader spectrum of themes than the recent studies on the data problem in pragmatics, namely, explorations by Pons Bordería (2008) and Jucker (2009) on discourse markers and historical speech act research, respectively.

1.2. On conceptions of the semantics–pragmatics interface in the studies of the book

All chapters of the present book are devoted to linguistic phenomena which have their own semantic and pragmatic aspects depending on one approach or another. Nevertheless, some chapters focus on the (formal or model-theoretic) characters of the objects of their studies and are not too specific regarding particular pragmatics theories, indicating only general factors of the use of language like the hearer's viewpoint, communicative skills and background assumptions. A conception of pragmatics as the study of language in use, however, is one of the few points that all pragmatists share (Németh T. and Bibok 2004: 227; Pons Bordería 2008: 1353). These constituents of language use seem to be suitable for purposes of indicating a necessary pragmatic addition even to precise and fine-grained semantic analyses of the definiteness effect and indexicals.

Other chapters concentrate on the pragmatic side, leaving semantic representations somewhat undetailed, or attempt to equally elaborate both sides of the semantics–pragmatics interface. The authors of these chapters use a wide range of pragmatics approaches: Gricean pragmatics, neo-Gricean theories (including optimality theoretic pragmatics), Levinson's theory of presumptive meanings, relevance theory, lexical pragmatics, historical pragmatics, and interactional pragmatics such as conversation analysis. In order to handle a phenomenon under investigation several papers argue in favor of one or another of these approaches, showing that this favored approach also requires some refinements, or even combine approaches in order to get more reliable and plausible solutions.

Because of the different approaches to different object theoretical issues, one cannot expect a common definite delimitation of the two linguistic subfields. This could have been achieved only if, for instance, all chapters had been oriented to the component of the utterance meaning which is called *what is said* and which is explored in the semantic minimalism vs. contextualism debate (cf. Jaszczolt, in press). Incidentally, what can seem to be fairly surprising for those who are accustomed to this opposition is that Wedgwood (2007) states that the whole outlook of Cappelen and Lepore's (2005) semantic minimalism is in essence very similar to that of relevance theory occupying a contextualist stance. In particular, the notion of minimal semantic content is largely equivalent in function to the notion of encoded meaning in relevance theory, but the former is propositional while the latter is not.

Consequently, despite their different topics and approaches, all of the issues the contributions to the present volume attempt to solve do not only belong to semantics or pragmatics but are also situated at the interface of semantics and pragmatics. Instead of a unified view of the dividing line between semantics and pragmatics, a number of points of contact and transitions are inevitably emerging when one deals with issues of meaning. While the papers in the present volume have significant contributions to various problems currently discussed in the semantics and pragmatics literature, an overall view of an intensive interaction emerges not only between semantics and pragmatics, but also between the whole of grammar and pragmatics. The authors repeatedly demonstrate and exemplify that pragmatics and semantics, including what is called formal semantics, necessarily complement each other in a broader conception of contextualism.

1.3. Methodological findings in the volume

We think that our volume presents achievements which go beyond those of current approaches to linguistic data because the contributions contain conscious reflections on the data problems listed in (i)–(iii) above. They are made through actual object theoretical research which involves and contrasts two linguistic subfields of their own techniques and methods of data gathering and handling. At the same time, some papers apply specific metatheoretical tools such as Lehmann's (2004) functional view of data, Steen's (2007) categorization of data, and Kertész and Rákosi's (2008d) plausible reasoning.

As to question (i) in 1.1, i.e. "What constitutes data and evidence in linguistic theories?", it is clear from the chapters of the book that the common distinction of sources of data collection, i.e. introspection, corpora and experiments (cf. Jucker 2009), is not sufficient. Contributors to this volume rely on a truly wide range of data sources, including, among other things, various types of experiments (cf. minimal pair experiments, thought experiments, pragmatically relevant psycholinguistic experiments), linguists' intuitions and intuitions of speakers who are not trained as linguists, written and spoken, monolingual and parallel corpora, dictionaries, previous results and analyses as well as comparisons with other languages. A special kind of data deserves peculiar attention, which has not been considered to any great extent thus far by those working at the semantics–pragmatics interface. Namely, there is a way in which one can access speaker intuitions through an analysis of the co-construction of syntactic units by two or more speakers in conversation when participants themselves orient to the interactional achievement of meanings. Beside such a pluralism of data, two statements have to be stressed. First, despite the existence of a widely propagated assumption that linguistic intuition is not reliable, but data gained from corpora are, no general claim can be made that a type of data is inherently better than or supersedes another type of data. However, in cases that are too fine-grained for introspection, experimental approaches to issues in the semantic–pragmatic interface may offer critical data. Second, there are limits to all forms of data, including even corpora. Corpora have to be used with an at least as great caution as intuitive data, and the limitations of corpus studies are clearly evident, for instance, in studies of the relative contribution of decoded and inferred conceptual material to the content of an utterance or in cases when examples from corpora can be interpreted in pragmatically or contextually different ways. Therefore, the various types of data have to be considered necessarily complementary. In fact, they are intertwined in a complex way. Taking, again, corpora and corpus studies as an example, one should bear in mind the fact that the data contained in linguistic corpora are data which are presumably judged well-formed by some speakers, so corpora also originate from intuition. What is more, the thorough analysis of contexts (real and constructed) seems to be of primary importance in all fields of pragmatics where one wants to find data concerning inferred meanings, i.e. meanings that are not present explicitly in linguistic forms.

In connection with question (ii) in 1.1, i.e. "What kind of relationship is there between data/evidence and hypotheses of linguistic theories?", the authors agree that data can have several functions in linguistic theorizing:

they can simultaneously be regarded both as the empirical basis for theory formation and as tools of testing in various phases of theory formation, and data have a special function in reporting on research as well. At the same time, data are theory- and problem-dependent. The relationship between theory and data is cyclic and even prismatic (in Kertész and Rákosi's (2008e) sense), and it is always the actual aims, problems and argumentation processes that determine what "things" can serve as data in what functions.

With regard to (iii) in 1.1, i.e. "What is the relationship between evidence and the rest of data in linguistic theories?", and also to (i), the metatheoretical relevance of the well-known type–token distinction is put forward. Ignorance, false judgments or deficient analyses of data as separate tokens cannot destroy a theory. What counts as evidence (i.e. a crucial empirical basis) for theory construction is only a set, or a type, of data considered in their totality.

2. Chapter by chapter synopsis of the book

The 10 papers constitute chapters of the book divided into three parts according to their object theoretical topics as follows: *Issues of referentiality, Scalar implicatures* and *Pragmatic ways from words to constructions and utterances.* Let us briefly overview the individual chapters in this arrangement.

2.1. Issues of referentiality

The subject of *Márta Maleczki's* paper is the definiteness effect in existential sentences. An existential construction exhibits the definiteness restriction if the DP called *pivot* and denoting the entities whose existence is claimed cannot be a proper name or a pronoun, or if the affected DP contains a common noun, it cannot be preceded by definite or universal determiners in neutral contexts. Maleczki compares three previous studies on definiteness effect in English existential sentences (Keenan 2003; Beaver, Francez and Levinson 2006; Ward and Birner 1995) from both theoretical and methodology points of view. These studies differ from each other in types of data and methods of data analysis as well as in the linguistic nature of the proposed explanations of the discussed phenomenon. They use data drawn from corpora or intuition, apply statistical methods, context analysis or the minimal pair method contrasting well-formed and ill-formed strings. Their conclusions are formulated in traditional syntactic/semantic, formal semantic or pragmatic terms. To evaluate these different types of research, the author handles three apparent dichotomies, namely, rules vs. tendencies, semantics vs. pragmatics, data bases vs. intuitions, and establishes four options concerning the nature of the rules which generate human language structures. The option fitting the results gained by the thorough analysis of the three approaches and of the relevant English data, to which some important data from Hungarian are also added, is the following: the sharp semantic property characterizing the allowed DPs in the existential constructions is the determiners' $cons_2$ property (conservative on the second argument, also called anticonservativity property). The exemptions from the restriction due to this semantic property are fake data in that they do not belong to the proper existential constructions. This is supported from three sides: the semantic condition put on the interpretation of the existential sentences, the productivity criterion, and the Hungarian counterparts show equally well that the *there*-sentences with a definite pivot are not *par excellence* existential sentences. However, the occurrence of the definite DPs in *there*-sentences is systematic enough to be explained by pragmatic considerations: the referent of the pivot can be interpreted as *hearer-new* (at least in some respects).

In the next chapter, *Zoltán Vecsey* questions one aspect of Kaplan's (1989a, b) model-theoretic view of indexicals. According to the double index theory, indexicals are evaluated with respect to two different collections of parameters: contexts and circumstances. First, contexts determine the content of characters. Second, for each structured proposition, circumstances yield truth values or truth conditions. While there is a general consensus that modal, tense and locational operators can explicitly shift the circumstantial parameters of the evaluation process, opinions differ on the possibility of context-shift. Kaplan claims that operators which would modify the contextual behavior of characters do not exist in natural languages such as English. Others maintain that context-shifting operators exist in some languages, perhaps even in English (Schlenker 2003a, b; Anand and Nevis 2004; Nishiguchi 2007). Sidelle (1991), Bezuidenhout (2003) and Recanati (2004) are of the persuasion that contexts can be shifted without the presence of any operators. In their view, there are specific communicative settings in which contexts shift freely. After a brief account of operator theoretic strategy, the author discusses the following communicative situations as the putative cases of free context-shifting: recorded messages, post-it notes, fiction, historical present and free indirect discourse. Then he raises an important question concerning the relationship between the theory and the data at his disposal: what is the theoretical status of the conclusions one draws from this restricted range of empirical data? He sees the methodological significance of empirical data not as derived from their epistemological properties, but as a consequence of their argumentative function. Viewed from this perspective, what is of primary importance is that once a research object has become part of an argumentative chain, then it should be acknowledged, at least provisionally, as datum. Therefore, he elaborates an alternative critical approach which does not depend directly on empirical counterexamples, but which is able to predict and explain the existence of such counterexamples. Vecsey reshapes the Kaplanian framework at the most general level supplying the contextual parameters with a particular pragmatic component. Non-Kaplanian contexts, where shifting is possible, come "in double packages". The first context is *c*, in which an indexical expression occurs. The second context is *c**, which functions as a proxy of *c*. The role of the proxy context *c** is to provide one or more parameters for the indexical. Not any context can function as a proxy for *c*. There must be a passage between *c* and *c** and this passage is pragmatic. The possibility of the passage depends on contextual factors such as general communicative skills, conventionalized norms of reasoning, conventionalized norms of using syntactic structures, implicature patterns, and background assumptions.

In the third paper of Part I, *Thorstein Fretheim* challenges the dominant view that demonstratives, both complex and simplex ones, are directly referential terms that pick out an individual (Kaplan 1989a, b; Recanati 1993). Like relevance theorists (Sperber and Wilson 1995; Carston 2002), who hold that semantic representations resulting from decoding of linguistic material are notoriously gappy compared to the proposition the speaker intends to express, he believes that the speaker's intention plays a crucial role in the (context-sensitive) interpretation of any utterance, including the interpretation of the reference of any demonstratives that an utterance may contain. In both English and Norwegian, grammatically definite demonstratives are semantically underspecified with regard to whether the reference is to an object or to a type of entity defined in terms of certain properties. However, his exploration of a parallel corpus revealed that there is a much greater tolerance for definite demonstratives that are intended to represent a *type* of entity in English, while in Norwegian there is a tendency to avoid use of definite demonstratives under such circumstances, preferring the indefinite demonstrative determiner corresponding to English *such* when the referent is a type of thing. The author strengthens his generalizations about systematic differences in usage between English and Norwegian pointing to some other linguistic phenomenon in English and Norwegian that might be related to the noted tendency, namely, the speaker's pronominal options in equative sentences and in left-dislocation structures where the pronoun and the dislocated phrase are traditionally taken to be coreferential. Data gained from informants suggests a causal relationship between a speaker's choice between a personal and a non-personal pronominal copy of a left-dislocated noun phrase and the ontological value of the entity so represented. An intraclausal, non-personal pronoun encodes the information that the entity represented is a property instantiated by tokens, while a personal pronoun is consistent with either a token-level or a type-level interpretation, depending on whatever input guides the pragmatic process of reference resolution for the addressee. This applies equally to English and Norwegian, but it was shown that a few combinations of formally indefinite, left-dislocated noun phrases and non-personal pronominal copies are grammatical in Norwegian but ungrammatical in English, and, conversely, it was shown that personal pronouns that agree in number with the dislocated phrase have a wider range of distribution in English than in Norwegian. As to the methodological point of this chapter, Fretheim combines the use of diverse research methods in an attempt to improve our knowledge of what demonstratives do for us. Intuitive judgments are central throughout the paper. In addition, however, he deploys results from the study of a bilateral translation corpus of English and Norwegian texts, while being aware of the limitations of strict corpus studies which are probably nowhere more evident than in studies of the relative contribution of decoded and inferred conceptual material to the content of an utterance. In another section of his paper he tests his own intuitions against those of a small group of native informants who were not trained as linguists.

2.2. Scalar implicatures and beyond

Napoleon Katsos and *Richard Breheny* experimentally investigate the semantics and pragmatics of scalar expressions and numerals, a much-discussed issue on the semantics–pragmatics interface. The authors first summarize the theoretical positions. According to what they call *implicature* accounts (e.g. Atlas and Levinson 1981; Horn 1989; Levinson 2000; Chierchia 2004), disjunctions, quantifiers and numerals are all scalar expressions, and the upper-bound interpretation is derived from a lower-bound semantic meaning by means of a scalar implicature. According to what they call *anti-implicature* accounts (e.g. Sadock 1984; Carston 1998; Guerts 1998; Breheny 2008), the upper-bound 'exactly N' interpretation of numerals does not depend on a scalar implicature, and it is the lower-bound one 'at least N' that must be derived from it in some way. With respect to the issue of numerals and scalars, the authors show how various theories ascribe different aspects of meaning to semantics and pragmatics. They also document the emerging consensus that theories about this issue as well as others on the semantics–pragmatics interface should be psycholinguistically as well as linguistically valid. The authors then go on to review the extensive recent literature on empirical investigations of the meaning of numerals and scalars. The authors themselves also present one offline and one online self-paced reading experiment, both of which investigate the processing of logical scales (existential/universal quantifier; disjunction/conjunction) and numerals by adult native speakers of English. These experiments have indicated that adults are sensitive to contextually induced expectations of informativeness when interpreting both logical scales and numerals offline, but the online task shows that the time-course of these interpretations is different. These results cannot be attributed to the extra-linguistic factors suggested as explanations of the pattern of acquisition. However, in attempting to adduce these data as evidence for or against particular theories, the authors run into conceptual difficulties. They see, in many cases, the question of whether data disconfirm a theory depends crucially on whether they make additional assumptions that are not necessarily integral to that theory. In particular, they discuss how the introduction of contrast sets might give rise to processing costs, and how costly the processes are by which senses are derived from one another. In doing so, the authors uncover issues on which many theories are non-committal but which could greatly influence the interpretation of the relevant experimental findings. The authors conclude that deriving straightforward empirically testable predictions from anti-implicatures accounts requires further conceptual and experimental work. Nevertheless, Katsos and Breheny have already demonstrated how experimental approaches to issues in the semantic–pragmatic interface may corroborate intuitions and offer critical data in cases that are too fine-grained for introspection.

In the second paper of Part II, *Reinhard Blutner* aims to argue for optimality theory as a conceptual framework that can help to close the gap between experimental pragmatics and neo-Gricean theories of pragmatics. The author demonstrates that optimality theoretic pragmatics has the potential to account both for the synchronic and the diachronic perspective in pragmatics. In discussing modern pragmatic theories, he shows that relevance theory and Levinson's theory of presumptive meanings account for the resolution of the conflict between effort minimization and effect maximization in different ways. The crux of both approaches can be translated in optimality theoretic pragmatics by making use of particular linking constraints. This translation makes the advantage of both approaches visible: both conform to the incremental, online character of natural language interpretation. Another important issue in Blutner's article concerns the proper interpretation of bidirectional optimality theory, either as a psychologically realistic online mechanism or as an offline phenomenon that relates to the fossilization of certain pragmatic effects. Accepting that both possibilities are real to some extent, the impending question is the distribution of labor between online processes (calculating optimal outcomes) and offline processing (fossilization processes). This question is asked for standard scalar implicatures, as well as for other types of pragmatic inferences such as semantic broadening, certain types of manner-implicatures and inferences in connection with pronoun/reflexives interpretation. Concerning the role of data at the semantics–pragmatics interface, the author discusses recent work on the phenomenon of delayed comprehension and delayed production. This is a phenomenon which was not discussed within experimental pragmatics so far, though the importance of the problem was clearly recognized within optimality theoretic pragmatics. A careful discussion of this problem is required in order to differentiate between the two central models: the online processing model and the fossilization account. Although the author argues in favor of the fossilization view, he also emphasizes that it requires further experimentation in order to reach a definite decision. The essence of the fossilization view concerns the observation that the borderline between semantics and pragmatics is transparent in at least one direction: tendencies predicted from pragmatics (conversational implicatures) may become *frozen* in the semantic part of knowledge representation. This directly affects the nature of the semantics–pragmatics interface. The author demonstrates that psycholinguistic data are required to test hypotheses about the underlying cognitive architecture. It is pointed out that the concept of fossilization can help to understand the idea of naturalization and (cultural) embodiment in the context of natural language interpretation.

2.3. Pragmatic ways from words to constructions and utterances

In her historical pragmatics paper *Katalin Nagy C.* intends to reconstruct a part of the history of the Catalan "*anar* 'go' + Infinitive" construction as well as discuss methodological issues concerning the role of context and data that can be used for assigning meanings in historical texts. In order to determine what conceptual content the medieval Catalan construction has, the author relies on the following: (i) a similar construction, namely, the Spanish "*ir (a)* 'go (to)' + Infinitive", whose history is better known and fits the universal tendency of the development of GO verbs in the languages of the world, (ii) other medieval Catalan and Spanish constructions with infinitive (henceforth: Inf) which show similarity in their functions and contexts, and (iii) linguistic clues which help assign meanings to historical occurrences. Semantic change in grammaticalization develops at the semantics–pragmatics interface inasmuch as originally pragmatic contents become semantic contents. The cognitive basis of semantic change in grammaticalization can be identified only if one manages to find reliable linguistic clues and contextual factors which can reveal something about the meaning of lexical units or constructions. The author emphasizes that data originating from the investigation of occurrences in their broad contexts can override previous claims about meanings, formulated on the basis of the exclusive analysis of narrow contexts. The results throw a new light on the history of the Catalan GO-construction. The origin of the Catalan GO-past can be related to the salience of the meaning component 'intention', suggesting that Detges's (2004) inchoative aspect hypothesis is mistaken. Historical occurrences of the Catalan "*anar* 'go' + Inf" refer to completed actions and not to their beginning. "GO + Inf" in medieval texts describes the action as a whole, and the occurrences are often followed by a description of the consequences. The use of this periphrasis suggests that the action had been completely performed and that the performance of the action was more dynamic and intentional than usually. This hypothesis seems to be confirmed by the conceptual affinity of "GO + Inf" and "THINK OF + Inf", both of which contrast with "BEGIN TO/OF + Inf". In order to reveal the cognitive background of semantic change as well as the cognitive development of lexical units undergoing grammaticalization, the author relies on a detailed contextual analysis for which she clarifies the conception of context. On the basis of Diewald's (2002) and Heine's (2002) works, she makes a distinction between two types of contexts: those which offer ambiguity and thus trigger grammaticalization, and those which exclude the original lexical meaning of the grammaticalizing item and thus serve as evidence of previous semantic change. Katalin Nagy C. further distinguishes between narrow context, which she defines grammatically, and broad context, which does not only refer to textual circumstances but also includes encyclopedic information and inferences in context. Applying a thorough contextual analysis as well as taking into consideration linguistic clues the author demonstrates that semantic change in grammaticalization can only be investigated at the semantics–pragmatics interface. From a methodological point of view, the careful contextual analysis has proved to be the most important methodological device in historical pragmatics.

Károly Bibok sets forth in detail a lexical-constructional account of syntactic alternations that eliminates the shortcomings of the lexical (Levin and Rappaport Hovav 1995; Rappaport Hovav and Levin 1998) and constructional (Pustejovsky 1995; Goldberg 1995) conceptions but exploits their advantages. In the creation of his theory Bibok relies upon the analysis of three syntactically alternating Hungarian verb classes. They include manner-of-motion verbs, verbs of sound emission, and the class of spatial position verbs, which has not been investigated yet in the Hungarian literature at all. As to the application of the lexical-constructional theory to these Hungarian verb classes, the results include the following: (i) underspecified meaning representations predict constructional meanings appearing due to syntactic alternations, (ii) the lack of alternations can be explained by specific meanings that verbs have due to idiosyncratic lexicalizations, and (iii) the analysis of some verb classes handled separately in previous research can be generalized further: they can be collectively referred to as one group through a meaning scheme (template) containing the shared properties of the verb classes. Establishing lexical-semantic representations of alternating and non-alternating verbs in a study at the interface of lexical semantics and lexical pragmatics, Bibok contributes to the elaboration of the lexicon in which, on the one hand, a number of words do not encode full-fledged concepts and, on the other hand, encyclopedic information or information concerning the use of language can be fixed with lexical entries. Such a lexicon is considered a promising starting point for lexical pragmatics. Reflecting consciously on methodological aspects of his research, the author uses the well-known type–token distinction for metatheoretical purposes. Ignorance or false judgments and analyses of data as separate tokens do not destroy a theory. Data considered a set or a type count as evidence (i.e. as a crucial empirical basis). Moreover, theory and data are interconnected. Not only does a theory depend on a type (or several types) of data, but what counts as data is theory-dependent as well (Lehmann 2004). On the basis of his paper, Bibok can state that the lexical-constructional approach to syntactic alternations determines what kind of examples one should take into consideration as data for what kind of word meanings, and how meanings in (explanatory) dictionaries can be used as data. Since examples from real use of language are always bound to corresponding situations, they cannot be related immediately to underspecified meanings. Finally, Bibok offers his theory to be compared to a larger body of theoretical and practical issues to reach a more *plausible* theory in Kertész and Rákosi's (2008d) sense, according to which an argumentation can be held to be a plausible one if it does not lead to a thoroughgoing certainty but has some degree of it. From the theoretical point of view, the author demonstrates the extendibility of the lexical-constructional approach into lexical pragmatics, which holds that as words have underspecified, although semantically and pragmatically enriched meaning representations, they reach their full meanings in corresponding contexts through considerable pragmatic inference. From the practical point of view, the plausibility of the lexical-constructional approach converted into a full-fledged lexical pragmatic theory can be increased by considering that human and machine disambiguation or semantic annotation of words in corpora cannot be solved on the basis of the traditional dictionary model of meaning representation but what is offered by Fellbaum et al. (2005: 37) is that "Annotators and automatic systems need the option to select either a cluster of specific senses or a single, broader sense, where specific meaning nuances are contained but hidden".

Enikő Németh T. examines in a complex approach what lexical-semantic factors influence the occurrence of verbs with implicit direct object arguments in Hungarian and how they do that. The verbs studied in her paper have rich lexical-semantic representations which constrain the arguments by means of selection restrictions, lexical stereotypes, prototypical structures of the categories very strongly. The lexical-semantic representation of these verbs can be interpreted in two ways: either the actions or events designated by the verbs are in the focus of attention or the object as well. This twofold interpretability makes it possible for these verbs to occur with implicit direct objects. If only the actions or events are in the focus of attention, the direct object arguments can be left lexically unrealized. The information whether the arguments at stake are of a particular type or a token of a type or a unique token involved in the selection restrictions can also be accessed as background information, and the omitted objects can be identified with this background information. However, in many cases information stored in the lexical-semantic representations of the verbs is not sufficient in itself to license the verbs' occurrence with implicit direct object arguments. One has to take into consideration morphosyntactic (indefinite/definite conjugations) and pragmatic (contextual) factors to a necessary extent as well assuming an interaction between the lexical-semantic representations of the verbs, grammar and pragmatics. On the basis of these results the author has two conclusions. First, the use and identification of implicit direct objects should be conceived as a phenomenon at the semantics–pragmatics interface or even at the grammar–pragmatics interface. Second, the division of labor between lexical semantics, grammar and pragmatics in the use and interpretation of implicit arguments is under the control of an economy balance, i.e. they are guided by the cognitive principle of relevance (Sperber and Wilson 1995: 260). Reflecting on the methodological aspects of her research, the author discusses the views on functions and sources of data (Lehmann 2004; Kertész and Rákosi 2008e) and demonstrates what relationships and overlaps can be assumed between these functions and sources without any inconsistency. The use of data from various direct sources in her research eliminates the disadvantages of the individual particular sources. The author also highlights what problems arise if one applies raw data in pragmatically oriented research, and how these problems can be solved by applying thought experiments in the research and presentation of the research as well. Finally, she also concludes that her particular practice in the research supports Kertész and Rákosi's (2008e) approach according to which the relationship between the theory and data should be considered cyclic and prismatic, and it is always the actual aims, problems and argumentation processes of the research or the presentation of the research that determine what can serve as data in what functions in a particular phase of the research and the presentation of the research.

In his chapter *Michael Haugh* explores the way in which speaker intuitions about what is said can be elucidated through an analysis of a particular interactional phenomenon, the co-construction of syntactic units by two or more speakers in conversation. Previous work has generally treated co-construction as a syntactic phenomenon with little analysis of semantic and pragmatic contributions to the joint production of utterances. Data from interactions illustrating both the semantic and pragmatic underpinnings of co-constructions are thus examined by the author. First, it is demonstrated that co-construction in fact lies at the syntax–semantics–pragmatics intersection and should be analyzed as such. Second, it is argued that co-constructions actually constitute evidence of participants orienting to (speaker) meanings rather than just syntax in interaction. It is suggested that such an analysis may support a conceptualization of what is said that is more empirically robust than previous approaches to eliciting speaker intuitions. And, third, it is argued in Haugh's paper that while interactional data and analysis may seem primarily of interest to researchers in pragmatics, there is greater potential than generally accepted for semantics to be informed by such research and methods. Admitting interactional data and analyses into debates at the interface of semantics–pragmatics may seem, at first glance, unnecessary or even counter-productive, particularly for those embedded in a more formal perspective on semantics. The author argues that introducing this kind of interactional perspective allows us to more readily access speaker intuitions and thereby bring to the fore tacit conceptions that underlie the semantics–pragmatics distinction (Szabó 2005: 7–8). Yet while interactional data and analysis can arguably provide an alternative perspective on the semantics–pragmatics interface, which complements existing approaches, there are two possible stumbling blocks to integrating such approaches. First, it should not be automatically assumed that findings from one methodological approach are necessarily commensurable with findings arising from another methodology. As the underlying epistemological and ontological commitments of interactional methodologies such as conversation analysis and those of philosophical pragmatics and formal semantics are arguably different, the implications of admitting interactional data and analysis into debates about the semantics–pragmatics interface need to be first carefully considered. A second potential stumbling block is that it is often very time-consuming to identify phenomena of interest in natural data, which results in the use of fairly small datasets in most interactional analyses. As Jucker (2009) points out, small datasets lack generalizability as they cannot generally yield statistically convincing results. In Haugh's analysis of co-constructions, for instance, while a strong trend emerges for participants to orient to co-constructions as what the first speaker has said, the relatively small set of examples examined means no generalizable conclusions can yet be reached. Therefore, the author suggests that interactional data and analysis in addition to intuited or experimental data, if used judiciously, provide a complementary perspective on the semantics–pragmatics interface.

The chapter by *Attila L. Nemesi* draws attention to the essential role of hyperbole in everyday communication. The author evaluates critically the developments of previous research on hyperbole with special regard to data collection and interpretation and offers some new insights from his own analyses of spoken Hungarian. Although the use of the term has a long tradition from ancient rhetoric, and the pervasive frequency of hyperbole is well documented (Kreuz et al. 1996), very little interest has been devoted to its pragmatic nature. To answer the question of what aspects of hyperbole or, in a wider perspective, figurative language are semantically specified and which aspects come about through pragmatic processes, first, the author considers it necessary to separate the issue of production and interpretation, and, second, to adopt a tenable view on the correct division of labor between semantics and pragmatics in the explanation of the two issues. In accordance with these aims, the author concludes that hyperbole disproportionately augments or reduces some element of the real state of affairs, emphasizing the role of the semantic (quantitative and evaluative) scales along which reality is distorted by the exaggeration. As for the production of hyperbole, the in-depth analysis of its lexico-grammatical repertoire and the relevant quantitative/evaluative scales is delegated to semantics, while the job of pragmatics is outlined as involving the study of its occurrence, interaction with other forms of figurative language, discourse goals, reflexive markers, typical genres, and so on. As for the interpretation, the author defends the "conventional meaning first" approach in a Gricean (1975) spirit against Gibbs's (1994, 2002) direct access hypothesis and relevance theory, but he borrows the idea of weak implicatures from Sperber and Wilson (1990, 1995). In the methodological part of his research, Nemesi estimates the data collection methods of several scholars who addressed the question of hyperbole production or reception building upon Steen's (2007) categorization. Though the author prefers observable verbal data taken from spoken corpora, he has no reason to question the usefulness of imagined and meta data for particular purposes. However, he emphasizes that human beings are not good enough at describing certain aspects of their own language production and cognitive processes, and written scenarios prepared for eliciting verbal or meta data might be too artificial to evoke reliable answers from the subjects. Corpus-based studies have fine prospects within pragmatics not only in research on hyperbole production (individual, cross-cultural, cross-gender differences, overstatement-prone genres such as stand-up comedy, talk show and everyday storytelling, metapragmatic awareness, etc.) but in research on its interpretation (children's understanding of hyperbole, style attribution and other perlocutionary effects, listeners' responses to overstatement, etc.) as well. In summary, the author considers the validity of data as depending on the aim of research.

3. Conclusions

On the basis of the results of 10 contributions to the present volume it can be concluded that, first, by consciously reflecting on methodological aspects of data use and applying metatheoretical tools, the object theoretical research at the semantics–pragmatics interface is more reliable, systematic and has more explanatory power than without it. Second, the questions concerning data and evidence can really be answered only through particular object theoretical investigations such as those reported on in the chapters of this volume.

Acknowledgements

The publication of the present volume was partly supported by the Research Group for Theoretical Linguistics of the Hungarian Academy of Sciences at the Universities of Debrecen, Pécs and Szeged, Hungary.

All papers in the present volume were peer-refereed. We wish to thank the reviewers for their willingness to read papers in short time and their helpful, valuable comments and remarks. So, we are grateful to Barbara Abbott (Michigan State University, USA), Anne Bezuidenhout (University of South Carolina, USA), Noel Burton-Roberts (Newcastle University, UK), Gabriele Diewald (Leibniz Universität, Germany), Susan M. Fitzmaurice (University of Sheffield, UK), Daniel García Velasco (University of Oviedo, Spain), Raymond Gibbs (University of California, USA), Robert M. Harnish (University of Arizona, USA), Seizi Iwata (Osaka City University, Japan), Matthew Juge (Texas Sate University, USA), Ferenc Kiefer (Research Institute for Linguistics, Hungary), Manfred Kienpointner (University of Innsbruck, Austria), Mikhail Kissine (University of Brussels, Belgium), Neal Norrick (University of Saarland, Germany), Roger Kreuz (University of Memphis, USA), Theeraporn Ratitamkul (Chulalongkorn University, Thailand) and Yves Roberge (University of Toronto, Canada).

Of course, our greatest thanks are due to the authors of this book for their exemplary and ready cooperation to observe the deadlines and to comply with the reviewers' and editors' requests for necessary revisions regarding both the content and the format of their papers.

We are also grateful for the assistance we got from the linguistic team of the Mouton de Gruyter Publishers. We thank MSP series editor Istvan Kecskes for his encouragement and providing all the necessary information concerning the content as well as the format for putting a volume together in the Mouton Series in Pragmatics.

Finally, the editors would like to say a big thank you to each other for their patience, support and efforts to edit this book and to continue their harmonious family life even during the stressful moments of the editing process.

References

Anand, Pranav and Andrew Nevins
2004 Shifty operators in changing contexts. In *Proceedings of the 14th Conference on Semantics and Linguistic Theory*, Kazuha Watanabe and Robert B. Young (eds.), 20–37. Ithaca, NY: Cornell Linguistic Publications.

Atlas, Jay David and Stephen C. Levinson
1981 It-clefts, informativeness and Logical Form. In *Radical Pragmatics*, Peter Cole (ed.), 1–61. New York: Academic Press.
Beaver, David, Itamar Francez and Dmitry Levinson
2006 Bad subject: (Non-)canonicality and NP distribution in existentials. In *Proceedings of Semantics and Linguistic Theory XV*, Effi Georgala and Jonathan Howell (eds.), 19–43. Ithaca, NY: Cornell Linguistic Publications.
Bezuidenhout, Anne
2003 Context-shifting. Invited paper read at conference on philosophy of language, Yale University, November 7–9. http://www.cas.sc.edu/ling/faculty/bezuidenhout/Context_shifting.pdf.
Borsley, Robert D. (ed.)
2005 *Lingua* 115 (11), Special issue on Data in theoretical linguistics.
Breheny, Richard
2008 A new look at the semantics and pragmatics of numerically quantified noun phrases. *Journal of Semantics* 25: 93–140.
Cappelen, Herman and Ernie Lepore
2005 *Insensitive Semantics: A Defense of Semantic Minimalism and Speech Act Pluralism.* Oxford: Blackwell.
Carston, Robyn
1998 Informativeness, relevance and scalar implicature. In *Relevance Theory: Applications and Implications*, Robyn Carston and Seiji Uchida (eds.), 179–236. Amsterdam: Benjamins.
Carston, Robyn
2002 *Thoughts and Utterances: The Pragmatics of Explicit Communication.* Oxford: Blackwell.
Chierchia, Gennaro
2004 Scalar implicatures, polarity phenomena, and the syntax/pragmatics interface. In *Structures and Beyond: The Cartography of Syntactic Structures, Vol. 3 (Oxford Studies in Comparative Syntax)*, Adriana Belletti (ed.), 39–103. Oxford: Oxford University Press.
Detges, Ulrich
2004 How cognitive is grammaticalization? The history of the Catalan *perfet perifràstic*. In *Up and Down the Cline: The Nature of Grammaticalization*, Olga Fischer, Muriel Norde and Harry Perridon (eds.), 211–227. Amsterdam: Benjamins.
Diewald, Gabriele
2002 A model for relevant types of contexts in grammaticalization. In *New Reflections on Grammaticalization,* Ilse Wischer and Gabriele Diewald (eds.), 103–120. Amsterdam: Benjamins.

Fellbaum, Christiane, Lauren Delfs, Susanne Wolff and Martha Palmer
2005 Word meaning in dictionaries, corpora and the speaker's mind. In *Meaningful Texts: The Extraction of Semantic Information from Monolingual and Multilingual Corpora*, Geoff Barnbrook, Pernilla Danielsson and Michaela Mahlberg (eds.), 31–38. London: Continuum.

Geurts, Bart
1998 Scalars. In *Lexikalische Semantik aus kognitiver Sicht*, Petra Ludewig and Bart Geurts (eds.), 95–118. Tübingen: Gunter Narr.

Gibbs Jr., Raymond W.
1994 *The Poetics of Mind: Figurative Thought, Language, and Understanding.* Cambridge: Cambridge University Press.

Gibbs Jr., Raymond W.
2002 A new look at literal meaning in understanding what is said and implicated. *Journal of Pragmatics* 34: 457–486.

Goldberg, Adele E.
1995 *Constructions: A Construction Grammar Approach to Argument Structure.* Chicago, IL: University Press of Chicago.

Grice, H. Paul
1975 Logic and conversation. In *Syntax and Semantics, Vol. 3: Speech Acts*, Peter Cole and Jerry L. Morgan (eds.), 41–58. New York: Academic Press.

Heine, Bernd
2002 On the role of context in grammaticalization. In *New Reflections on Grammaticalization,* Ilse Wischer and Gabriele Diewald (eds.), 83–102. Amsterdam: Benjamins.

Horn, Laurence R.
1989 *A Natural History of Negation.* Chicago, IL: University of Chicago Press.

Jaszczolt, Katarzyna M.
in press Semantics and pragmatics: The boundary issue. In *Semantics: An International Handbook of Natural Language Meaning*, Klaus von Heusinger, Paul Portner and Claudia Maienborn (eds.). Berlin/New York: Mouton de Gruyter.

Jucker, Andreas
2009 Speech act research between armchair, field and laboratory: The case of compliments. *Journal of Pragmatics* 41: 1611–1635.

Kaplan, David
1989a Demonstratives. In *Themes from Kaplan*, Joseph Almog, John Perry and Howard Wettstein (eds.), 481–563. Oxford: Oxford University Press.

Kaplan, David
1989b Afterthoughts. In *Themes from Kaplan*, Joseph Almog, John Perry and Howard Wettstein (eds.), 565–614. Oxford: Oxford University Press.

Keenan, Edward
2003 The definiteness effect: Semantics or pragmatics? *Natural Language Semantics* 11: 187–216.
Kepser, Stephan and Marga Reis (eds.)
2005 *Linguistic Evidence: Empirical, Theoretical and Computational Perspectives*. Berlin/New York: Mouton de Gruyter.
Kertész, András and Csilla Rákosi
2008a Daten und Evidenz in linguistischen Theorien: Ein Forschungsüberblick. In *New Approaches to Linguistic Evidence: Pilot Studies*, András Kertész and Csilla Rákosi (eds.), 21–60. Frankfurt am Main: Lang.
Kertész, András and Csilla Rákosi
2008b Conservatism vs. innovation in the (un)grammaticality debate. In *New Approaches to Linguistic Evidence: Pilot Studies*, András Kertész and Csilla Rákosi (eds.), 61–84. Frankfurt am Main: Lang.
Kertész, András and Csilla Rákosi
2008c Conservatism vs. innovation in the debate on data in generative grammar. In *New Approaches to Linguistic Evidence: Pilot Studies*, András Kertész and Csilla Rákosi (eds.), 85–108. Frankfurt am Main: Lang.
Kertész, András and Csilla Rákosi
2008d Introduction: The problem of data and evidence in theoretical linguistics. In *New Approaches to Linguistic Evidence: Pilot Studies*, András Kertész and Csilla Rákosi (eds.), 9–18. Frankfurt am Main: Lang.
Kertész, András and Csilla Rákosi
2008e Megjegyzések a nyelvészeti adatok és evidencia problémájáról folyó vita jelenlegi állásához [Remarks on the current discussion on linguistic data and evidence]. *Magyar Nyelv* 104: 274–286, 385–402.
Kreuz, Roger J., Richard M. Roberts, Brenda K. Johnson and Eugenie L. Bertus
1996 Figurative language occurrence and co-occurrence in contemporary literature. In *Empirical Approaches to Literature and Aesthetics*, Roger J. Kreuz and Mary Sue MacNealy (eds.), 83–97. Norwood, NJ: Ablex.
Lehmann, Christian
2004 Data in linguistics. *The Linguistic Review* 21: 175–210.
Levin, Beth and Malka Rappaport Hovav
1995 *Unaccusativity: At the Syntax–Lexical Semantics Interface.* Cambridge, MA: MIT Press.
Levinson, Stephen C.
2000 *Presumptive Meanings: The Theory of Generalized Conversational Implicature.* Cambridge, MA: MIT Press.

Németh T., Enikő and Károly Bibok
2004 Guest editors' note. *Acta Linguistica Hungarica* 51: 227–229.
Nishiguchi, Sumiyo
2007 Covert emotive modality is a monster. In *Lecture Notes in Artificial Intelligence: New Frontiers in Artificial Intelligence. Joint JSAI 2006 Workshop Post-Proceedings*, Takashi Washio, Ken Satoh, Hideaki Takeda and Akihiro Inokuchi (eds.), 191–204. Berlin: Springer.
Penke, Martina and Anette Rosenbach (eds.)
2007 *What Counts as Evidence in Linguistics. The Case of Innateness.* (Benjamins Current Topics 7.) Amsterdam: Benjamins.
Pons Bordería, Salvador (eds.)
2008 *Journal of Pragmatics* 40(8), Special issue on Empirical data and pragmatic theory.
Pustejovsky, James
1995 *The Generative Lexicon.* Cambridge, MA: MIT Press.
Rappaport Hovav, Malka and Beth Levin
1998 Building verb meanings. In *The Projection of Arguments: Lexical and Compositional Factors*, Miriam Butt and Wilhelm Geuder (eds.), 97–134. Stanford: Center for the Study of Language and Information.
Recanati, François
1993 *Direct Reference: From Language to Thought.* Oxford: Blackwell.
Recanati, François
2004 Indexicality and context-shift. Paper presented at the *Workshop on Indexicals, Speech Acts, and Logophors.* Harvard University, 20 November 2004.
Sadock, Jerry
1984 Whither radical pragmatics? In *Meaning, Form and Use in Context*, Deborah Schiffrin (ed.), 139–149. Washington D.C.: Georgetown University Press.
Schlenker, Philippe
2003a Indexicality, logophoricity, and plural pronouns. In *Research in Afroasiatic Grammar II (Selected Papers from the Fifth Conference on Afroasiatic Languages, Paris, 2000)*, Jacqueline Lecarme (ed.), 409–428. Amsterdam: Benjamins.
Schlenker, Philippe
2003b A plea for monsters. *Linguistics and Philosophy* 26: 29–120.
Sidelle, Alan
1991 The answering machine paradox. *Canadian Journal of Philosophy* 81: 525–539.
Sperber, Dan and Deirdre Wilson
1990 Rhetoric and relevance. In *The Ends of Rhetoric: History, Theory, Practice*, John Bender and David Wellbery (eds.), 140–156. Stanford, CA: Stanford University Press.

Sperber, Dan and Deirdre Wilson
1995 *Relevance: Communication and Cognition.* 2nd edition with a Postface. Oxford: Blackwell.
Steen, Gerard J.
2007 *Finding Metaphor in Grammar and Usage: A Methodological Analysis of Theory and Research.* Amsterdam: Benjamins.
Stefanowitsch, Anatol and Stefan Th. Gries (eds.)
2007 *Corpus Linguistics and Linguistic Theory* 3(1), Special issue on Grammar without grammaticality.
Sternefeld, Wolfgang (ed.)
2007 *Theoretical Linguistics* 33(3), Special issue on Data in generative linguistics.
Szabó, Zoltán Gendler
2005 Introduction. In *Semantics versus Pragmatics*, Zoltán Gendler Szabó (ed.), 1–14. Oxford: Clarendon Press.
Ward, Gregory and Betty Birner
1995 Definiteness and the English existential. *Language* 71: 722–742.
Wedgwood, Daniel
2007 Shared assumptions: Semantic minimalism and Relevance Theory. *Journal of Linguistics* 43: 647–681.

Part One
Issues of referentiality

On the definiteness effect in existential sentences: Data and theories

Márta Maleczki

1. Introduction

In this paper, a well-studied but still problematic linguistic phenomenon, the definiteness effect is investigated by comparing some theoretically and methodologically very different approaches. All of the three papers which are the focus of the present article intend to restrict their data set to existential sentences. Beaver, Francez and Levinson (2006) use a large corpus, apply statistical methods, and their conclusion is formulated in traditional syntactic/semantic terms. Keenan (2003) offers a strictly formalized semantic definition, argues explicitly against pragmatic approaches, and uses the well-known minimal pair method contrasting well-formed and ill-formed strings (data and judgments are supposedly his own). Ward and Birner (1995) argue for a pragmatic explanation, their data are drawn from a corpus, but no statistical methods are used in the analysis; instead, the relevant examples of the corpus are examined in their contexts, applying traditional common sense reasoning.

1.1. Background

Since Milsark's frequently cited dissertation (Milsark 1974) it has been observed in several languages that there are certain linguistic environments where a class of nominal expressions is not tolerated. Since definite DPs are among the unaccepted nominal phrases, the phenomenon was dubbed *the definiteness effect.* Existential constructions exhibit this restriction most strikingly (although they are not the only construction where the definiteness effect occurs in English either):

(1) *There are some/two/at least four mighty grass snakes (in the moor).*

(2) **There are the/every/both mighty grass snakes (in the moor).*

During the last few decades several enterprises have been published with the purpose of giving an explanation to the contrast between (1) and (2), relying on syntactic, semantic, or pragmatic means, or through some mixture of these; see a recent survey given by Frances (2009). In this paper syntactic considerations play only a marginal role, and the semantic and pragmatic explanations examined here will be reconciled. The main motivations and aims leading to matching the semantic and pragmatic accounts are summarized in the next subsection.

1.2. The aims and structure of the paper

In this paper the definiteness effect is examined only in *there*-sentences, concentrating on the results of the three papers mentioned at the outset. The motivation is methodological in nature, which is reflected in the main questions addressed, which are the following:

Does the definiteness effect originate in pragmatics or semantics? Does the origin of the data on the basis of which the different investigations are carried out influence the final conclusions of the research? What types of linguistic constraints exist, and what type does the definiteness effect belong to?

The answers are roughly the following. The conclusions of the research papers examined here are strongly influenced by the range and origin of the data they are drawn from. A data set that is larger than the set of *par excellence* existential sentences necessarily evokes conclusions according to which the constraints the definiteness effect arises from are tendency-like (Beaver, Francez and Levinson 2006) or pragmatic (Ward and Birner 1995). However, if the data set contains only existential sentences proper then the definiteness effect can be grasped by pure semantic notions in a strictly formalized way (see Keenan 2003). Thus, it seems crucial to find an independent characterization of the set of existential sentences. Accordingly, the structure of the paper is as follows.

The paper consists of three main parts: in the first one (section 2) the characteristic properties of existential sentences and the definiteness effect are presented, and the main tenets of the three papers mentioned above are studied. In the second part (section 3) some basic theoretical questions are addressed, and the analyses presented in the first part are discussed accordingly. In section 4 I return to linguistics proper, and on the basis of the results of section 3 I formulate some conclusions on the nature of the definiteness effect and the range of data exhibiting it. These conclusions are supported by some interesting data from Hungarian. In section 5 the results are summarized and their connection with the theoretical considerations of section 3 is discussed.

2. Existential sentences and the definiteness effect

In the first two subsections of section 2 the main properties of existential sentences and the problems of the definiteness effect are outlined. The presentation of these very puzzling phenomena is extremely sketchy, since the only purpose of 2.1 and 2.2 is to make understandable the remaining three subsections, where three theoretically and methodologically different solutions to the problem of the definiteness effect are discussed. The aim of the whole section 2 is to provide a basis for the methodological investigations and theoretical conclusions of sections 3 and 4.

2.1. What is an existential sentence?

(3) *There are some mighty grass snakes (in the moor).*

McNally (2008) identifies existential sentences on the basis of two main criteria. One is syntactic, and the other is semantic in nature. The syntactic criterion says simply that the existential construction is *special* in all languages as opposed to the structure that can be called the *canonical* sentence form in the given language. The particulars in which existential constructions deviate from the canonical linguistic forms vary according to the syntactic peculiarities of the languages. For instance, in languages where expletives exist, in existential constructions an expletive phrase is present (*there* in English). The expletive can possibly collapse with a locative phrase, whose occurrence is also characteristic of these constructions. If there is a verb at all in the existential constructions of a given language, it is usually the copula, or some other "bleached" predicate expressing the mere (non-)existence of the entities named by the nominal expression.

The nominal phrase denoting the entities whose existence is claimed (or negated) is called *pivot*; any linguistic material other than the pivot or the existential verb (adverbial or prepositional phrases, relative clauses, etc.) is named *coda*. This is the *terminology* used when describing this type of sentences, but existential sentences do not have either a syntactic or a semantic analysis that can be called "standard" or "widely agreed upon" in the case of English *there*-sentences either (see a thorough survey of existing analyses in Frances 2009). Crosslinguistic investigations show that existential constructions occur in great varieties in the languages of the world; as Francez (2009: 2) notes, "pivots are the only elements that are both universally present and obligatory in the clause across languages". This fact explains why their shared syntactic characterization cannot be more specific than merely stating that they are non-canonical constructions.

The non-canonical property of existential clauses can be manifested simply in a special array of the constituents of sentences, as in the case of Hungarian, which is a discourse configurational language where word order is not constrained by syntactic categories or roles. Hungarian existential sentences differ from their canonical counterparts only in the order of the words (accompanied possibly by some minor differences in their intonation patterns). The sentence in (4) is the Hungarian counterpart of (3), while (5), which seems merely a permutational variant of (4), is not existential:[1]

(4) *Van néhány hatalmas sikló a mocsárban.*
is some mighty grass.snake.NOM the moor.INE
'There are some mighty grass snakes in the moor.'

(5) *Néhány hatalmas sikló a mocsárban van.*
some mighty grass.snake.NOM the moor.INE is
'Some mighty grass snakes are in the moor.'

The intonational difference is that in (5) a partial[2] eradicating stress occurs on the first syllable of *mocsárban* 'in the moor', while this type of stress is present on *van* 'is' in (4). The consequence of these minor changes is that (5) becomes a canonical locative sentence, which is shown plainly by the fact that the locative phrase *a mocsárban* 'in the moor' cannot be omitted from it.

According to the view McNally (2008) accepts, there is another, semantic criterion if a sentence is to be qualified as existential. It says that an existential statement never implies anything beyond the mere existence of the entities named by the pivot nominal. Thus, (6) is not existential (example (1c) in McNally 2008):

---

1 The glosses are not intended to capture all morphological properties of Hungarian words but indicate the necessary ones for the present purposes. The abbreviations used in the glosses throughout this paper are the following: 3PL = third person plural, 3SG = third person singular, INE = inessive, NOM = nominative, PL = plural, SUB = sublative, SUP = superessive.

2 An "eradicating stress" always appears on the first syllable of a word, similarly to the normal word stress pattern in Hungarian. Its distinguishing property is that a really eradicating stress makes the regular word initial stresses entirely disappear from **all** the following items. I call the stress present in (4) and (5) partial because its eradicating power extends only to the immediately following lexical item.

(6) *There stood in the corner an empty coat rack and umbrella stand.*

The comment on the sentence in (6) is that "thanks to the verb, it entails something more than mere existence or presence" (McNally 2008). Evidently, this criterion rules out all *there*-sentences containing a non-existential main verb, and perhaps this was the main motivation for introducing it. However, the formulation itself refers to a general semantic property, which will be considered here a basic semantic requirement about the entities the pivot nominal may denote in existential sentences. Since this criterion will be the basis of one of the main claims of the paper, for the purposes of further references it is formulated as in (7):

(7) Semantic criterion: the statement an existential sentence expresses cannot entail anything other of the entities the pivot nominal denotes than their mere existence or presence somewhere.

This semantic feature should be present simultaneously with the special syntactic form in order to set apart existential *there*-sentences from the canonical sentences expressing existence on the one hand (see (8)) and from the canonical locative sentences on the other (see (9)):

(8) *Carnivorous flowers exist.*

(9) *Some carnivorous flowers are there/in the moor.*

In sum, if either the non-canonical structure condition or the semantic condition formulated in (7) is not met, the sentence is not existential. From this it follows that a construction could be labeled as existential neither on the basis of its syntactic form alone, nor merely on the basis of its truth conditions. This point should be emphasized because it has crucial consequences for evaluating the generalizations and conclusions based on the data gained by different methods (see section 3).

Returning to the Hungarian examples above, the semantic criterion is fulfilled by (4) exactly as in (3), but not by (5), where the nominal phrase tends to have a strong (partitive) interpretation. Thus, the claim that the existential structure is expressed in Hungarian by a special ordering of the words is supported from the semantic side as well. See some more Hungarian data in section 4.2.

2.2. The definiteness effect

A construction exhibits the definiteness restriction if a DP[3] (the pivot in the existential sentences) cannot be a proper name or a pronoun, or if the affected DP contains a common noun, it cannot be preceded by definite or universal determiners in neutral contexts (that is, in contexts where nothing else is implied than the mere stating of the semantic content of the sentence).

Investigations concerning the definiteness effect have been extended to several languages. When this phenomenon is examined in any language, at least the following three basic questions emerge. First, is there a phenomenon in the given language which can be labeled as definiteness effect? Second, if the first question is answered affirmatively, in what linguistic environments (in what structures, or with words having what properties) does the definiteness effect arise? Third, what are the relevant properties which a DP must have in order to be admitted in the contexts showing the definiteness effect? The last question is frequently put inversely: what are the distinguishing properties which exclude a DP from the contexts where the restriction holds?

The two formulations of the last question raise a methodological issue as well: is the direct characterization (that is, trying to find the properties which allow a DP to occur in a context exhibiting the definiteness restriction) superior to the indirect characterization (which seeks the distinguishing properties of the DPs banned from the relevant contexts), or vice versa? Putting it more succinctly, are the allowed DPs to be characterized, or the disallowed ones?

Another methodological and theoretical issue is what type of characterization is needed in order to grasp the very essence of the definiteness effect: syntactic, semantic or pragmatic (or what combination of these)? Arguments could be gained from the coverage of data, or from theoretical considerations. From the point of view of the data the winning type of characterization would be the one that could account for the most linguistic data, supplied with an explanation for the allowed and the disallowed expressions equally well. From the theoretical point of view the best solution is the most

---

[3] There is no agreement among semanticists concerning the categorial notation of the pivot. For instance, Beaver, Francez and Levinson (2006) refer to it as NP, while Keenan (2003) as DP. Although this may well reflect something of the authors' theoretical attitude, it is a question not bearing upon the present issue. Thus, the DP-notation will be preferred here without argumentation, except where the viewpoint of authors are discussed who use the NP-notation.

simple and coherent one, which is based on a (possibly well-formalizable) model assuring a strong explanatory force.

In this paper, three very different articles are examined and compared with respect to their data bases, methods, theoretical bases, and results. One is a formal semantic approach applying a direct semantic characterization (Keenan 2003). The other is a pragmatic investigation, which uses non-standard existential sentences (with definite pivot DPs) as data base, but results in a direct characterization (Ward and Birner 1995). The third paper characterizes along the same set of traditional syntactic, semantic and pragmatic properties both the types of DPs which are excluded from the contexts showing the definiteness restriction and which are allowed in these contexts; data are gained from a large corpus by statistical methods (Beaver, Francez and Levinson 2006).

The next three subsections present the basic ideas and results of these papers; the methodological problems are discussed in section 3.

2.3. A formal semantic approach to the definiteness effect (Keenan 2003)

Keenan (2003) argues that the definiteness effect can be grasped by a formally well-definable semantic property of the determiners. He follows Barwise and Cooper (1981) in working in the framework of the theory of generalized quantifiers, but while Barwise and Cooper (1981) identified the property of the determiners which allows them to occur in existential sentences as intersectivity, Keenan (2003) argues that the relevant property is the $cons_2$ (conservative on the second argument, also called anticonservativity) property. In order to make clear the intuitive content of this formal property, recall that in the theory of generalized quantifiers the meaning of determiners (D) is regarded as a relation between two sets: the first set (A) is given by the denotation of the common noun occurring in the subject DP,[4] while the second set (B) is given by the denotation of the nucleus, that is, by the main verbal phrase of the sentence. The $cons_2$ property of determiners is characterized by Keenan (2003) in the following way:

(10) $DAB \Leftrightarrow D(A \cap B)B$

[4] Of course, there are more exact semantic definitions for including the cases when there is no determiner in the DP; however, these details will be omitted here. This is justified because Keenan (2003) does not consider the cases of bare nouns at all (neither the case when the DP consists of proper names, nor when it contains bare common nouns).

This equivalence can be exemplified by (11) and (12) below (*iff* is a shorthand notation for *if and only if* in the following):

(11) *Some boys snore* is true iff *some* ***snoring boys*** *snore* is true.

(12) *At least two but at most twenty cats are on the roof* is true iff *at least two but at most twenty* ***cats on the roof*** *are on the roof.*

The $cons_2$ property determines a subcategorization on the category of determiners, since it is not a universal property of them:

(13) It is not the case that
Every boy snores is true iff *Every* ***snoring boy*** *snores* is true.

(14) It is not the case that
Both cats are on the roof is true iff *Both* ***cats on the roof*** *are on the roof* is true.

The determiner *every* is clearly not $cons_2$, since, taking the example (13), *every snoring boy snores* is a tautology, while *every boy snores* is a contingent (either true or false) proposition. The same can be said about the sentences in (14); in addition, the conditions under which *both*-phrases may be interpreted in them are not the same: in the first *cat*-sentence in (14) there are only two (relevant) cats in the universe (of discourse), while in the second sentence the set of cats may contain more elements on condition that they are not on the roof, since the presupposition is induced by the expression *both cats on the roof.*

On the basis of the $cons_2$ property it is possible to give an account not only of the fact that DPs with symmetric determiners are allowed as pivots in existential sentences (see Barwise and Cooper 1981[5]), but also of the allowed appearance of DPs consisting of *only/just/mostly* + bare common noun (noun phrase with no determiner) in existential constructions:

(15) *There were only naughty kids in the movie.*

(16) *There are just /mostly freshmen in that course.*
(example (38) in Keenan 2003)

Intuitively, Keenan's (2003) $cons_2$ property means that the denotation of the whole VP (which in existential constructions is given by the coda, or, if

---

5 The relevant equivalences are DAB ⇔ DBA ⇔ D(A∩B)(A∩B) with the notation (10) is given above.

there is no coda, by the predicate *exist*) may be relevant for the truth conditions of the statement. This is clearly so in the case of examples (15), (16) above: for instance, in order to check the truth conditions of (15), we must take into account each person in the movie, because even one of them who is not a naughty kid falsifies the statement. This type of determiner would be excluded by the intersectivity property by which only the intersection of the denotation of the N constituent of the DP and the denotation of the VP plays a role in the truth conditions of existential statements (see footnote 5). On the other hand, the $cons_2$ property does not differ from the intersectivity with respect to the truth-conditionally relevant part of the denotation of the N, because it says that the relevant part of the set denoted by the noun is part of the VP-denotation as well (see the definition in (10)).

In sum, Keenan (2003) claims that $cons_2$ is the property on the basis of which the determiners which are allowed in existential constructions can be characterized exhaustively: this property is characteristic to all determiners called existential or weak in the literature, and none of the strong or truly quantificational determiners are $cons_2$; moreover, he proves that the Boolean compounds of existential determiners are also $cons_2$ (see (12)). Thus, all DPs with a $cons_2$ determiner are allowed in existential constructions, while determiners which do not exhibit this property do not occur in *productive* existential sentences. A more detailed discussion of Keenan's (2003) productivity criterion for existential sentences will be presented in section 3.2.2.

2.4. A pragmatic explanation based on corpus data (Ward and Birner 1995)

Ward and Birner (1995) presented the first corpus-based analysis of the definiteness effect. It is methodologically interesting that they sought examples that (seemingly) hurt the definiteness effect. The investigations of the paper are based on approximately 100 existential *there*-sentences where some kind of definite determiner occurs in the pivot nominal phrase. These sentences are drawn from a NASA document containing more than a million words of transcribed oral data.

The conclusion of the authors is not that there is no definiteness restriction in existential sentences. On the contrary, they claim that the data can be explained in a coherent way if the definiteness restriction is derived from the incompatibility between some cognitive properties belonging to the pivot in existential sentences on the one hand and to the definite NPs on the other. This means that the licensing condition for the pivot NP is not indefiniteness or weakness or some similar semantic property; moreover, some pragmatic properties offered in the literature are also excluded by counterexamples. Ward and Birner (1995) argue that the licensing condition is that the referent of the pivot NP should be interpreted as *hearer-new* (at least in some respects). If this requirement is fulfilled in some way or other, the pivot NP can have even a definite (strong) determiner.

A typical example is when a definite NP is used in an existential sentence in order to remind the hearer of something which is presupposed to be known by her. In that case it is not the entities the NP denotes that are new to the hearer but their occurrence in the given context (example (8b) from Ward and Birner 1995: 726).

(17) *I'd love to get away from my job, the kids, the bills... I've thought of chucking it all and going to Hawaii. But there are the kids to consider.*

Another type of data is, for instance, when the definite NP is licensed in an existential sentence because the discourse referents it introduces are new token instances of a known type (Ward and Birner 1995: 732, example 21):

(18) *There was the usual crowd at the beach today.*

Ward and Birner (1995) show that possibly different continuations of this sentence prove that the NP *the usual crowd* refer both to a type (hearer-old, so it licenses the definite article) and a token (hearer-new, so it licenses the *there*-construction). All in all, five types of instantiations of the dual cognitive status of the definite NPs in pivot position are identified (new token instances of a known type, hearer-old entities treated as hearer-new, hearer-old entities newly instantiating a variable, hearer-new entities with uniquely identifying descriptions, false definites). From our point of view the essence of the paper is that the definiteness effect is explained on pragmatic (more exactly, cognitive) grounds: noun phrases occurring as pivots always introduce hearer-new referents, even if they contain a definite determiner.

The method Ward and Birner (1995) apply is that after extracting the deviant data (*there*-sentences with definite pivot NPs) from the corpus, they are subjected to a careful analysis in their contexts. The analyses are carried out by the usual common sense reasoning, relying on data from the linguistic literature and constructed examples as well. More on this method will be said in section 3.2.3.

2.5. Comparative statistical analyses of large corpora (Beaver, Francez and Levinson 2006)

As the previous sections made it clear, existential sentences are similar to (canonical) locative sentences in some respects: both types of sentences can be built up from a (nominative) DP, a copula, and a locative PP. The most striking and distinguishing property of English existential constructions is that they always contain an expletive *there*-element at the very beginning of the sentence; this is followed by the copula, and the pivot nominal is always placed after the copula (whereas this DP must occur before the copula in canonical sentences). The locative (full) PP appears on the right periphery of both constructions; it is obligatorily present in canonical locative sentences, while its occurrence is optional in the existential constructions. This short reminder to these differences is important because these properties become crucial when algorithms are sought which are intended to set apart the two constructions. For Beaver, Francez and Levinson (2006) it is necessary to apply syntactic criteria in order to find existential constructions because they apply statistical analyses to enormous corpora. Although a purely syntactic basis for identifying existential constructions seems insufficient if we accept the characterization as described in 2.1 (according to which a semantic criterion is also necessary), the discussion of this problem (and some other deficiencies related to it) is deferred to section 3.2.1.

Put briefly, the searching algorithm Beaver, Francez and Levinson (2006) used identifies a construction as existential only if it has the form THERE'S|IS|ARE [NP pattern] IN. The initial assumption is that the characterizing properties of pivot NPs can be discovered by contrasting them with the NPs occurring in canonical locative sentences; so the other pattern they simultaneously examine is [NP pattern] IS|ARE IN. These syntactic schemes are in good accordance with our theoretical starting point, which is based on the well-known observation that existential sentences have special syntactic properties compared with canonical sentences (see section 2.1). Beaver, Francez and Levinson (2006) assume that the markedness of existential constructions is the basis on which the regularities in the occurrence of the different types of NPs (the definiteness restriction) can be explained. The theoretically based expectations of the authors (which are to be supported by the corpus data presented in their paper) are that the best candidates for fulfilling the role of the pivot in an existential construction are the NPs which have the least subject-like properties. This is certainly a well-motivated expectation in the light of the existing literature on existential sentences; for instance, it is fully compatible with the argumentation by which the pivot NP denotes a property (McNally 2009); or with the assumptions according to which pivots play the role of the main predicate in existential sentences (Frances 2009). The novelty of the work presented by Beaver, Francez and Levinson (2006) lies neither in their initial assumptions, nor in their conclusion (which meets the expectations), but in the way the results are justified: the authors carry out a contrastive corpus analysis with the help of statistical methods.

The most interesting detail in this research is not that linguistic corpora are used that are larger than the ones that have ever been used to study these phenomena, but that it is a comparative work in two ways. First, within a language the existential and the canonical forms are compared with respect to the type of the subject NPs occurring in them. Second, the first type of comparative analysis is carried out within three languages (English, Dutch, and Russian). In this way, the results reinforce the authors' markedness hypothesis crosslinguistically: in all the three languages the bad subjects are the good pivots, and good subjects tend to occur in the canonical locative sentences.

Beaver, Francez and Levinson (2006) also address the question whether the definiteness restriction is a categorical ban or whether it is rather a tendency. They claim that it is only a tendency (although a very strong one), and they think that their corpus-based analysis supports this claim (the validity of this conclusion is discussed in section 3.2.1). It turns out from the statistical analysis that all types of NPs have occurrences both in the *there*-sentences and in the canonical versions. However, the ratio of their occurrences in *there*-sentences as compared with their occurrences in the canonical locative forms shows not only that in the existential sentences mostly indefinite (weak) NPs occur, but also that these NPs are not very welcome in the canonical subject position. Consequently, an interesting empirical generalization comes to light due to the analysis performed in the way it is done: a kind of *anti-definiteness effect* has been discovered. This is a tendency observable in canonical sentences, and it is parallel with the definiteness effect, but in the opposite way: NP types which occur most frequently as pivots in the *there*-sentences scarcely occur as subjects in the canonical locative constructions. Thus, a kind of complementary distribution of the different types of NPs is observable with respect to the constructions they are likely to occur.

3. The evaluation of the different methods and results

In this part, the methods and results of the three papers presented above are discussed. The opinion formed on the basis of comparing and evaluating the different types of analyses will be reinforced by some interesting empirical data from Hungarian in section 4.

3.1. Theoretical background

Our initial assumption is simple, it is shared by the great majority of linguists (a notable exception is Sampson 2007) and leads us quickly to the point:

(19) Human languages are structured.

In the broadest sense, this claim amounts to admitting that for any natural language it is possible to pick up some elements from its vocabulary and arrange them in such a way that the resulting string will not be accepted as an expression of that language by any native speaker of it. This idea can be made more precise if we treat human languages in the same way as formal languages: a formal language L is a set of strings generated by its grammar G_L from a finite set V of symbols. L is generally assumed to be permutationally not closed. This means that G_L select a (non-empty) proper subset L of V* (where V* is the set of all possible sequences made of the elements of V). Thus, the explication given for (19) reduces to the claim that $L \subset V^*$, and the grammar G_L of L is nothing else than the means to selecting this subset from the whole set of strings that can be built from the elements of V.

This formal approach to human languages may seem simplifying to trivialities, but a closer examination reveals that there are some hidden assumptions lurking in the background which are far from being trivial. Starting at the very beginning, if we take a language to be a *set* of sequences of symbols, we should be able to identify its elements. In the case of natural languages this should happen in a way that makes possible to tell apart the well-formed sequences belonging to the language from the ones not belonging to it. That is, the set of ill-formed strings should be discernible on the basis of the characterization given for the well-formed sentences.[6] However, although there are numerous sequences of V* that can be judged

6 This is the informal explication of the property formulated in the theory of formal languages as natural languages belong to *recursive* languages, which constitute a proper subset of the *recursively enumerable* languages.

unequivocally in this respect, we are always able to find strings of symbols which are held (a) well-formed by some native speakers, and ill-formed by others, (b) well-formed in some contexts, but ill-formed in others, (c) well-formed in some respects (e.g. syntactically), but ill-formed in others (e.g. semantically). This uncertainty in judgments raises at least the following issues:

Is the "well-formed" vs. "ill-formed" opposition a dichotomy, drawing a sharp line between the well-formed and ill-formed linguistic expressions, or is the distinction gradual, meaning that a string of symbols can be more or less well-formed?

In what sense can a string of linguistic symbols be well-formed or ill-formed?

It is supposed (moreover, proven by Pereira 2000, cited in Pullum 2007: 34) that at least two kinds of grammatical well-formedness can be differentiated: syntactic and semantic. The role of pragmatics is very interesting in this respect: the circumstances (the linguistic and non-linguistic contexts, (hidden) biases of the speaker, etc.) of the use of utterances can significantly strengthen or diminish their acceptability; actually, to such an extent that grammaticality judgments can be altered (not only semantic judgments but syntactic as well). This fact seems to prove that the dividing line between the set of well-formed and ill-formed sequences of symbols is far from being sharp.

Bearing this in mind, we have theoretically at least the following options concerning the nature of the rules which build human language structures:

1. The structure building rules of human languages are fuzzy in the sense that they are not "input-output" type or other well-definable rules but their character is similar to some (statistical) tendency.
2. The structure building rules are sharply definable, but the categories they are to be applied to are fuzzy. As a result, if the categorial status of an element is uncertain, it also becomes uncertain whether a rule that is sensitive to categories is applicable or not.
3. The structure building rules are sharp, the categories they apply to are well-definable sets, but because of the (verbal and non-verbal) context of utterances, or because of the presence of other interacting (sharp) grammatical rules the illusion of exemptions arises. If this is the case, the (fake) exemptions should be systematic enough that they should be explained by other grammatical or pragmatic rules.

4. The above mentioned three possibilities (or two of them) may be simultaneously present in universal grammar, and inside a given language as well.

Sorace and Keller (2005) argue convincingly that it is characteristic to human languages that their rules come in two main varieties: there are clear-cut rules on the basis of which the acceptability judgments are fairly unequivocal (these they call hard constraints), and rules which can be overridden easily by contextual factors, resulting in a gradience of acceptability judgments (soft constraints). On the basis of this typology of rules, the case mentioned under point 3 above might arise from soft constraints, which, as opposed to hard constraints, can be strongly influenced by contextual factors. Although it might happen in principle that what is a hard constraint in language A is a soft constraint in language B, crosslinguistic evidence shows that hard constraints are universally hard, and one of the distinctive features of soft constraints is that they exhibit great variation across languages (for more details, see Sorace and Keller 2005).

This survey of some of the problems affecting the very essence of linguistic theories and methods is admittedly brief. However, these issues will not be dwelt on here, partly because of space limitations, and partly because their mere enumeration supplies us with some central notions along which it is possible to compare and evaluate the different methods and results presented in section 2.

3.2. Linguistic data and theoretical conclusions

If we try to evaluate the approaches presented in section 2 on the basis of what is described in 3.1, the following observations can be made.

3.2.1. Rules or tendencies? Beaver, Francez and Levinson (2006)

The work presented by Beaver, Francez and Levinson (2006) seems to support the first option formulated above on the possible nature of the rules of human languages: the authors are convinced that they proved that the definiteness effect is a tendency (although a strong tendency, they admit), and not a rule based phenomenon. The data presented in the article seemingly support this view, however, the evidence based on them is not convincing, for the following reasons.

The main problem is a descriptive mismatch: the linguistic material the conclusion is drawn from is not quite the one the authors aim to investigate, due to the large and mechanically examined data base. It seems a trivial requirement that if some research is oriented to discovering the rules (or tendencies) occurring in existential clauses, then the data set representing the existential constructions should contain existential constructions. Now, if we take a closer look at the pattern Beaver, Francez and Levinson (2006) use in order to find the existential structures of the corpora, it turns out that the syntactic scheme "THERE'S|IS|ARE [NP pattern] IN" gives a condition which is neither necessary nor sufficient for identifying existential clauses. The reasons can be summarized as follows.

First, there are infinitely many existential sentences not containing an *in* preposition in the coda, or not containing a coda at all, so a reasonable assumption is that the large corpora examined here also contain some. Unfortunately, these have no chance to be included into the data set of the existential constructions. This fact demonstrates that the pattern given for existential constructions gives a non-necessary (too strict) criterion. However, this would not influence the reliability of the results on condition it could be proven that the data given by this pattern constitute a representative sample of existential constructions. Unfortunately, this remains an open question.

Second, recall the semantic criterion that also has to be met in order to identify existential sentences: nothing is to be involved by an existential claim beyond the mere existence of the entities the pivot denotes. Constructions qualified as existential by the pattern above may contain several instances which would turn out to be not existential if we examined them more closely. Something is done in this respect when Beaver, Francez and Levinson (2006) apply a statistical sampling method to sift out the truly locative *there*-sentences from the relevant data. However, there are various possibilities to infer from a *there*-sentence more information than the mere availability of some entities, see e.g. the 100 sentences examined by Ward and Birner (1995). Thus, a syntactic pattern like the one above will presumably match a significantly large number of *there*-sentences which cannot be considered existential on the basis of the semantic criterion given in (7). So, the pattern does not give a sufficient condition either (it is too lax).

Of course, this objection can emerge only if we accept the semantic criterion the existential sentences are characterized by in section 2.1. If this is dropped, then the context of *there*-constructions becomes irrelevant, and all sentences matching the pattern "THERE'S|IS|ARE [NP pattern] IN" will qualify as existential. Notice, however, that this entails that the definiteness effect is expected to work as a context-independent structural rule, that is, as a hard constraint in the terminology introduced by Sorace and Keller

(2005). But, as Ward and Birner (1995) have demonstrated, the emergence of the definiteness effect as a ban on the occurrence of definite DPs is heavily dependent on the context, moreover, on the lexical meaning of the words occurring inside the *there*-sentences, see (18). Consequently, the definiteness effect cannot be expected to exhibit the characteristic features of a hard constraint. Thus, the conclusion according to which the definiteness effect is a tendency and not a rule is derivable from the clash between the (hidden) assumption implicit in the method that the data are selected by and the well-documented context-sensitivity of the definiteness effect: since the data are gained as they are (by pattern matching, without referring to the context), they will necessarily contain sentences which would be qualified as non-existential by the semantic criterion given by (7). Consequently, any rule pertaining to existential sentences characterized by the two conditions given in section 2 can be expected to behave like a tendency with respect to the set of sentences gained by applying only one of the two conditions, which therefore constitutes a superset of the set of existential sentences. Thus, the tendency-like character of the definiteness effect does not follow from the nature of existential sentences but from the methods the authors apply in order to find the existential sentences of the corpora. This would not be so if the data had been gained from some other type of definition for existential sentences (for instance, one including the semantic criterion (7)). It is to be admitted, though, that working with a more sophisticated definition could set insurmountable problems for statistical analyses.

It is important to note here that although the inference to the *nature* of the rule that results in the definiteness effect cannot be considered justified merely on the basis of the research presented by Beaver, Francez and Levinson (2006), the very essence of the paper is convincing, and the data presented there certainly can serve as a useful background at least for some of the theories on the semantic structure of existential sentences. The main finding of the paper, specifically, that good pivots are bad subjects, gives justification for theories that treat pivots as properties or predicates (see e.g. McNally 2009, Frances 2009). Moreover, a new empirical generalization arose as a side effect of the corpus analysis, because not only the existence of the definiteness effect is proven by the data but an equally convincing piece of evidence has been found in support of the existence of an inverse restriction (see section 2.5 above). In sum, Beaver, Francez and Levinson's (2006) paper contains a corpus analysis that can provide valuable data based support for justifying certain theoretical assumptions on the nature of existential sentences.

3.2.2. *Semantics or pragmatics? A theoretically based approach: Keenan (2003)*

The algebraic semantic approach offered by Keenan (2003) belongs to the third group mentioned in 3.1: a sharply defined semantic property is discovered, which results in well-delineated (sub)categories, and possible exceptions are excluded by a productivity criterion. The claims of the paper are formalized and proven in an independently existing logical framework, namely, the theory of generalized quantifiers. The formal background makes it possible to find and characterize the property of the DPs licensed as pivots in existential constructions in a mathematically exact way. Keenan (2003) argues that the $cons_2$ algebraic property he defines as given in (10), repeated here as (20), characterizes the determiners of the DPs occurring in existential constructions most exhaustively and in the simplest possible way.

(20) $DAB \Leftrightarrow D(A \cap B)B$

This property divides the category of DPs into two disjoint sets, the members of one are allowed, while the members of the other are (presumably) excluded from the existential constructions (for more details, see section 2.2.3). This might suggest that the definiteness effect is a hard constraint: it is a clear yes/no question whether a determiner has the $cons_2$ property or not, and if it does, it is allowed to occur as a pivot nominal, while if it does not, it is not allowed. However, as Ward and Birner (1995) demonstrated through data gained from a fairly large corpus, there are *there*-sentences where definite determiners (which do not have the $cons_2$ property) occur as pivot. In order to eliminate the controversy, we have to look at the range of data the two papers use. This will be done in the last part of this section.

Keenan's (2003) paper raises three basic methodological issues which are also our present concern.

The main question of the paper is whether the definiteness effect is semantic or pragmatic in nature. Keenan's (2003) paper is designed overtly against the pragmatic explanation Zucchi (1995) offers, and his answer is that the most adequate way this restriction can be accounted for is in terms of the algebraic semantic properties of the determiners. The algebraic approach has the advantage, among others, that the set of data (the range of the determiners allowed in pivot nominals) that can be explained on the basis of the $cons_2$ property is significantly larger than the data set Zucchi (1995) can account for on the basis of pragmatic considerations.

The second theoretical issue Keenan (2003) addresses is the question of direct or indirect characterization, that is, whether the definiteness effect should be given by explicating the properties which characterize the allowed DPs in the pivot position, or by discovering the features of the disallowed DPs. Keenan (2003) chooses the former option (direct characterization), supporting it with a cognitively based argument. His line of reasoning is that since it is evident that we learn our native tongue by acquiring rules that allow us to make well-formed expressions, and not rules that exclude expressions as non-well-formed, the more sound method when describing a natural language is certainly the one which characterizes the expressions that are well-formed (as opposed to exploring the properties of expressions disallowed in a construction).

The third issue is the question of the data. Keenan's (2003) initial linguistic data are the well-known minimal pairs similar to (1) and (2) in 1.1, and beside such pairs several well-formed expressions are created by him, a native speaker, during the argumentation. He relies on no corpora and no judgments of other speakers. The only data type occurring in the paper is the type of constructed examples. However, Keenan (2003) does pay attention to the question of data by introducing a very simple criterion: the existential *there*-sentences he aims to give an account of should be productive. This means that they should have negated and interrogative forms (with no additional changes in the meaning of the affirmative version beyond what the meaning of the negation or question itself causes in it). The aim of this requirement is to exclude the *there*-sentences where special contextual effects are present (list contexts, reminder contexts, and presentative superlatives are explicitly mentioned in the paper).

This criterion proves to be highly relevant if we check the data analyzed by Ward and Birner (1995) against it. Let us see, for instance, the type of the reminder *there*-sentences, whose function is to call the hearer's attention to known entities in a new context (example (17) in 2.4, repeated here as (21)):

(21) *I'd love to get away from my job, the kids, the bills... I've thought of chucking it all and going to Hawaii. But there are the kids to consider.*

The interrogative (*Are there the kids...?*) and the negative (*There aren't the kids...*) versions of (21) are supposedly not acceptable in any contexts, and if they become somehow acceptable, they certainly will not have the reminder meaning.[7] So, the reminder uses of definite DPs in *there*-sentences

[7] I suppose that the productivity criterion fails in the case of this type of examples, although the *Aren't there the kids to consider?* version is acceptable with the intended (reminder) meaning by some English native speakers. I think that

are excluded from the existential sentences by the productivity condition. Presumably, most of the other types of examples studied in Ward and Birner (1995) are excluded by virtue of this criterion.[8] It would be a task for further research to check this surmise against a broader set of data based on native speakers' intuitions. It is certain, however, that if the productivity condition removes from the set of relevant data the *there*-sentence types with a definite pivot DP that Ward and Birner (1995) analyze the controversy mentioned at the outset of this section would disappear. For the purposes of the present paper what is important is that this *might be* the case. On the basis of this observation it becomes evident that the data sets Keenan (2003) and Ward and Birner (1995) work with belong to different types of *there*-sentences, and the productivity-criterion Keenan (2003) stipulates results in a narrower set of *there*-sentences than the set Ward and Birner (1995) examine. For this narrower set, referred to as proper existential sentences below, the $cons_2$ property can in principle work as a hard constraint, while the larger data set of *there*-sentences might require another type of explanation.

---

the productivity criterion is to be meant in the sense of "full productivity"; thus, the failure of the negated *or* the interrogative *or* the negative-interrogative versions each by itself hurts the productivity requirement.

8 The other type of *there*-sentences with definite pivots cited in section 2.4 seems more resistant to the productivity test: the negated and interrogative forms seem acceptable (*Was there the usual crowd at the beach today? There wasn't the usual crowd at the beach today.*) The productivity of this type of existential sentences, however, is not in contradiction with the semantic property of $cons_2$, if we take into consideration the lexical meaning of the word *usual* (and the words similar to it in their relevant meaning component, e.g. *obligatory, expected, required*, etc.), for the following reasons. Take the canonical sentence *The ususal crowd was at the beach.* The contribution of the word *usual* to the meaning of the DP is to connect it to the predicative expression in a way that the whole sentence means that 'the crowd usual **at the beach** was at the beach', so no part of the denotation of the noun (*crowd*) will be relevant for the truth conditions beyond the one the predicative phrase (*be at the beach*) applies to as well. Notice that the unicity condition usually induced by definite descriptions cannot arise here because of the repetitive component in the lexical meaning of *usual.* This means that it is only the denotation of the common noun phrase *crowd that is usual at the beach* is what counts here (and not the whole denotation of *crowd*). But the $cons_2$ property says exactly this, if we place the counterpart words of our example into the scheme given in (10): *The usual crowd is at the beach* is true exactly when *The usual crowd at the beach is at the beach.*

It is important to notice that the *there*-sentences examined by Ward and Birner (1995) do not meet the second, semantic criterion for existential sentences put forward in section 2 above, either: they imply something beyond the mere existence or presence of entities. The very purpose of that paper is to find the shared feature of the definite pivots licensing these implications. This purpose is reached by carrying out careful pragmatic analyses resulting in an arrangement of the data (*there*-sentence containing a definite pivot NP) into five groups (see more details in section 2.4 above). If we examine how these analyses are performed we arrive at our third basic question, addressed next, in the following subsection.

3.2.3. Data bases or intuitions? Ward and Birner (1995)

One of the most frequently addressed basic methodological problems of linguistics is that the traditional, intuition based treatment of linguistic data raises the question of reliability. The main objection to this method is that constructed data gained on the basis of intuitive judgments may be subject to (unintended) manipulations on the part of the linguists creating them. Unfortunately, this might happen and actually does happen: Pullum (2007) cites some shocking examples from the literature.

What is to be emphasized here is that unwanted subjectivity in the treatment of data cannot be eliminated by merely relying on (analyses of) data drawn from existing linguistic corpora. This has been demonstrated in section 3.2.1 by showing some incompatibilities between a theoretical conclusion drawn by Beaver, Francez and Levinson (2006) and the data (gained by a corpus analysis) their conclusion is based on.

The first relevant work on existential sentences carried out on the basis of a corpus was Ward and Birner's (1995) paper. It is quite understandable that the temptation was too great to resist it: the question whether it is really the case that definite NPs cannot occur in *there*-sentences seemed to be possible to be answered decisively by examining a large corpus. The approximately 100 instantiations of *there*-sentences with a definite pivot NP they found meant apparently a great challenge for maintaining the empirical generalization called the definiteness effect. Ward and Birner (1995) met the challenge and gave a pragmatic explanation to the definiteness restriction, deriving it from the incompatibility of the cognitive status of the discourse referents introduced by existential sentences on the one hand, and the cognitive status of the entities referred to by definite NPs on the other (see more details in section 2.4 above).

What interests us at present is what can be gained by the use of a linguistic corpus. The ready answer is, of course, that it is data that can be gained. If so, the next question is why use corpora for gaining data when native speakers' intuition is available, and data need not be searched for but can simply be evoked? There are at least two important types of answers to this question. The first is that we might come across data which we could not evoke (easily) on the basis of our intuition. The second is that relying on corpus data we are able to eliminate the uncertainties of judgments and the manipulative uses of the data gained on the basis of native speakers' intuition. The latter answer is evidently based on the assumption that linguistic intuition is not reliable, but data gained from corpora are. As for the second part of this assumption, we have already shown in section 3.2.1 that corpora should be used with an at least as great caution as intuitive data. In addition, recall the fact that the data contained by linguistic corpora are data which are presumably judged well-formed by some speakers, so corpora also originate from intuition.

Our concluding (rhetorical) question in this section is that if intuition is not reliable when gaining linguistic data, why does it become reliable when drawing conclusions from the data? Ward and Birner (1995) do not apply statistical methods, they analyze on the basis of their own linguistic intuition the linguistic instances which the corpus supplied them with. They examine the contexts and the contents of their data with the aid of argumentations that are based on simple common sense reasoning, and their results are quite convincing. Keenan (2003) also argues convincingly on the basis of his constructed data. Thus, we have a pragmatic approach based on corpus data which seemingly contradict the definiteness restriction, and a formal semantic approach based on constructed examples. The latter says that it is the $cons_2$ algebraic property of the determiner which allows a DP to appear as a pivot in an existential construction. The former says that the relevant condition is the hearer-new discourse referent introducing property and shows that the definite DPs occurring as pivots also have this property in some way or another. The possibilities for reconciling the results of the two papers are discussed in the following section.

Summing up the methodological moral of this section, it is evident that since intuition cannot be eliminated from scientific work in general, it cannot be eliminated from linguistics either. And if it cannot be eliminated when *reasoning* about data, why should we refrain from using it when *gathering* linguistic data? "The point is simply that general objections to the use of intuitions are rather foolish" (Borsley 2005: 1477). This opinion is presumably compatible with a standpoint like Pullum's (2007), who is definitely against using *false* data and argumentations, irrespective of whether their falsity originates from spurious intuitive judgments, or from some misinterpretation of the possibilities linguistic corpora can contribute to scientific analyses. Pullum (2007) argues that applying different methods simultaneously is possibly the most reliable way of doing linguistic research, since the results based on a certain method can control the results gained in some other way: for instance, corpus analysis can be used for supporting or discarding theoretical assumptions. Actually, both Ward and Birner (1995) and Beaver, Francez and Levinson (2006) use their corpus data essentially in such a way. The latter explicate overtly their expectations (based on theoretical considerations and constructed examples) that are to be supported by the corpus analysis. Ward and Birner (1995) attempt to provide a theoretically based explanation to an unexpected data set. Both papers contain an abundance of constructed examples besides the data gained from the corpora, and their theoretical assumptions are based on the existing (usually not corpus-based) literature. The next section gives a further instance of reconciling corpus data and constructed data; moreover, the conflict between the semantic and pragmatic approaches will be resolved as well.

4. Semantics and pragmatics reconciled

In this section some new considerations about the definiteness effect will be presented on the basis of comparing and reconciling the results of two papers, Keenan (2003) and Ward and Birner (1995), which are seemingly entirely different in their character: in the origin of their data, in their theoretical backgrounds, and in their conclusions. The claims resulting from this comparison are supported by some (constructed) Hungarian data in subsection 4.2.

4.1. Comparing the results of Keenan (2003) and Ward and Birner (1995)

Our question is whether Keenan's (2003) and Ward and Birner's (1995) solutions for explaining the definiteness effect can be reconciled in a way that this would result in a coherent picture. Our answer is yes, on the basis of the following considerations.

On the one hand, Keenan's (2003) generalization is about existential sentences, while Ward and Birner's (1995) data are not existential sentences if we take seriously the semantic criterion mentioned by McNally (2008). It was shown in 3.2.2 that the *there*-sentences containing a definite pivot

NP do not meet the productivity criterion provided by Keenan (2003) either. Thus, it seems that the $cons_2$ semantic property gives us the semantic criterion that is to be fulfilled by the determiners of the DPs occurring in *proper* existential constructions, that is, in *there*-sentences meeting McNally's (2008) semantic criterion and Keenan's (2003) productivity criterion. (It remains an open question at present what the exact relationship is between the data gained on the basis of only one of the two criteria.)

On the other hand, Ward and Birner (1995) give an explanation for a set of *exceptional there*-sentences. From their pragmatic analyses they infer a general property of existential sentences which is valid of some more *there*-sentences than the proper existential sentences characterized in the previous paragraph. Ward and Birner (1995) claim that the pragmatic explanation they give (hearer-new discourse referents are introduced) is capable to account for the definiteness effect and the exemptions from it equally. Notice the convergence of the conclusions drawn from a set larger than the existential sentences in the two corpus-based papers: Beaver, Francez and Levinson (2006) claim that the relevant property of the (not always indefinite) pivots is that they are bad subjects, while Ward and Birner (1995) emphasize the hearer-new status of the discourse referents introduced. Now, hearer-new information is typically conveyed by the predicate of sentences; while if something is a bad subject in a sentence, then it is similar to (a part of) the predicate. Moreover, the formal property given for the determiners allowed in existential sentences by Keenan (2003) states that from the denotation of the noun occurring in the pivot only that part is truth-conditionally relevant which is also the part of the extension of the predicative phrase. Thus, the three solutions examined here are not in contradiction, moreover, all three point in one and the same direction.

Returning to the two papers which are the main concern of this section, the first point to be emphasized is that they deal with different sets of data: as was shown in 3.2.2 Keenan (2003) gives a semantic characterization that is valid for a narrower set of *there*-sentences than the pragmatic characterization offered by Ward and Birner (1995). Thus, we can assume that there is a smaller set of *there*-sentences meeting the productivity criterion and the semantic criterion, and exhibiting the definiteness restriction as a rule that allows only DPs with a $cons_2$ determiner as pivots. This narrowly defined set of existential sentences can be extended to a larger set which includes the data Ward and Birner (1995) examine: if something more than a mere existential claim is expressed by a *there*-sentence, then, and only then, definite determiners also may occur in the pivot DPs. However, the occurrence of the definite DPs is constrained by a pragmatic principle: they must introduce discourse referents that are hearer-new at least in some respects. Since a contextual parameter (the hearer) is explicitly present in that requirement, the definiteness effect clearly works as a soft constraint with respect to this larger set of data.

In sum, assuming that both of the theories are correct, the general semantic property of pivot DPs in existential sentences is their determiners' $cons_2$ property, and their general pragmatic property is that they introduce hearer-new discourse referents.[9] The latter condition describes a larger set of data, while the former yields a data set that is presumably a proper part of the set given by the pragmatic criterion. These results are in good accordance with everything that is expected from a semantic and a pragmatic theory. However, the non-contradictoriness of the two properties and the part-of relation between the set of data they describe remain a conjecture as far as the hearer-new discourse referent property is not explicated as exactly as the $cons_2$ property. This should be the topic of a future, more formally oriented paper. At present, only a set of data will be presented here which supports this conjecture in an interesting way.

4.2. Data from Hungarian

An argument can be gained from Hungarian data in support of the view that the data set treated by Keenan's (2003) semantic approach covers proper existential sentences, and the *there*-sentences where a definite DP occurs as the pivot are not existential in the strict sense.

4.2.1. Existential sentences in Hungarian

Hungarian is a discourse configurational[10] and *pro*-drop language, so there is no syntactic pressure to apply expletives. Thus, Hungarian counterparts

---

9 The hearer-new property, in turn, makes the pivot nominal a "bad subject", so Beaver, Francez and Levinson's (2006) conclusion is also in harmony with this finding.

10 Discourse configurationality means that Hungarian has no distinguished syntactic positions for the subject, object, and main verb, etc. Instead, the sentential topic occurs obligatorily at the very beginning of declarative sentences (irrespective of whether it is the subject, object, etc.), the focused constituent always stands immediately before the verb, quantified expressions also have a distinguished position on the left periphery, and so on. Of course, none of these is an obligatory constituent, thus it may happen, for instance, that if a sentence

of English existential sentences do not contain expletive pronouns, and when deciding whether a Hungarian sentence is existential or not, we must rely first of all on the semantic criterion. However, when the semantic counterparts of English existential sentences are found, we can also observe some syntactic peculiarities of them. As it has been mentioned in section 2.1, the order of the words (accompanied by minor changes in the intonation contours) differentiates between a canonical locative and an existential sentence (examples (4) and (5) are repeated here as (22) and (23)):

(22) *Van néhány hatalmas sikló a mocsárban.*
is some mighty grass.snake.NOM the moor.INE
'There are some mighty grass snakes in the moor.'

(23) *Néhány hatalmas sikló a mocsárban van.*
some mighty grass.snake.NOM the moor.INE is
'Some mighty grass snakes are in the moor.'

The sentence type represented by (22) is the *par excellence* Hungarian existential construction. It will be frequently referred to as *van*-sentence below, after its definitive syntactic property, which is that the copula (*van* 'is') stands at the very beginning of the sentence.

There is a third typical construction beside the canonical locative and the *par excellence* existential sentences, expressing sometimes a meaning which is locative in its character (exemplified by (24) and (27)), and sometimes a more abstract meaning similar to the pure existential meaning (exemplified by (31)):

(24) *Ott/Itt van néhány hatalmas sikló a mocsárban.*
there/here is some mighty grass.snake.NOM the moor.INE
'Some mighty grass snakes are there in the moor.'

It is an interesting question what is the exact syntactic status of the word *ott* 'there' (or *itt* 'here') in sentences like (24), and it would be even more interesting to discover their exact semantic contribution to the meaning of this sentence type. The *ott* 'there' in (24) can be interpreted as a demonstrative pronoun, but it frequently turns out that a demonstrative meaning

contains no topic, the very first element will be a quantified expression, or if there is no quantified expression before the verb either, the first element of the sentence can be a focused expression, or if none of the distinguished constituents is present in the sentence, the verb will be the sentence-initial constituent. For more details, see e.g. É. Kiss (1987), (2002).

is not necessarily present in this construction (see examples (27) and (31) in section 4.2.2). However, since the present paper's aim is not to discuss questions of descriptive grammar of Hungarian, these issues will not be dwelt on here. What is relevant to our purposes is the mere fact that there is a third, non-canonical locative and not purely existential sentence type in Hungarian.[11]

4.2.2. *The definiteness effect in Hungarian*

As Szabolcsi (1986) observed, at least four classes of verbs (each of them a closed set) evoke the definiteness effect in Hungarian. In the present paper the topic is not the definiteness effect in general, thus, from the four verb classes only the one containing the copula will be relevant here.

In Hungarian, *van*-sentences always exhibit a very strong definiteness restriction which cannot be "neutralized" by the otherwise definiteness effect neutralizer focusing or progressive, see more details on the definiteness effect in Hungarian in Szabolcsi (1986):

(25) **Van a/minden/a három/mindkét vendég a kertben.*
is the/all/the.three/both guest.NOM the garden.INE

On the other hand, neither the canonical locative, nor the *ott-van*-sentences show the definiteness restriction:

---

[11] In fact, there is a non-standard version of existential sentences as well:

(i) *Néhány hatalmas sikló van a mocsárban.*
some large grass.snake.NOM is the moor.INE
'There are some large grass snakes in the moor.'

However, this sentence type will be neglected here, because the (pivot?) DP occupies a position which might equally well be the focus position (although intonation differences may be present). The version of existential sentences where the verb occupies the very first position (*van* – pivot DP – locative phrase, or *van* – locative phrase – pivot DP, called *van*-sentences) may be intonated as focused as well, but in their case the focus stress pattern is much more striking than in the case of (i)-type (DP – *van* – locative phrase) sentences. In the *van*-sentences the most neutral and natural intonation pattern always gets a proper existential interpretation, but this cannot be said about (i)-type sentences; so *van*-sentences will be considered as the standard versions of Hungarian existential constructions.

(26) *A/minden/a három/mindkét vendég a kertben van.*
the/all/the.three/both guest.NOM the garden.INE is
'The/all/the three/both guests are in the garden.'

(27) *Ott/Itt van a/minden/a három/mindkét vendég a kertben.*
there/here is the/all/the.three/both guest.NOM the garden.INE
'The/all/the three/both guests are there/here in the garden.'

If the definiteness effect is expected to occur systematically in existential sentences, then *ott-van*-sentences in Hungarian are either exceptions to this rule, or they are not existential. Since no *ott-van*-sentences show any kind of restriction similar to the definiteness effect, and their meaning is not purely existential as compared with the *van*-sentences, it is reasonable not to regard *ott-van*-sentences as existential constructions.[12] However, they are not canonical locative sentences either: as opposed to (23), the located individuals (the syntactic subjects) are not in the topic position. These syntactic observations are in accordance with the native speakers' intuition on their meaning, which was characterized above as overlapping sometimes with the canonical locative and sometimes with the existential meaning.

A further distinguishing property of *ott-van*-sentences is that while bare common nouns are perfectly acceptable in *van*-sentences, they are absolutely banned from *ott-van*-sentences:

(28) *Van vendég/virág/sündisznó a kertben.*
is guest/flower/hedgehog.NOM the garden.INE
'There are some guests/flowers/hedgehogs in the garden.'

(29) **Ott/itt van vendég/virág/sündisznó a kertben.*
there/here is guest/flower/hedgehog.NOM the garden.INE

4.2.3. Hungarian counterparts of English there*-sentences*

Our next step is to try to find the Hungarian counterparts of at least some types of English *there*-sentences. The theoretical motivation behind this enterprise can be summarized as follows.

Consider in language A a set of data which seems homogeneous from a given point of view (for example, the elements of the data set have the same

---

12 Maybe their meaning can be called *presentative*, however, I refrain from using this term without a clarification, because it is fairly overloaded with connotations originating from its various uses in the literature.

structure in some relevant sense), then examine whether the counterparts of these data in language B have a uniform structure as well. If they do, then either the examined set of data is really homogeneous, or there is some difference between the elements of the data set but it is expressed neither in language A nor in B by structural means. If, however, in language B a systematic structural difference can be observed between the elements of the set of data to which language A seems structurally insensitive, it is reasonable to assume that the data are not really homogeneous in A either.

Now if we try to find the Hungarian counterpart of a simple existential sentence and a *there*-sentence with a definite pivot DP, it turns out that they do not translate into one and the same construction in Hungarian. As we have seen, an existential *there*-sentence typically translates like a *van*-sentence, however, the well-formed Hungarian counterpart of the *there*-sentence in (17) and (21), repeated here as (30) is an *ott-van*-sentence (see (31); the *van*-sentence version (32) sounds extremely bad:

(30) *I'd love to get away from my job, the kids, the bills... I've thought of chucking it all and going to Hawaii. But there are the kids to consider.*

(31) *De ott vannak a gyerekek, akikre gondolni kell.*
but there are.3PL the kids.NOM who.PL.SUB consider must.3SG
'But there are the kids to consider.'

(32) *??De vannak a gyerekek, akikre gondolni kell.*
but are.3PL the kids.NOM who.PL.SUB consider must.3SG

Another example is (33), cited as (12c) by Ward and Birner (1995: 729) from Prince (1992):

(33) *There was the stupidest article on the reading list.*

The Hungarian counterpart of (33) is (34):

(34) *Ott volt a leghülyébb cikk az olvasmánylistán.*
there was.3SG the stupidest article.NOM the reading.list.SUP
'There was the stupidest article on the reading list.'

However, this is not a *van*-sentence in Hungarian, but an *ott-van*-sentence. Its *van*-sentence version is totally unacceptable:

(35) **Volt a leghülyébb cikk az olvasmánylistán.*
was.3SG the stupidest article.NOM the reading.list.SUP

It holds generally that when we try to find the Hungarian counterparts of the examples of Ward and Birner (1995), it turns out that they all can be given more properly as an *ott-van*-sentence than as an existential *van*-sentence. Even if some of them can be translated into a *van*-sentence, it sounds definitely worse than the *ott-van* version.

If we accept the reasoning presented at the beginning of this section, the data in (24)–(35) demonstrate that English *there*-sentences do not form a homogeneous class, and the *there*-sentences where the pivot has a definite determiner are not proper existential sentences. Of course, this is not surprising at all in the light of Keenan's (2003) productivity criterion and the semantic criterion stated in (7). However, since the final methodological conclusion of this paper is that the results of linguistic research are the more convincing the more types of data support them, crosslinguistic observations may become important. In our case they certainly deserve attention, because they reinforce the conclusions of section 4.1. The overall conclusions can be summarized as follows:

1. In proper existential sentences the definiteness effect works as a rule, and the licensing property of pivot DPs can be given by an as sharply defined semantic property as it is given by Keenan (2003). In Hungarian the proper existential sentences are the *van*-sentences.
2. The pragmatic explanation given by Ward and Birner (1995) covers a larger data set whose elements are not restricted to the *par excellence* existential sentences. On this set of *there*-sentences the definiteness effect works as a soft constraint in the sense of Sorace and Keller (2005), thus, requiring pragmatic explanations.

5. Summary

Turning now to the question of how our theoretical considerations given in 3.1 square with the results gained by the thorough comparative analysis of the different types of research and of some relevant English and Hungarian data, it is evident that our results fit the third option mentioned there, repeated in the following paragraph.

The structure building rules are sharp, the categories they apply to are well-definable sets, but because of the (verbal and non-verbal) context of utterances, or because of the presence of other interacting (sharp) grammatical rules the illusion of exemptions arises. If this is the case, the (fake) exemptions should be systematic enough that they should be explained by other grammatical or pragmatic rules.

The results of this paper fill this scheme in the following way. The sharp semantic property characterizing the allowed DPs in the existential constructions is the determiners' $cons_2$ property. The exemptions from the restriction due to this semantic property are fake data in that they do not belong to the proper existential constructions. This can be supported from at least three sides. The semantic condition put on the interpretation of the existential sentences, the productivity criterion, and the Hungarian counterparts show equally well that the *there*-sentences with a definite pivot are not *par excellence* existential sentences. However, the occurrence of the definite DPs in *there*-sentences is systematic enough to be explained by pragmatic considerations valid for existential sentences as well.

Acknowledgements

The research reported on in the present paper was supported by the Research Group for Theoretical Linguistics at the Universities of Debrecen, Pécs and Szeged, Hungary.

References

Barwise, Jon and Robin Cooper
1981 Generalized quantifiers in natural language. *Linguistics and Philosophy* 4: 159–219.

Beaver, David, Itamar Francez and Dmitry Levinson
2006 Bad subject: (Non-)canonicality and NP distribution in existentials. In *Proceedings of Semantics and Linguistic Theory XV,* Effi Georgala and Jonathan Howell (eds.), 19–43. Ithaca, NY: CLC Publications.

Borsley, Robert D.
2005 Introduction. *Lingua* 115: 1475–1480.

É. Kiss, Katalin
1987 *Configurationality in Hungarian.* Dordrecht: Reidel.

É. Kiss, Katalin
2002 *Hungarian Syntax.* Cambridge: Cambridge University Press.

Frances, Itamar
2009 Existentials, predication and modification. *Linguistics and Philosophy* 32: 1–50.

Keenan, Edward
2003 The definiteness effect: semantics or pragmatics? *Natural Language Semantics* 11: 187–216.

McNally, Louise
2008 Existential sentences. In *Semantics: An International Handbook of Natural Language Meaning*, Claudia Maienborn, Klaus von Heusinger and Paul Portner (eds.). Berlin/New York: Mouton de Gruyter.

McNally, Louise
2009 Properties, entity correlates of properties, and existentials. In *Quantification, Definiteness, and Nominalization,* Anastasia Giannakidou and Monika Rathert (eds.) 163–187. Oxford: Oxford University Press.

Milsark, Gary
1974 Existential sentences in English. PhD dissertation. MIT.

Pereira, Fernando
2000 Formal grammar and information theory: Together again? *Philosophical Transactions of the Royal Society* 358: 1239–1253.

Pullum, Geoffrey K.
2007 Ungrammaticality, rarity, and corpus use. *Corpus Linguistics and Linguistic Theory* 3: 33–47.

Sampson, Geoffrey R.
2007 Grammar without grammaticality. *Corpus Linguistics and Linguistic Theory* 3: 1–32.

Sorace, Antonella and Frank Keller
2005 Gradience in linguistic data. *Lingua* 115: 1497–1524.

Szabolcsi, Anna
1986 From the definiteness effect to lexical integrity. In *Topic, Focus and Configurationality*, Werner Abraham and Sjaak de Meij (eds.), 321–348. Amsterdam: John Benjamins.

Ward, Gregory and Betty Birner
1995 Definiteness and the English existential. *Language* 71: 722–742.

Zucchi, Alessandro
1995 The ingredients of definiteness and the definiteness effect. *Natural Language Semantics* 3: 33–78.

On the semantics and pragmatics of shifted indexicals

Zoltán Vecsey

1. Introduction

1.1. Background: the basic tenets of the Double Index Theory

Influenced by Kamp's (1971) and Kaplan's pioneering work (1989a, b), the dominant view on the semantic interpretation of indexicals is based on the following familiar picture. Model-theoretic structures for indexical languages consist of two separable interpretive domains: contexts of occurrence (c) and circumstances of evaluation (i). Contexts are conceived of as collections of different parameters which are needed to determine the denotations of indexical expressions. Such collections could be minimally represented by quintuples of the form $\langle s, t, l, w, g \rangle$, where s is an agent, t is a point of time, l is a location, w is a possible state of the world, and g is a (possibly partial) variable assignment function defined on the salient entities of w at t and l. Circumstances of evaluation could be symbolized usually with centered world–time tuples $\langle w, t \rangle$, but if the complexity of the evaluated context requires this, they may also include further parameters. The number and kind of additional parameters do not influence substantially the model-theoretic role of circumstances. That role consists in assigning truth values to the contents of sentences which contain one or more indexical expressions. In the classical Kaplanian conception, sentential contents are structured propositions. If we accept this account, we can say that circumstances settle truth values for propositions.

The model-theoretic interpretation of indexical languages is then basically a two-step procedure. In the first step of the interpretation process indexicals are evaluated with respect to a particular collection of relevant contextual parameters. The evaluated objects are conceived of traditionally as conventionalized meanings or lexical entries. Kaplan (1989a: 505) calls such objects characters. As an example, consider the contextual occurrence of three paradigmatic indexicals in an intended model M[1,2]:

---

1 In this paper I concentrate mainly on the behavior of *pure indexicals*. One distinguishing property of pure indexicals is that their denotations are determined automatically in each context. This means that in normal speech situations the successful use of pure indexicals does not require the presence of non-linguistic

(1) a. $[[I_g]]^c = \mathrm{AUTH}_g(c)$
b. $[[here_g]]^c = \mathrm{LOC}_g(c)$
c. $[[now_g]]^c = \mathrm{TIME}_g(c)$

In (1a), (1b), and (1c) characters are evaluated with respect to their context of occurrence. It is commonly assumed that the context of occurrence *c* and the assignment function *g* of the model *M* together determine the content (denotation) of paradigmatic indexicals. So given an appropriate assignment function *g*, the content of the personal pronoun *I* is the agent of *c*, the content of the locative adverb *here* is the most salient location of the occurrence of *here* in *c*, and the content of the temporal adverb *now* is the most salient moment of time selected by the occurrence of *now* in *c*. Other indexicals such as *today* or *actual* are supposed to behave in the same way.

The second step in the interpretation process identifies an actual or counterfactual circumstance with respect to which it is possible to ask for the truth values {1, 0} of structured propositions. In intended models, circumstances coincide with the actual world and time $<w_a, t_a>$, that is to say, with *our* actual world. Circumstances may be identified in other admissible models with counterfactual worlds and time points.

Ultimately, then, indexicals and indexical sentences are evaluated with respect to two different collections of parameters: contexts and circumstances. First, contexts determine the content of characters. Second, for each structured proposition, circumstances yield truth values or truth conditions. The emerging picture is one of double indexing:

(2) Step One:
a. $[[I_g]]^c = \mathrm{AUTH}_g(c)$
b. $[[here_g]]^c = \mathrm{LOC}_g(c)$
c. $[[now_g]]^c = \mathrm{TIME}_g(c)$

Step Two:
d. $[[I\ am\ here\ now_g]]^{c,\,i} = 1$ iff $\mathrm{AUTH}_g(c)$ is at $\mathrm{LOC}_g(c)$ and at $\mathrm{TIME}_g(c)$ in w_i.

---

demonstrations. Denotations are determined by character-context pairs alone. The exact list of pure indexicals is somewhat controversial, but it undoubtedly includes the following few words: *I, here, now, actual, today* and *tomorrow.* Note that in uses of *here* and *now* the size of the automatically determined place and time might be occasionally vague. On the interpretation of this vagueness, see Kaplan (1989a: 491) and Predelli (2005: 40–75).

2 By an intended model I mean simply a model whose domain consists of some set of objects of the actual world.

Given an intended model *M*, the index *c* in (2a–d) represents in each case the actual context in which the evaluated expressions occur. Indexicals may denote different objects in different contexts, but it seems that every particular context determines the denoted objects completely and definitely. The personal pronoun *I*, for example, necessarily denotes in each of its occurrences the person who utters it. If you are the only utterer of *I* in *c*, *I* cannot denote me truly in that very context.

This observation is the basis of the Kaplanian Reference Principle, according to which pure indexicals are directly referential expressions (Kaplan 1989a: 492, 1989b: 569). The principle of direct reference claims that indexical denotations are directly determined with respect to the relevant parameters of the actual context of their occurrence. The mechanism of the determination is called direct, since the denoted objects become part of the propositions without the mediation of other propositional constituents. It is irrelevant how characters find their denoted objects. Although their referential behavior may be governed by descriptive rules, these rules are not part of the constituent structure of propositions. The character of *I*, for example, may be identified roughly with the descriptive rule *search for the person who is speaking or writing.* At the level of propositions, however, only the person denoted by *I* may have any model-theoretic significance.

If the Reference Principle is correct, then it is clear that the determination of the content of indexicals cannot be influenced by counterfactual circumstances. Moreover, it seems that when an indexical expression denotes an object in an intended model *M*, then it must denote the same object in all possible models *M**. Therefore, taking into consideration the structure of intended models, $[[a_g]]^{c,\,i} = \mathrm{DEN}_g\,(c)$ may be regarded as a generally valid rule for determining indexical denotations.

This rule does not mean, in and of itself, that circumstances cannot have an autonomous function in the process of evaluation. As stated above, circumstances might be relevant to assigning truth values to propositions. Consider the sentence in (2d). According to this example, the proposition expressed by *I am here now* should come out true in such contexts where the utterer of the sentence is at the location of the utterance at the time of the utterance in the world of the utterance. It is not hard to see that in intended models every context meets these requirements. Uttered sentences are bound with necessity to their actual agent, location and time parameters. So the question arises: could we have any model *M** in which the sentence *I am here now* may be uttered falsely? On Kaplan's view, such models do not exist. The reason for this is that a counterfactual circumstance in which the utterer is not at the location and time of the utterance would contain an impossible world parameter. If one would try to detach the agent parameter from the location and time parameters, the resulting picture would be obviously incoherent. Viewed from this perspective, $[[I\ am\ here\ now_g]]^{c,\,i} = 1$ counts as a logical truth in model theory.[3] But now consider the sentence type *Britney is here now* occurring in a particular context *c*:

(3) $[[Britney\ is\ here\ now_g]]^{c,\,i} = 1$ iff Britney is at LOC_g (c) and at $TIME_g$ (c) in w_i

In an intended model *M*, the proposition expressed by *Britney is here now* is true if and only if Britney is at the location and time of the context *c*. Example (3) illustrates this simple case.[4] Suppose that *Britney is here now* is indeed true in *c*. However, if the sentence were evaluated with respect to an arbitrary model *M**, and Britney were at another location at the time *t* of *c*, then the proposition expressed in *c* would be false. The example shows clearly the truth-conditional effect of circumstances. It is easy to recognize that, with their varying world and time parameters, circumstances of evaluation may alter the truth values of propositions.

Recent work on the Double Index Theory concentrates mainly on one related issue. There is presently a general consensus that modal, tense and locational operators can explicitly shift the circumstantial parameters of the evaluation process. Opinions differ, however, on the possibility of context-shift. Because of his Reference Principle, Kaplan denied the existence of context-shifting operators.[5] Recently, several researchers, among others Schlenker (2003b), Nishiguchi (2007), and Predelli (2008), have argued against this claim. They offered empirical evidence showing that in some natural languages contexts can be shifted by sentential operators. Others insisted that contexts may also be shifted without such operators. In their view, there are specific communicative settings in which contexts shift freely.

---

[3] Note that *I am here now* counts as a logical truth only if it is conceived of as an *utterance type*. If *I am here now* is conceived of as an *occurrence of a sentence type*, then it may be evaluated in some cases as false. In a model *M**, for example, in which no one exists, the occurrence of *I am here now* would express a false proposition.

[4] Here I take for granted that (i) as a directly referential expression the proper name Britney denotes Britney constantly across contexts and circumstances and (ii) it is used unambigously in *c*.

[5] Kaplan (1989a: 510) calls operators that attempt to modify contexts *monsters*.

1.2. Aims and the structure of the paper

In the sections below I focus my discussion on these two forms of context-shifting. The structure of the paper is as follows. In section 2.1, I provide an overview of the possible sources and effects of context-shifting. After outlining the basic problem, in section 2.2, I give a brief account of operator theoretic strategy. Section 2.3 turns to putative cases of free context-shifting. In section 3, I discuss the methodological issues of the relationship between linguistic theories and empirical data. In section 4, reflecting on a methodological observation, I elaborate a general constraint on the mechanism of shifting. My central claim is that, in addition to the behavior of the relevant contextual parameters, the possibility of context-shift depends essentially on a specific pragmatic factor. Finally, section 5 gives a summary of the main message of the paper.

2. At the semantics–pragmatics interface: context-shifting

2.1. The Fixity Thesis and its critics

Let us first examine briefly the relatively uncontroversial case of circumstance-shifting. Consider the following example:

(4) a. $[[$*Britney is here now*$_g]]^{c,\, i} = 1$
b. $[[$*Necessarily, Britney is here now*$_g]]^{c,\, i} = 0$

In (4a) the proposition expressed by *Britney is here now* is supposed to be true relative to a given collection of contextual and circumstantial parameters. In (4b) the necessity operator modifies the world and time parameter of the original circumstance of evaluation to the effect that the singular proposition about Britney should come out true with respect to all possible $<w, t>$ tuples. But it is beyond reasonable doubt that Britney's location in space and time is a contingent matter. She could have been at other places at the time of the utterance of the sentence *Britney is here now.* This is why in (4b) the proposition expressed by *Necessarily, Britney is here now* must be false. The most natural explanation is to conclude that the truth value difference between (4a) and (4b) arises because of the circumstance-shifting effect of the necessity operator.

The explanation becomes more controversial, however, if we turn to the case of the interaction between sentential operators and contextual parameters. On the one hand, one might think that there is no way for operators to act on contexts, because when operators begin their work the content of the characters in the embedded sentences is already secured. In fact, this is Kaplan's view. On the other hand, one might assume that context-shifting is governed by the same scopal mechanisms as circumstance-shifting. It is plausible to expect, solely on syntactic grounds, that within their scope operators can manipulate contexts in the same way as circumstances.

As for the first view, Kaplan (1989a: 510) illustrates the immunity of the content of characters to varying contexts with the locational operator *in some contexts it is true that.* According to his interpretation, there is a sharp contrast between the acceptability conditions of (5a) and (5b):

(5) a. [[*I am tired now*$_g$]]$^{c,\,i}$ = 1 iff $AUTH_g$ (c) is tired at LOC_g (c) and at $TIME_g$ (c) in w_i

b. * [[*In some contexts it is true that I am tired now*$_g$]]$^{c,\,i}$ = 1 iff $AUTH_g$ (c) is tired at LOC_g (c*) and at $TIME_g$ (c*) in w_i

In an intended model *M, I am tired now* is true if and only if the utterer in the actual context of the occurrence of the sentence is tired at the time of the utterance. The truth conditional structure of the expressed proposition seems to be represented appropriately by (5a).

With respect to the same model, (5b) seems to assume that there is at least one arbitrary context *c** significantly different from the actual context *c*, and in this context the utterer of the sentence is tired at the time of the utterance. At first blush this assumption is harmless. The property of being tired may be truly self-attributed by agents in different contexts. Accordingly, the proposition expressed by *In some contexts it is true that I am tired now* seems to be true if and only if the agent denoted by *I* is at the appropriate location and time and she is tired. So far, so good.

But on closer examination, (5b) is hard to interpret as a correct truth conditional structure, because the indexical expressions *I* and *now* in the embedded sentence cannot denote arbitrary objects. If I am tired now, I am tired in my actual context *c*. I could not be at the location of *c** at this very moment. Contrary to this fact, (5b) assumes that it may be true that I am now in *c** and I am tired there.

This demonstrates that the context indicated by the locational operator and the context of the indexicals in the embedded sentence are not the same. Therefore, one might conclude that *In some contexts it is true that* is a true context-shifing operator. The problem is that the proposition expressed by *In some contexts it is true that I am tired now* cannot be true, since the operator in question cannot interact with the content of *I* and *now.* (5b) is unacceptable, because according to the Reference Principle *I* and *now* are invariably connected to the agent and time parameters of their actual context *c*.

The upshot of the Kaplanian reasoning is that operators which attempt to modify the content of the indexicals do not exist in natural languages such as English. The main point of the Kaplanian view concerning the impossibility of context-shift is aptly summarized by Schlenker (2003b: 29) as follows:[6]

(6) *Fixity Thesis*: The denotation or propositional contribution of an indexical expression *a* is fixed solely by the actual context of occurrence *c*, and cannot be influenced by any sentential operators.

Note that the first part of the Fixity Thesis is in essence the semi-formal version of the general rule $[[a_g]]^{c,\,i} = DEN_g(c)$ stated above. The second part of the thesis implies the impossibility of operator controlled context-shift with respect to the determination of characters.

Interestingly, in the last few years a number of empirical surveys have come to the conclusion that there are natural languages which falsify the Fixity Thesis.[7]

According to the data collected by Speas (2000), first and second person pronouns in Navajo can be interpreted from the point of view of the agent, not from the point of view of the subject, when they occur within a direct discourse complement. This suggests that at least one form of context-shift is allowed in the semantics of Navajo. And similarly, Schlenker (2003a, b) argues at length that in Amharic the denotation of the first and second person pronouns may be shifted in reported speech acts.[8] Furthermore,

---

6 For my own purposes I modified the words of the original Schlenkerian version of the thesis. The term *fixed* is used here in the sense of *determined.* The Fixity Thesis is restated by Cable (2005).

7 Kaplan (1989a: 510–511) calls attention to the fact that in using a metalinguistic device contexts can be explicitly shifted:

There *is* a way to control an indexical, to keep it from taking primary scope, and even to refer it to another context (this amounts to changing its character). Use quotation marks. If we *mention* the indexical rather than *use* it, we can, of course, operate directly on it. Carnap once pointed out to me how important the difference between direct and indirect quotation is in

Otto said 'I am a fool.'
Otto said that I am a fool.

8 Amharic is a Semitic language spoken in North Central Ethiopia.

Anand and Nevins (2004) claim that optional shifting is possible for indexicals in Zazaki and Slave speech reports.[9]

What is more interesting is that some researchers maintain, in contrast with Kaplan, that the Fixity Thesis is false, even for English. Israel and Perry (1996), Schlenker (2003b), and Nishiguchi (2007) are of the opinion that in English one can find a couple of non-traditional context-shifting operators. One common feature of these works is that they do not radically deny the Kaplanian insights. Rather, they concentrate on exceptional or ambiguous cases. The basic pattern of this variant of shifting seems to be the following:

(7) $[[\mathrm{OP}a_g]]^{c,\,i} = \mathrm{DEN}_g(c) / \mathrm{DEN}_g(c^*)$

(7) symbolizes an interpretive option according to which an indexical expression in English either denotes an object of its actual context *c*, or it denotes an object of the shifted context *c**. OP here plays the role of the non-traditional context-shifting device. If (7) represents a real possibility, then we should have to revise some parts of the traditional model-theoretic semantics of indexicals.

The Fixity Thesis was criticized from another point of view by Sidelle (1991), Bezuidenhout (2003), and Recanati (2004). These authors argue for the possibility of operator free context-shifting. According to this alternative view, contexts might be shifted without the presence of any sentential operator. It is supposed that there are typical communicative situations in which indexicals denote obligatory objects of shifted contexts. If one evaluates recorded messages, post-it notes or fictional discourses, it is observable that indexicals switch their denotations from *c* to *c**. In all such situations, there is supposedly an implicit communicative convention in force. Indexicals in recorded messages, for example, have to be evaluated typically with respect to an intended context after the recording. Indexicals occurring in fictional discourses denote objects which belong to the domain of fiction, and so on. Although there are important variations between the individual cases, the general scheme is the following:

(8) In a typical communicative situation SIT_x it is appropriate to evaluate an indexical expression *a* as $[[a_g]]^{c,\,i} = \mathrm{DEN}_g(c_x)$.

[9] Zazaki is an Indo-Iranian language spoken mostly in Turkey. Slave is an Athabaskan language spoken in Canada. For more details, see Anand and Nevins (2004: 37).

As we have seen, the controversy about the possibility of context-shift revolves around three theses. Kaplan claims that operators which would modify the contextual behavior of characters do not exist in natural languages such as English. Others maintain that context-shifting operators exist in some languages, perhaps even in English. And some researchers are of the persuasion that contexts can be shifted without the presence of any operators. The adherents of the second and third theses attempt to prove that the Fixity Thesis is not crosslinguistically true. Let us investigate their proposals somewhat more closely.

2.2. Context-shift under the influence of sentential operators

The Amharic indexical first person pronoun is probably the best documented counterexample to the Fixity Thesis. Schlenker (2003b: 31) proposes to analyze the following speech situation.[10]

(9) *Situation to be reported*: John says: *I am a hero.*
 a. *English*: $John_1$ says that he_1 is a hero.
 b. *English*: *$John_1$ says that I_1 am a hero.
 c. *Amharic*: *ǰon ǰəgna nə-ññ yɨl-all*
 John hero be.PF.1SO 3M.say.AUX.3M
 '$John_1$ says that he_1 is a hero.' (lit.: '$John_1$ says that I_1 am a hero.')

The reported speech in (9a) is, of course, unproblematic. In (9b), however, English does not allow for the indexed pronoun to denote the subject of the matrix sentence, because *I* must denote the agent of the actual context. Therefore, there arises a discrepancy between the denotation of *John* and the established rule $[[I_g]]^{c,\,i} = AUTH_g\,(c)$.

In contrast to English, the Amharic first person pronoun may denote the agent of the reported speech act rather than of the actual speech act. That is, it can denote John. Schlenker points out that in (9c) the attitude operator modifies the content the character of *I*. Thus, the embedded clause *I am a hero* expresses the singular proposition *that John is a hero*. If Schlenker's data were obtained from a reliable source,[11] then it is plausible to claim, as Schlenker does, that in Amharic the operator SAY is able to modify the

[10] See also Anand and Nevins (2004: 26).

[11] As regards the sources of Amharic data, Schlenker enumerates several authentic informants in his study. See Schlenker (2003b: 68).

character of *I* in embedded sentences, which casts doubt on the crosslinguistic validity of the Fixity Thesis.

An alternative interpretation would be that in the example above the embedded clause were quoted. But, according to Schlenker, this interpretation is not possible in Amharic attitude reports. In this respect Amharic is similar to English. In spoken English *I* or *you* cannot normally be quoted in indirect discourse. Otherwise, the following sort of exchange might occur: "'Mary didn't hear what John told her 'you' should bring' should mean 'Mary didn't hear what John told her *she* (= Mary) should bring', contrary to fact" (Schlenker 2003b: 69).

The presence of a quoted indexical element in attitude reports is not permitted, either in Amharic or in English.

One further set of data strengthens the assumption made by Schlenker. According to Schlenker, it has been observed that in other syntactic positions the Amharic first person pronoun denotes the agent of its actual context. If *I* occurs in subject position in a matrix sentence, for example, then it denotes invariably the actual agent of the uttered sentence. This means that the Amharic counterpart to *I* behaves in an appropriate environment like a standard English indexical expression. With these sets of empirical data, Schlenker can plausibly argue that the reported speech in (9c) is a real instance of operator controlled shifting.

Operator controlled shifting has been observed recently in other natural languages such as Zazaki and Slave. Based on their empirical research, Anand and Nevins (2004) claim that in Zazaki all indexical expressions are, in principle, shiftable. That is, the Zazaki counterparts to English *I*, *you*, *here*, or *yesterday* all have the option of shifting when they occur within the scope of the attitude verb *vano* 'say'.

Let us take again as an example the indexical *I*. According to the interpretation of Anand and Nevins (2004: 22), the evaluation of the first person pronoun in the scope of *vano* offers the following option:

(10) *Situation to be reported*: Hesen said: *I am rich.*
  a. *English*: Hesen$_1$ said that he$_1$ is rich.
  b. *English*: *Hesen$_1$ said that I$_1$ am rich.
  c. *Zazaki*: *Hɛseni$_j$ (mi$_k$-ra) va kɛ ɛz$_{j/k}$ dɛwletia*
  Hesen.OBL (I.OBL.to) said that I rich.be.PRES
  'Hesen$_1$ said that he$_1$ is/I$_1$ am rich.'

In English, (10a) reports correctly the *de se* attitude of the subject of the matrix sentence (Hesen). (10b), however, represents a misleading report, because the English indexical *I* denotes the agent of the reporting context, not the agent (Hesen) of the original speech situation. Interestingly, the evaluation rules of Zazaki indexicals allow both forms of reporting. In (10c) the embedded clause mirrors an ambiguity concerning the effects of context-shifting. In the first case, context-shifting is blocked, and the attitude holder (Hesen) is denoted by the third person pronoun *he*, as is usual in English. In the second case, where shifting is allowed, the content of the character of the first person pronoun *I* is modified, and it also denotes the attitude holder. Anand and Nevins (2004: 24) maintain that the source of this ambiguity lies in the grammar of Zazaki. According to their view, there are data to support this claim. As in the Amharic example, the crucial point is, again, that shifted indexicals in Zazaki cannot be quotations. The best evidence for this is that A-extraction is prohibited in direct quotations, but it is possible out of complements of attitude verbs with shifted indexicals. Consider the following illustration from Anand and Nevins (2004: 24):

(11) *Situation to be reported*: Hesen said: *The girl that I kissed is pretty.*
a. *English and Zazaki*: *The girl that Hesen said, "I kissed *t*" is pretty.
b. *Zazaki*: *čɛnɛkɛ [kɛ Hɛseni va mɨ t paci kɛrda] rindɛka*
girl that Hesen said I *t* kiss did pretty.be.PRES
'The girl that Hesen said {Hesen, I} kissed is pretty.'

This example makes it probable that the shifting effect in (10c) depends on the grammatical features of the attitude verb *vano* rather than on the mechanism of quoting. If this is so, then on the basis of its grammar the Zazaki counterpart of English *say* may function as a context-shifting operator.

Roughly the same could be said about the Slave attitude verb *hadi* 'say'. There are, however, two minor differences between Zazaki and Slave. In Slave only the first person pronoun can be shifted in the scope of *hadi*, and the shift is always obligatory. On the other hand, the Slave counterpart to English *want* can optionally modify the content of the character of the first person pronoun, and the counterpart to *tell* can influence optionally all embedded pronouns.

At the end of their investigation, Anand and Nevins (2004: 36) draw the tentative conclusion that the observed cases demonstrate the existence of Zazaki and Slave context-shifting operators. It would follow from this that the Fixity Thesis must be abandoned as a valid principle in these languages.

As regards the shifting possibilities in English, the empirical support from recent hypotheses is not so convincing. Schlenker (2003b) and Nishiguchi (2007) try to prove that there are also context-shifting operators for

English indexicals. Let us turn first to Schlenker's argumentation. Schlenker's (2003b: 64) main argument is based on the following temporal example:[12]

(12) *Situation to be reported*: John has told me repeatedly over the years: *I was sick the day before yesterday/two days ago.*
   a. *The day before yesterday*: * John has told me repeatedly over the years that he was sick the day before yesterday.
   b. *Two days ago*: John has told me repeatedly over the years that he was sick two days ago.

According to Schlenker's interpretation, the report in (12a) is not acceptable, because the indexical phrase *the day before yesterday* denotes directly a day relative to the actual context of its occurrence, while the temporal modifier *over the years* denotes an indeterminate period of time. Thus, the direct denotation of the indexical phrase creates a conflict with the indeterminacy of the temporal modifier.

Clearly, it cannot be the case that John was sick the day before yesterday (= $[[\textit{the day before yesterday}_g]]^{c,\,i} = \mathrm{TIME}_g(c)$) over the years. This conflict is absent in (12b). The explanation is straightforward. Schlenker points out that *two days ago* can be evaluated with respect to the indeterminate period of time of the reported speech act. That is, the evaluation of *two days ago* does not depend on the time parameter of its actual context. It can denote any salient day. If John was sick on July 27, 2008, then *two days ago* in (12b) may denote this day. If John was sick on July 27, 2009, then *two days ago* in (12b) may denote this day.

Schlenker concludes from this fact that the contextual content of the indexical phrase *two days ago* can be modified by appropriate sentential operators such as TELL or SAY. If this is a reasonable account, then the Fixity Thesis is false even for English. In the case of English, however, it is not so easy to disprove the Fixity Thesis. Minimally, three powerful objections could be formulated against Schlenker's negative conclusion.

---

[12] A misleading remark must be corrected here. Schlenker (2003b: 30) claims that according to the Kaplanian account, context-shifting operators do not and could not exist in natural languages. Kaplan makes, in fact, a more careful observation. He states that there are no operators which could modify the content of characters *in English*. Fortunately, Schlenker later corrects his former interpretation and makes the following correct remark: "Kaplan grants that operators that shift the context of evaluation of an indexical are perfectly well-formed from a logical standpoint, but he claims that such monstrous operators do not exist in English and *could not even be added* to it." (Schlenker 2003b: 36).

First and foremost, it might be said that the expression *two days ago* is a bad example to begin with, because it is not directly referential in the Schlenkerian reading *the day before yesterday*. Recall what the Reference Principle states. As we have seen, Kaplan (1989b: 569) pointed out that indexicals are directly referential expressions, and thus their semantic values are determined completely and definitely by the parameters of their actual context of occurrence. Note, however, that in contrast to *the day before yesterday*, the phrase *two days ago* does not contain any directly referential expression. Although the semantic value of the phrase depends in part on the time parameter of the actual context, it does not depend directly on it. This means that in order to ascertain the propositional contribution of this phrase, one should make a detour through the whole proposition. Therefore, it seems dubious whether *two days ago* belongs to the class of Kaplanian indexicals. It is more probable that it plays the function of a predicate modifier which merely restricts the denotation domain of a predicate: $\mathrm{PRED}_{\text{two days ago}}$.[13]

Second, in a similar way, it may be argued that *two days ago* is an anaphoric expression rather than indexical. Anand and Nevins (2004: 25) claim that the denotation of *two days ago* may depend on the denotation of *over the years*. This would mean that the supposed sensitivity of *two days ago* to the sentential operator in (12b) is in fact a sensitivity to its anaphoric antecedent. In this case, the anaphoric linking function would indicate that the linked element gets its semantic value in an indirect way and that would be incompatible again with the Reference Principle.[14]

Third, as von Stechow (2003: 380) argues, the alleged facts of shifting may be explained through the mechanism of feature deletion under semantic binding. Von Stechow rejects the Schlenkerian theory, according to which operators can shift the contextual parameters of the evaluation process. Instead of this, he proposes a view that treats the symptoms of shifting as an effect of feature deletion at the logical forms of sentences. According to this approach, operators such as TELL or SAY can never act on the expressions of embedded sentences. If *two days ago* alters its value as in (12b), then it is due to binding by the matrix verb. That is, in (12b) the tense of the main clause must be co-indexed with the tense of the embedded *two days ago*, roughly in the following way:

---

13 A further possibility is that *two days ago* is a perspectival expression in the sense of Bezuidenhout (2005).

14 A similar line of thought is to be found in Ball (2006).

(12) b.' *Two days ago*: John has told$_{PAST}$ me repeatedly over the years that he was sick [two days ago$_{\text{PRES}}$]$_{PAST}$.

On this alternative interpretation the acceptability of (12b') is ensured by the deleted PRES feature and the co-indexed items. The main advantage of von Stechow's solution is that in explaining the mechanism of tense-shift it avoids the need to attribute indexical features to the non-indexical expression *two days ago*.

Yet, in spite of these obvious objections, some researchers try to defend Schlenker's theory. For instance, Nishiguchi (2007) offers a number of examples in defense of context-shifting operators in English. Perhaps the most promising among them is the example of implicit agent modality. Nishiguchi (2007: 195) claims that expressions of implicit modality are able to shift the time parameter of the actual context of an indexical sentence. Covert attitudes such as *I am sorry*, *I regret*, or *happily* are supposed to function as sentence operators.

According to Nishiguchi, context-shift occurs if two conditions are fulfilled: (i) The agent has a negative presupposition with respect to the obtaining of an event or state of affairs, and (ii) the sentence contains an expression of implicit modality. The speech situation in (13) seems to satisfy both of these conditions:

(13) *State of affairs*: It is cold outside.
  a. *Presupposition*$_{AUTH}$: It will be not cold outside.
  b. I am sorry that it has become cold outside.

Unfortunately, it is hard to know what to make of this example, because (13a) has nothing to do with the phenomenon of context-shift. Let us suppose for a moment that *I am sorry* functions as an operator and the adverb *outside* in its scope is a Kaplanian indexical.[15] Then, according to Nishiguchi's conception, the operator *I am sorry* should have to modify the actual time parameter of *outside*. But how would this happen? It cannot, because the evaluation of the expression *outside* is not dependent on the time parameter of its context at all. If *I am sorry* is indeed an operator, then it can perhaps interact with the tense feature of the embedded clause. It is not an implausible hypothesis that attitude expressions may function as tense-shifting devices. This aspect of the example is, however, wholly irrelevant to the issues of the shifting possibilities of indexicals.

---

[15] Following Bezuidenhout (2005), I would say that *outside* is not an indexical but a perspectival.

One can see from the above data that the crosslinguistic status of the Fixity Thesis is still an unsettled issue. Operator controlled shift seems to occur in some natural languages. In English, however, it is more difficult to find acceptable examples which would cast doubt on the Kaplanian theory of indexicals. With this result at hand, we find ourselves in a somewhat perplexing situation. We have found empirical research data which seem to provide strong evidence against a plausible model-theoretic principle. Examples collected from Navajo, Amharic, Slave and Zazaki native speakers appear to undermine the crosslinguistic validity of the Fixity Thesis. It is clear that the resolution of this conflict would require further investigations concerning the relationship between formal models and linguistic data. Below, in sections 5 and 6 I will suggest an appropriate strategy to this end. But before that goal can be achieved, we need a general overview of the mechanisms of free context-shift.

2.3. Evidence for free context-shift

The first part of the Fixity Thesis states that the content of an indexical expression *a* is determined solely by the parameters of the actual context in which it occurs. In recent years, this part of the Kaplanian view has been challenged as well. There is a growing body of empirical observations which seems to deny the distinctive role of the actual context in determining contents.

Many researchers, including Sidelle (1991), Bezuidenhout (2003), Recanati (2004) and Predelli (2005), are of the opinion that under certain interpretive conditions indexicals might be shifted from *c* to *c** freely, without using sentential operators. According to the proposed approach, there are communicative situations in which the occurrence of an indexical expression can be interpreted successfully only if the actual context is replaced with a new collection of parameters in the interpretive process.

Examples of free context-shifting include among others the following communicative situations: (i) recorded messages and post-it notes, (ii) fiction, (iii) historical present, and (iv) free indirect discourse.[16]

[16] This list is not in any sense comprehensive. Some situations of translating, advertising or nonquotational echoes may exemplify the operator free type of shifting, too. But first, the scenes where free shift appears most obviously are represented by the above examples. And second, these are the examples which are treated most frequently in contemporary literature. In this section, I attempt to demonstrate that the examples in (i)–(iv) have a common structure.

The first question which comes to mind on looking at these examples is the following: what does it mean that the denotation of *a* in *c* in a particular communicative situation SIT_x may be determined by the parameters of an alternative context *c**?

The general answer has the following form. Kaplan (1989a: 509) emphasized that from a model-theoretic point of view in intended models the class of contexts should be narrowed down to include only the proper ones. Proper contexts are quintuples <*s*, *t*, *l*, *w*, *g*>, where *s* is at *t* at *l* in the world state *w*, and *g* is an arbitrary variable assignment function. That means that proper contexts straightforwardly supply the parameters which are needed to determine the denotations of indexicals involved in them. If *a* is interpreted with respect to a proper context *c*, then the resulting content will be automatically truth evaluable. It is reasonable to suppose that in everyday exchanges indexicals occur overwhelmingly in proper contexts.

But in some communicative situations *c* may lack one or more of the relevant parameters for the evaluation of *a*. That is, in a particular SIT_x *c* may be qualified as an improper context. In spite of the missing parameters of *c*, however, the sentence which contains *a* remains truth evaluable, since SIT_x does not block the first step of the evaluation process. On the contrary, the process remains normal, so that SIT_x supplements the missing parameters of *c* by the proxy parameters of *c**. A proxy parameter should be thought of as equivalent in its role to a particular parameter of the actual context. Thus, in the end, *c* fixes the denotation of *a* with the partial contribution of *c**. So, as usual, in the second step of the evaluation process the sentence containing *a* may get its truth value relative to a possible circumstance *i*. Let us investigate the role of proxy parameters on concrete examples.

(i) Recorded messages and post-it notes

On the basis of Sidelle (1991), Predelli (2005: 51–53) analyzes the evaluation of *now* in a situation where a man – let's call him Jones – intends to inform his wife that she is to meet him at 11 p.m. Let us suppose that Jones is at home at 8 a.m. He records the sentence (14a) below, and hopes that his wife will be at home at 5 p.m.

(14) *Situation to be evaluated*: Jones records a message at 8 a.m. for his wife who is expected to arrive home at 5 p.m.

a. I am not here *now*, meet me in six hours at the airport.

b. $SIT_{recording}$: $[[now_g]]^{c,\,i} = TIME_g(c_{intended})$

If *now* were evaluated with respect to its actual context *c* in (14a), then it would denote 8 a.m. Intuitively, this would be an empirically inadequate result, since in this case the intended time of the meeting would be 2 p.m. But we have seen that Jones wants to meet his wife at 11 p.m. Moreover, the first part of (14a) would be false or paradoxical with respect to *c*, for it would express the proposition *that Jones is not at home at 8 a.m.* Therefore, the denotation of *now* must be determined by the time parameter of the context *c**, in which the recorded message is intended to be heard. The proxy parameter of this shifted context is 5 p.m. If Jones' wife hears the message at 5 p.m, she will understand correctly that her husband will expect her at the airport at 11 p.m. Accordingly, (14b) represents a case of free context shift for *now*.

It is important to note that although it involves a context-shift, the example above does not contradict the Kaplanian Reference Principle, in the sense that in (14b) *now* is still a directly referring expression. The only difference is that in the actual context of the recording, the denotation of *now* is determined not as TIME_g (c), but as TIME_g (c_{intended}). In spite of this partial shift, the denoted object is determined definitely and finally. To see this, let us suppose that Mrs. Jones arrives home later than 5 p.m. If she heard the message, say, at 6 p.m., then she would think that she should be at the airport at midnight. This would be simply a misinterpretation. Since the denotation of *now* has already been determined by the proxy parameter of the shifted context, it cannot be influenced by such contingencies as the thoughts and intentions of Mrs. Jones.

Post-it notes can give rise to similar phenomena. Consider the following example (Corazza, Fish and Gorvett 2002: 5):

(15) *Situation to be evaluated*: Jones writes a note and attaches it to the office door of his colleague Smith.

a. *I* am not in.

b. $\text{SIT}_{\text{writing}}$: $[[I_g]]^{c,\,i} = \text{AUTH}_g\,(c_{\text{intended}})$

Apparently, the first person pronoun denotes Jones in the context of writing, since Jones is the agent of the context. But according to Jones's communicative intention, *I* should denote his colleague Smith in the written sentence. This means that in the described situation the proxy parameter (Smith) should take over the role of the original agent parameter (Jones). In other words, if a reader understands the proposition expressed by (15a) correctly, then she should realize that the proposition expressed by the sentence *I am not in* is about Smith. It is important to stress that the reader should follow this interpretation even if she knows that the note was written originally by Jones.

(ii) Fiction

As Recanati (2004), Voltolini (2006) and Predelli (2008) observe, free context-shift happens often in fictional discourses. According to them, a fictional sentence which contains an indexical expression involves two different kinds of context. The primary context is *c*, the actual context of the occurrence of the indexical sentence. The secondary context is a pretended or imaginary context *c**, the context of the fictional discourse. Let us see what happens with the first person pronoun if it occurs at the beginning of a novel:

(16) *Situation to be evaluated*: The novelist writes the following sentence on the first page of her novel.

a. *I* escaped from the prison.

b. $\mathrm{SIT}_{\mathrm{fictional}}$: $[[I_g]]^{c,\,i} = \mathrm{AUTH}_g\,(c_{\mathrm{fiction}})$

In (16a) the act of writing provides the parameters which are needed to determine the denotation of the first person pronoun. Naturally, with respect to the actual context of writing, *I* denotes the novelist. But, from an empirical point of view, this interpretation seems to be wrong, since the singular proposition expressed by (16a) does not contain the novelist among its constituents. This proposition contains instead a fictive person. *He* escaped from the prison. This person belongs to the secondary context of the fiction which was created by the act of writing. The example suggests clearly that the denotation of *I* should be determined by this secondary context. Let us call it c_{fiction}. Thus, the proxy parameter of c_{fiction} for the determination of *I* is the agent of the fictional discourse. (16b) illustrates schematically this variant of free context-shift.

(iii) Historical present

Similar situations arise in some cases of historical narration. In recent years, the behavior of indexicals in historical discourses has elicited great attention. Several authors, among others Bezuidenhout (2003), Recanati (2004), and Voltolini (2006), agree on the possibility of free context-shift in these discourses. Historical present sentences interact, of course, with the time parameter of their actual context. With minor modifications, the following example is taken from Voltolini (2006: 25):

(17) *Situation to be evaluated*: In a lecture on history the following sentence occurs. (The lecture was given on July 27, 2008.)

a. *Now* Hitler begins his invasion of the USSR.

b. $\text{SIT}_{\text{historical}}$: $[[now_g]]^{c,\,i} = \text{TIME}_g\,(c_{\text{history}})$

It is easy to realize that the *now* in (17a) cannot denote the time parameter of the context in which it occurs. Evidently, Hitler did not begin his invasion on July 27, 2008. In (17a) *now* denotes, instead, June 22, 1941, the starting day of the invasion of the USSR. There is a risk of confusion if we interpret the sentence otherwise. This suggests that we must somehow identify the intention of the lecturer. If he intends to denote with *now* June 22, 1941, then we should follow him in this respect.

The denotation of *now*, however, does not depend exclusively on our mind reading abilities. Rather, the whole communicative situation must be taken into consideration. We all know that historical discourses deal with historical facts, even if they use the present tense. So *now* is embedded in a whole discourse in which the frame of time is structured otherwise than in everyday discourses. In this time frame the default context of *now*, namely c, may be shifted to c_{history} in a way which is represented by (17b). Clearly, (17b) is silent about the exact mechanism of context-shift, it shows solely that in $\text{SIT}_{\text{historical}}$ it is appropriate to evaluate *now* with respect to a shifted context c_{history}. But for our purposes this is a close enough approximation. We have presented a case where communicative success depends again on the presence of a proxy parameter.

(iv) Free indirect discourse (FID)

Bezuidenhout (2003) and Sharvit (2004) noticed recently that FID may generate occasionally free context-shift. FID is a literary form of narration in which the reader or listener is confronted with the inner thought of a person. It is interesting that in FID not all indexicals shift at once. Indexical pronouns are evaluated according to the above mentioned general rule $[[\alpha_g]]^{c,\,i} = \text{DEN}_g\,(c)$, while locational and temporal indexicals are allowed to alter their denotations with recourse to proxy parameters. (18) is a paradigmatic example:[17]

[17] The original example is to be found in Sharvit (2004).

(18) *Situation to be evaluated*: Jones stared at me.

a. I would resign today(, he thought).

b. SIT_{FID}: $[[\textit{today}_g]]^{c,\,i} = \text{TIME}_g\,(c_{\text{FID}})$

(18a) stands for the inner thought of Jones. The first person pronoun *I* denotes the reportee, but the context of the temporal indexical is shifted. *Today* represents a shifted time parameter where Jones locates himself, which does not coincide with the time parameter of the reportee. Accordingly, (18b) illustrates how the context of *today* shifts in (17a).

With the examples of (14)–(18) above, I wanted to demonstrate that paradigmatic cases of free context-shift for English indexicals exhibit the common structure SIT_x: $[[a_g]]^{c,\,i} = \text{DEN}_g\,(c_x)$. Within this structure *x* denoted in each case a typical kind of communicative situation. In all probability, structurally similar situations exist in most natural languages. The ground for this assumption is that the existence of these situations does not depend directly on language-specific rules which govern the behavior of context sensitive expressions. These situations come into being rather as a peculiar effect of improper contexts. Improper contexts, as we have seen, are semantically deficient in the sense that they lack one or more parameters which would be needed to settle the determination of contents completely. The content of characters must be somehow determined, however, before they are loaded into propositions of the usual kind. Thus, agents and recipients in improper contexts have no choice but to involve proxy parameters in their utterances and interpretations. This seems to be a trivial requirement for successful communicative interactions, not only in English, but in many other languages as well. If this assumption is accurate, then free context-shift must be indeed a very widespread linguistic phenomenon.

Let us stop here for a brief summary. The results of the first four sections are the following. It appears that the Fixity Thesis is not a crosslinguistically valid principle, because in some languages sentential operators can act on the content of indexicals. It is hard to find, however, convincing examples of indexical-modifying operators in English. Context-shift occurs more probably in operator free communicative situations. As we have seen, both forms of context-shifting – operator controlled and free shift – might be supported by data gathered from empirical sources.

In summarizing our results it is important to bear in mind, however, that we have dealt up to this point only with a small set of examples. Moreover, the examples we have referred to included only a restricted range of linguistic data. This raises an important question concerning the relationship between our theory and the data at our disposal: what is the theoretical status of the conclusions we draw from this restricted range of empirical data? In the following two sections, I provide some suggestions on how to answer this question.

3. Metatheoretical reflections on linguistic theories and data

3.1. A note on the relationship between linguistic theories and empirical data

At this point, there are two motives for making a brief note on the relationship between formal models and data.

On the one hand, we have established above that the crosslinguistic status of the Fixity Thesis is currently unstable. Although English indexicals appear to behave as Kaplanian model theory predicts, it turned out that the counterparts of English indexicals may be shifted occasionally by sentential operators in some other languages. In this respect, Navajo, Amharic, Slave and Zazaki data provided clear counterevidence to the Fixity Thesis.

On the other hand, we saw that improper contexts were *entia non grata* in the framework of the Kaplanian model theory. Kaplan excluded the possibility of semantically deficient contexts primarily on logical grounds. He thought it to be a matter of logical necessity that indexical sentences such as *I am here now* cannot be uttered falsely. In his view, every possible context of occurrence must guarantee that *I*, *here*, *now* and other indexical expressions denote their objects determinately. Non-denoting occurrences of these words would clash with the meaning conventions embodied in their characters. Therefore, Kaplan regarded the rule $[[a_g]]^{c,\,i} = \mathrm{DEN}_g\,(c)$ generally valid. But the validity of this rule may be questioned, since in some communicative situations it should be replaced by the rule $[[a_g]]^{c,\,i} = \mathrm{DEN}_g\,(c_x)$. This is what free context-shift cases demonstrated.

Putting these two motives together we can ask the question in what sense the examples above constitute counterevidence to the main thesis of the Kaplanian model theory. I suppose that Schlenker (2003b), Nishiguchi (2007) and many others would say that the data obtained from surveys of other languages and the examples in English may undermine the fundamentals of the Kaplanian approach. These researchers would claim that empirical findings provide counterevidence to the Kaplanian theory in the sense that they disprove or disconfirm the generalizability of its basic statements.

There is nothing peculiar in this methodological attitude. A pervasive assumption in this area of research is that theoretical statements which purport to express universal laws do not tolerate exceptions. It is not particularly important here how a given law becomes endowed with empirical import. In model-theoretic semantics, as in other branches of theoretical linguistics, universal laws may be achieved either by inductive or deductive procedures. Both methods can undoubtedly yield testable empirical generalizations. But what is more interesting is that the validity of an already existing law is assumed to depend on data which are gathered from empirical sources. The relationship between data and theory is thought to be twofold: in positive cases, empirical data confirm the theory, in negative cases, empirical data disconfirm the theory. Naturally occurring data are conceived as externally and objectively accessible phenomena. Thus, it is often assumed without reflection that it follows from the epistemological status of empirical data that they can function as confirming or disconfirming evidence for theoretical statements.

Schlenker (2003b) and Nishiguchi (2007) appear to think, for example, that a few Amharic and English data provide sufficient evidence to disconfirm Kaplan's Fixity Thesis. The structure of their main argument is as follows. If the Fixity Thesis states that the denotation of an indexical expression is determined by its actual context of occurrence, then this statement must be considered a universal law. Universal laws do not tolerate exceptions. There are Amharic and English data, however, which demonstrate that in special syntactic environments the denotations of indexical expressions may be determined by shifted contexts. So, the data in question function as exceptions. Therefore, we are entitled to conclude that the Fixity Thesis is not a universal law.

I do not mean to suggest that this line of reasoning is fundamentally flawed. It would be idle to question that empirical data of this kind play a decisive role in defending, modifying or rejecting existing theories. I want merely to point out that there is a viable alternative to this methodological stance. To sketch the alternative requires a small change in perspective.

It is customary to think that the methodological significance of empirical data stems from their epistemic properties. Speech events, inscriptions and other kinds of empirical data are thought to belong to the observable and theory-independent domain of reality. In the traditional sense of the empiricist notion of reality, they are real-world phenomena constituted from such material substances as sound waves in the air or ink marks on a piece of paper. Material substances of this kind are seen as the external causes of our sensory perceptions. This means that at this fundamental epistemological level empirical data may be taken to be the externally anchored starting points for all scientific research methods.

One important part of this popular methodological stance is that the empirical notion of datum is explained in a simplistic and reductive manner. Something may be accepted as a datum only if it can be reduced to, or identified with, a particular material substance with epistemologically significant properties. The problem with this reductive explanation is that in certain cases it may be highly difficult to ascertain whether a particular research object meets these criteria. Are mental objects of introspection, then, empirical data according to this approach? Or, what is the methodological status of grammaticality judgments in this respect? If grammaticality judgments can be thought of as empirical data, what would be their material substance? And what is the methodological value of linguistic data produced by computer simulations?[18]

Instead of attempting to answer these difficult questions, I propose to change slightly the current theoretical perspective.

In an interesting paper, Lehmann (2004) maintains that what constitutes a datum is not its epistemic properties but its function. Following his approach, we can say that for an object to count as an empirical datum it must fulfill an argumentative function in a particular field of research. We can argue with Lehmann (2004: 181) in the following way:

> Nothing is in and of itself a datum; instead, it is a datum for somebody (or for a scientific community) in some perspective. [...] Something is not a datum by virtue of corresponding to some elementary observation, like the "protocol sentences" of the logical positivists. On the contrary, it may be highly abstract. It may nevertheless function as a datum in some research that assigns it the role of unquestionable evidence in the argumentation. Thus, something is not in and of itself a datum, but it is a datum relative to some particular empirical research.

It is worth noticing that Lehmann provides in this passage a non-reductionist, functional explanation for the notion of datum. The first sentence of the passage suggests that the problem of data should be treated from a relativistic point of view, but we do not have to follow Lehmann in this risky direction. It deserves more attention that Lehmann's approach assigns an explicit argumentative function to data. This opens an alternative theoretical perspective for us. The proposed alternative view is that we see the methodological significance of empirical data not as derived from their epistemological properties, but as a consequence of their argumentative

---

[18] For a discussion of this type of data, see the remarks of Penke and Rosenbach (2007: 12).

function. Viewed from this perspective, the epistemological commitments of a given linguistic theory are of secondary importance. What is of primary importance is that once a research object has become part of an argumentative chain, then it should be acknowledged, at least provisionally, as datum.

We must guard, however, against two possible misunderstandings. First, it does not follow from the functional explanation that for a given linguistic theory any arbitrary object in the research domain could serve as datum. On the contrary, objects need to possess a dedicated argumentative function, and the argumentative function they possess must be relevant to one or more statements of the theory. This relevance requirement restricts significantly the number and kind of data candidates.

Second, the functional approach does not imply in itself that objects which function as data must provide in every concrete case conclusive evidence or counterevidence for a given hypothesis or theory. In ideal theoretical situations, where the justificatory relations of the research are maximally transparent, data may serve as conclusive evidence for or against a theoretical construction. But in the vast majority of cases, data cannot resolve conclusively the conflict between rival hypotheses or theories, since justificatory relations in linguistics are usually far from transparent.

Thus, we should not assume that there is always a particular set of data which may be identified with the evidential base of a given linguistic hypothesis or theory. The evidential relationship between data and theoretical statements is not so direct: the truth values of the statements of the theory are only provisionally determined by the available data.[19] This is so be-

[19] One line of research which places special emphasis on the analysis of this property of data originates from Rescher (1976). According to Rescher (1976: 10), data structures do not possess pre-established scientific values once and for all times. They provide only provisional support for the mechanisms of scientific reasoning. This means that data structures should be regarded as more or less plausible candidates for theoretical constructions. In the course of scientific reasoning, the initial plausibility of a given set of data may be increased or reduced. Theoretical statements are also associated with variable degrees of plausibility. From this point of view, it is appropriate to say that a given theoretical statement becomes acceptable only if it attains a relatively high degree of plausibility. It should be mentioned here that Rescher's metascientific insights have been reworked and applied to theoretical linguistics in recent works of Kertész and Rákosi (2005, 2006). Kertész and Rákosi (2005, 2006) concentrate primarily on specific case studies, but their analyses are based on general theoretical insights. I think the success of their application shows, at least, that the

cause data can affect truth values only through their function in argumentative chains, and this function changes continuously during the research process. As the research process progresses, for example, certain data may alter or even lose their truth-conditional function. But the opposite is also possible: certain types of data which were regarded formerly as irrelevant to the research project may acquire unexpectedly a genuine truth-conditional function. One of the main advantages of the functional explanation of data is that it helps to bring to light this important fact.

3.2. Formalizing the results

After this brief methodological detour, we can return to our main theme. As we have seen above, Schlenker (2003b), Nishiguchi (2007) and others claim that empirical data may provide sufficient evidence to disconfirm Kaplan's Fixity Thesis. Of course, in a very general sense of empirical data, their claim is uncontroversial. If there are natural speech data which appear to contradict the first or the second part of the Fixity Thesis, then the Kaplanian account is empirically inadequate.

This strong conclusion may be mitigated to some extent if we hold that empirical data are only functionally connected to the truth values of theoretical statements. Obviously, I do not want to suggest that Kaplan's account can be defended against the criticism outlined above. On the contrary, I tend to think that the Fixity Thesis is the weakest point of his Double Index Theory. Nevertheless, I want to maintain that the target of the criticism is not the right one.

The functional explanation of data highlighted the fact that an object may count as datum at a given stage of research in virtue of its argumentative status. Going one step further, we can conjecture that at different stages of a given research process different types of objects might count as datum. Similar considerations are relevant to the notion of empirical evidence: at different theoretical levels, different types of objects might play the role of empirical evidence. Now, let us revise the Kaplanian account and its critique in the light of these considerations.

First of all, one should not forget that model-theoretic investigations in semantics set out usually from a restricted experiential basis. It is well known that Kaplan (1989a, 1989b) examined only a few concrete examples from everyday English. He simply neglected the fact that in ordinary inter-

---

Rescherian approach is compatible with current theories in formal semantics, but to argue for this point would take us too far afield.

actions there is a great variety of linguistic constructions relevant to the theory of indexicals.[20] His work focused primarily on the structural and modal features of contexts and circumstances. He was deeply persuaded that the contextual and logical connections between character, content and truth cannot be influenced by the contingencies of communicative actions.[21] Thus, his main aim was to elaborate a theoretical framework devoid of the muddled world of actions and then construe within this framework a consistent formal language for indexical expressions. The invented language was based essentially on the vocabulary of classical first-order predicate logic.

Although Kaplan presented some pieces of his formal framework in a colloquial style, we should keep in mind that the Fixity Thesis belongs to the pure formal level of the Double Index Theory. In order to see this, let us formalize the initial thesis. Remember that the first part of the thesis states that the denotations of characters are determined by their actual context of occurrence, and the second part declares the impossibility of context-shift with respect to characters. After separating the two parts, we get the following result:

(19) *The Fixity Thesis formalized*:
  a. $([[a_g]]^{c,i} = DEN_g(c)) = 1$
  b. $([[OP\ (a_g)]]^{c,i} = DEN_g(c^*)) = 0$

Adherents of the operator theoretic strategy, as we already know, maintain that the second part of the schematic presentation of the thesis is not valid. According to their diagnosis, sentential operators may interact with charac-

[20] Two earlier proposals in the same spirit can be found in Lewis (1970) and Hintikka (1979). "(1) What sort of thing is a meaning? (2) What is the form of semantic rules whereby meanings of compounds are built from the meanings of their constituent parts? It is not my plan to make any strong empirical claim about language. To the contrary: I want to propose a convenient format for semantics general enough to work for a great variety of logically possible languages" (Lewis 1970: 18). "For of course we can study certain aspects of the rules governing the use of language in abstraction from the idiosyncrasies of the people using it. This feat is no more remarkable, I am tempted to say, than studying syntax in isolation from the idiosyncrasies of handwriting and typeface" (Hintikka 1979: 18).

[21] Consider a famous Kaplanian maxim often cited in the present-day literature on indexicals: "Logic and semantics are concerned not with the vagaries of actions, but with the verities of meanings." (Kaplan 1989b: 584–585)

ters which occur in their scope, and this syntactic interaction results occasionally in context-shift. Thus, they opt for an alternative version of (b) with variable truth values:

(19) b'. $([[\mathrm{OP}\ (a_g)]]^{c,\,i} = \mathrm{DEN}_g\,(c^*)) = 0/1$.

Schlenker would surely contend that we should accept (b') instead (b) because of the evidential force of natural language examples produced by native Amharic and English speakers. Amharic examples demonstrate unambiguously that some attitude operators are able to elicit semantic effects pertaining to the determination of indexical denotations. This means that there are Amharic attitude verbs that quantify over contexts instead of circumstances. If Schlenker's analysis is on the right track, certain English attitude verbs can produce analogous effects. All of this seems to provide sufficient evidence for (b').

But what reason do we have for thinking that the empirical data presented by the adherents of the operator theoretic strategy are pertinent to (b) at all?

The formula (b) illustrates how the characters of indexicals behave in interpretive models composed from contexts and circumstances. In particular, it illustrates that characters are in principle immune to operator controlled context-shifting attempts. It is important to see, however, that as a logico-semantic thesis (b) is not a simple generalization of empirical observations. Quite the contrary, it must be conceived as a corollary of higher-order laws which govern the semantic relations between indexical expressions and objects or states of affairs. As already indicated, one of these laws is the Reference Principle. Other laws concern, for example, the cognitive significance of indexical thoughts or the role of directing intentions in the determination of denotations (See Kaplan 1989a: 530 and 1989b: 587–588). This demonstrates clearly that (b) is settled at a theoretical level where natural language examples may play only an indirect evidential role.

I suspect that the Schlenkerian intuitions concerning the invalidity of (b) are credible. There is something wrong with (b). If so, it should be replaced by (b'). Nevertheless, I think that it is a methodological mistake to argue for (b') directly with empirical data.

What of the first part of the schematic presentation of the Fixity Thesis? The formula (a) illustrates that it is an essential feature of characters that they denote objects in their actual context of occurrence. Actual contexts are supposed to be proper contexts, in the sense that they provide in any case the objects characters are searching for. What (a) says is that contents can be generated only in this way.

But, again, there are natural language examples which can be regarded as exceptions to (a). It is assumed that in improper contexts characters are allowed to denote objects which belong to their proxy contexts. Thus, Bezuidenhout, Recanati and other theorists would opt for an alternative version of (a). In their version the denotation rule would be provided with variable truth values:

(19) a'. $([[a_g]]^{c,i} = DEN_g(c)) = 1/0$

Note that (a') specifies only partially how some theorists think about the possibility of free context-shift. It does not show the hidden factors which cause the failure of (a). As we have seen, free context-shift presupposes the presence of improper contexts which create idiosyncratic communicative situations. The success of the determination of sentential contents in these situations is supposed to depend crucially on the communicative intentions of the agents and the interpretive skills of the recipients. Bezuidenhout, Recanati and others seem to think that these success conditions are manifested by the examples gathered from the empirical domain of language use. According to their view, recorded messages, sentences from fictional language and other examples help to make explicit the hidden structure of the situations where (a) does not hold. Then, referring to the naturalness and obviousness of these examples, they conclude that in some situations proxy contexts play a supplementary role in determining the contents of characters. This provides sufficient reason to move from (a) to (a').

Given this familiar methodological strategy, we can repeat our former question: in what sense are the empirical data mentioned by free context-shifting theorists relevant to the validity of (a)?

I fear that such types of empirical data are of little relevance to the theoretical status of (a). That is to say, they have little *direct* relevance to (a). Recall that (a) and (b) are intended equally as schematic generalizations. From this it follows that they are settled at the same theoretical level. If they are settled at the same theoretical level, they must be interconnected with the same higher-order semantic and logical laws. Obviously, as theoretical generalizations which aim at truth, they are also interconnected with the validity/invalidity of these higher-order laws. From the validity or invalidity of the Reference Principle, for example, we can directly deduce the validity or invalidity of (a) and (b). This would be a methodologically legitimate operation, since we would investigate conceptual connections between general claims with conceptual means. But it is questionable how empirical data might be incorporated into the implementation of this conceptual framework.

In my view, the common mistake behind the proposals (a') and (b') is purely methodological rather than substantive. Both proposals leave out of consideration that even in model-theoretic approaches to semantics there are different levels of argumentation. There is nothing inherently wrong in making use of natural language examples for testing existing model-theoretical principles. But before the testing is done, the target of the criticism must be properly identified.

A little reflection is enough to see what has gone wrong here. Everyone would agree that Kaplan's Fixity Thesis is not an *a priori* principle, since it is based partly on an *a posteriori* analysis of the behavior of indexical expressions. This means that it is related to the ways indexicals are used in natural languages by competent agents. And it reflects also the ways indexical propositions are conveyed in everyday communicative exchanges. But, as we have seen, it can be pointed out that the theoretical level at which Kaplan's thesis is settled cannot be confronted *immediately* with the opaque processes of natural language use. It seems to me that there is a methodological mismatch in the arguments which try to prove the opposite.

Note again that my central objection to the proposals (a') and (b') is methodological in nature. I think that we have to find a more appropriate procedure to argue for the credibility of (a') and (b'). The positive part of my criticism is then the following. First, we should reassess the problematical consequences of the Fixity Thesis on the abstract level of the representation of contexts and circumstances. Second, we should elaborate an alternative critical approach to Kaplan's thesis which does not depend directly on empirical counterexamples, but which is able to predict and explain the existence of such counterexamples.

4. The pragmatic constraint on shifting

Let us start with quoting a significant passage from Cresswell (1979: 138–139): "It seems to me impossible to lay down in advance what sort of thing is going to count as a context of use. [...] The moral here seems to be that there is no way of specifying a finite list of contextual coordinates."[22]

Cresswell rightly complains that the notion of context is fraught with indeterminacies. In fact, contexts are not natural kinds out in the world. One cannot observe and catch contexts and then separate out their functional constituents as, for instance, biologists used to dissect insects. The notion of context is a theoretical artifact and as such its denotational structure cannot

---

[22] On the background to this passage, see Lewis (1980: 86–87).

be depicted in a theory-free manner. This counts as a notorious problem for truth-conditional semantics in general and it also poses a considerable challenge for model-theoretic investigations.[23]

Fortunately, there is a way out of the awkward situation described by Cresswell, for we can stick to a particular framework and use the notion of context in harmony with its conceptual stipulations. Thus, we can specify a finite list of contextual parameters without postulating thereby a neutral or absolute notion of context. This is only a partial solution for Cresswell's problem, but it is a solution worth considering seriously.

This means in our case that we may stick to the Kaplanian framework and represent contexts as quintuples of the form <*s*, *t*, *l*, *w*, *g*>. One important stipulation here is that such a list of contextual parameters must be sufficient to determine the denotations of all indexical expressions. A further stipulation is that contexts are structured properly such that any occurrence of *I* denotes the agent *s* of the actual context. And similarly *now* is supposed to denote automatically the time *t* of the actual context, *here* is supposed to denote the location *l* of the actual context, and so on.

Given these stipulations, the question arises whether the Kaplanian notion of context is suitable for accounting for all possible occurrences of indexical expressions. Kaplan believes that the answer is a categorical Yes, but I am persuaded that the right answer is No.

Two possible types of occurrence case are relevant here. The first type of case arises when one of the parameters is missing from the quintuple <*s*, *t*, *l*, *w*, *g*>. Let us suppose, for example, that the first person pronoun *I* occurs in *c*, but the agent *s* is absent in *c*. Thus, *I* would have to be evaluated with respect to the parameter structure <_, *t*, *l*, *w*, *g*> where the blank space would symbolize the missing agent parameter. Kaplan would maintain that this type of case is impossible on logical and metaphysical grounds, but we should not forget that this verdict follows from his initial stipulations.

The second type of case occurs when a context requires definitely that the quintuple <*s*, *t*, *l*, *w*, *g*> be supplemented with an additional parameter. Let us suppose, for example, that the first person pronoun *I* occurs in *c*, but the agent *s* of *c* takes over the semantic function of the agent s_1 of c* in *c*. In this case the correct formal representation of *c* would be <*s*, s_1, *t*, *l*, *w*, *g*>, and *I* would denote s_1. Kaplan's response would be that this type of case is incredible, because the first person pronoun in *c* denotes always the agent *s*,

---

[23] A lot of literature is devoted to this problem. See, among others, the works of Gauker (1998), Lewis (1980) and Predelli (2005).

quite independently of the distribution of semantic functions. But this verdict would follow again from his initial stipulations.

It is easy to see that the Fixity Thesis stands or falls with these background stipulations. If we accept that the Kaplanian parameter structure <*s*, *t*, *l*, *w*, *g*> is sufficient for the evaluation of all possible contextual occurrences of indexical expressions, then we must hold that the formalized version of the Fixity Thesis is valid. That is, we must hold that the formulas (a) and (b) represent true laws.

If, on the other hand, we are inclined to think that the Kaplanian parameter structure is not capable of covering all possible occurrences of indexicals, then we must conclude that the Fixity Thesis is not universally valid. Though this conclusion does not prove in itself that the alternative formulas (a') and (b') are true, it gives them undoubtedly some positive support.

I think the intuition behind this latter opinion is powerful enough to base on it a new critical approach. So I take it as an open possibility that the parameter structure <*s*, *t*, *l*, *w*, *g*> may sometimes provide too much, sometimes too little to the correct evaluation of indexical expressions. This means that some contexts may contain more parameters than required by the evaluation principles. And the opposite is also possible: some contexts may contain too few parameters to offer an adequate evaluation for an occurrence of a given indexical expression. The possibilities in question do not depend directly on the accessibility of supporting empirical evidence, for at least two reasons. First, there is no need to point to empirical counterexamples in order to recognize the restrictiveness of the Kaplanian stipulations. We see by simple inspection that several expression-context combinations are ruled out by the proposed parameter structure. Second, even if one took into account empirical counterexamples, that would lead to *questionable* results, since, as we have seen, the evidential relationship between empirical data and theoretical claims is not fully transparent.

Supposing that some of these possibilities may actually occur, we cannot evade the issue of non-Kaplanian contexts. The task is then to explain how these improper, non-Kaplanian contexts might be integrated into the conceptual framework outlined so far.

In my view, the best method to reshape critically the Kaplanian framework at the most general level is to supply the parameter structure <*s*, *t*, *l*, *w*, *g*> with a particular pragmatic component. The main advantage of this strategy is that it preserves the explanatory power of the model-theoretic account, and, at the same time, it helps to explain the basic mechanism behind the phenomenon of context-shift without relying essentially and directly on empirical data.

I do not intend to use the notion pragmatic in a very specific sense, since I will not engage in the incredibly complicated semantics versus pragmatics debate here. I will merely draw attention to a potential explanatory component that has hitherto been left out of interpretive models. But before turning to a clarification of the notion particular pragmatic component, let us consider the following passage from a recent paper of Vanderveken (2008: 12): "Agents personally and voluntarily make their own attempts. Whoever attempts to make an attempt makes it. Agents make attempts in order to reach an objective. Whoever attempts to make an attempt succeeds in making that attempt, but he can fail to reach his objective. In such a case his attempt is unsatisfied."

The literature on speech act theory has already devoted a lot of attention to the issue of success conditions of intentional acts. From this point of view, there is nothing new in Vanderveken's observation. It is more interesting that at the end of his discussion Vanderveken (2008: 24) comes to the following conclusion: "One should reinforce the theoretical approach to conversation by integrating semantics and pragmatics within a general formal discourse pragmatics studying the logical structure and dynamics of all types of dialogues with a proper conversational goal."[24]

One aspect of this conclusion is highly relevant to our topic. In Kaplan's model-theoretic framework, occurrences of indexicals and indexical sentences are represented as if they were detached from the communicative attempts of agents. Strictly speaking, occurrences of expressions in contexts are not true conversational units in this framework at all. They do not represent observable realizations of speech acts. This is why the Kaplanian principles are insensitive to the pragmatic aspects of communication.

But what should we do if non-Kaplanian contexts of occurrence are indeed possible? This is where Vanderveken's claim becomes important, since we have found a specific theoretical area with respect to which the integration of semantics and pragmatics seems to be desirable. In any case, my claim is that we need a particular pragmatic component if we want to give a unified account of how indexical expressions and indexical sentences can be evaluated in non-Kaplanian contexts.

The reason for this is relatively simple. Non-Kaplanian contexts, where shifting is possible, come in double packages. The first context is c in which an indexical expression a occurs. The second context is c^* which functions as a proxy of c. The role of the proxy context c^* is to provide one or more parameters for the evaluation of a. It is important to see that if c is given, c^*

[24] For an earlier approach to this theme, see Vanderveken (2004).

cannot be arbitrarily determined. Not any context can function as a proxy for *c*. There must be a connection or passage between *c* and *c**. And my contention is that the passage is pragmatic.

The pragmatic account I am proposing looks roughly like this. Non-Kaplanian contexts require a special passage between related pairs of contexts. If *a* occurs in *c*, and *a* can be evaluated only with the (partial) contribution of *c**, then both contexts must be accessible for the evaluation process. But the character of *a* and the parameter structures of *c* and *c** in themselves do not explain how this can happen. It is not entirely clear what enables that the denotation of *a* be determined despite the deficiencies of *c*. It also needs to be explained how the appropriate proxy for *c* can be selected. The most plausible explanation of these unclarities is that the possibility of the passage depends on an explanatory component which lies outside of the parameter structures of *c* and *c**. Or, to be more precise, there is a set of explanatory components which members make the passage either individually or collectively possible.

It is beside the point to provide a fine-grained identity criterion for these explanatory components. There is no need to be too specific here. It is enough to allude to a few plausible candidates.

(i) Agents and recipients possess *general communicative skills* which are needed to use and interpret indexicals and indexical sentences successfully in non-Kaplanian contexts.
(ii) In certain situations, there are *conventionalized norms of reasoning* in force that yield the result that the communicative attempts of agents will be satisfied.[25]
(iii) There are also *conventionalized norms of using syntactic structures* that help to determine the denotations of characters in non-standard cases.
(iv) Agents and recipients may use *implicature patterns* to establish connections between non-Kaplanian contexts and their proxies.
(v) The propositions indexical sentences express can be understood sometimes only relative to certain *background assumptions*.

The explanatory components mentioned in (i)–(v) can be conceived of as constituents of non-Kaplanian contexts. It is somewhat embarrassing that some of them have clearly non-extensional features. Skills and norms, for example, cannot be analyzed using exclusively model-theoretic terms.

[25] For this, see the argumentation in Corazza, Fish and Gorvett (2002).

Background assumptions may be even more problematical in so far as they represent intensional mental states. It does not follow from this, however, that they cannot be integrated into the framework of interpretive models.

Here is one way to proceed. Let us refer comprehensively to these contextual constituents under the symbol *p*. Then we can say that in non-Kaplanian contexts the correct evaluation of indexicals depends on the presence or absence of *p*. If *a* occurs in a non-Kaplanian context *c*, and *p* is present in *c*, then there is a passage from *c* to *c** and the denotation of *a* becomes determined through the passage. In the absence of *p*, the passage is closed and *a* remains unevaluated.

There are two equivalent options to formalize the result. The first option is that we supplement the Kaplanian parameter structure with *p*: $<s, t, l, w, g, p>$. Or, alternatively, we can say that an interpretive model may consist occasionally of three parts: *c*, *p* and *i*. I will adopt this latter option.

Remember that the reason behind the introduction of *p* was that it may provide a methodologically acceptable argument for the possibility of context-shift. Thus, we have to concentrate primarily on the role *p* plays in arguing for (a') and (b'), regardless of the exact nature of *p*.

In other words, the account presented here is methodological (or structural) rather than substantive. It makes clear that both variants of context-shift are constrained pragmatically. We can model the supposed interpretive relationship between characters, contexts and their proxies with the following schema:

(20) *The pragmatic constraint on context-shift:*

If in a given context *c* $[[\text{OP}\ (a_g)]]^{c,\,i} = \text{DEN}_g\,(c^*)$ or $[[a_g]]^{c,\,i} = \text{DEN}_g\,(c^*)$ is the case, then to evaluate *a* correctly in *c* there must be a pragmatic passage *p* between *c* and *c**.

Obviously, our schema does not disconfirm the Fixity Thesis. It expresses only a conditional claim: *if* shifting is possible at all, then its mechanism obeys the constraint exhibited by *p*. But I am presuming, with Schlenker and many others, that the antecedent of this conditional is true. Thus, there seems to be no obstacle to present the constrained mechanism of shifting in a concise form:

(21) *Generalized formulas for shifting*:

(a'') $[[\text{OP}\ (a_g)]]^{c,\, i[c\rightarrow p\rightarrow c^*]} = \text{DEN}_g\,(c^*)$

(b'') $[[a_g]]^{c,\, i[c\rightarrow p\rightarrow c^*]} = \text{DEN}_g\,(c^*)$

(a'') and (b'') demonstrate that contextual modifications of characters are licensed at the abstract level of parameter structures. In particular, they show – contrary to the Kaplanian stipulations – that some pragmatic factors may intrude into the first step of the evaluation process of indexicals. But notice that the correctness of (a'') and (b'') depends partly on the presumed truth of the antecedent *if shifting is possible at all.*

5. Conclusion

The extent to which this paper presents a mixture of formal and pragmatic perspectives may be unusual to some readers. I admit that there is a terminological tension in the proposed account, but we should not forget that context-shift is, in itself, a rather unusual phenomenon. If a particular pragmatic factor helps to understand better the complicated mechanism of context-shift, then I think it should be involved in the explanation. Moreover, as we have seen, we can also formalize the pragmatic constraint on shifting. A non-reductionist, functional explanation of empirical data shows how this theoretical move can be carried out. The functionalist approach to linguistic data may be regarded, therefore, as the basic methodological precondition for developing an adequate (non-Kaplanian) theory of shifted indexicals. The final consequence of this is that model-theoretic evaluations of context sensitive expressions should consist of various kinds of data ranging from syntactic and semantic features of expression types to formalizable, pragmatic elements of language use.

Acknowledgements

The research reported on in the present paper was supported by the Research Group for Theoretical Linguistics at the Universities of Debrecen, Pécs and Szeged, Hungary.

References

Anand, Pranav and Andrew Nevins
2004 Shifty operators in changing contexts. In *Proceedings of the 14th Conference on Semantics and Linguistic Theory*, Kazuha Watanabe and Robert B. Young (eds.), 20–37. Ithaca, NY: Cornell Linguistic Publications.

Ball, Derek
2006 Bound variables and monstrous semantics. Paper presented at *The 34th Annual Meeting of the Society for Exact Philosophy.* Princeton, 6 March 2006.

Bezuidenhout, Anne
2003 Context-shifting. Invited paper read at conference on philosophy of language, Yale University, November 7–9. http://www.cas.sc.edu/ling/faculty/bezuidenhout/Context_shifting.pdf.

Bezuidenhout, Anne
2005 Indexicals and perspectivals. *Facta Philosophica* 7: 3–18.

Cable, Seth
2005 *Binding local person pronouns without semantically empty features.* Ms. http://people.umass.edu/scable/papers/binding-local-pronouns.pdf.

Corazza, Eros, William Fish and Jonathan Gorvett
2002 Who is I? *Philosophical Studies* 107: 1–21.

Cresswell, Max J.
1979 The world is everything that is the case. In *The Possible and the Actual: Readings in the Metaphysics of Modality*, Michael J. Loux (ed.), 129–145. Ithaca, NY: Cornell University Press.

Gauker, Christopher
1998 What is a context of utterance? *Philosophical Studies* 91: 149–172.

Hintikka, Jaakko
1979 Language-Games. In *Game-Theoretical Semantics: Essays on Semantics by Hintikka, Carlson, Peacocke, Rantala and Saarinen*, Esa Saarinen (ed.), 1–26. Dordrecht: Reidel.

Israel, David and John Perry
1996 Where monsters dwell. In *Logic, Language, and Computation*, Volume 1, Jerry Seligman and Dag Westerstdahl (eds.), 303–316. Stanford: Center for the Study of Language and Information.

Kamp, Hans
1971 Formal properties of 'now'. *Theoria* 37: 223–273.

Kaplan, David
1989a Demonstratives. In *Themes from Kaplan*, Joseph Almog, John Perry and Howard Wettstein (eds.), 481–563. Oxford: Oxford University Press.

Kaplan, David
1989b Afterthoughts. In *Themes from Kaplan*, Joseph Almog, John Perry and Howard Wettstein (eds.), 565–614. Oxford: Oxford University Press.

Kertész, András and Rákosi, Csilla
2005 Whole-part and part-whole inferences in generative and cognitive linguistics. *Acta Linguistica Hungarica* 52: 221–280.

Kertész, András and Rákosi, Csilla
2006 Inconsistency and plausible reasoning in an analysis of German affricates. A case study in the philosophy of linguistics. *Language Sciences* 28: 386–423.
Lehmann, Christian
2004 Data in linguistics. *The Linguistics Review* 21: 175–210.
Lewis, David
1970 General semantics. *Synthese* 22: 18–67.
Lewis, David
1980 Index, context, and content. In *Philosophy and Grammar*, Stig Kanger and Sven Öhman (eds.), 79–100. Dordrecht: Reidel.
Nishiguchi, Sumiyo
2007 Covert emotive modality is a monster. In *Lecture Notes in Artificial Intelligence: New Frontiers in Artificial Intelligence. Joint JSAI 2006 Workshop Post-Proceedings*, Takashi Washio, Ken Satoh, Hideaki Takeda and Akihiro Inokuchi (eds.), 191–204. Berlin: Springer.
Penke, Martina and Anette Rosenbach
2007 *What Counts as Evidence in Linguistics?* Amsterdam: Benjamins.
Predelli, Stephano
2005 *Contexts. Meaning, Truth, and the Use of Language.* Oxford: Clarendon Press.
Predelli, Stephano
2008 Modal monsters and talk about fiction. *Journal of Philosophical Logic* 3: 277–297.
Recanati, François
2004 Indexicality and context-shift. Paper presented at the *Workshop on Indexicals, Speech Acts, and Logophors.* Harvard University, 20 November 2004.
Rescher, Nicholas
1976 *Plausible Reasoning.* Assen: Van Gorcum.
Schlenker, Philippe
2003a Indexicality, logophoricity, and plural pronouns. In *Research in Afroasiatic Grammar II (Selected Papers from the Fifth Conference on Afroasiatic Languages, Paris, 2000)*, Jacqueline Lecarme (ed.), 409–428. Amsterdam: John Benjamins.
Schlenker, Philippe
2003b A plea for monsters. *Linguistics and Philosophy* 26: 29–120.
Sharvit, Yael
2004 Free indirect discourse and de re pronouns. In *Proceedings of the 14th Conference on Semantics and Linguistic Theory*, Kazuha Watanabe and Robert B. Young (eds.), 305–322. Ithaca, NY: Cornell Linguistic Publications.

Sidelle, Alan
1991 The answering machine paradox. *Canadian Journal of Philosophy* 81: 525–539.

Speas, Margaret
2000 Person and point of view in navajo. In *Papers in Honor of Ken Hale*, Andrew Carnie, Eloise Jelinek and Mary Willie (eds.), 19–38. Cambridge, MA: MIT Press.

Stechow, Arnim von
2003 Feature deletion under semantic binding: tense, person, and mood under verbal quantifiers. In *Proceedings of the Thirty-Third Annual Meeting of the North East Linguistic Society*, Makoto Kadowaki and Shigeto Kawahara (eds.), 379–404. Amherst, MA: University of Massachusetts.

Vanderveken, Daniel
2004 Success, satisfaction and truth in the logic of speech acts and formal semantics. In *Semantics: A Reader*, Steven Davis and Brendan S. Gillon (eds.), 710–734. Oxford: Oxford University Press.

Vanderveken, Daniel
2008 Towards a formal pragmatics of discourse. Forthcoming in the *Proceedings of the International Colloquium Logic and Dialogue.*

Voltolini, Alberto
2006 Fiction as a base of interpretation contexts. *Synthese* 153: 23–47.

Demonstratives and reference to individuated objects vs. reference to properties of objects: A contrastive analysis

Thorstein Fretheim

1. Introduction

1.1. Background

According to the direct reference program of analytical philosophy of language (Kaplan 1989a, 1989b; Recanati 1993), the descriptive meaning of a definite description that is used referentially is truth-conditionally irrelevant: it contributes no constituent to the propositional content of the utterance.

The following data was found in ter Meulen (1995: 339).

(1) a. *The president is getting old.*
 b. *The president of the club is John.*

The referentially used definite description in (1a) contains a noun, *president*, which is a truth-conditionally irrelevant description of the referent according to the direct reference theory, while the actual referent of the term is a constituent of the propositional content of an utterance of (1a). In contrast, the definite description in (1b) is predicatively used, so being the president of the club is a truth-conditionally relevant attribute of the person called John.

Demonstratives, whether complex ones consisting of a determiner and minimally a head noun or a pronoun unaccompanied by a descriptive item, are said to be directly referential terms that invariably supply a referent to the propositional content, and whose descriptive elements never figure in the content of the utterance. Consider sentence (2), an utterance of which involves two jointly performed operations that will enable the hearer to identify the object the speaker is drawing the hearer's attention to: (i) the linguistic stimulus with the description of the person referred to, and (ii) the speaker's simultaneous gestural demonstration in the direction of this person.

(2) *That man by the window next to the exit looks as if he's going to pass out any minute.*

An utterance of (2), accompanied by the speaker's gaze and gesture, expresses a singular proposition (Kaplan 1989a, 1989b). The underlined complex demonstrative in (2) includes a post-nominal modifying phrase *by the window next to the exit* with spatial indications that help the hearer identify the location of the intended referent, but the linguistic meaning of the underlined referential term contributes nothing to the propositional content of the utterance. Given the speaker's demonstration of where the hearer is supposed to look to identify the referent, an utterance of the shorter sentence (3), accompanied by the speaker's nodding in the direction of the referent, would have expressed the same proposition as (2) under the same circumstances, and so would (4) if the description *with a white beard* is one that truthfully causes the hearer to pick out the individual referred to.

(3) *Hé looks as if he's going to pass out any minute.*

(4) *That man over there with the white beard looks as if he's going to pass out any minute.*

Being located by the window next to the exit is a transient attribute of the man referred to, having a white beard is a somewhat more stable attribute of this individual, but neither attribute supplies a truth condition to the singular proposition expressed by an utterance of (2) or (4). The addressee of any one of the linguistic forms of (2), (3) or (4) identifies a unique referent through the processing of a visual stimulus that the utterance and the accompanying gesture direct the addressee's vision to.

King (2001) challenges the direct reference account of demonstratives. He draws what is for him an important distinction between using a complex demonstrative with a so-called *perceptual intention* in an act of rigid reference, as in the case of the alternative linguistic forms of (2), (3) or (4), and on the other hand using it with a *descriptive intention* in an act of non-rigid reference. King points out that there are uses of complex demonstratives that are problematic for the direct referent theorists and he therefore proposes to replace the direct reference account by a quantificational account that is argued to work even for those cases where the speaker uses a complex demonstrative to refer to an object she perceives. His own quantificational approach is claimed to offer an adequate account of all uses of complex demonstratives, whether or not a deictic demonstration is employed together with the linguistic description. He cites several cases where the use of a complex demonstrative is, as he says, not referential, let alone directly referential, including (5), (6) and (7).

(5) *That hominid who discovered how to start fires was a genius.*

(6) *Every father dreads that moment when his oldest child leaves home.*

(7) *Most avid snow skiers remember that first black diamond run they attempted to ski.*

King offers three different quantificational accounts of complex demonstratives, explaining his reasons for favoring one of them, but the only aspect of his work on demonstratives that concerns me here is his insistence that they are used either referentially or non-referentially, an assumption denied by the direct reference theorists.

King recognizes one fundamental difference between definite descriptions and complex demonstratives, or 'that'-phrases as he prefers to call them. He holds that "demonstrations or speaker's intentions have a semantic role when accompanying the latter but not when accompanying the former" (King 2001: 27). This, he says, is why one can say *That car is nicer than that car* when looking at cars in a lot filled with new cars, but one cannot say *#The car is nicer than the car.* His explanation for this difference is that "the phrase 'that *F*' can be used several times in a situation in which there are many *F*s to talk about distinct *F*s" (King 2001: 27), but "the semantics of 'the' does not allow a role for demonstrations or speaker intentions" (King 2001: 28). It is true that the definite article lacks the deictic as well as the anaphoric properties of demonstrative determiners or pronouns, but referential interpretation of definite descriptions relies on the hypotheses the addressee forms about the communicator's intentions just as much as does referential interpretation of demonstratives. A couple of concrete examples of sentences occurring in King's own monograph may be used to demonstrate my point.

(8) *The second sort of intention is closely related to the first.*
(King 2001: 29)

(9) *Again, I simply mention these possibilities to give the reader the sense of the available theoretical space.* (King 2001: 33)

The reference of *the second sort of intention* in (8) cannot be determined until we read on and find out how King presents this "second sort of intention". In contrast to this, the reference of the definite description *the first* appearing at the end of (8) can be established at that point in the text where (8) occurs. It is a sort of intention described in the paragraph that takes up most of page 29 of his book. King can simply spare his readers from going through a full repetition of key notions related to this "first sort of intention", and he can spare himself the gratuitous effort of writing something that simply recapitulates what the preceding paragraph was all about. He may use a brief referring expression that vastly underdetermines the reference, because he relies on his readers' ability to infer the intention behind his term *the first*, where the adjective *first* is simply a metatextual indicator of a specific order of presentation, not the encoder of a concept that plays a semantic role in relation to the pragmatically derived content of (8).

The reader's interpretation of the reference of the definite description *the available theoretical space* in (9) depends, among other things, on how we saturate the anaphorically used demonstrative determiner *these* in the earlier complex demonstrative *these possibilities* and bring the sort of possibilities activated in our minds to bear on the interpretation of the underlined description. The noun *possibilities* in (9) is a truth-conditionally irrelevant item in the direct-reference sense, just like the adjective *first* (and *second*) in (8). There was no previous mention of *possibilities*. The reader has to figure out what the author intends to refer to with the complex demonstrative *these possibilities*, which will have consequences for the reader's pragmatic processing of the later definite description *the available theoretical space* and determination of its reference.

King also uses *the theory* as a referential term a few times in his book, but with varying reference. On every occurrence the reader has to use whatever contextual assumptions are available to draw inferences about the author's intention to refer to one specific theory.

The dominant view, among philosophers and linguists, has been that demonstratives, both complex and simplex ones, are directly referential terms that pick out an individual, while definite descriptions are used either referentially to designate an individual or attributively to designate whoever or whatever satisfies the description (Donnellan 1966). While I agree with King that there are both referential and non-referential uses of complex demonstratives, I believe that the speaker's intention plays a semantic role in the (context-sensitive) interpretation of any utterance, including the interpretation of the reference of any definite descriptions or demonstratives that an utterance may contain. I side with the relevance theorists (Sperber and Wilson 1995; Carston 2002), who hold that semantic representations resulting from decoding of linguistic material are notoriously gappy compared to the proposition the speaker intends to express. The pragmatic processes that mediate between sentence meaning and propositional content are of two kinds. Some are triggered by something in the linguistic structure, like the ellipsis associated with *the first* in example (8), which we understand to refer to a sort of intention due to information in the earlier phrase *the second sort of intention*; others result from top-down pragmatic processes, so-called free enrichment (Carston 2002; Recanati 2004), as when the reader depends on global inferences to resolve the reference of the conceptually meager definite description *the theory.* Wilson and Sperber (2004: 607) say, "Relevance theory may be seen as an attempt to work out in detail one of Grice's central claims: that an essential feature of most human communication is the expression and recognition of intentions."

According to Relevance Theory, the encoded linguistic meaning of a sentence just provides the addressee with a blueprint that guides and constrains the pragmatic interpretation of the utterance of the sentence, on the one hand by supplying concepts directly to the proposition expressed and on the other hand by directing the addressee to a context whose exploitation in the pragmatic process of utterance interpretation is likely to make the utterance optimally relevant to the addressee. A stimulus, whether linguistic or non-linguistic, is optimally relevant to an individual if its inferential interpretation yields a sufficient number of cognitive effects for the least processing cost.

1.2. Methodological issues

We have seen that an author like King (2001) preaches one thing about definite descriptions in contrast to demonstratives but uses definite descriptions in his own text which contradict his beliefs and undermine his arguments. The rather obvious lesson to learn from this discrepancy between armchair theorizing and theory formation based on observation of linguistic data is that serious attention to what may be found in a corpus of written or spoken language can have a sobering effect on one's conviction that intuition or imagination must be allowed to define what belongs to the language whose system of rules and principles one is exploring and what falls outside that system. It may be tempting to hold on to some sweeping generalization because its truth has what the investigator judges to be advantageous implications, while its falsity implies, in the most perilous case, the overthrow of a cherished theoretical perspective. Real progress, in linguistics as in other empirical sciences, is impossible without documented empirical support. A fresh look at factually occurring data as opposed to data ingeniously made up and tailored to one's theoretical needs will sometimes bring disorder bordering on chaos into the investigator's work, but there is no viable alternative, taking shortcuts means cheating.

Consideration and appreciation of attested data is all the more important for linguists trying to tackle issues at the interface between the language system and the thought system, notably the study of the way that pragmatic (extra-linguistic) input complements verbal input in the creation and the comprehension of communicated content. Generative grammarians of the traditional sort have typically been concerned with the question of the degree to which their contrived sentence forms strike them as being intuitively well-formed or ill-formed. What happens when linguists of the same methodological persuasion enter into studies that relate directly to the semantics–pragmatics interface is that they are forced to operate with an idealized communicator and an idealized addressee who have to worry about not just grammaticality or the lack of such but also the individual utterance's intuitively determined appropriateness relative to a set of potential contexts of utterance, of which exactly one is selected by the model addressee. Armchair linguists theorizing about the balance between linguistic meaning and inferred meaning in utterance interpretation not only have to invent their objects of study, they also have to invent more or less likely contexts for their invented data, possibly based on information derived from a contrived type of discourse that the investigator has put together so as to make it resemble real discourse.

Nevertheless, corpus linguistics in its purest form also has its clear shortcomings when utilized without caution and to the exclusion of other methodological avenues, and the limitations of strict corpus studies are probably nowhere more evident than in studies of the relative contribution of decoded and inferred conceptual material to the content of an utterance. The informative intention of a speaker cannot be grasped through direct observation of discourse features. An analyst cannot explain, simply by looking at some corpus material, how the hearer accesses those contextual assumptions that must be brought to bear in pragmatic interpretation of a given utterance so that the hearer's expectations of relevance are satisfied.

Linguistic experiments designed for the purpose of eliciting judgments or other kinds of response from test subjects make use of invented data but one advantage of experimental work of this sort is that it is strictly forbidden to try to influence the informants' reactions in advance of the test and a capital sin to tamper with the data obtained. Experimenters usually have some precise predictions at the outset about the reaction patterns of the informants but they are not in a position to filter out reactions that are adverse to their predictions.

In this paper I am going to combine the use of diverse research methods in an attempt to improve our knowledge of what demonstratives do for us. To this end I am examining data from two specific languages, Norwegian and English, and addressing the question of the contribution of the English and the Norwegian demonstratives to the hearer's pragmatic computation of the propositional content of an utterance. Intuitive judgments will be central throughout, but in addition I am deploying results from the study of a bilateral translation corpus, a parallel corpus of English and Norwegian texts, in section 2, while in section 3 I am testing my own intuitions against those of a small group of native informants who were not trained as linguists. Lexical marking of a nominal constituent as a non-referential term is found to be a more frequent phenomenon in Norwegian than in English discourse. This generalization is supported by the corpus study reported in section 2 as well as the informant tests described in section 3. The linguistic data focused on in the latter section is restricted to syntactic constructions with a left-dislocated phrase. There is an interesting formal difference between a personal and a non-personal pronoun as *in situ* copy of the dislocated phrase in otherwise identical sentences, and my Norwegian informants' reactions to this difference between a personal and a non-personal pronoun *in situ* are in conformity with the Norwegian tendency to encode the information that the demonstrative is non-referential.

1.3. Aims

I shall use the present study of demonstratives to show that definite demonstrative phrases are used indiscriminately as referential and non-referential terms in English, and I shall substantiate my claim that non-referential use of definite demonstrative phrases is a less frequent phenomenon in Norwegian than in English discourse. In both languages grammatically definite demonstratives are semantically underspecified with regard to whether the reference is to an object or to a type of entity defined in terms of certain properties. However, speakers of Norwegian seem to prefer to differentiate formally between demonstratives used to represent objects and demonstratives used to represent properties instantiated by one or several objects, even if the linguistic resources available are the same, or approximately the same, in English and Norwegian.

My concern is with indefinite and definite demonstratives. While the latter category is familiar to every person reading this, the category of indefinite demonstrative items includes one central member in English, the grammatically indefinite demonstrative determiner *such*, which has received little attention from linguists. Heim (1982: 309) says that deictic and anaphoric uses of referring expressions have at least one thing in common: "neither is possible with an indefinite." The word *such*, however, is a grammatically indefinite demonstrative indexical. It can be used deictically or anaphorically, like the definite demonstrative indexicals *this* and *that* and the corresponding plural forms, but *such* is inherently marked as grammatically indefinite. There is no **the ideas such as these*, **the such ideas* or **such the idea* compared to the well-formed indefinites *ideas such as these*, *such ideas* and *such an idea*, respectively. *Such* instructs the addressee to seek out a context-dependent property to be attributed to the higher-order entity that the *such*-phrase designates.[1] Take a look at another sentence found in King's book on complex demonstratives.

(10) *In such a case, I will say that the speaker has a past perceptual intention.* (King 2001: 29)

Finding an antecedent for the anaphoric determiner *such* in (10) is a prerequisite to the reader's comprehension of what the phrase *such a case* designates, and when the anaphor is saturated, this phrase supplies a truth condition to the proposition expressed. The immediately preceding sentences (on page 29 of King's book) tell us that the definite description *the speaker* in (10) refers to (a variable) someone who has a current intention to talk about something he perceived in the past, and the adverbial adjunct *in such a case* points to antecedent information in the form of a little story invented by the author to illustrate what he means by *past perceptual intention*, a term he is going to use on several occasions later in the book. He could have replaced (10) by (11) without losing any information, but (11) would not necessarily have expressed the same proposition as (10).

(11) *In this case, I will say that the speaker has a past perceptual intention.*

Taken literally, (11) seems to say that the speaker has a past perceptual intention in the single case described in the previous discourse. The reader would probably still have inferred that the predication is meant to hold not just in this particular case but also in what will be loosely understood to be similar cases, because the illustration he offered antecedently could certainly have been replaced by a different one that shared with it those elements that interest the author. Thus we have no problem activating the

1 What I am saying about *such* in this paper does not apply to the role of this word as intensifier, as in *It was such fun* or *It's such a nuisance.*

implicitly conveyed assumption that the author intends the reader to generalize to similar cases. This generalization is included in the hearer's context-free semantic representation of (10), however, where *such a case* stands for 'this case and similar cases' by virtue of the linguistic meaning of *such*.

My exploration of a bi-directional translation corpus, the Oslo Multilingual Corpus (OMC) – http://www.hf.uio.no/ilos/OMC – revealed that indefinite *such*-phrases and noun phrases with a definite demonstrative determiner are frequently interchangeable, and when they are, the preponderant type of situation is not that *such* loses its role as property-denoting indexical but that the communicators intend their definite demonstrative determiners *these* and *those* to represent a property instantiated by objects sharing that property.

When a Norwegian source text in my corpus contains an indefinite demonstrative item corresponding to English *such*, the English target text quite frequently does not contain *such* at all but one of the definite demonstratives *these* or *those*. Conversely, definite *these* and *those* in English source texts are frequently translated by one of the forms of the Norwegian lexical counterpart of *such*. This does not mean that the translations are bad or inaccurate. My objective is to demonstrate the validity of the following four claims: (i) the indefinite demonstrative determiner encodes the information that the noun phrase is used non-referentially, (ii) definite demonstratives do not encode the information that they are used referentially, (iii) although the contribution of a given definite demonstrative to the truth-conditional content of an utterance is not determined by the linguistic semantics of the demonstrative phrase in either of the two languages compared, there is a higher frequency of definite demonstratives with a pragmatically inferred, non-referential truth-conditional value in English than in Norwegian discourse, and (iv) the non-referential value seems to be relatively more often expressed semantically in Norwegian, due to a more widespread use of the indefinite demonstrative determiner in Norwegian than in English discourse.

Is the observed difference between English and Norwegian usage to be discussed in section 2.2 an isolated quirk which one should not view as a reflection of a more general difference between English and Norwegian grammar, or between certain conventions of usage pertaining to the two languages? Or is there a chance that this difference might be related to some other linguistic phenomenon, maybe a feature of grammar where English and Norwegian behave differently? This issue is given consideration in section 3, where two possible candidate phenomena are proposed and examined, the left-dislocation construction and equative sentences.

2. Grammatically definite and grammatically indefinite demonstratives in English and Norwegian discourse

2.1. Use of a parallel corpus

That the contribution of grammatically definite and grammatically indefinite demonstrative phrases to the propositional content of utterances overlaps to the extent it does would have been concealed to me if I had not exploited the avenues to insight that a corpus offers the linguistic researcher.

I am focusing rather more on the use of plural demonstratives than singular ones in the present paper. Convincing illustrations of the systematic truth-conditional vagueness of definite demonstrative determiners in English are much more numerous in the OMC when the determiner is plural *these* or *those* than when it is singular *this* or *that. These Ns* must often be interpreted pragmatically in the same way as *this type of N* or *such Ns*. The designatum is typically a property instantiated by more than one thing.

The overlapping use of definite and indefinite demonstratives when the designatum is a property of objects of the same type is a discourse phenomenon that I stumbled upon by accident a few years ago when I was looking for something entirely different in the Oslo Multilingual Corpus. Later I was pleased to find that Cornish (1999) had noticed some occurrences of French definite demonstrative noun phrases of the type *ces Ns* whose function was similar to that of English *such Ns*, and when I consulted the Oslo Multilingual Corpus to look for French, Norwegian and German renderings of English *such*-phrases, I found that French occurrences of indefinite demonstrative phrases with *tel* or *pareil* as determiners were much less frequent than English *such Ns* and definitely rare compared to both the Norwegian and the German indefinite property-denoting demonstratives, which are *slik*, or the more colloquial *sånn*, in Norwegian, and *solch* in German.

The English translators' frequent preference for a definite demonstrative form even if the Norwegian source text has an indefinite demonstrative *slik/sånn* corresponding to *such*, and the Norwegian translators' preference for the indefinite demonstrative when the English source text contains a definite one, these are entrenched patterns of usage which suggest that for practical purposes, the grammatically definite demonstratives and the grammatically indefinite property-denoting demonstratives constrain the recipient's search for the right interpretation as much as is needed, given a pragmatic theory like Relevance Theory, which emphasizes the balance between decoding and inference in the hearer's computation of the explicitly communicated content of an utterance.

2.2. Definite demonstratives in English, indefinites in Norwegian

43 English source text occurrences of the demonstrative indexicals *these*, *those*, *this* and *that* in the Oslo Multilingual Corpus (determiners or pronouns), out of a total of 198 occurrences of these forms, were translated into Norwegian as *slike*, *sånne* ('such', pl.), *slikt*, *sånt* ('such', sg. n.), or *slik*, *sånn* ('such', sg. m. or f.). 39 of these 43 tokens were plural forms, in source text and target text, and the remaining 4 were singular forms.

35 source text occurrences of Norwegian *slike*, *sånne*, *slikt*, *sånt*, *slik*, *sånn*, out of a total of 186, were translated as *these*, *those*, *this* or *that*. 26 of these 35 tokens were plural forms and 9 were singular forms.

77 of the 186 Norwegian tokens of indefinite demonstrative determiners or pronouns were translated as English *such*, the most direct or literal translation possible. Subtracting the 35 cases of a switch to a definite demonstrative, we are left with 74 tokens of Norwegian indefinite determiners or pronouns in my corpus that were not translated into English as anything comparable to a demonstrative, whether definite or indefinite.

Not a single occurrence of any of the four Norwegian definite demonstratives *disse* ('these'), *de* ('those'), *dette* ('this', n.) or *denne* ('this', m. or f.), was translated as English *such*, and just one occurrence of *such* in English source texts, out of a total of 149 (including quite a few with a clear intensifier function; cf. note 1), was translated as a definite demonstrative determiner in the corresponding Norwegian target text.

Of the 198 occurrences of English definite demonstrative determiners or pronouns, 121 were translated into Norwegian directly as definite demonstrative determiners or pronouns. I judged 85 of those 121 tokens to be of the referential kind, while the remaining 36 were, as far as I could tell, non-referential.

Just a handful of examples of definite vs. indefinite demonstrative asymmetries between English and Norwegian source texts and target texts can be presented here. Occasionally a comparison will be made between English, Norwegian and German. In (12), the Norwegian translation of *these intentions* in the final sentence contains the indefinite and property-denoting anaphoric determiner *slike* ('such') instead of the definite demonstrative determiner that is the direct counterpart of English *these*. The Norwegian translation of the final sentence in (12) with the plural demonstrative phrase is given after the icon "→", which will henceforth be used to indicate that the translation is from the language represented before this symbol to the language or languages represented after it.

(12) (FF1)

"Intentions," he said as though the word intrigued him, "yes, intentions. But you see, John, there are a lot of intentions in the minds of a lot of people vis-à-vis this country, not all of them friendly. But we can't propose policy, measures or counter-measures on the basis of these intentions ..."

→

(FF1TN)

"... Men vi kan ikke foreslå politiske skritt, foranstaltninger og mot-foranstaltninger på grunnlag av slike intensjoner ..."
'... but we cannot propose political steps, measures and counter-measures on the basis of such intentions'

The antecedent of the anaphoric demonstrative *these* of *these intentions* in the English source text contains information about unspecified people's unfriendly intentions toward a contextually given country. Apart from the antecedent mention of intentions that are not friendly, no specific intentions which might direct the reader to an interpretation of *these intentions* as a set of identifiable intentions are mentioned here or in the lines preceding (12) in the OMC text labeled (FF1). The Norwegian translator notices this fact and changes the definite demonstrative of the source text into an indefinite demonstrative phrase with the property-denoting determiner *slike* ('such', pl.). A direct translation of the English proximal demonstrative *these* as Norwegian *disse* ('these') would not have been incorrect but the translator probably judged a switch to an anaphoric determiner that rules out a referential interpretation to mirror the original English author's intention more directly. The translator may have felt that *slike intensjoner* (such-pl. intention-pl.indef) is a more idiomatic rendering of *these intentions* than the alternative *disse intensjonene* (these intention-pl.def) would have been, and I concur with that judgment.

(13) expresses the thoughts of an investigator of a series of murders. The sentences following "→" are the German and Norwegian translations of the final period starting with the demonstrative *these cases* in the English source text.

(13) (PDJ3)

... it was unlikely that his holiday would be interrupted by the need to take even a cursory glance at the Whistler, Norfolk's notorious serial killer, dead or alive. He had been at his work for fifteen months now

and the latest victim – Valerie Mitchell wasn't it? – was his fourth. *These cases were invariably difficult, time-consuming and frustrating, depending as they often did more on good luck than good detection.*

→

(PDJ3TD)

… *Solche Fälle waren zumeist schwierig, zeitaufwendig, mühevoll, …*
such cases were mostly difficult time-consuming frustrating

→

(PDJ3TN)

… *Slike saker var erfaringsmessig vanskelige, tidkrevende og*
such cases were experience-wise difficult time-consuming and
frustrerende, …
frustrating

The predication starting with the demonstrative *these cases* is not about those four murder cases mentioned in (13), it is about serial killings in general. While it would have been possible for the German and the Norwegian translators to maintain the definite demonstrative form used by the original author – *diese Fälle* and *disse sakene*, respectively – both translators apparently felt it was more natural to shift to an indefinite demonstrative phrase with the plural indefinite determiner forms *solche* for German and *slike* for Norwegian.

Proof that the English definite demonstrative *these cases* in (13) must be given a non-referential interpretation for logical reasons is offered by the quantifier expressions *invariably* in English and *zumeist* ('mostly') in German. The somewhat freer Norwegian translation *erfaringsmessig* ('from experience', 'experience-wise') of the adverb *invariably* also defies a referential interpretation of the subject noun phrase. Although a definite demonstrative form instead of indefinite *slike saker* ('such cases') would probably not have led the readers astray, my judgment is that the Norwegian definite demonstrative *disse sakene* ('these cases') would not be as relevant in (13) as the English source-text form *these cases*. The co-occurrence of *disse* and the adverb *erfaringsmessig* creates a sense of discord that might garden-path readers who process the definite demonstrative as a referential term on the first pass but are forced to associate *disse sakene* with the general concept SERIAL KILLINGS as soon as they encounter the word *erfaringsmessig*. The linguistic semantics is the same for English *these* and Norwegian *disse*, so tokens of these definite demonstratives may be interpreted referentially or non-referentially in both languages, depending on the hearer's contextual assumptions brought to bear in the reference resolution process. There is a difference in usage, however, and data from the OMC suggests that this difference is intimately tied to a more widespread use of the Norwegian indefinite demonstrative determiner *slike* ('such', pl.) than the corresponding English determiner *such*. The lexical meaning of the indefinite, property-designating determiner precludes an interpretation of the demonstrative phrase as a referential term, and this determiner is frequently the preferred form in Norwegian translations of the English determiner *these* in the OMC.

(14) is an example of a translation that goes in the opposite direction, from Norwegian to English, hence the backward-pointing "←". The complex demonstrative *these tiny pieces* looks like a term that refers to a mentioned set of objects, and there is nothing in the following predicate phrase to stop a reader of the English translation from thinking that the subject term is used referentially. On the other hand, the preceding text shows that the antecedent of *these tiny pieces* is the non-count noun *clay*, mentioned twice in successive bare noun phrases, and immediately before (14) there was a mention of the fact that clay can be broken up into smaller and smaller pieces.

(14) (JG1TE)

These tiny pieces can never be joined together again to make something else.

←

(JG1)

... og slike ørsmå leirklumper kan ikke "kneppes" sammen igjen
and such tiny clay-lumps can not be-buttoned together again
til nye gjenstander.
to new objects
'... and such tiny lumps of clay cannot be buttoned together again to form new objects'

The question the reader has to resolve in the process of reference assignment is this: Does *these tiny pieces* take scope over *never* and refer to a set of individuated pieces of clay, or are the scope relations reversed so that the demonstrative subject phrase designates a general concept within the scope of the negation operator?

These tiny pieces in the target text of (14) is referentially underdetermined, not just because there is no overt mention of the concept CLAY in that descriptive phrase but also because it contains the indexical *these* followed by the plural form of a noun. There is no accessible antecedent in the form of a plural expression that refers to individuated lumps of clay. A reader will presumably be able to see straight away that the predication is not about some specific lumps that cannot ever be joined together in the way described, it is a general statement about any little piece of clay. The author intends his readers to form a mental representation of pieces of clay that are similar to such pieces as were described in the previous text. The translation would have been less than optimally relevant if the average English reader were to associate the demonstrative *these tiny pieces* with a *de re* interpretation on the first pass. However, the form *these tiny pieces* was evidently felt to give the reader sufficient linguistic guidance so that the same proposition was understood to be conveyed in the translation as in the Norwegian original with its property-denoting demonstrative determiner *slike* ('such') instead of definite *disse* ('these') and the plural indefinite nominal form *leirklumper* (clay-lump-pl.indef) instead of the definite alternative *leirklumpene* (clay-lump-pl.def).

My occupation thus far has been with complex demonstratives, not demonstrative pronouns. The demonstrative data examined has mainly consisted of an anaphoric determiner and its complement, minimally a head noun, but the remaining examples to be offered in this section involve demonstrative pronouns. There are a few tokens in the OMC of the use of demonstrative *those* (never *these*) in a syntactic position otherwise reserved for indefinites, as seen in the existential-presentational construction of (15).

(15) (MW1)
We never did, of course, but there were those who did.

Not surprisingly, the German translation of the second conjunct in (15) is *aber es gab genug andere, die es getan haben* ('but there were others who did'), with the indefinite *andere* ('others') where the source text had the definite demonstrative *those*. Similarly, the Norwegian translator of (15) decided to respect the indefiniteness condition and rendered *those* in (15) as *noen* ('some'). It appears that the existential-presentational form is in order if the post-verbal noun phrase can be associated with an existential quantifier; a grammatically indefinite form is not required in English.

(16) is another example of an existential-presentational construction with a definite demonstrative in the position otherwise reserved for indefinite quantified expressions. This illustration is not from the OMC; it was uttered by Barack Obama in his speech in Denver on the 28th of August 2008 (BBC International News Channel).

(16) *I know there are those who dismiss these beliefs.*

Those in (16) does not refer to a unique group of people, and the context available to me as TV viewer also did not help me narrow down the reference of *these beliefs* to a set of specific beliefs rather than, more vaguely, a sort of belief antecedently mentioned by the then Democratic presidential candidate. (17), where *those* is in the canonical subject position as the agentive argument of the transitive verb *dismiss*, does not permit the interpretation intended by Obama.

(17) *I know that those dismiss these beliefs.*

Here the speaker's intention must have been to use demonstrative *those* as a referential term which depends for its intended interpretation on information derived via association with a linguistic antecedent or else made accessible via direct perception. In (16), however, the only information encoded by *those* that an addressee must consider in his estimation of the contribution of that word to the content of the utterance is the feature plural, the rest follows from our common knowledge that only human beings are able to dismiss a belief.

(18) is another example of a pronominal indexical that is grammatically definite in English (*this*) but grammatically indefinite in Norwegian (*sånt*, 'such', sg. n.). This is one of the fairly rare examples in the OMC of singular forms that exhibit the noted asymmetry between the two languages with respect to the distribution of grammatically definite and grammatically indefinite forms. The translation is from Norwegian to English. *This* in the target text represents a kind of venture.

(18) (KF1TE)
I've gradually become good at <u>this</u>.
←
(KF1)
Jeg er blitt dyktig til <u>sånt</u> etter hvert.
I am become skilled to such-SG.N gradually
'I have gradually become skilled at such things.'

The sg. n. form of the Norwegian indefinite property-denoting indexical – *sånt* – is a pronoun that may be used to represent abstract entities of various sorts. In order to succeed in giving the Norwegian sentence an adequate English form, a translator will either have to give up the pronominal form and write *such things*, or give up the grammatical indefiniteness and use a definite demonstrative pronoun, either *this* or *that*. The translator opted for the latter strategy. *This* in the English target text and *sånt* ('such') in the Norwegian source text receive their truth-conditional value from pragmatic interpretation of the immediately preceding discourse where there is a reference to the fact that the narrator, a professional thief, gets a kick out of appraising the value of gems worn by ladies he encounters.

3. Personal vs. non-personal pronouns – a litmus test for referentiality?

We have seen that English-speaking people do not mind using a complex demonstrative with a grammatically definite determiner to designate a higher-order entity defined in terms of some salient property, while users of Norwegian tend to avoid use of definite demonstratives under such circumstances, preferring the indefinite demonstrative determiner corresponding to English *such* when the referent is a type of thing. It would strengthen my generalizations about systematic differences in usage between English and Norwegian if I could point to some other linguistic phenomenon in English and Norwegian that might be related to the noted tendency for Norwegian translators of English texts to prefer indefinite *such*-phrases where English has a grammatically definite complex demonstrative and the tendency for English translators to prefer definite demonstratives where the Norwegian source text has a *such*-phrase.

I reckoned that it might be profitable to take a look at the speaker's pronominal options in equative sentences and in left-dislocation structures where the pronoun and the dislocated phrase are traditionally taken to be coreferential.

I find it useful to begin my account by repeating the examples (la) and (lb) found in ter Meulen (1995: 339), where a definite description was used referentially in the former but predicatively in the equative construction of (lb).

(1) a. *The president is getting old.*
    b. *The president of the club is John.*

The right pronominal form for the definite description *the president* in (la) is the personal pronoun *he*, as in the left-dislocation sentence of (19a), but the left-dislocation structure of (19b) with an *in situ* pronominal copy *he* is not well-formed.

(19) a. *The president, he's getting old.*
     b. **The president of the club, he's John.*

This difference between *he* as the right choice of pronoun in (19a) but an unacceptable choice in (19b) may tell us something about the ontological value of what the dislocated term refers to. A personal pronoun is permitted *in situ* in some kinds of equative left-dislocation sentences in English, but it will normally be a bad choice when the predicate nominal is a proper name as in (19b) (cf. Declerck 1983). The *in situ* pronoun in (19b) should be non-personal *that*, not personal *he*.

There is just a minimal formal difference between English (20) and (21), but while (20) is a copula sentence of the equative sort, (21) with the pronominal copy *he* instead of *that* shows that (21) is of the ascriptive sort.

(20) *The man with the white shirt, that's Julie's brother.*

(21) *The man with the white shirt, he's Julie's brother.*

(21) is a predication about the individual described as the man wearing a white shirt, and the message is simply that the man with the white shirt is in a brother relation to Julie, who may have other brothers in addition to this man. In (20), *Julie's brother* and the left-dislocated nominal *the man with the white shirt* express predicates satisfied by the same uniquely identifiable individual. The difference in the pronominal forms, *that* against *he*, offers the addressee the information that the dislocated phrase in (20) represents a stage-level predicate (Carlson 1980) satisfied by the referent, while the formally identical dislocated phrase in (21) is a referential term whose descriptive meaning is truth-conditionally irrelevant according to Kaplan's direct-reference account, because the reference is to the individual said to be Julie's brother and the description of the man could have been replaced by any other description that would cause the hearer to identify the right person.

Personal pronouns obey number agreement rules, non-personal[2] pronouns do not. Imagine that the speaker of (22a) is pointing to his two daughters, using the plural demonstrative pronoun *these* deictically. English non-personal pronouns, appropriate for reference to higher-order entities of different sorts, include the two singular demonstratives *this* and *that*, but (22b) is not an acceptable alternative to (22a) in this equative construction. A plural pronoun and plural concord in the verb is required. The singular

2 I prefer the term *non-personal* to *impersonal*, because *impersonal* is frequently used with reference to a pronoun like *one* in English or *man* in German or the Scandinavian languages.

form *this* in (22b) cannot co-occur with the plural form of the coreferential predicate nominal.

(22) a. *These are my daughters, Tina and Simone.*
b. **This is my daughters, Tina and Simone.*

The sg. verb form *is* is likely to contribute significantly to our intuitive discomfort with (22b), but I would also like to think that it may be a salient factor that speakers of English frequently use plural definite demonstratives non-referentially. Data to be presented below will be seen to strengthen this presumption.

Norwegian equative sentences do not tolerate a personal subject pronoun. One might presume that the lack of plural concord in Norwegian verbs makes the non-personal, singular form *dette* ('this') in (23b) more palatable than the corresponding form *this* in (22b). However, the pronoun *dette* appearing in (23b) is not just a permissible form, the plural personal pronoun *disse* ('these') is no option at all in the Norwegian translation of (22a).

(23) a. **Disse er døtrene mine, Tina og Simone.*
these COP daughter-PL.DEF mine-PL Tina and Simone
b. *Dette er døtrene mine, Tina og Simone.*
this COP daughter-PL.DEF mine-PL Tina and Simone

Similarly, (24a) with plural concord is the only alternative in English, but the non-personal form *det* ('that') must be used at the expense of the plural form *de* ('those') in the Norwegian translation of (24) presented as (25).

(24) a. *Those are the generals.*
b. **That is the generals.*[3]

(25) a. **De er generalene.*
those COP general-PL.DEF
b. *Det er generalene.*
that COP general-PL.DEF

A Norwegian non-personal pronoun like *dette* ('this') in (23b) or *det* ('that') in (25b) is neuter and singular. These items encode the information that the referent is not a first-order entity (cf. Borthen 2004). While a non-personal

---

[3] It appears that the number disagreement between subject and nominal predicate is easier to accept for some speakers if we replace *that is* with *that's*. The contracted form *'s* is possibly less conspicuous as a singular form than the full form *is*.

form is the only safe choice of pronominal subject in a Norwegian equative sentence and the plural forms *disse* ('these') in (23a) and *de* ('those'/'they') in (25a) are but downright ungrammatical, English permits, or even demands, use of a personal subject pronoun that marks the grammatical distinction between singular and plural, as shown in (22a) and (24a).

Let us now turn from equatives to sentences with a left-dislocated *such*-phrase. There are at least two parameters that affect a Norwegian speaker's preference for either a personal or a non-personal pronominal form when the antecedent is a Norwegian *such*-phrase that designates a type of entity: animate vs. inanimate and subject vs. non-subject. We may start by looking at English (26) where the *in situ* pronominal copy of the dislocated phrase is a prepositional object whose referent is animate.

(26) a. **Such people*$_i$, *it's a fantastic experience to co-operate with that*$_i$.
b. *Such people*$_i$, *it's a fantastic experience to co-operate with them*$_i$.

Although *such people* is a term that designates a type of person rather than a set of individuals, the only legitimate pronominal copy of *such people* in (26) is the personal, plural pronoun *them* occurring in (26b); non-personal *that* is ruled out. Norwegian, however, permits a choice between non-personal *det* ('that'), in (27a), and personal *dem* ('those'/'them'), in (27b).

(27) a. *Sånne folk*$_i$, *dét*$_i$ *er det fantastisk å samarbeide*
such-PL.INDEF people-INDEF that is it fantastic to co-operate
med.
with
b. *Sånne folk*$_i$, *dém*$_i$ *er det fantastisk å samarbeide*
such-PL.INDEF people-INDEF them is it fantastic to co-operate
med.
with
'It's a fantastic experience to co-operate with such people.'

Thus, a speaker of Norwegian may use the non-personal pronoun *det* ('that') to signal her intention to designate any person who satisfies the predicate resulting from pragmatic processing of the relation between the anaphor *sånne* ('such') and its selected antecedent. (27a), where the non-personal demonstrative pronoun is topicalized and the supposedly coreferential *such*-phrase dislocated, was judged to be more natural than (27b) by five out of seven speakers of Norwegian who were consulted; the remaining two informants felt that (27a) and (27b) were equally natural, and they did not perceive a difference in meaning between them. When asked, they felt there was no communicated difference between a non-specific reading of the dislocated constituent in (27a) and a specific reading in (27b).

In contradistinction to my informants' reactions to (27a) and (27b), the same seven speakers of Norwegian did discern a difference in meaning between (28a) with non-personal *det* ('that') and (28b) with personal *dem* ('them'/'those').

(28) a. *Sånne folk, det etterlyser vi.*
such-PL.INDEF people that seek we
b. *Sånne folk, dem etterlyser vi.*
such.PL.INDEF people them seek we
'We're looking for such people.'

One interesting thing to notice about the verb *etterlyse* ('seek', 'look for', possibly, but not necessarily, something lost) is that it permits a range of context-sensitive, *ad hoc* conceptual interpretations (cf. Carston 2002) of its lexical meaning. It might be that the speaker and the people she represents are trying to track down certain fugitives and turn them over to the police, or it might be that they are looking for someone to fill a vacancy and would be interested in whoever might possess the qualities solicited. It is possible to associate the dislocated phrase in (28) either with people whose existence is presupposed and who resemble, in some salient respect, certain individuals mentioned in the antecedent structure, or else to associate that phrase with some potentially existent people who possess certain desiderata, people as yet unknown to the agents. My seven informants were sensitive to the difference between searching for people whose identity is familiar to speaker and hearer and searching for unknown people who meet certain standards, and they all associated the plural pronoun *dem* in (28b) with the former, and the non-personal pronoun *det* in (28a) with the latter interpretation.

The dislocated subject noun phrase in (29) contains the Norwegian property-denoting determiner *sånn* ('such', sg., m.) and a head noun of the inanimate sort. (29a) with the non-personal neuter pronoun *in situ* appears to be the unmarked alternative for some native speakers; (29b) where the pronoun *den* ('that', m.) and the predicative adjective *dyr* ('expensive', m.) agree in number and gender with the noun *mat* ('food', m.) is nevertheless a fully acceptable alternative to (29a). Some of my informants said they might use (29a) and (29b) interchangeably.

(29) a. *Sånn mat, det er veldig dyrt i Norge.*
such-SG.M food-M that-N COP very expensive-N in Norway
b. *Sånn mat, den er veldig dyr i Norge.*
such-SG.M food-M that-M COP very expensive-M in Norway
'Such food is very expensive in Norway.'

Both in (29a) and (29b), the dislocated phrase (and the pronominal copy in the subject position) designate a particular culinary product. Unlike verbs, Norwegian adjectives exhibit gender concord with the grammatical subject, a formal distinction with no semantic implications in (29).

Formal definiteness in a dislocated phrase fully determines the Norwegian speaker's choice of subject pronoun, there is absolutely no leeway here: personal *den* ('that', m.), agreeing with the m. head noun *mat*, is obligatory when the form of the dislocated phrase is definite, as in (30) where the well-formed alternative of (30b) has a generic flavor.

(30) a. **Maten, det er veldig dyrt i Norge.*
food-M.DEF that-N COP very expensive-N in Norway
b. *Maten, den er veldig dyr i Norge.*
food-M.DEF that-M COP very expensive-M in Norway
'The food is very expensive in Norway.'

The subject referent is animate in (31), but the dislocated phrase is the same indefinite demonstrative phrase as in (27) and (28). When the verb is in the active voice, the personal plural pronoun *de* ('they') is the only well-formed alternative.

(31) *Sånne folk, de/*det lærer aldri.*
such-PL.INDEF people-INDEF they/*that learn never
'Such people, they never learn.'

Although *det* is not an acceptable substitute for *de* in (31), it is possible to place a non-personal pronoun in the subject position of a passive sentence with a dislocated *such*-phrase that denotes an animate entity, as seen in (32), where the speaker's choice between a non-personal *det* ('that') and a plural *de* ('they') as pronominal copy of the dislocated noun phrase again appears to have no impact on the explicitly communicated content of the utterance. Both mean 'it happens every day that people with certain (discourse-given) talents are being discovered'; the universal quantifier of the temporal adjunct *hver dag* ('every day') takes the wide scope in (32) regardless of whether the subject pronoun is non-personal *det* as in (32a) or personal *de* as in (32b).

(32) a. *Sånne talenter, det oppdages hver dag.*
such-PL.INDEF talent-PL.INDEF that discover-PASSIVE every day
b. *Sånne talenter, de oppdages hver dag.*
such-PL.INDEF talent-PL.INDEF they discover-PASSIVE every day
'Such talents are being discovered every day.'

Non-personal *det* ('that') in (32a) is an overt sign that the subject phrase designates a type of person defined in terms of the attribute that the determiner *sånne* ('such') represents. The personal pronoun *de* ('they') in (32b) may otherwise be used referentially, but the presence of its indefinite antecedent *sånne talenter* ('such talents') in (32b) overrules that interpretation. We witness once more that Norwegian grammar permits use of a non-personal pronoun where English grammar requires a personal pronoun agreeing in number with the plural noun phrase in the dislocated position, as shown in (33b) compared to the ill-formed version of (33a).

(33) a. **Such talents, that is being discovered every day.*
b. *Such talents, they are being discovered every day.*

The pronoun *they* in (33b) is normally consistent with either a referential or a non-referential interpretation, but the latter prevails in this example due to the linguistic semantics of the indefinite, dislocated phrase *such talents* plus the fact that it is hard to associate the predicate phrase with a *de re* interpretation of the subject referent for pragmatic reasons. If the context is fixed, even (34), where the demonstrative phrase is *these talents*, expresses the same proposition as (33b).

(34) *These talents, they are being discovered every day.*

(34) is not about specific individuals who are discovered every day. *These* represents a salient attribute ascribed to some (talented) people, like *such* in (33b). Both the plural pronoun *they* and the dislocated demonstrative phrase *these talents* may function as referential terms if there is no linguistic or contextual evidence against such an interpretation. However, (34) seems to be an exact parallel to the OMC example (13) presented in section 2.2 – *These cases were invariably difficult, time-consuming and frustrating,...* – where the presence of the adverb *invariably* precludes a referential interpretation of the demonstrative in the subject position, and where the context available to the reader prompts the correct assumption that *these cases* denotes any murder case where the crime is committed by a serial killer.

In English and Norwegian alike, the appearance of a non-personal pronoun as the pronominal copy of a left-dislocated noun phrase is a sufficient condition for a non-referential interpretation, but non-personals are used a lot more in Norwegian than in English. As long as the dislocated phrase is not formally definite and its pronominal copy is not the subject of a verb in the active voice, the Norwegian speaker is free to use non-personal *det* to indicate that the designatum is a type of entity defined in terms of a contextually accessible property. One consequence of this is that, if the Norwegian speaker's intention is to convey that the discovery of new talents is something that happens every day, which is how (32a) and (32b) will be read, it will be counterproductive to use a definite complex demonstrative and a plural pronominal copy similar to the English forms in (34). Norwegian (35) is a strictly literal glossing of English (34). It is hard to avoid construing the definite complex demonstrative and the plural pronoun *de* ('they') in (35) as (co-)referential terms that pick out a set of discourse-activated individuals all of whom are claimed to be discovered anew on a daily basis – a truly odd statement. (35) is not a relevant linguistic form if the speaker's intention is to communicate that discoveries of talented people with certain contextually determinable attributes are made every day.

(35) #*Disse talentene, de oppdages hver dag.*
these talent-PL.DEF they discover-PASSIVE every day
#'These talents$_i$, they$_i$ are being discovered again and again, every day.'

As the acceptability of the Norwegian sentence form of (32b) shows, the *in situ* personal pronoun *de* ('they') does not by itself encode the information that the referent is a set of tokens but the Norwegian combination of a dislocated definite demonstrative phrase and a personal pronominal copy in (35) favors a referential (*de re*) interpretation so much that all my informants judged the normal non-referential (*de dicto*) interpretation of the corresponding argument in English (34) to be completely inaccessible when the Norwegian sentence form is (35).

The answer to the question posed in the heading of this section is that neither a personal nor a non-personal English or Norwegian pronoun operates in a fashion that makes their semantic effect as predictable as the effect of applying litmus paper under acidic or basic conditions. In both languages, a non-personal pronoun does provide a guarantee that the designated entity is of the higher-order sort but a personal pronoun underdetermines the hearer's choice between a referential and a non-referential interpretation.

I believe the difference in the English and Norwegian use of definite and indefinite demonstratives and the difference in the use of personal and non-personal pronominal copies of dislocated demonstratives in the two languages to have a basis in an aptitude for speakers of Norwegian to express overtly the difference between referential and non-referential use, a bias not found to the same extent with speakers of English.

4. Conclusion

My exploration of a parallel corpus described in section 2.2 led me to the conclusion that there is a much greater tolerance for definite demonstratives that are intended to represent a **type** of entity in English than in Norwegian discourse. On the other hand, there appears to be rather more use of the indefinite property-denoting determiner corresponding to English *such* in Norwegian discourse. Data discussed in section 3 suggests that there is a causal connection between a speaker's choice between a personal and a non-personal pronominal copy of a left-dislocated noun phrase and the ontological value of the entity so represented. An intraclausal, non-personal pronoun encodes the information that the entity represented is a property instantiated by tokens, while a personal pronoun is consistent with either a token-level or a type-level interpretation, depending on whatever input guides the pragmatic process of reference resolution for the addressee. What I am saying here applies equally to English and Norwegian, but it was shown in section 3 that a few combinations of formally indefinite, left-dislocated noun phrases and non-personal pronominal copies are grammatical in Norwegian but ungrammatical in English, and conversely it was shown that personal pronouns that agree in number with the dislocated phrase have a wider range of distribution in English than in Norwegian.

One feature of English grammar that may be conducive to the preference for a personal pronoun is the phenomenon of number agreement in English verb forms. Linguistic choices that were mainly a matter of the degree of suitability of different types of demonstrative noun phrases in section 2.2 were seen to affect grammatical well-formedness in section 3, where I demonstrated how the choice between a personal and a non-personal pronoun impacts on the grammaticality of sentences with a left-dislocated noun phrase. The data discussed in section 3 shows how the behavioral tendency to use definite demonstratives freely as non-referential terms in English and the tendency to use an indefinite demonstrative for this purpose in Norwegian can even intrude into the grammatical systems of the two languages.

English finite verbs exhibit an opposition between singular and plural agreement with a 3rd person subject, in contrast to the absence of concord marking in Norwegian verbs. This difference in the grammars of the two languages may shed some light on the question why a speaker of English is permitted to use an equative sentence like *These are the candidates* but not **This is the candidates* with a non-personal demonstrative pronoun that neutralizes the sg.–pl. opposition, while a speaker of Norwegian expresses the same thought by saying *Dette er kandidatene* (lit: this is the candidates) with a non-personal subject. However, this difference between subject–verb agreement in English and its absence in Norwegian does not explain why a Norwegian string like **Disse er kandidatene* (lit: these are the candidates) is an ill-formed alternative to the sentence with the non-personal pronoun *dette* ('that').

Norwegians are rather more inclined to use the indefinite, property-denoting demonstrative than speakers of English, they may use non-personal pronominal copies in some left-dislocation constructions where English requires the personal alternative, and they have to use a non-personal subject pronoun in equatives. In my view these are all manifestations of a single phenomenon, the tendency for Norwegian speakers to mark by conventional linguistic means the distinction between referential and non-referential use of nominal expressions. I believe the mandatory non-personal subject pronoun in Norwegian equatives to be grounded in a very strong Norwegian tendency to express overtly that the noun phrase represents a property of objects rather than the objects *per se*.

Acknowledgements

I am indebted to Kaja Borthen, Chris Wilder and Jeremy Hawthorn, to three anonymous reviewers for their productive comments and criticism, and above all to the editors of this volume, Enikő Németh T. and Károly Bibok, for their help and encouragement.

References

Borthen, Kaja
2004 The Norwegian type-anaphor *det*. In *DAARC 2004: 5th Discourse Anaphora and Anaphor Resolution Colloquium*, António Branco, Tony McEnery and Ruslan Mitkov (eds.), 79–85. Lisbon: Edições Colibri.
Carlson, Gregory N.
1980 *Reference to Kinds in English*. New York: Garland Press.
Carston, Robyn
2002 *Thoughts and Utterances: The Pragmatics of Explicit Communication*. Oxford: Blackwell.

Cornish, Francis
1999 *Anaphora, Discourse, and Understanding: Evidence from English and French*. Oxford: Oxford University Press.
Declerck, Renaat
1983 'It is Mr Y' or 'He is Mr Y'? *Lingua* 59: 209–246.
Donnellan, Keith
1966 Reference and definite descriptions. *Philosophical Review* 77: 281–304.
Heim, Irene
1982 The semantics of definite and indefinite noun phrases. PhD dissertation, Amherst, MA: University of Massachusetts.
Kaplan, David
1989a Demonstratives. In *Themes from Kaplan*, Joseph Almog, Howard Wettstein and John Perry (eds.), 481–563. Oxford: Oxford University Press.
Kaplan, David
1989b Afterthoughts. In *Themes from Kaplan*, Joseph Almog, Howard Wettstein and John Perry (eds.), 565–614. Oxford: Oxford University Press.
King, Jeffrey C.
2001 *Complex Demonstratives: A Quantificational Account*. Cambridge, MA: The MIT Press.
Recanati, François
1993 *Direct Reference: From Language to Thought*. Oxford: Blackwell.
Sperber, Dan and Deirdre Wilson
1995 *Relevance: Communication and Cognition*. Oxford: Blackwell. (2nd edition with a Postface).
ter Meulen, Alice
1995 Semantic constraints on type-shifting anaphora. In *The Generic Book*, Gregory N. Carlson and Francis Jeffry Pelletier (eds.), 339–357. Chicago, IL: The University of Chicago Press.
Wilson, Deirdre and Dan Sperber
2004 Relevance Theory. In *The Handbook of Pragmatics*, Laurence R. Horn and Gregory Ward (eds.), 607–632. Oxford: Blackwell.

Part Two
Scalar implicatures and beyond

Two experiments and some suggestions on the meaning of scalars and numerals

Napoleon Katsos and Richard Breheny

1. Introduction

A debate in the semantics/pragmatics literature concerns the meaning of numerals, and whether the *exactly N* interpretation is derived from the lower-bound *at least N* by means of scalar implicature. Recent cross-linguistic research in language acquisition indicates that the *exactly N* interpretation of numerals is acquired earlier than the upper-bound interpretation of scalar expressions such as the existential quantifier and disjunction, and this is taken by some as evidence of the different nature of numerals and scalar expressions. Others argue for the uniformity of scalars and numerals, suggesting that the difference in the pattern of acquisition is due to extra-linguistic factors related to more general cognitive development. We present one off-line and one on-line self-paced reading experiment which investigate the processing of logical scales (existential/universal quantifier; disjunction/conjunction) and numerals by adult native speakers of English. These experiments indicate that adults are sensitive to contextually induced expectations of informativeness when interpreting both logical scales and numerals off-line, but the on-line task shows that the time-course of these interpretations is different. These results cannot be attributed to the extra-linguistic factors suggested as explanations of the pattern of acquisition. Overall, we aim to demonstrate how experimental approaches to issues in the semantics–pragmatics interface may corroborate intuitions and offer critical data in cases that are too fine-grained for introspection.

1.1. Scalar expressions

Grice's first maxim of quantity, "Make your contribution as informative as is required for the current purposes of the exchange" (Grice 1989: 26), has been systematically exploited to account for how the informational load of utterances can be strengthened via pragmatic implicature (Gazdar 1979; Horn 1972, 1984; Levinson 1983 i.a.). Certain linguistic expressions can form scales that are ordered in terms of the informational strength of utterances that contain them. The scale of the existential and universal quantifier and that of disjunction and conjunction are two of the cases widely discussed in the literature. For the first scale, the universal quantifier is informationally stronger than the existential, since if it is true that *all Fs are G*, it is also true that *some Fs are G*, but not vice versa. Similarly for conjunction and disjunction, if it is true that *p and q*, it follows that *p or q*, but not vice versa.

Logically speaking, asserting the weaker term of a scale, such as by saying "some Fs are G", is compatible with a scenario in which a stronger term holds, in this case a scenario in which all Fs are G. However, given the first maxim of quantity that requires speakers to be as informative as is necessary in a given context, the assertion of an utterance containing the weaker term where the stronger proposition would provide more relevant information will prompt the listener to reason as follows: if the speaker could have made the stronger claim, she would have done so. Hence, by asserting the weaker term, she is communicating that the stronger claim does not hold.[1] The implicature associated with this maxim is called *scalar implicature.*

Whether scalar implicature is considered a default inference (Chierchia 2004), a generalised conversational implicature (Gazdar 1979; Horn 1992, 2005 i.a.), or a nonce-inference (Atlas 2005; Carston 2002; Hirschberg 1991; Geurts 1998; Sperber and Wilson 1986/1995 i.a.), or a combination thereof (Recanati 2003, Levinson 2000), most accounts of scalar implicature currently available rely on considerations of informational strength and relevance to the topic of the conversation. The success of such approaches is partly due to the observation that scalar implicatures do not arise in contexts where the implicature would not contribute to making the utterance more informative. Such contexts can be introduced by previous discourse. As we can see in (1) and (2), there are contexts where interlocutors are interested in the logically strongest information possible, and hence an implicature would increase the amount of contextually relevant information communicated by the speaker. Let us call such contexts *upper-bound contexts*, and the interpretation of the scalar expressions with an implicature the *upper-bounded* interpretation. Now compare these contexts with (1') and (2'), respectively:

---

1 To be precise, the speaker is communicating that she does not know that the stronger claim is true. If the speaker is assumed to be an expert on the topic of the conversation, then the listener may further infer that the speaker knows that the stronger claim does not hold.

(1) *A: How well did Peter do at his exams?*
B: He passed some of them with distinction.

(1') *A: How does Peter need to do at his exams to get a scholarship?*
B: He has to pass some of them with distinction.

(2) *A: Who is interviewing prospective students?*
B: Taylor or Powell from the Board of Admissions.

(2') *A: Who is available to interview prospective students?*
B: Taylor or Powell from the Board of Admissions.

Should the scalar expressions in (1') and (2') be given an upper-bound interpretation? There is widespread agreement in the literature that scalar implicatures should not be available in discourse contexts where the information encoded by the plain meaning of the scalar expression ("at least one", for *some*; "p or q or both", for *p or q*) is sufficient for addressing the discourse goal. This can be traced to the formulation of the first maxim of quantity itself, where contributions must be as informative as it is required *for the purposes of the exchange*. Thus, for (1'), it is beside the point to consider whether Peter does not have to obtain distinctions in every one of his exams in order to get a scholarship.[2] Similarly, for (2'), either one of Taylor or Powell would be sufficient for interviewing students and it is irrelevant to consider whether both of them are available. Let us then call contexts where computing an implicature would be superfluous *lower-bound contexts*.

A second observation in support of implicature accounts is that the interpretation of scalar expressions is dependent on the direction of the entailment of the linguistic structure. Implicatures are routinely found in upward entailing structures like the assertions in (1) and (2). However, in downward entailing structures, for instance in the antecedent of conditionals or under the scope of negation, the direction of entailment in the scale is reversed and scalar implicatures are not available:

2 Note that according to theoretical accounts that allow for scalar implicatures to be generated in embedded positions, such as under the scope of a modal (Chierchia, 2004; Levinson, 2000; Recanati, 2003 i.a.), the embedded implicature in this case would be that Peter has to pass some but not all of the tests, rather than that he does not have to pass all of the tests. The difference between the two implicatures is irrelevant in this case, as all accounts predict that implicatures are not generated in what we called lower-bound contexts.

(3) a. *If Peter passes some of the tests with distinction, he will treat himself to a holiday in Greece.*
b. *If Taylor or Powell interviews prospective students, then the Board of Admissions will be content.*

The crucial property of downward entailing structures is that utterances containing the otherwise weaker scalar terms become informationally stronger. In these cases the sub-clauses containing *some* and *or* receive interpretations compatible with, respectively, Peter passing all the tests with distinction, and both Taylor and Powell interviewing prospective students.

There are further properties of scalar implicature that merit an elaborate discussion, such as reliance on the speakers' epistemic state, and availability in certain embedded positions (see Geurts 2009; Russell 2006; i.a.). For the purposes of this paper, we wish to highlight that considerations of informational strength, relevance, and of the structural properties of the sentence are crucial for the interpretation of scalar expressions such as the existential quantifier *some* and disjunction.

Up to this point we have been talking about meaning and interpretation without too much concern about the difference between these terms. It is possible to flesh out this difference and say that, according to most theories in the field, scalar expressions have lower-bound *meanings*. That is, the lexical entry for *some* encodes plain existential quantification and the lexical entry for *or* encodes inclusive disjunction. We can further say that scalar expressions can have upper-bound *interpretations* – "some but not all", "either one but not both" – that are derived from the lexical lower-bound meaning. The process by which this interpretation is derived invariably involves a scalar implicature arising out of considerations of informativeness (though, as we mentioned, the exact nature of such inferences is not an uncontroversial issue).

1.2. Numerals: some similarities and some differences with scalar expressions

It can be shown that the interpretation of numerals is sensitive to similar considerations of informativeness as that of other scalar expressions. In fact, numerals have been treated as the paradigmatic case of scalar expression in the neo-Gricean literature (Atlas and Levinson 1981; Gazdar 1979; Horn 1972; i.a.), and are still considered by some as the scalar term *par excellence* (Chierchia 2004). According to such accounts, the lexical meaning of numerals is the lower-bound "at least N", and the scalar implicature contributes an "at most N" inference, in order to derive the upper-bounded interpretation "exactly N" as in (4):

(4) *A: How is George doing?*
B: He has won three games in the first set.

Crucially, the step from "at least three" to "exactly three" is motivated by considerations of informativeness: if the speaker knew that George had won four or more games in the first set, she should have said so. The fact that the speaker did not say so allows the listener to infer that this is not the case. In (4) the utterance containing the numeral is preceded by an upper-bound context. Compare this with (4'), where the preceding utterance sets a lower-bound context by introducing a goal that can be addressed by an "at least" interpretation of the numeral:

(4') *A: What does George have to do in order to put up a decent performance?*
B: He has to win three games in the first set.

Again, the numeral need not receive an upper-bound interpretation, which would be to the effect that George does not have to win four games in the first set in order to put up a decent performance, since this would be irrelevant for the purposes of addressing the question. Similarly, in downward entailing structures, numerals can receive the lower-bound "at least N" interpretation:[3]

(5) *If George wins three games in the first set, he will have put up a decent performance.*

However, several researchers (Carston 1998; Geurts 1998; Horn 1992; Sadock 1984 among others) have pinpointed a number of differences between numerals and other scalar expressions. Even in logical contexts such as mathematical statements, in which linguistic expressions are presumably used only with the logical-semantic meaning, numerals are used with an upper-bound interpretation, as otherwise 3+3 = 5 ought to be valid (Sadock 1984). Horn also highlights asymmetries with respect to which aspect of an expression's meaning can be denied (examples are based on Horn 1972):

---

[3] If anything, we get a so-called 'scale reversal' implicature to the effect that it is not true that if George wins *two* games in the first set he will have put up a decent performance (see Horn, 1989).

(6) *A: Do you have two children?*
B1: No, three.
B2: ?Yes, (in fact) three.

(7) *A: Did many of the guests leave?*
B1: ?No, all of them.
B2: No, just a few of them.
B2: Yes, (in fact) all of them.

A negative response to (6A) is compatible with having derived the upper-bound "exactly N" interpretation of the numeral, while a negative response to the scalar quantifier *many* can only be understood as "fewer than many" (7B2) rather than "more than many" (7B1). Moreover, Carston (1998) argues that numerals may have an "at most N" interpretation (8) which cannot be construed from an "at least" meaning, and is not available without special intonation for other scalar terms:

(8) *Mary: How many guests can I bring with me?*
Jane: You may bring three guests.

In the same vein of pointing out differences between scalar quantifiers and numerals, Geurts (1998) argues that numerals have different distributions and combine differently with modifiers:

(9) *Bill is hosting at least {?many/three} relatives*
Bill is hosting less than {?a few/three} relatives
Bill is hosting exactly {?a few/?some/?many/three} relatives

The fact that numerals allow for explicit modification by *precisely* and *exactly* suggests that they have a punctual meaning, i.e. they identify a precise point in the numerical scale.

This list of observations that differentiate scalar expressions from numerals is not exhaustive, nor is it necessarily convincing. Besides the standard neo-Gricean literature, Levinson (2000) and Chierchia (2004) put forth proposals that still argue for the view that the meaning of numerals is lower-bound "at least N", and the upper-bound is a derived interpretation that involves scalar implicature. We will refer to any approach that maintains that numerals and scalar expressions share the same meaning, the lower-bound one, and that upper-bound interpretations are achieved through scalar implicature, as an *implicature approach.*

But what are the alternatives? According to Sadock (1984), Koenig (1991), Scharten (1997), Geurts (1998, 2006), Breheny (2008) and others, numerals have an upper-bound "exactly N" meaning. These "exactly N" approaches have to deal with deriving the other interpretations. For example, Geurts (2006) puts forth a *polysemy* position, whereby numerals have an "exactly N" primary meaning, the "at least N" interpretation is derived by a standard type-coercion process, and the "at most N" interpretation is pragmatically derived. On a different approach, Breheny (2008) suggests that the "at least" interpretations can be derived as special cases of specific interpretations of the numerically quantified noun phrase. Breheny argues that when they are specifically construed, weak noun phrases can undergo a form of existential closure on the specific domain, particularly in embedded contexts. In the case of numerically quantified noun phrases, this existential-closure effect gives rise to an "at least" interpretation.

According to a third view, the *underspecification* view, the meaning of numerals is neutral towards any of the potential interpretations. The meaning of numerals is an abstract representation that is each time specified in contextually appropriate senses as "exactly N", "at least N", or "at most N". Proponents of this approach include Atlas (2005) and Carston (1985, 1998).

1.3. Aims of the present investigation

Further discussion of the theoretical literature would unveil further differences. But we will stop at this point, since we can identify at least one critical prediction with respect to the upper- and lower-bound interpretation of numerals. According to *implicature* approaches, the process that derives upper-bound interpretations from lower-bound meanings for scalar expressions is also involved in numeral interpretation. According to polysemy, existential closure, and underspecification approaches, the process that derives upper- and lower-bound readings of numerals should be different to the process of generating a scalar implicature in standard scalar expressions.

The main aim of this chapter is to empirically address this issue, which is central to some theories of the semantics–pragmatics interface. But how does one go about testing such claims empirically? And does one care about empirically testing this or any other claim about meaning? At least some researchers have taken a categorical stance: Carston (2004), Chierchia (2004), Levinson (2000), and Sperber and Wilson (1986/1995) claim that their accounts should enjoy psycholinguistic as well as linguistic validity. They view their theories not as accounts of an abstract system but of the actual, psychologically real competence native speakers have with regard to semantics and pragmatics. As a result, there is currently a growing experimental literature, which is directly motivated by the theoretical linguistic debate.

The rest of this chapter is set out as follows. In section 2, we review this literature, examining the evidence from child language acquisition (section 2.1) and from adult processing studies (section 2.2). In section 3, we discuss the predictions generated by existing theories as to the way in which adults process scalars and numerals (section 3.1), and examine the findings of two experiments designed to test these predictions, an off-line study (section 3.2) and a study on the time-course of processing (section 3.3). In section 4, we discuss how the competing theories may be reconciled with the experimental data. Finally, we conclude (section 5) by examining how this investigation, and its methodology, relates to the general issue of investigating the semantics–pragmatics interface.

2. A brief overview of the experimental literature

In this section, we summarize recent experimental work bearing upon the meaning of scalars and numerals. First we examine the evidence from acquisitional studies, then we turn to the investigations of adult performance.

2.1. Existing evidence from child language acquisition

In an investigation that has motivated much recent work, Noveck (2001) studied the acquisition of scalar expressions by French-speaking children. The fundamental finding was that children first acquire the lower-bound interpretation of the existential quantifier and modal expressions and only later do they acquire the upper-bound ones. Following up on this study, Papafragou and Musolino (2003) compared the acquisition of the existential quantifier to the acquisition of numerals, using variations of the truth-value judgment task (Crain and Thornton 1998 i.a.). They presented children and adults with an act-out scenario where it was obvious that the strong term of the scale was applicable, e.g. a puppet had to tell what happened in a scenario where all of three horses jump a fence. Participants were then presented with an utterance containing the weak term of the scale of the existential/universal quantifier or a numeral, e.g. *some of the horses jumped the fence*, *two of the horses jumped the fence*. Participants may interpret the scalar terms with their lower-bound meaning, "at least one and even all" and "at least two", which is compatible with the scenario they witnessed. In this case, they will accept this utterance as true, even if it is underinformative. Alternatively, they may interpret the scalar terms with an upper-bounded reading and generate the scalar inferences "some but not all", "exactly two". In this case, participants will reject the utterances since they are inconsistent with the scenarios they saw. The study by Papafragou and Musolino showed that adults reject more than 90% of underinformative utterances on either scale. Five-year-old children reject very few underinformative utterances for the existential/universal quantifier scale (12.5%), corroborating previous findings by Noveck (2001). Crucially for our topic of interest, children do reject 65% of underinformative utterances with numerals. Further studies by Guasti et al. (2005), as well as Pouscoulous et al. (2007) and Hurewitz et al. (2006), have shed more light on both the ages at which children reject underinformative utterances with scalar expressions and the reasons why they may do so. All these studies confirm the finding that children acquire the upper-bound meaning of numerals earlier than that of the existential quantifier and disjunction.

A straightforward interpretation of this finding is that numerals, unlike scalars, do not have a lower-bound meaning and an upper-bound interpretation achieved by scalar implicature. Rather children start with an upper-bound meaning for numerals, and this is the reason why they perform better on the underinformative utterances as well as in a variety of similar tasks (e.g. Musolino 2004).

However, one can resist this conclusion on several grounds. First, there might well be extra-linguistic factors why the upper-bound interpretation of numerals is acquired earlier than for other scalars, namely numerical literacy. The amount of exposure and training that five-year-old children receive with numerals, greater than that with inexact quantifiers, could contribute to better performance on the tasks at hand. Another argument, implicit in Guasti et al. (2005), is that children process numerals like other scalars, but acquire the relevant informativeness scale for numerals earlier than the scale for inexact quantifiers. In their account, scales are specified in the lexical entry of each scalar term. For cognitive, biological or cultural reasons, it may be that children form the entailment scale of numerals earlier than the scale for quantifiers and for disjunction, which would explain the results in question. This proposal is supported by evidence that upper-bound interpretations of other scales such as the modals *may/must* appear even later than for the inexact quantifier (see for example the studies reported in Noveck 2001), indicating that there are scale-specific effects in acquisition.

2.2. Existing evidence from adult processing

The extra-linguistic factors that have been invoked to explain the acquisition data are not pertinent to competent adult native speakers, for whom one can assume that all scales are fully lexicalised and who are equally familiar with numerals as with inexact quantifiers and sentential operators such as disjunction and conjunction. Let us then review some recent experimental findings on the processing of scalars by adults that will provide us with processing predictions.

As with acquisition, there is a growing number of investigations of how adults process scalar terms, starting with the studies of Noveck (2001), Noveck and Posada (2003) and Bott and Noveck (2004). In a series of single utterance verification studies, Noveck and colleagues built on a paradigm by Smith (1980) which presented participants with utterances using a scalar term, e.g. *Some elephants have trunks*, without any preceding scenario. These utterances are underinformative given world-knowledge that all elephants have trunks. When presented with a scalar term and asked to make a truth-judgment, respondents may answer by generating the implicature and arriving at an upper-bound interpretation, or just by using the lower-bound meaning of the term. Noveck (2001) found that about 60% of underinformative utterances are rejected by adults who are logically competent in a variety of other reasoning tasks, indicating that these adults derived the upper-bound interpretations.

What is of particular interest is that in such paradigms one can measure how much time participants require in order to respond. Noveck and Posada (2003) and Bott and Noveck (2004) found that participants who derive the upper-bound interpretation of scalar expressions require more time than participants who do not, even though both groups of participants are equally competent and equally quick in several control conditions.

Moreover, in a series of studies, Katsos, Breheny and Williams (2005a, 2005b), Breheny, Katsos and Williams (2006) and Katsos (2006, 2008) investigated the effect of contextually induced expectations of informativeness on processing scalar expressions. For example, Katsos (2006) established that participants interpreted scalar terms with upper- or lower-bound interpretations depending on the context. Short discourses were created as in (10a) and (10b), which are upper-bound and lower-bound, respectively:

(10) a. *The Head of the Department asked her secretary: Who is giving a lecture on Nuclear Physics for undergraduates? Her secretary replied: Williams or Tyler from the Research Laboratory.*

b. *The Head of the Department asked her secretary: Who is available to give a lecture on Nuclear Physics for undergraduates? Her secretary replied: Williams or Tyler from the Research Laboratory.*

In a metalinguistic judgment task, participants were asked to read these short texts and to rate on a 7-point Likert scale whether the disjunction was exclusive ("p or q but not both") or inclusive ("p or q or even both"). Additionally, in a sentence completion task participants were asked to fill in a verb at the end of the last sentence of the same texts (where it was assumed that a verb marked for singular number would indicate an exclusive interpretation of the disjunction, and a verb marked for plural would indicate an inclusive interpretation). In both tasks it was found that participants consistently preferred exclusive interpretations in upper-bound contexts and inclusive ones in lower-bound contexts. The pattern of results for the disjunction was obtained both in English and Greek (Katsos, Breheny and Williams 2005a); moreover, an off-line metalinguistic judgment task in English showed that participants were sensitive to the upper- and lower-bound interpretations of the existential quantifier as well.

Disjunctions and existential quantifiers in such contexts were then further studied using self-paced reading tasks (Katsos 2006; Katsos, Breheny and Williams 2005b), where it was found that scalar terms were read more slowly in the upper-bound condition than in the lower-bound one. Breheny, Katsos and Williams (2006) included additional control conditions for the existential quantifier and obtained the same results. Moreover, it was found that one can introduce considerations of informativeness, even in the absence of discourse context, by manipulating whether the existential quantifier is positioned utterance-initially or utterance-finally. Overall, the self-paced reading studies indicate that processing scalar expressions with their upper-bound interpretations is more time-consuming than processing them with their lower-bound meaning. This finding corroborates the results of the utterance evaluation studies by Noveck and Posada (2003) and Bott and Noveck (2004), and is also consistent with ongoing work on the processing of scalars using the visual-world eye-tracking paradigm (Huang and Snedeker 2009).

3. An empirical study in the semantics–pragmatics interface: numerals versus scalars

In this section, we present additional experimental findings on the processing of numerals and scalars by adult speakers. However, first we wish to compare the precise predictions on this point arising from the various theoretical approaches that have been mooted.

3.1. Predictions on the processing of numerals and scalars by adults

We are now ready to spell out predictions concerning the processing of numerals and scalars by adults. In section 1.2 we saw that the standard neo-Gricean literature (Atlas and Levinson 1981; Gazdar 1979; Horn 1972 i.a.), as well as Levinson (2000) and Chierchia (2004), advocates a common view, arguing that the semantic meaning of numerals and scalar expressions is the lower-bound "at least N"/"at least some"/"either p or q or even both" and that upper-bound interpretations are derived by means of a scalar implicature. We called this view the *implicature* view. At the psycholinguistic level, this view predicts that the interpretation of scalars and numerals alike should be sensitive to considerations of informativeness, and that reading time of existential quantifiers, disjunctions and numerals in contexts which are biased towards the upper-bound interpretations should be slower than in contexts which are biased towards the plain lower-bound meaning.

According to the coercion/polysemy, existential closure, and underspecification views (Sadock 1984; Koenig 1991; Horn 1992; Scharten 1997; Carston 1998; Geurts 1998, 2006; Breheny 2008; i.a.), numerals have a different semantics to scalars. This is as far as the consensus goes in the non-implicature view. Significant differences can be found when looking at the specifics of each account: for coercion/polysemy accounts the upper-bound meaning is the starting point and the lower-bound interpretation is derived from the upper-bound by a process similar to type-coercion, while for underspecification accounts all interpretations are derived by pragmatic processes from a more abstract underlying representation. For existential closure accounts, the effect is achieved through some mechanism at the pragmatic interface operating on the linguistically determined meaning of the utterance. For Breheny (2008), the mechanism in question is simply domain restriction. While domain restriction occurs in virtually all contexts, regardless of whether an upper- or lower-bound interpretation is being derived, in the existential closure cases domain restriction involves extra pragmatic inferences (presupposition accommodation) and this factor should in fact make the lower-bound reading more costly, if anything. In other existential closure accounts, such as are suggested in Kratzer (2003), the details of the closure mechanism are not specified other than as operations that apply post-grammatically. Even so, such mechanisms would make the "at least" reading no less costly than the "exactly" reading, and possibly more so.

We will collectively refer to these accounts as *anti-implicature* accounts, on the grounds of their shared prediction for either equal reading time between upper- and lower-bound contexts for numerals, or longer reading time for lower-bound ones.

3.2. Off-line sensitivity to contextually induced upper- and lower-bound interpretations

In the first study we investigated the prediction that is shared by all accounts, namely whether contextually induced expectations of informativeness affect the interpretation of numerals as they have been shown to affect scalars. We created short texts for three types of expressions: numerals, disjunctions, and quantifiers. Each text was rendered in two versions. In one version there was a question that required the informationally strongest interpretation of the answer, therefore biasing towards the upper-bound interpretation of the expression (see 11a, 12a, 13a). In the other version of the text there was a question that could be sufficiently addressed by the lower-bound interpretation of the expression (see 11b, 12b, 13b). We asked participants to evaluate on a 7-point Likert scale whether the critical expression had the upper- or lower-bound interpretation.

Method

Participants

The participants were 24 graduate and undergraduate students of the University of Cambridge (mean age 25;1, range 20–29). 17 of them were female. Participants were paid £7 for participating in one hour of experimental tasks in total.

Design and Materials

For each type of expression we created twelve short question/answer pairs in two conditions, the upper-bound and the lower-bound condition. In the upper-bound condition (henceforth UB; see 11a, 12a) the first utterance was a mention-all or exhaustive question which asks the addressee to give as much information as she can (see van Rooy and Schulz 2006). Assuming that the addressee is cooperative and suitably expert on the topic of the conversation, the answer to such questions will be interpreted as being the most informative interpretation possible. In the case of a disjunctive noun phrase or an existential quantifier, this will result in the upper-bound interpretation "p or q but not both" and "some but not all the Fs", respectively. In the lower-bound condition (henceforth LB; see 11b, 12b), the first utterance is a mention-some or non-exhaustive question that asks the addressee to give enough information to address a specific goal set up by the discourse context. In these contexts, the disjunctive noun phrase and the existential quantifier obtain the lower-bound interpretations "p or q and even both" and "some and even all the Fs", respectively. We created 12 short question/answer texts in UB and LB conditions for the numerals in a similar way (13a, 13b):

(11) a. (Upper-bound *or*) *The Dean asked: Who is interviewing prospective students? Her secretary replied: Taylor or Powell from the Board of Admissions.*
b. (Lower-bound *or*) *The Dean asked: Who is available to interview prospective students? Her secretary replied: Taylor or Powell from the Board of Admissions.*

(12) a. (Upper-bound *some*) *Tracy asked Georgette: How well did Peter do with the exams he had to take? Georgette replied: He managed to pass some of the tests with distinction.*
b. (Lower-bound *some*) *Tracy asked Georgette: How does Peter need to do on the exams to get a scholarship? Georgette replied: He has to pass some of the tests with distinction.*

(13) a. (Upper-bound numeral) *At the pistol shooting range, Mary inquired: How is my husband doing so far? The instructor told her: He has hit four targets in the bull's-eye.*
b. (Lower-bound numeral) *At the pistol shooting range, Mary inquired: How well does my husband have to have to do to qualify for an advanced license? The instructor told her: He has to hit four targets in the bull's-eye.*

In total, we used 36 critical items, 12 for each type of expression. A list of all the items is available from the first author. The items for each type of expression were randomly divided into two groups of 6. One presentation list was created by taking the UB items from Group 1 and the LB items from Group 2, and another list was created using the remaining versions of each text. Each presentation list therefore contained 6 items in each condition. The order of the items in each list was independently randomized. We further split the participants for each of the two lists into three groups. One group first completed the task on disjunctions, then on quantifiers, and then on numerals. The other two groups in each list completed the tasks in cyclically permuted orders. This was done to control for the possibility that prior experience in one task would affect performance in the other two tasks. The tasks together took around 30 minutes to complete.

Procedure

Participants were given a booklet with the items and were told that they would read short texts that consist of a question and an answer. For each type of expression they were given separate but similar instructions. They were told that the answer always contained a phrase with a disjunction or an existential quantifier or a numeral, depending on the task. For example, for the task on the disjunctions, they were told that, when asked *Who is John dating?*, an answer could be *Mary or Jane.* Participants were asked to rate on a 7-point Likert scale on a horizontal line whether they believe that the answer implies "Mary or Jane **but not both of them**", or whether they believe that the answer implies "Mary or Jane **and even both of them**". The leftmost part of the scale (1) was glossed for the lower-bound interpretation using abstract letters (*A or B or even both*), and the rightmost (7) was glossed for the upper-bound (*A or B but not both*). Participants were also told that the point in the middle of the scale, (4), indicated that they had no preference.

For the other types of expressions there was a similar example and the corresponding upper- and lower-bound interpretation glosses were used ("some but not all", "some and even all"; "at least N", "exactly N").

Results and discussion

Table 1. Ratings of numerals and scalars in upper- and lower-bound contexts on a 7-point scale

	Upper-bound context (SD)	Lower-bound context (SD)
All expressions	5.63*** (0.98)	2.7 *** (0.99)
Numerals	6.35*** (0.81)	2.36*** (0.93)
Disjunction	5 *** (0.96)	2.85** (0.91)
Existential Quantifier	5.48*** (0.72)	2.89*** (1.00)

Asterisks indicate level of significant difference from '4', chance performance, at the .001 (***) and the .01 (**) level. SD = Standard Deviation

The ratings on the interpretation of the expressions can be seen in Table 1. Analyses of Variance were conducted in which subjects and items were treated as random factors. For the subjects analysis the between-subjects factor was Presentation List, and for the items analysis the between-items factor was Item Group. In both analyses the within-subjects/items factors were Expression type (3: numerals, disjunctions, quantifiers) x Context (2: Upper-bound, Lower-bound). Because the assumption of sphericity was not met by the data, we report the results of the tests with the Huynh-Feldt correction. There was a main effect of Context ($F1(1,22) = 293.44$, $p < .001$; $F2(1,10) = 351.57$, $p < .001$). A main effect of Expression type was significant in the items analysis, but not in the subjects analysis ($F1(2,22) = 2.26$ n.s.; $F2(2,9) = 8.34$, $p < .01$). The interaction between Expression and Context was significant ($F1(2,44) = 11.77$, $p < .001$; $F2(2,20) = 6.18$, $p < .01$). Planned comparisons indicate that all expressions were rated significantly higher in upper-bound contexts than in lower-bound ones; for the numerals $F1(1,22) = 168.01$, $p < .001$; $F2(1,10) = 193.6$, $p < .001$; for disjunctions $F1(1,22) = 56.78$, $p < .001$; $F2(1,10) = 26.33$, $p < .001$; for the quantifiers $F1(1,22) = 123.66$, $p < .001$; $F2(1,10) = 82.83$, $p < .001$.

Furthermore, unplanned comparisons by means of pairwise t-tests indicate that numerals were rated higher in the upper-bound context than either disjunctions ($t1(23) = 5.58$, $p < .001$; $t2(11) = 5.01$, $p <.001$) or quantifiers ($t1(23) = 4.07$, $p < .001$; $t2(11) = 3.78$, $p < .005$), whereas there was no significant difference between disjunctions and quantifiers ($t1(23) = 1.66$ n.s.; $t2(11) = .769$ n.s.). Further analyses did not reveal any reliable differences in lower-bound contexts (since 6 unplanned comparisons were performed in total, the confidence interval was adjusted to .0083 according to the Bonferroni correction for chance capitalization).

The fact that numerals were rated higher in the upper-bound context was not expected, and it might be taken as an indication that numerals are more susceptible to contextual bias than disjunctions and quantifiers. However, a study designed to test this claim, i.e. whether numerals are more sensitive to UB and LB contexts than other expressions, should have the scalar (disjunctions and quantifiers) and the numeral items embedded in identical discourses, rather than different ones. This would be possible especially with regards to quantifiers and numerals, which are semantically related expressions. For example, four conditions for such an item are given in (14):

(14) a. (Upper-bound *some*/numeral) *Tracy asked Georgette: How well did Peter do with the exams he had to take? Georgette replied: He managed to pass {some of the/four of the} tests with distinction.*

b. (Lower-bound *some*/numeral) *Tracy asked Georgette: How does Peter need to do on the exams to get a scholarship? Georgette replied: He has to pass {some of the/four of the} tests with distinction.*

As it is, this off-line study is only an indication that all three expressions are sensitive to the specific UB/LB contexts that were constructed for each of them. The difference in degree of sensitivity could be partly attributed to the different materials used for each expression type rather than solely to the effect of context and expression type.

Overall, we can conclude that there is evidence that contextually introduced considerations of informativeness consistently bias hearers towards the upper- and lower-bound interpretations of numerals, disjunctions and quantifiers. To the best of our knowledge, this comes as the first empirical confirmation of a prediction that is widely shared in the theoretical literature.

3.3. The time-course of upper- and lower-bound interpretations

We now turn to investigate the process by which the upper-bound and lower-bound interpretations are derived. According to the implicature view, all three expressions involve a lower-bound semantic meaning and an upper-bound interpretation derived through scalar implicature. Previous findings on the processing of scalar terms, reviewed in section 2.2, indicate that upper-bound interpretations of scalars are processed more slowly than lower-bound ones. Thus this view predicts that upper-bound interpretations of numerals, disjunctions, and quantifiers should all be read more slowly than the corresponding lower-bound interpretations.

On the anti-implicature view, this should not obtain. But what precisely should obtain is not necessarily clear, since the specific predictions rely on a number of assumptions on the time-course of the alternative processes invoked, namely type-coercion, domain restriction and underspecification. Domain restriction and underspecification accounts seem to suggest that both interpretations should be read equally quickly, since the domain of application or the underspecified meaning have to be specified for both upper- and lower-bound interpretations (albeit resulting in different interpretations). A polysemy account, on the other hand, might predict longer reading times in the lower-bound context, if deriving this interpretation requires an additional time-consuming process (type-coercion) compared to deriving the upper-bound interpretation. Thus, at this stage we will only claim that according to anti-implicature accounts numerals should not show the upper-/lower-bound asymmetry that scalars do, and we will further explore the particulars of these accounts in section 4. Schematically, then, these predictions are as shown in Table 2.

Table 2. Predictions of implicature and anti-implicature accounts

Implicature view			
	Reading time	UB > LB for both scalars and numerals	
Anti-implicature view			
	Reading time	Scalars: UB > LB	Numerals: UB ≤ LB

To compare these hypotheses, we ran a self-paced reading experiment.

Method

Participants

Thirty participants were drawn from the University of Cambridge graduate and undergraduate pool of students (mean age: 23;8, range 19–27; 18 were females). All participants had normal or corrected-to-normal vision and did not have a history of language disorders. Participants were paid £7 for participating in one hour of experimental tasks in total.

Design and Materials

We used the same 36 critical items that we employed in Experiment 1, 12 items for each type of expression (disjunctions, quantifiers and numerals), in the same two conditions, upper-bound and lower-bound contexts. The items for each type of expression were randomly divided into two groups of 6. One presentation list was created by taking the UB items from Group 1 and the LB items from Group 2, and another list was created using the remaining versions of each text. Each presentation list therefore contained 6 items in each condition for each type of expression. 60 items were added to each list, which were fillers or the critical items of other experiments. The order of the items in each list was independently randomized. Each presentation list was read by 15 participants. Comprehension was checked by administering 32 questions, 12 of which were on critical items. The answers to the comprehension questions were not related to the upper- or lower-boundedness of the interpretation of the critical expressions. Segmentation of the items was such that only the critical expressions appeared in the segment containing them.

Procedure

The experiment was run using Superlab software. Participants were told that they had to answer accurately questions pertaining to texts that they would read on the computer. They were told that they would read short texts presented segment by segment. After reading each segment carefully they were told to press the left mouse button to see the next one using their habitual mouse hand. They were instructed to read each segment only once and not try to memorise it, but also that they should fully understand each segment before advancing to the next one. The segments were presented in black font against a white background, in the centre of the screen. There was no delay between the pressing of buttons and the presentation of segments. The time to read each segment was recorded by Superlab software (which provides accuracy within 1ms). Answers to comprehension questions were also recorded by the software. The experiment took between 25 and 35 minutes to complete, including five practice items at the beginning and one rest break halfway through. The post-experiment interview revealed that no participant had become aware of the purpose of the experiment. Participants' accuracy on the comprehension questions was 90%, with accuracy rates being similar in each presentation list. One participant who scored significantly lower than the rest was excluded from the final sample and replaced.

Results

The reading times for the region preceding the critical segments, the regions containing the critical segments, and the following regions constituted the data for analysis. The effect of outliers was curtailed in two stages. First, any values below 200ms were excluded, since they probably reflected mechanical responses. Also, excessively long reading times, assumed to be due to processes other than the ones of interest, were excluded. The exclusion value was calculated as approximately 2.5 times the mean segment time over all participants for each of the three regions (preceding, critical, following). Once this had been done, individual cut-off values were calculated for each participant as the mean plus 2 standard deviations over all 36 items (disregarding expression type and context). Any value exceeding the cut-off was replaced with the cut-off value. The assumption was that, although such long responses may reflect the processes of interest, their effects should be curtailed in order that the response time distribution should not be overly skewed. Over all participants, around 4% of the data were either removed or replaced by the cut-off value. In the preceding, critical and following region, each type of expression was affected as follows: numerals 3.1%, 3.2%, 5%; disjunctions: 6%, 3.2%, 5.2%; quantifiers: 3.2%, 3%, 5%. The reading time results for the critical regions as well as the preceding/following regions can be found in Table 3.

Table 3. Reading time for the regions of the critical expressions and the preceding/following regions in upper- and lower-bound contexts (in milliseconds; Standard Error of the Mean reported in brackets)

		Preceding	Critical	Following
Numerals	UB	546 (43)	804 (57)	778 (66)
	LB	559 (43)	810 (59)	788 (64)
Disjunctions	UB	768 (59)	800 (63)	786 (65)
	LB	772 (52)	754 (56)	756 (68)
Quantifiers	UB	536 (41)	717 (62)	743 (68)
	LB	532 (45)	669 (60)	730 (63)

Analyses of Variance were conducted in which subjects and items were treated as random factors. For the subjects analysis the between-subjects factor was Presentation List, and for the items analysis the between-items factor was Item Group. In both analyses the within-subjects/items factors were Expression type (3: numerals, disjunctions, quantifiers) x Context (2: upper-bound, lower-bound). Because sphericity is not assumed in the data we report the results with the Huynh-Feldt correction. With regards to the regions preceding the critical region, ANOVAs reveal a main effect of Expression type ($F1(2,29) = 38$, $p <.001$; $F2(2,11) = 15.49$, $p < .005$) with disjunctions being particularly slow. This seems to be due to the difference in segment length between disjunctions (mean segment length 21.3 characters including spaces) and the other two expression types (mean segment length for numerals and quantifiers 10.7 and 10.5 characters, respectively, including spaces). There was no main effect of Context, nor was the interaction between Expression type and Context significant (all Fs < 0.5).

Let us now turn to the critical regions. There was a main effect of Context ($F1(1,28) = 18.81$, $p < .001$; $F2(1,10) = 29.58$, $p < .001$). There was a tendency for the main effect of Expression type to reach significance by subjects, but not by items ($F1(2,28) = 2.97$, $p = .059$; $F2(2,9) = 1.95$ n.s.). The interaction of Context and Expression type was significant ($F1(2,56) = 3.52$, $p < .05$; $F2(1.7,17.3) = 11.84$, $p < .001$). Planned comparisons showed that disjunctions were read more slowly in the upper-bound contexts relative to the lower-bound contexts ($F1(1,28) = 8.46$, $p < .01$; $F2(1,10) = 12.54$, $p < .01$) and so were quantifiers ($F1(1,28) = 14.8$, $p <$; $F2(1,10) = 55.51$, $p < .001$). However, this difference did not obtain for numerals ($F1(1,28) = .14$ n.s.; $F2(1,10) = 1.35$ n.s.). That is to say, the upper- and lower-bound interpretations of numerals are processed in comparable time.

With regard to the regions following the critical region, numerically the upper-bound contexts were slower than the lower-bound contexts for quantifiers and disjunctions, whereas for numerals the opposite was the case. However, Analyses of Variance indicate that no main effects or interaction were near significance (all Fs < 2).

Before discussing the implications of these results, one issue that needs to be addressed is related to the length of the preceding regions for upper- and lower-bound contexts. For the disjunctions, the items were constructed in such a way that the region preceding the region that contains the critical expression was identical in upper- and lower-bound contexts. However, this was not always the case for numerals and quantifiers. Out of the 24 items (12 for each type of expression), there were differences in length of the preceding region for 10 (7 numeral items, 3 quantifier items). For the quantifiers, the mean segment length of all 12 items was 10.6 characters (including spaces) in upper-bound and 10.5 in lower-bound contexts, a rather insignificant difference. For the numerals, however, the mean length of the preceding segment was 9.7 characters (including spaces) in upper-bound and 11.8 in lower-bound contexts. Hence, there may be some concern that for the numerals in particular this difference in length of the preceding regions might affect the reading time for the critical regions. This could be possible if the longer segments required more reading time, which was not manifest in the region itself, but rather spilled over to the next region, i.e. the critical region of interest containing the numeral expression. If this were the case, then it is possible that a difference in reading time between upper- and lower-bound contexts for the numerals, comparable to the one observed for disjunctions and quantifiers, is masked by a reading time penalty that arises from the difference in length of the preceding region.

To address this concern, we performed a regression analysis to determine the predictiveness of the length of the preceding region on critical region reading times. This analysis was done over all 12 numeral items for each participant. The length of preceding region was the predictor variable, and the critical region reading time was the dependent variable. These analyses were far from significance, both by subjects and by items (both Fs < 1), indicating that the absence of a slowdown between upper- and lower-bound contexts for numerals should not be attributed to different preceding region segment length. It is therefore indicated that numerals are not processed similarly to disjunctions and quantifiers given contextually introduced expectations of informativeness.

An unexpected finding that ought to be mentioned is that, in the original analysis, the main effect of Expression type in the critical regions almost reached significance in the by-subjects analysis. What is particularly striking is the difference between the two most semantically related expressions, numerals and quantifiers, which turns out to be significant ($F1(1,59) = 13.967$, $p < .001$; $F2(1,23) = 5.59$, $p < .03$). The fact that numerals take longer to process than *some* cannot be attributed to segment size of the critical region: the mean critical segment length was actually much greater for *some* (19.6 characters including spaces) than for numerals (11.8 characters including spaces). The difference in segment length would have led one to expect the opposite reading time pattern from that obtained. Hence, the greater reading time for numerals must be due to some other cause.

This difference was neither predicted, nor does it seem possible to retrospectively account for it in a straightforward manner. We would be inclined to look for the causes of this effect in the processes of accommodating into the discourse model a quantifier which does not specify the numerosity of entities involved versus a numeral that mandates a specific numerosity. In the numeral case, regardless of whether the eventual interpretation is "exactly N" or "at least N", the discourse model must be updated with a specific number of entities rather than the underspecified amount that would be accommodated by an utterance of *at least some* or *some but not all*. Such an explanation would be related to the semantics of the type of expressions, and does not bear upon whether the upper-bounded interpretation is achieved via an implicature or otherwise.

All that was predicted by the implicature and anti-implicature accounts was whether reading time would be differentially affected for numerals and *some* when the expectations of contextual relevance change — not that one type of expression would take longer time overall. Hence, this finding requires further inquiry, conceptually as well as experimentally.

4. Implications of the experimental findings for theories of scalar and numeral meanings

This paper set out to empirically investigate the semantics and pragmatics of scalar expressions and numerals, a much-discussed issue on the semantics–pragmatics interface. To summarize the theoretical positions, according to what we called *implicature* accounts (Atlas and Levinson 1981; Gazdar 1979; Horn 1972, 1989; Levinson 2000; Chierchia 2004; i.a.) disjunctions, quantifiers and numerals are all scalar expressions, and the upper-bound interpretation is derived from a lower-bound semantic meaning by means of a scalar implicature. According to what we called *anti-implicature* accounts (Sadock 1984; Koenig 1991; Horn 1992; Scharten 1997; Carston

1998; Geurts 1998, 2006; Breheny 2005 i.a.) the upper-bound "exactly N" interpretation of numerals does not depend on a scalar implicature, and it is the lower-bound one "at least N" that must be derived from it in some way.

In the first off-line study we found that the interpretation of all these types of expression is governed by contextually induced expectations of informativeness, empirically confirming an intuition that is widely shared in the literature. This finding applies at the level of the eventual interpretation of an expression and not at the level of the processes that derive this interpretation. In a second on-line study we found that the upper- and lower-bound interpretations of disjunctions and quantifiers are not processed in equal time, with the upper-bounded interpretation being read more slowly than the lower-bounded interpretation. This finding conforms with previous studies (Bott and Noveck 2004; Breheny, Katsos and Williams 2006 i.a.) that show that generating a scalar implicature is time-consuming. However, we also found that the upper-bounded, "exactly" interpretation of numerals requires no more reading time than the lower-bounded, "at least" one. At this stage, we take this as evidence that the "exactly N" interpretation of numerals does not involve a scalar implicature, contrary to implicature accounts.

The on-line results are compatible with evidence from acquisition. Studies that compared the acquisition of numerals and scalars (Foppolo, Guasti and Chierchia in press; Papafragou and Musolino 2003; Pouscoulous and Noveck in press i.a.) have found that children start with the lower-bounded interpretation of scalars and only later acquire the upper-bound one. With numerals, however, children start with the "exactly N" interpretation. As we have seen in section 2.1, some researchers have argued against using this finding as evidence that numerals are not scalar expressions. There might be extra-linguistic factors involved that make children acquire the upper-bound interpretation of numerals earlier than for other scalars, namely training and familiarity with numerical literacy and the earlier lexicalization of the relevant entailment scale for numerals. These factors, however, are not likely to be involved in adult populations, where the relevant scales of all scalar terms ought to be maximally lexicalized, and familiarity with numerals should match familiarity with other scalar expressions. Overall, we believe that the objections raised against the acquisition data do not obtain for the adult findings.

Hence, given the assumption in the current experimental pragmatic literature that implicatures are costly in terms of processing resources, our data weigh against implicature accounts for numerals – a conclusion which is also reached in recent investigations with eye-tracking paradigms in children and adults (Huang, Snedeker and Spelke in press; Huang and Snedeker 2009). However, we would like to conclude this paper with a discussion of two issues. The first issue is whether implicatures *per se* are costly, and if not, what implications this would have for the interpretation of our findings. Independently of this, a second issue is whether the data offer evidence in favour of any particular versions of anti-implicature accounts over others.

With regards to the first issue, an important question in the emerging experimental pragmatics literature is: why should implicatures be costly? There is by now ample evidence that pragmatic processes in themselves are not necessarily costly in processing terms. For example, work in metaphor comprehension (Gibbs and Tendahl 2006; Glucksberg 2003 i.a.) indicates that pragmatic interpretations that are sufficiently biased by the context can be understood virtually automatically, without any special processing cost. So why should implicatures specifically be costly?

Multiple suggestions can be made, with different effects on the conclusions we drew for numerals. First, it can be considered that scalar implicatures are in effect metalinguistic inferences that require the addressee to take into account the alternative utterances the speaker might have employed in order to interpret the actual utterance, and also to consider the overarching discourse goals and the speaker's epistemic state. One or more of these high-order mental processes could be time-consuming, hence rendering implicatures costly. An implicature account would postulate that these higher-order processes are involved in the upper-bound interpretation of numerals too, and so the absence of a processing cost for numerals would then indeed be compatible with our conclusion that numerals do not involve an implicature.

Another hypothesis is related to the negative component of the scalar implicature ("p or q but **not** both" for the disjunction; "some but **not** all" for the existential quantifier). Since Chase and Clark (1972), there is a general consensus in the literature that negation gives rise to processing costs, and this would lead one to expect a processing delay if indeed listeners implicitly or explicitly entertain the negation of the stronger proposition. With regard to the topic at hand, according to implicature accounts the upper-bound interpretation of numerals also involves a negative component ("not more than N"), and hence our initial conclusion is supported under this hypothesis. However, it should be noted that at the level of linguistic theorizing, negation is not indispensable in the process of deriving implicatures, since there are ways to compute a scalar implicature without employing any negative inference (see Breheny 2008). Moreover, there is also evidence that other conversational implicatures which clearly do not involve negation, such as the causal/temporal implications of the conjunction, require processing resources as well (Noveck 2006), thus rendering the negation account of implicature cost rather implausible.

A third suggestion by Noveck and colleagues, in terms of a Relevance theory framework as outlined by Wilson and Sperber (2003), is that pragmatic inferences that prompt the listener to depart from the first accessible interpretation are generally costly, involving attentional processes which require resources exceeding those necessary for grammatical operations. The processing cost of rejecting and entertaining interpretations other than the first accessible one is offset by gains in terms of contextual effects. Hence the cost involved in generating scalar implicatures would not be specific to implicature but would extend to all interpretative processes that require enriching the first accessible interpretation (see Noveck 2006 for conjunction, Noveck, Bianco and Castry 2001 for metaphor). In cases where there is no apparent processing cost for generating an enriched interpretation, this must be because, due to independent factors (e.g. a strongly biasing context), the enriched interpretation has become the most accessible one. Hence, the *prima facie* contradictory evidence that certain pragmatic operations are not costly is attributed to contextually-triggered re-ranking of the order of accessibility. For the case at hand, this account of processing costs suggests that whereas for scalars the first accessible interpretation is the lower-bound one, for numerals it is the upper-bound one, again supporting our initial conclusion that the upper-bound interpretation of numerals does not involve implicature.

A fourth suggestion is that, regardless of the description of the phenomenon at the linguistic level, the two (or more) interpretations of scalars and numerals are treated as ambiguous senses of the same lexeme at the psycholinguistic level. The slowdown in the upper-bound interpretations reflects the activation of the non-dominant reading of an ambiguous expression, relative to the quick reading time required for the dominant lower-bound reading. If this is so, then the absence of a slowdown in the upper-bound interpretation of numerals perhaps suggests that either there is no dominant reading, or that the process by which upper- and lower-bound readings are computed is not akin to lexical disambiguation. In either case, these findings underscore the differences between scalars and numerals.

We would like to explore in some detail a fifth alternative that seems to be a promising avenue for research. It might be that it is not the implicature itself that is costly, but rather the operations that it initiates on the discourse model currently being built. To illustrate this, consider an utterance of the form, *some of the Fs G-ed.* When participants interpret this without an implicature, they introduce into their mental model of the discourse the set of Fs who G-ed. When they interpret this with an implicature, they have not only to introduce the set of Fs referred to but also partition it in two non-empty subsets. The predicate G will then hold for only one of the subsets. An alternative way to conceptualize this, but to the same effect, is to say that participants have to introduce a set of Fs that G-ed and additionally accommodate a set of Fs that did not G. Thus the interpretation with an implicature implies the existence of a contrast set for which predicate G will not hold.

The suggestion that it is the process of introducing contrast sets rather than the implicature itself that induces a processing cost is compatible with two sets of experimental findings. First, there is substantial evidence in the psycholinguistic literature on processing syntactically ambiguous sentences that participants disprefer a reading that forces them to accommodate a contrast set. In terms of Referential Theory in particular (Crain and Steedman 1985; Altmann and Steedman 1988; i.a.), given a structurally ambiguous sentence, the principle of Parsimony enjoins the listener to choose the interpretation associated with the fewest unsatisfied presuppositions (where *presupposition* is used not in the technical sense of linguistic theory but in the sense of introduction of discourse entities). More recently there have been direct demonstrations that, even in structurally unambiguous sentences, introducing contrast sets through restrictive relative clauses gives rise to processing costs (Grodner, Gibson and Watson 2005). These costs are expressed as reading time delays in self-paced reading of restrictive relative clauses. For example, the sentence *A director that the critics praised at a banquet announced...* implicates the existence of another director that was not praised. A processing cost is obtained when such sentences are compared with identical non-restrictive relative clauses which do not implicate the existence of a contrast set (*A director, who the critics praised at a banquet, announced...*). In another condition, the restrictive relative clause was preceded by a context that introduced two salient referents in advance of the critical region (e.g. *A group of film critics praised a director at a banquet and another director at a film premiere*). As predicted, the processing cost disappeared in the condition where the contrast set implicated by the restrictive relative clause was already established at the point when the clause was processed.

A further consideration in support of the contrast set account of processing cost is that, once a contrast set is established, inferential processes that are dependent on the second maxim of quantity (which requires speakers not to be over-informative, much as the first maxim requires them not to be under-informative) are initiated at the earliest possible stage, without giving rise to any processing cost (Sedivy 2002; Sedivy et al. 1999). It seems quite plausible, therefore, that an account along these lines might be able to explain the processing cost involved in these scalar implicatures.

If the reason why implicatures are costly is indeed related to the accommodation of contrast sets, then this would have radical implications on how to interpret the results of these studies. As we have seen, a lower-bound interpretation of *some of the Fs G-ed* introduces into the discourse model a set of Fs that G-ed. The predicate will then hold for any number of them. However, an upper-bound interpretation normally introduces a set of Fs that G-ed, and also a contrast set of Fs that did not G. The slowdown observed in processing the upper-bound interpretation may be an integral property of the scalar implicature, as suggested by the first three hypotheses we considered, or it may be the result of introducing additional contrast sets into the discourse model. Critically, neither the lower-bound "at least four Fs G-ed" nor the upper-bound "exactly four Fs G-ed" interpretation implies the existence of a contrast set of Fs that did not G. If indeed the delay in generating implicatures is due to the introduction of contrast sets, then the absence of this delay for the numerals does not imply the absence of an implicature.

Finally, independently of this discussion, a second issue is whether the data we obtained could be adduced as evidence in favour of any particular of anti-implicature accounts over others. One relevant factor in this discussion is whether an anti-implicature account postulates that both upper- and lower-bound interpretations are derived from some underspecified meaning or whether the lower-bound is derived from the upper-bound. Given the underspecification account, a straightforward processing prediction would be that the appropriate interpretation would be chosen by a similar process for each of the possible interpretations, thus predicting no difference in reading time, all things being equal, for "exactly N", "at least N" or even "at most N" interpretations.

It is also quite probable that some polysemy proposals which derive the lower-bound interpretation from the upper-bounded one would make similar predictions. For instance, Geurts (2006) suggests that the lower-bound interpretation is derived from the upper-bounded one as a matter of regular type-coercion akin to that which relates the quantificational and predicational interpretations of *a man*. While conceptually prior to the lower-bounded interpretation, the upper-bounded interpretation need enjoy no particularly special status in an account of on-line processing. It could be that regular coercions are simply listed in the lexicon. If so, then the processing predictions of the type-coercion account would most likely line up with those of the underspecification account in our study.

However, there is ample data in the experimental literature that different sense-alteration processes have different time-courses. For example, research on the processing of systematic polysemy indicates that certain forms of metonymy are harder to process than others. A body of eye-tracking studies (summarized in McElree, Frisson and Pickering 2006) find that logical metonyms (*The gentleman started Dickens while waiting for a friend to arrive* = "started reading the work of Dickens") are more costly than conventional interpretations (*The gentleman spotted Dickens while waiting for a friend to arrive* = "spotted Dickens, an actual person"), because they involve additional computational stages. Interestingly, standard metonyms (*The gentleman read Dickens while waiting for a friend to arrive* = "read the work of Dickens") are as easy to process as conventional interpretations. Hence, any polysemy account of numerals would need to specify the precise nature of the sense alternation that is involved in deriving one interpretation from the other, and then relate this to other sense alternation processes whose psycholinguistic profile is already established.

At this stage, it is worth also discussing further what the predictions of an ambiguity account would be. For several theoretical and meta-theoretical reasons (see Geurts 1998 and the original discussion in Grice 1989, as well as Sadock 1978) lexical ambiguity is not preferred as a linguistic explanation. At the processing level, however, there is nothing to stop us considering what the processing of scalars and numerals would be if the possible interpretations were just ambiguous senses. In this case, the interpretations would not be related to each other by means of deriving one from the other in any psychologically real way, and the (statistically) dominant sense should be faster with the non-dominant slower even in contexts that suitably bias for each reading. At this stage there is very little work with regard to the statistical distribution of the interpretation of scalars and numerals (for a notable exception see Bultinck 2005), and it is difficult to postulate which interpretation is dominant. The fact that for the quantifiers and disjunctions lower-bound interpretations are faster than the upper-bound ones, even though both are appropriately biased towards in their respective contexts, perhaps suggests that the former reading is dominant. Consequently, the absence of such a difference for numerals suggests that no reading is dominant or that ambiguity is not the relation that characterizes upper- and lower-bound interpretations. However, in order to investigate the ambiguity hypothesis, we should again highlight that it is preferable to test quantifiers and numerals in identical contexts, such as those suggested in (14) above.

As to the existential closure account set out in Breheny (2008) and Kratzer (2003), the mechanism required to derive the "at least" readings may add to the cost of processing if presupposition accommodation is required in each case, or it may be that existential closure is rather an automatic process.

5. Implications for empirical investigations of the semantics–pragmatics interface

With respect to the issue of numerals and scalars, we have seen how various theories ascribe different aspects of meaning to semantics and pragmatics. We have also documented the emerging consensus that theories about this, as well as other issues on the semantics–pragmatics interface, should be psycholinguistically as well as linguistically valid.

We have then gone on to review the extensive recent literature on empirical investigations of the meaning of numerals and scalars, in addition to presenting novel work on that topic. Generally it is clear that psycholinguistic studies of these entities can reveal clear patterns both in acquisition and in adult performance, and thus greatly augment our understanding of the relation between semantics and pragmatics in these domains.

However, in attempting to adduce these data as evidence for or against particular theories, we run into conceptual difficulties. We see that, in many cases, the question of whether data disconfirm a theory depends crucially on whether we make additional assumptions that are not necessarily integral to that theory. In particular, we discussed how the introduction of contrast sets might give rise to processing costs, and how costly the processes are by which senses are derived from one another. In doing so, we uncovered issues on which many theories are noncommittal, but which could greatly influence the interpretation of the relevant experimental findings.

Overall, it seems that deriving straightforward empirically testable predictions from anti-implicature accounts requires further conceptual and experimental work. We hope that this chapter will raise enough questions to lead to further investigations of this nature in the experimental pragmatics and semantics paradigm.

Acknowledgement

The authors would like to acknowledge the support of the Arts and Humanities Research Council (Ref: AH/E002358/1).

References

Altmann, Gerry and Mark Steedman
1988 Interaction with context during human sentence processing. *Cognition* 38: 419–439.

Atlas, Jay David and Stephen C. Levinson
1981 It-clefts, informativeness and Logical Form. In *Radical Pragmatics*, Peter Cole (ed.), 1–61. New York: Academic Press.

Atlas, Jay David
2005 *Logic, Meaning and Conversation: Semantical Underdeterminacy, Implicature, and their Interface*. Oxford: Oxford University Press.

Bott, Lewis and Ira Noveck
2004 Some utterances are underinformative: The onset and time course of scalar inferences. *Journal of Memory and Language* 51: 437–457.

Breheny, Richard
2008 A new look at the semantics and pragmatics of numerically quantified noun phrases. *Journal of Semantics* 25 (2): 93–140.

Breheny, Richard, Napoleon Katsos and John Williams
2006 Are generalised scalar implicatures generated by default? An on-line investigation into the role of context in generating pragmatic inferences. *Cognition* 100 (3): 434–463.

Bultinck, Bert
2005 *Numerous Meanings: The Meaning of English Cardinals and the Legacy of Paul Grice*. Oxford: Elsevier.

Carston, Robyn
1985 A reanalysis of some 'quantity implicatures'. Unpublished ms., University College London.

Carston, Robyn
1998 Informativeness, relevance and scalar implicature. In *Relevance Theory: Applications and Implications*, Robyn Carston and Seiji Uchida (eds.), 179–236. Amsterdam: John Benjamins.

Carston, Robyn
2002 *Thoughts and Utterances: The Pragmatics of Explicit Communication*. Oxford: Blackwell.

Carston, Robyn
2004 Review of Stephen C. Levinson *Presumptive Meanings: The Theory of Generalized Conversational Implicature*. *Journal of Linguistics* 40: 181–186.

Clark, Herbert H. and William G. Chase
1972 On the process of comparing sentences against pictures. *Cognitive Psychology* 3: 472–517.

Chierchia, Gennaro
2004 Scalar implicatures, polarity phenomena, and the syntax/pragmatics interface. In *Structures and Beyond: The Cartography of Syntactic*

Structures, Volume 3 (Oxford Studies in Comparative Syntax), Adriana Belletti (ed.), 39–103. Oxford: Oxford University Press.

Chierchia, Gennaro, Stephen Crain, Maria Teresa Guasti, Andrea Gualmini and Luisa Meroni
2001 The acquisition of disjunction: evidence for a grammatical view of scalar implicatures. In *Proceedings of the 25th Annual Boston University Conference on Language Development (BUCLD 25)*, Anna H.-J. Do, Laura Domínguez and Aimee Johansen (eds.), 157–168. Somerville, MA: Cascadilla Press.

Crain, Stephen and Mark Steedman
1985 On not being led up the garden path: the use of context by the psychological parser. In *Natural Language Parsing: Psychological, Computational and Theoretical Perspectives*, David Dowty, Lauri Karttunen and Arnold Zwicky (eds.), 320–358. Cambridge: Cambridge University Press.

Crain, Stephen and Rosalind Thornton
1998 *Investigations in Universal Grammar: A Guide to Experiments on the Acquisition of Syntax and Semantics*. Cambridge, MA: MIT Press.

Crain, Stephen, Andrea Gualmini and Luisa Meroni
2000 The acquisition of logical words. *LOGOS and Language* 1: 49–59.

Foppolo, Francesca, Maria Teresa Guasti and Gennaro Chierchia
in prep. Scalar implicatures in child language: failure, strategies and lexical factors.

Gazdar, Gerald
1979 *Pragmatics: Implicature, Presupposition and Logical Form*. New York: Academic Press.

Geurts, Bart
1998 Scalars. In *Lexikalische Semantik aus kognitiver Sicht*, Petra Ludewig and Bart Geurts (eds.), 95–118. Tübingen: Gunter Narr.

Geurts, Bart
2006 Take "five": the meaning and use of a number word. In *Indefiniteness and Plurality*, Liliane Tasmowski and Svetlana Vogeleer (eds.), 311–329. Amsterdam: Benjamins.

Geurts, Bart
2009 Scalar implicature and local pragmatics. *Mind and Language* 24: 51–79.

Gibbs, Raymond and Markus Tendahl
2006 Cognitive effort and effects in metaphor comprehension: Relevance Theory and psycholinguistics. *Mind and Language* 21 (3): 379–403.

Glucksberg, Sam
2003 The psycholinguistics of metaphor. *Trends in Cognitive Science* 7: 92–96.

Grice, H. Paul
1975/89 Logic and conversation. In *Studies in the Way of Words*, 22–40. Cambridge MA: Harvard University Press.

Grodner, Daniel, Edward Gibson and Duane Watson
2005 The influence of contextual contrast on syntactic processing: evidence for strong-interaction in sentence comprehension. *Cognition* 95: 275–296.

Guasti, Maria Teresa, Gennaro Chierchia, Francesca Foppolo, Andrea Gualmini and Luisa Meroni
2005 Why children and adults sometimes (but not always) compute implicatures. *Language and Cognitive Processes* 20 (5): 667–696.

Hirschberg, Julia
1991 *A Theory of Scalar Implicature*. New York: Garland.

Horn, Laurence R.
1972 *On the Semantic Properties of Logical Operators in English*. UCLA dissertation, distributed by Indiana University Linguistics Club, 1976.

Horn, Laurence R.
1984 Towards a new taxonomy for pragmatic inference. In *Meaning, Form and Use in Context: Linguistic Applications (GURT '84)*, Deborah Schiffrin (ed.), 11–42. Washington D.C.: Georgetown University Press.

Horn, Laurence R.
1989 *A Natural History of Negation*. Chicago, IL: University of Chicago Press.

Horn, Laurence R.
2005 The border wars: a neo-Gricean perspective. In *Where Semantics Meets Pragmatics*, Ken Turner and Klaus von Heusinger (eds.), 21–48. Oxford: Elsevier.

Huang, Yi Ting, Jesse Snedeker and Elizabeth Spelke
in press What exactly do numerals mean? *Language*

Huang, Yi Ting and Jesse Snedeker
2009 Online interpretation of scalar quantifiers: Insight into the semantics–pragmatics interface. *Cognitive Psychology* 58 (3): 376–415.

Hurewitz, Felicia, Anna Papafragou, Lila Gleitman and Rochel Gelman
2006 Asymmetries in the acquisition of numbers and quantifiers. *Language Learning and Development* 2: 77–96.

Katsos, Napoleon
2006 Experimental investigations on the effects of structure and context on the generation of scalar implicatures. PhD thesis, University of Cambridge.

Katsos, Napoleon
2008 The semantics/pragmatics interface from an experimental perspective: the case of scalar implicature. *Synthese* 165: 358–401.

Katsos, Napoleon, Richard Breheny and John Williams
2005a Interaction of structural and contextual constraints during the on-line generation of scalar inferences. In *Proceedings of GLOW 28*, University of Geneva.
Katsos, Napoleon, Richard Breheny and John Williams
2005b The interaction of structural and contextual constraints during the on-line generation of scalar inferences. In *Proceedings of the 27th Annual Conference of the Cognitive Science Society*, Bruno G. Bara, Larry Barsalou and Monica Bucciarelli (eds.), 1108–1113. Mahwah, NJ: Erlbaum.
Koenig, Jean-Pierre
1991 Scalar predicates and negation: punctual semantics and interval interpretations. In *Papers from the 27th Regional Meeting of the Chicago Linguistics Society (CLS27),* Lise M. Dobrin, Lynn Nichols and Rosa M. Rodriguez (eds.), *Part 2: Parasession on Negation*, 140–155. Chicago, IL: Chicago Linguistics Society.
Kratzer, Angelika
2003 Scalar implicatures: are there any? Presentation at Workshop on Polarity, Scalar Phenomena, and Implicatures, University of Milan-Bicocca, June 18, 2003. Accessed via SemanticsNet.
Landman, Fred
2000 *Events and Plurality*. Dordrecht: Kluwer.
Levinson, Stephen C.
1983 *Pragmatics*. Cambridge: Cambridge University Press.
Levinson, Stephen C.
2000 *Presumptive Meanings: The Theory of Generalized Conversational Implicature*. Cambridge, MA: MIT Press.
McElree, Brian, Steven Frisson and Martin J. Pickering
2006 Deferred interpretations: why starting Dickens is taxing but reading Dickens isn't. *Cognitive Science* 30: 113–124.
Musolino, Julien
2004 The semantics and acquisition of number words: integrating linguistic and developmental perspectives. *Cognition* 93: 1–41.
Noveck, Ira A.
2001 When children are more logical than adults. *Cognition* 86: 253–282.
Noveck, Ira A., Maryse Bianco and Alain Castry
2001 The costs and benefits of metaphor. *Metaphor and Symbol* 16: 109–121.
Noveck, Ira A. and Andres Posada
2003 Characterising the time course of an implicature. *Brain and Language* 85: 203–210.

Noveck, Ira A.
2006 Going beyond the initial developmental findings on implicature. Presentation at 'Crosslinguistically robust stages of children's linguistic performances', Universidade Nova de Lisboa, 6–8 July 2006.

Papafragou, Anna and Julien Musolino
2003 Scalar implicatures: experiments at the semantics/pragmatics interface. *Cognition* 86: 253–282.

Pouscoulous, Nausicaa and Ira A. Noveck
in press Going beyond semantics: the development of pragmatic enrichment. In *Advances in Child Language*, Susan Foster-Cohen (ed.). London: Palgrave Macmillan.

Pouscoulous, Nausicaa, Ira A. Noveck, Guy Politzer and Anne Bastide
2007 A developmental investigation of processing costs in implicature production. *Language Acquisition* 14: 347–376.

Richardson, J. F. and A. W. Richardson
1990 On predicting pragmatic relations. In *Proceedings of the 16th Annual Meeting of the Berkeley Linguistics Society: Parasession on the Legacy of Grice*, Kira Hall, Jean-Pierre Koenig, Michael Meacham, Sondra Reinman and Laurel Sutton (eds.), 498–508. Berkeley, CA: Berkeley Linguistics Society.

Recanati, François
2003 Embedded implicatures. *Philosophical Perspectives* 17: 299–332.

van Rooy, Robert and Katrin Schulz
2006 Pragmatic meaning and non-monotonic reasoning: the case of exhaustive interpretation. *Linguistics and Philosophy* 29: 205–250.

Russell, Benjamin
2006 Against grammatical computation of scalar implicatures. *Journal of Semantics* 23: 361–382.

Sadock, Jerry
1978 On testing for conversational implicature. In *Syntax and Semantics 9: Pragmatics*, Peter Cole (ed.), 281–297. New York: Academic Press.

Sadock, Jerry
1984 Whither radical pragmatics? In *Meaning, Form and Use in Context*, Deborah Schiffrin (ed.), 139–149. Washington D.C.: Georgetown University Press.

Scharten, Renate
1997 Exhaustive interpretation: a discourse-semantic account. PhD thesis, Katholieke Universiteit Nijmegen.

Sedivy, Julie C.
2002 Invoking discourse-based contrast sets and resolving syntactic ambiguities. *Journal of Memory and Language* 46: 341–370.

Sedivy, Julie C., Michael K. Tanenhaus, Craig G. Chambers and Gregory N. Carlson
1999 Achieving incremental semantic interpretation through contextual representation. *Cognition* 71: 109–147.

Smith, Carol L.
1980 Quantifiers and question answering in young children. *Journal of Experimental Child Psychology* 30: 191–205.

Sperber, Dan and Deirdre Wilson
1986/95 *Relevance: Communication and Cognition*. Oxford: Blackwell.

Wilson, Deirdre and Dan Sperber
2003 Relevance theory. In *Handbook of Pragmatics*, Laurence R. Horn and Gregory L. Ward (eds.), 607–632. Oxford: Blackwell.

Some experimental aspects of optimality theoretic pragmatics

Reinhard Blutner

1. Introduction

Experimental pragmatics is an exciting and growing research field which builds a bridge between pragmatics and psycholinguistics. As Noveck and Sperber (2005) formulate it, properly devised experimental evidence can be highly pertinent to the discussion of pragmatic issues, and pragmatics might greatly benefit from becoming familiar with relevant experimental work and from contributing to it.

Recent approaches to experimental pragmatics (Bezuidenhout 2002; Bezuidenhout and Cutting 2002; Noveck and Sperber 2005; Garrett and Harnish 2007) are mainly concentrated on the investigation of scalar implicatures. Characteristically, the interpretive perspective (hearer's view) is taken in this research. A theoretical main issue is to decide between two rivaling theories: Sperber and Wilson's (1986/1995) relevance theory and Levinson's (2000) theory of presumptive meanings or generalized conversational implicatures. Levinson claims that generalized conversational implicatures are calculated automatically – i.e. without demanding much processing resources. In contrast, relevance theory argues that the calculation is controlled and is strongly influenced by the available processing resources.

Neo-Griceans (e.g. Atlas and Levinson 1981; Horn 1984; Blutner 1998; Atlas 2005; Horn 2005) are typically ignored in this research. A typical defense for this pretermission is that neo-Gricean theories are normative theories that do not directly make predictions about processing. Unfortunately, this argument exaggerates the philosophical issue of distinguishing between the normative and the naturalistic realm. Surely, these two aspects of understanding human actions can be clearly separated from each other. However, that does not mean they predict different action patterns in most cases. The idea of a rational world is not so irrational to be excluded in ordinary affairs. Evolutionary game theory has presented us with many examples demonstrating that the reasonable is naturally arising (Axelrod 1984).

The aim of this article is to close the gap between experimental pragmatics and neo-Gricean theories of pragmatics. The version of neo-Gricean pragmatics I will consider here is called optimality theoretic pragmatics. While the automatic/controlled issue of processing has dominated the recent theoretical debate, optimality theoretic pragmatics will raise several additional issues. One new issue concerns the asymmetries between comprehension and production. How to explain the experimentally observed asymmetries and what is their status in theories of language acquisition? Seeing comprehension and production as different optimization processes, a further research topic concerns the question of how the two optimization processes are integrated with each other (bidirectional optimization). That relates to the psychological reality of bidirectional optimization in the domain of pragmatics. The role of psycholinguistic data at the semantic–pragmatic interface is of crucial importance in this connection. The posed architectural decision cannot be made without a sound experimental background.

Another important point concerns the nature of conventionalization (or fossilization) in pragmatics – an issue that deserves much more attention both theoretically and empirically. The occurrence of conventionalization/fossilization relates to a phenomenon investigated at the semantics–pragmatics interface. Again, intuitive decisions of competent speakers/listeners are not sufficient for grounding the needed theoretical decisions. We have to ask for possibly rather indirect experimental decision criteria.

Optimality theory will be used in this article both in the *broad sense* of a general methodology dealing with resolving conflicting constraints by using universal optimization procedures and in the *narrower sense* of developing an explicit model that concerns the essentials of neo-Gricean pragmatics. In the following section, I give a concise introduction to the basic conceptions of optimality theoretic pragmatics, and I explains the idea of unidirectional and bidirectional optimization. In section 3 the three main views conforming to a naturalistic pragmatics are discussed: (a) relevance theory, (b) Levinson's (2000) theory of presumptive meanings, and (c) the neo-Gricean approach. I show how the idea of optimal interpretation can be used to restructure the core ideas of these three different approaches. It is important to have the general methodology of optimality theory in order to see (i) the uniform basis these models have with regard to the semantics–pragmatics interface, (ii) the particular differences and relationships between the different models. Further, the general setting of optimality theory helps to formulate the mechanism of *fossilization* – a mechanism that enables an automatic transfer between two basically different ways of interpreting bidirectionality.

Section 4 explains the idea of fossilization in more detail and directly addresses an issue at the semantics–pragmatics interface. It is pointed out how the general setting of cultural evolution can help to make the idea of fossilization precise. Further, a series of important theoretical and methodological problems is raised – mainly concerning the distribution of labor between online processes (optimization procedures) and offline processing (fossilization processes). In section 5 I discuss a series of experimental findings that are relevant with regard to the semantics–pragmatics interface, especially concerning the relationship between online processes at the interface and fossilization phenomena. Section 6 draws some general conclusions about the need of psycholinguistic data in order to answer basic questions about the cognitive architecture and about the integration of the synchronic and the diachronic perspective in the context of natural language interpretation.

2. Optimality theoretic pragmatics

Optimality theory is an approach to embodied cognition in the sense of Anderson (2003). It combines the advantages of constraint-based, symbolic models with the advantages of neuronal network models of cognition (cf. Smolensky and Legendre 2006). Further, it has the capacity to model cultural evolution and to solve the symbolic grounding problem (e.g. Harnad 1990; Boersma and Hayes 2001). In the study of natural language, optimality theory was successfully applied to the main linguistic disciplines of phonology, morphology and syntax, and also to the explanation of natural language acquisition and other performance traits. Optimality theoretic pragmatics is an application of this integrated approach to Gricean pragmatics. It has its origin in the attempt to explain certain phenomena of lexical pragmatics (Blutner 1998) and is inspired by the optimal interpretation approach proposed by Hendriks and de Hoop (2001) and Zeevat's (1999) theory of explaining presupposition triggers.

In the broad view of optimality theory, this framework can be seen as a general framework that systematizes the use of optimization methods in linguistics.[1] One component of optimality theory is a list of tendencies that hold for observable properties of a language. These tendencies take the form of violable constraints. Because the constraints usually express very general statements, they can be in conflict. Conflicts among constraints are resolved because the constraints differ in strength. Minimal violations of

[1] A recent overview is given in Smolensky and Legendre (2006). For optimality theoretic pragmatics, the reader is referred to Blutner and Zeevat (2004) and Blutner, de Hoop and Hendriks (2005).

the constraints (taking their strength into account) define optimal conflict resolutions.

Standard, optimality theory specifies the relation between an input and an output. This relation is mediated by two formal mechanisms, GEN and EVAL. GEN (for Generator) creates possible output candidates on the basis of a given input. EVAL (for Evaluator) uses the particular constraint ranking of the universal set of constraints CON to select the best candidate for a given input from among the candidate set produced by GEN. In phonology and syntax, the input to this process of optimization is an underlying linguistic representation. The output is the (surface) form as it is expressed. Hence, what is normally used in phonology and syntax is unidirectional optimization. Obviously, the point of view of the speaker is taken. This contrasts with optimality theoretic semantics where the view of the hearer is taken (de Hoop and de Swart 2000; Hendriks and de Hoop 2001).

Bidirectional optimization (Blutner 1998, 2000) integrates the speaker and the hearer perspective into a simultaneous optimization procedure. In pragmatics, this bidirectional view is motivated by a reduction of Grice's maxims of conversation to two principles: the R-principle, which can be seen as the force of unification minimizing the speaker's effort, and the Q-principle, which can be seen as the force of diversification minimizing the auditor's effort. In the next section we will explain the relationship between the neo-Gricean view and optimality theoretic pragmatics in a bit more detail. In this section, I will introduce the heart of this approach – bidirectional optimization. Further, I will give a very schematic example in order to illustrate some characteristics of bidirectional optimality theory.

In the so-called strong version of bidirectional optimality theory, the following clause applies:

(1) Strong Bidirectionality: A form-interpretation pair <*f*, *m*> is considered to be (strongly) optimal iff
   a. Interpretive Optimization: no other pair <*f*, *m*'> can be generated that satisfies the constraints better than <*f*, *m*> and
   b. Expressive Optimization: no other pair <*f* ', *m*> can be generated that satisfies the constraints better than <*f*, *m*>.

The idea behind interpretive optimization is to select the most coherent interpretation. What is meant by coherence has to be expressed by particular optimality theoretic constraints, such as formulated by Zeevat (2007), for instance. Hence, the principle of interpretive optimization is a very abstract one which has to be supplemented by a system of ranked constraints in order to constitute a system that is able to express something like Horn's (1984) R-principle. The simultaneous use of expressive optimization can be seen as similar to the role of Horn's (1984) Q-principle – it acts as a blocking mechanism which blocks all the outputs which can be expressed more economically by an alternative linguistic input. Again, what counts as more economical has to be expressed by the system of constraints. This formulation makes it quite clear that the neo-Gricean framework can be conceived of as a bidirectional optimality framework which integrates the speaker and the hearer perspective. Whereas the R-principle compares different possible interpretations for the same syntactic expression, the Q-principle compares different possible syntactic expressions that the speaker could have used to communicate the same meaning.

The following example gives a simple illustration of how the theory works and how the required ingredients look like. Assume we have two forms f_1 and f_2 which are semantically equivalent, i.e., they bear the same truth conditions. Technically, this means that GEN associates the same interpretations with them, say m_1 and m_2. We stipulate that the form f_1 is less complex (less marked) than the form f_2 and that the interpretation m_1 is less complex (more coherent) than the interpretation m_2. This is expressed by two markedness constraints: F for forms and M for interpretations – F prefers f_1 over f_2 and M prefers m_1 over m_2. This is indicated by the two leftmost constraints in Table 1. The two stars (*) relating to the form-meaning pairs $<f_2, m_1>$ and $<f_2, m_2>$ in the column for "F" indicate that the form f_2 violates a complexity constraints for forms. Similarly, the two stars relating to the form-meaning pairs $<f_1, m_2>$ and $<f_2, m_2>$ in the column for "M" indicate that the interpretation m_2 violates a complexity constraint for forms.

Table 1. Markedness and linking constraints in a 2-forms × 2-interpretations design

	F	M	F→M	*F→*M	F→*M	F*→M
$<f_1, m_1>$					*	
$<f_1, m_2>$		*	*			
$<f_2, m_1>$	*			*		
$<f_2, m_2>$	*	*				*

Besides the markedness constraints, so-called linking constraints can be formulated. There are precisely four independent linking constraints in the present example. The linking constraint F→M says that simple (unmarked)

forms express simple interpretations. The constraint *F→*M says that complex forms express complex interpretations. The two remaining linking constraints express the opposite restrictions. In the present case linking constraints can be seen as lexical stipulations that fix a form-interpretation relation in an instance-based way.[2]

From the differences of markedness given by the constraints F and M the ordering relation between form-meaning pairs can be derived as shown in Figure 1. The preferences are indicated by arrows in a two-dimensional diagram. Such diagrams give an intuitive visualization for the optimal pairs of (strong) bidirectional optimality theory: they are simply the meeting points of horizontal and vertical arrows.[3] The optimal pairs are marked with the symbol ✌ in the diagram.

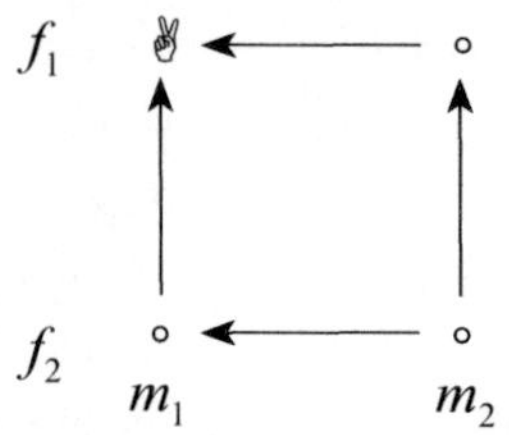

Figure 1. Diagram to illustrate strong bidirectionality

The scenario just mentioned describes the case of total blocking where some forms (e.g., **furiosity*, **fallacity*) do not exist because others do (*fury, fallacy*). However, blocking is not always total but may be partial. This means that not all the interpretations of a form must be blocked if another form exists. McCawley (1978) collects a number of examples demonstrating the phenomenon of partial blocking. For example, he observes that the distribution of productive causatives (in English, Japanese, German, and other

---

2 The so-called phenomenon of *harmonic alignment* of two scales (Prince and Smolensky 1991, Aissen 2003) means that items which assume comparable positions in both scales are considered most harmonic. Taking a first scale F of exactly two items ($f_1 < f_2$) and second scale M of likewise two items ($m_1 < m_2$), harmonic alignment is precisely the piece of information expressed by the two linking constraints F→M and *F→*M. It is straightforward how this simple schema can be generalized to the general case.

3 Dekker and van Rooy (2000), who introduced these diagrams, gave bidirectional optimality theory a game theoretic interpretation where the optimal pairs can be characterized as so-called Nash Equilibriums.

languages) is restricted by the existence of a corresponding lexical causative. Whereas lexical causatives – e.g. (2a) – tend to be restricted in their distribution to the stereotypical causative situation (direct, unmediated causation through physical action), productive (periphrastic) causatives tend to pick up more marked situations of mediated, indirect causation. For example, (2b) could have been used appropriately when Black Bart caused the sheriff's gun to backfire by stuffing it with cotton.

(2) a. *Black Bart killed the sheriff.*
    b. *Black Bart caused the sheriff to die.*

To make things concrete we can take f_1 to be the lexical causative form (2a), f_2 the periphrastic form (2b), m_1 direct (stereotypic) causation and m_2 indirect causation.

Typical cases of partial blocking are found in morphology, syntax and semantics. The general tendency of partial blocking seems to be that "unmarked forms tend to be used for unmarked situations and marked forms for marked situations" (Horn 1984: 26) – a tendency that Horn (1984: 22) terms "the division of pragmatic labor".

There are two ways of avoiding total blocking within the bidirectional framework and to describe Horn's division of pragmatic labor. The first possibility makes use of linking constraints and fits the intended form-interpretation relation by stipulating the appropriate ranking of the constraints such that partial blocking comes out. Let us assume that the two linking constraints F→M and *F→*M are higher ranked (are more important) than the rest of the constraints. This can be depictured as in Figure 2a. Hence, strong bidirectionality can be taken as describing Horn's division of pragmatic labor when the appropriate linking constraints are dominant.

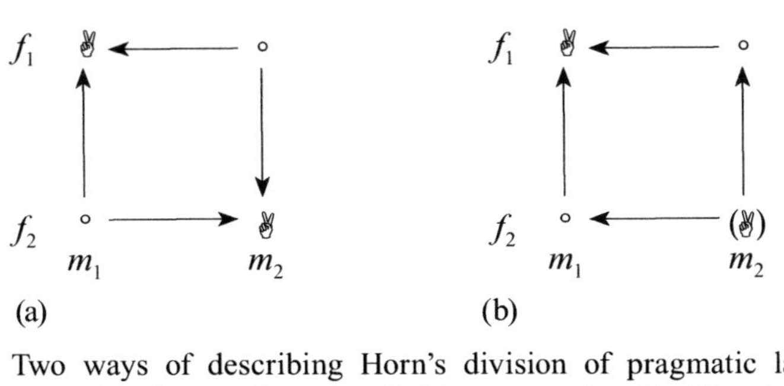

Figure 2. Two ways of describing Horn's division of pragmatic labor: (a) by assuming the two dominant linking constraints F→M and *F→*M and strong bidirectionality; (b) by assuming the markedness constraints F and M and weak bidirectionality

The second possibility is to weaken the notion of (strong) optimality in a way that allows us to derive Horn's division of pragmatic labor by means of the *evaluation procedure* and without stipulating particular linking constraints. Blutner (2000) proposes a *weak* version of two-dimensional OT, according to which the two dimensions of optimization are mutually related. The definition for super-optimality is as follows:

(3) Weak Bidirectionality (Super-Optimality): A form-interpretation pair <*f*, *m*> is considered to be super-optimal iff

  a. Interpretive Optimization: no other *super-optimal* pair <*f*, *m*'> can be generated that satisfies the constraints better than <*f*, *m*>;

  b. Expressive Optimization: no other *super-optimal* pair <*f*', *m*> can be generated that satisfies the constraints better than <*f*, *m*>.

This formulation looks like a circular definition, but Jäger (2002) has shown that this is a sound *recursive* definition under very general conditions (well-foundedness of the ordering relation). The important difference between the weak and strong notions of optimality is that the weak one accepts super-optimal form-meaning pairs that would not be optimal according to the strong version. It typically allows marked expressions to have an optimal interpretation, although both the expression and the situations they describe have a more efficient counterpart.

Figure 2b shows that the *weak* version of bidirectionality can explain the effects of partial blocking without the stipulation of extra linking constraints; especially it can explain why the marked form f_2 gets the marked interpretation m_2. This is a consequence of the *recursion* implemented in weak bidirectionality: the pairs <f_1, m_2> and <f_2, m_1> are *not* super-optimal. Hence, they cannot block the pair <f_2, m_2> and it comes out as a new super-optimal pair. In this way, the weak version accounts for Horn's pattern of *the division of pragmatic labor.*

The two parts of Figure 2 describe the same set of solution pairs but the calculation of the solutions is completely different in the two cases. In the first case unidirectional optimization (either hearer or speaker perspective) is sufficient to calculate the solution pairs. It is plausible to assume that this kind of optimality theoretic systems can be used to construct cognitively realistic models of online, incremental interpretation (cf. Blutner 2006, 2007). The second case – using the recursion of weak bidirectionality (super-optimality) – has a completely different status. Because of its strictly non-local nature the proposed algorithms that calculate the super-optimal solutions seem not to fit the requirements of a psychologically realistic model of online, incremental interpretation. Rather, the proper understanding of weak bidirectionality relates best to an off-line mechanism of bidirectional learning and fossilization. In a certain sense, it turns the pragmatic mechanism of conversational implicatures into a (fossilized) change of semantic information. Clearly, this relates to a mechanism at the semantic–pragmatic interface. The second half of section 4 explains this idea in detail.

3. Three variants of Gricean pragmatics

3.1. Methodological prerequisites

The *naturalization of pragmatics* refers to a research program that aims to provide a cognitively realistic picture of utterance interpretation and production. Hence, the proponents of this program such as relevance theorists take the stance of seeing natural language interpretation as a cognitive phenomenon and thus considering the basic principles of communication as a consequence of the nature of human cognition. A prerequisite of this program deals with the levels of cognitive representations and the boundary between semantics and pragmatics. As pointed out by Atlas and Levinson (1981), Bach (1994), Atlas (2005), and Jaszczolt (to appear) among others, there is a strong tendency among current researchers to follow the tradition of radical pragmatics and to accept the following three claims which crucially concern the nature of the semantics–pragmatics interface:

- There is a level of logical form or semantic representation. The representations of this level do not necessarily provide truth conditions. Rather, they underspecify truth-conditional content in a number of ways.
- There is a mechanism of enriching underspecified representations.[4] The result of enriching is propositional content. It expresses the utterance meaning of the relevant expression.
- There is a level of implicatures proper, understood as separate thoughts implied by the utterance. It is implicit propositional content that can be inferred from the explicit content mentioned in the second point.

Obviously, the consensus is about rejecting the Gricean doctrine of literal meaning (logical form conforms to literal meaning), accepting the role of underspecification (logical forms are underspecified with regard to the expressed semantic content) and acknowledging that implicature is a graded category (some implicatures are closer to LF than others). Obviously, this

[4] Sometimes this mechanism is called *development* of logical form.

view sharply contrasts with the paradigm of generative semantics – a view that tries to ground pragmatic phenomena by using particular syntactic stipulations. There are still representatives of this view in linguistics. For a critical discussion the reader is referred to Russell (2006).

Before we discuss three variations on Grice and the naturalization of conversational implicatures it is useful first to introduce the methodological distinction between *global* and *local* approaches to conversational implicatures (cf. Chierchia 2004). According to the global (neo-Gricean) view one first computes the (plain) meaning of the sentences; then, taking into account the relevant alternatives, one strengthens that meaning by adding in the implicature (Chierchia 2004: 42). This contrasts with the local view, which first introduces pragmatic assumptions locally and then projects them upwards in a strictly compositional way where certain filter conditions apply. Representatives of the global view are Atlas and Levinson (1981), Gazdar (1979), Horn (1984), Soames (1982), Krifka (1995), Blutner (1998), Sauerland (2004), Sæbø (2004), and (Benz 2006); the local view is taken by Chierchia (2004), Levinson (2000), and relevance theory (Sperber and Wilson 1986/1995, Carston 2002).

Usually, the globalists argue against the local view and the localists against the global view. I have argued at another occasions (Blutner 2006, 2007) that proper variants of both views are justified if a different status is assigned to the two views: global theories provide the standards of rational discourse and correspond to a diachronic, evolutionary scenario; local theories account for the shape of actual, online processing including the peculiarities of incremental interpretation. In this way, it can be claimed that seemingly conflicting approaches such as relevance theory and the neo-Gricean approach are much closer related than the proponents (and opponents) of these theories expected.

I will take the broad view of optimality theory in this section, seeing it as a general scheme that can be used for expressing many different and possibly diverging views. For instance, it is possible to give optimality theoretic reconstructions of a speaker-oriented normative pragmatics like the one developed by Grice. It is also possible to reconstruct hearer-oriented naturalistic pragmatics as in relevance theory (cf. Hendriks and de Hoop 2001; Zeevat 2007). These systems are important for online synchronic accounts of speaking and interpretation. Interestingly, the main aspects of Levinson's (2000) theory of presumptive meanings can also be mimicked in a closely related way. Perhaps more surprisingly, the reconstruction of the neo-Gricean systems of Atlas and Levinson (1981) and Horn (1984) is possible but crucially deviates from the reconstruction of Levinson (2000).

Similar to the reconstruction of relevance theory, the reconstruction of Levinson (2000) requires a unidirectional optimization mechanism. This contrasts with the restoration of the neo-Gricean systems which requires two opposing optimization principles (corresponding to the Q- and the I/R-principle). The integration of two simultaneous optimization procedures (speaker and the hearer direction) automatically leads to a bidirectional optimality theoretic pragmatics.

3.2. Relevance theory

Relevance theory assumes the representational/computational view of the mind, and, on this basis, gives a naturalization of pragmatics adopting Jerry Fodor's language of thought hypothesis (Fodor 1975). The central thesis of relevance theory is the communicative principle of relevance, according to which utterances convey a presumption of their own optimal relevance. In other words, any given utterance can be presumed:

(i) to be at least relevant enough to warrant the addressee's processing effort

(ii) to be the most relevant one compatible with the speaker's current state of knowledge and her personal preferences and goals.

From these two assumptions relevance theorists derive the following general procedure that the cognitive system follows in comprehending an utterance (cf. Sperber, Cara and Girotto 1995: 95): (a) test possible interpretations in their order of accessibility, (b) stop once the expectation of (optimal) relevance is satisfied (i.e. a certain context-dependent threshold value of relevance is reached). The procedure makes sure that the desired effect (a certain value of relevance) is reached with the minimal cognitive effort.

Obviously, relevance theory conforms to the localist approach and can be formulated in terms of unidirectional optimization. Let us stipulate a constraint EFFECT for describing the desired effect (a certain value of relevance) and a constraint EFFORT for describing the cognitive effort. Then the stipulation EFFECT >> EFFORT makes sure that the desired effect is reached with the minimal cognitive effort. Obviously, there are many questions left concerning the concrete content of the constraints EFFECT and EFFORT, the relevance theoretic literature contains a number of specifications. These specifications typically have the character of linking constraints. It might be interesting to investigate recent optimality theoretic models of pragmatics in the light of the general structure of relevance theory – a task that goes beyond what can be done in the present paper.[5]

Another important aspect concerns pragmatic acceptability. The relevance theoretic account of pragmatic (un)acceptability is worked out in connection with bridging phenomena (Wilson and Matsui 1998). In relevance theory, "unacceptability can result from (a) inadequate effects or (b) gratuitous effort" (Wilson and Matsui 1998: 19). That means there have to be thresholds for (a) effects and (b) effort, and when these thresholds are reached unacceptability results. This kind of argumentation is not possible within an optimality theoretic approach because in optimality theory the absolute strength of constraint violation is not of importance. What counts is the comparison with other expressions that lead to the same interpretation and the possibility of blocking an interpretation by a cheaper expression alternatives (e.g. Blutner 1998). It is an open issue to test the empirical consequences of this view.

3.3. Presumptive meanings

Levinson's (2000) theory of presumptive meanings is a chameleon that in a certain sense adapts general assumptions of relevance theory and in another sense crucially conflicts with this theory, for instance in assuming more than one basic principle (*maxim*) for formulating the interpretational mechanism. In short, these are the general assumptions:

---

[5] For instance, Zeevat (2002, 2007) reconstructed the presupposition theory as formulated by Van der Sandt (1992) and Heim (1982). In both these theories there are two preferences. The first one prefers identifying the induced presupposition in the context of the utterance (resolution), the second one prefers the addition of the presupposition to the global context (Heim) or to the highest accessible context where that is possible (Van der Sandt). Zeevat's reconstruction makes use of the following constraints that are used in finding an optimal interpretation: FAITH >> CONSISTENCE >> DO NOT ACCOMMODATE >> STRENGTH. CONSISTENCE demands that there is no conflict of the current utterance with what is known already, FAITH asks for the presence of the presupposed information at an accessible position, DO NOT ACCOMMODATE forbids the addition of the presupposed information and STRENGTH forbids interpretations if there are informationally stronger ones available. Obviously, FAITH and DO NOT ACCOMMODATE are constraints of type EFFORT while CONSISTENCE and STRENGTH are realizations of Type EFFECT. This violates the relevance theoretic scheme EFFECT >> EFFORT saying that all EFFECT-constraints outrank all EFFORT-constraint.

(i) Differing from both relevance theory and the standard neo-Gricean view, Levinson assumes *three* levels of meaning corresponding to coded meaning, utterance-type meaning and utterance-token meaning.

(ii) Coded meanings constitute what is normally called semantics, i.e. a convention of a language at a given time. In the present context it relates to the association of natural language forms with underspecified representations of meaning.

(iii) Utterance-type meanings are in correspondence with Grice' generalized conversational implicatures. More precisely, they are *fossilized* (or crystallized) invited inferences associated with certain lexemes or particular constructions. As a matter of preferred interpretation, they are calculated by a particular default mechanism which is relatively context-independent. It is in their nature that they may be cancelled. Basically, there are three such defaults or heuristics:
 – Q-heuristic: *What isn't said is not the case.*
 – I-heuristic: *What is expressed simply is stereotypically exemplified.*
 – M-heuristic: *What's said in an abnormal way isn't normal.*[6]

(iv) Utterance token meanings are invited inferences that have not been fossilized into commonly used implicatures. They are highly context-dependent and as such they may be based in encyclopedic knowledge or in situation-specific information.

(v) In contrast to utterance token meanings, which are calculated in a global manner, utterance type meanings (= presumptive meanings) are local, i.e. they arise at the point at which they are triggered (for instance, the word *some* triggers the default interpretation NOT ALL via the Q-heuristics). The feature of local pragmatics is essential to artificial intelligence pragmatics (e.g. Hobbs and Martin 1987) and likewise to relevance theory.

Presumptive meanings are identical with utterance type meanings and based on generalized conversational implicatures. The mechanics of these implicatures is very useful for understanding natural language interpretation, especially for explaining the predominantly incremental character of utterance comprehension. Like relevance theory Levinson's (2000) theory of presumptive meanings conforms to the localist approach and can be formulated in terms of unidirectional optimization. The defaults Q, I and M

---

[6] Levinson's M-heuristics should not be confused with the markedness constraint M introduced in Table 1.

can be formulated as optimality theoretic constraints. In case of two forms and two meanings (as considered in section 2; see Table 1), the I-heuristics conforms to the linking constraint F→M saying that simple (unmarked) forms express simple interpretations. Similarly, the M-heuristics is expressed by the constraint *F→*M saying that complex forms express complex interpretations. With only two forms and two meanings, the substance of the Q-heuristics is not really different from that of the M-constraint. To get an independent extensional expression of the Q-heuristics there needs to be more than two forms and two meanings.

An advantage of the present optimality theoretic approach is its general grounding in embodied cognition in general and in connectionist network research in particular. Using this methodology, we can achieve a clarification concerning the nature of *automatic* vs. *controlled processing. Automatic processing* is highly parallel, but limited in power. *Controlled processing* has powerful operations, but is limited in capacity (cf. Schneider and Shiffrin 1977). The distinction between these two types of processing has been used, for example, for modeling lexical access, visual perception, problem solving and parsing strategies in natural language processing. As demonstrated elsewhere (Blutner 2004; Smolensky and Legendre 2006), in cases where the constraint network is built with exponential weights[7] the energy landscape is structured like high mountains with an obvious path to the valley of the global energy minimum. Moreover, the stochastic solution algorithm yields robust results given some fluctuation of the parameters corresponding to attention. Hence we have the tentative characterization of automatic processing. In the other case, however, the energy landscape is flat and there are many walls of comparable height to cross before we see the valley of minimum energy. In this case, it is much more difficult for the solution mechanism to find the global optimum. Processing is slow and the attentional parameters may become much more influential. That corresponds to the traits of controlled processing.

Levinson claims that generalized conversational implicatures are processed automatically. Though Levinson does not discuss the implementation of his default mechanism in connectionist networks, this can be done, for example, along the lines demonstrated in Blutner (2004). What is requires then is a system of constraints with strict domination. That is exactly what Levinson is proposing: Q >> M >> I. Hence Levinson's assumption

---

7 This corresponds to a strict domination of constraints. Strict domination means that a violation of an arbitrary number of lower ranked constraints can never overpower to violation of ONE higher ranked constraint.

about the ranking of the constraints fits together with his assumption about the automaticity of processing assuming the proposed picture of embodied cognition. However, I doubt the automaticity of processing in connection with generalized conversational implicatures and, consequently, I also doubt the strictness of domination between the pragmatic constraints Q, M and I. Hence, the position of relevance theory – assuming controlled processing – is more appropriate when performance factors are under debate. The problem of finding the appropriate constraints is an open issue so far I can see. Neither relevance theory nor Levinson's generalized conversational implicatures are fully adequate at the moment.

3.4. Neo-Gricean approach

Neo-Griceans (Atlas and Levinson 1981; Horn 1984; Blutner 1998; Atlas 2005; Horn 2005) are assuming two countervailing optimization principles: the Q-principle and the R-principle.[8] The first is oriented to the interests of the hearer and looks for optimal interpretations; the second is oriented to the interests of the speaker and looks for expressive optimization. Here is a standard presentation of the two principles (cf. Horn 1984, 1989, 2004, 2005):

> **The Q-Principle** (Hearer-based):
> *Make your contribution sufficient!*
> *Say as much as you can!* (modulo R)
> (Grice's first quantity maxim and the first two manner maxims)
>
> **The R-Principle** (Speaker-based):
> *Make your contribution necessary!*
> *Say not more than you must!* (modulo Q)
> (Grice's second quantity maxim, relation maxim and the second two manner maxims)

It is tempting to identify the Q-principle with Levinson's Q-heuristic and the R-principle with the I-heuristics. However, they are not identical though there is a correspondence between them. The difference has to do with the different status of *principles* in the global, neo-Gricean pragmatics on the

---

[8] In optimality theory, these 'principles' correspond to different directions of optimization where the *content* of the optimization procedure is expressed by particular optimality theoretic constraints. This will be pointed out in more detail in the following section.

one hand and *heuristics* (*defaults*) in Levinson's local pragmatics on the other hand. According to the neo-Gricean picture the principles constitute a kind of communication game – either between real speakers and hearers or between fictive speakers and hearers in the mind of a language user. In this game both principles are applied in a recursive way (corresponding to the modulo-clause in the formulation of the principles). In Levinson's theory, no such interaction between real or fictive speakers/hearers takes place. Instead, presumptive meanings are default interpretations and they are processed in a nearly automatic way. No *mind reading* facilities are required here. The difference becomes quite clear when we give formalization in terms of unidirectional and bidirectional optimality theory.

In section 2, I have introduced weak bidirectionality and it was illustrated how this solution concept explains Horn's division of pragmatic labor. If we assume that the optimization procedure is supplemented by a system of ranked constraints – in order to provide the content of the optimization – then Horn's R-principle/Q-principle is in exact correspondence to interpretive/expressive optimization. Further, the modulo-clause in the formulation of the Q-/R-principle is explicitly expressed by the recursive term in formalism as can be seen from the definition given in (3).

An important question concerns the *status* of the theory with regard to synchrony versus diachrony. Obviously, both relevance theory and Levinson's theory of presumptive meanings take the synchronic view and both suggest a model of online language interpretation. Within the neo-Gricean camp, the situation is not so clearly decided. As mentioned in the introduction, prominent researchers take a normative stance. For instance, Horn (2005) claims the following:

> Grice's goal of developing an account of speaker meaning (of which implicature constitutes a proper subpart) is distinct from Relevance theorists' goal of developing a cognitive psychological model of utterance interpretation, which does not address the question of how and why the speaker, given what she wants to convey, utters what she utters. (p. 194)

However, we agree with Carston (2005) that this statement is too strong as it stands. I think that the difference between the normative stance and the naturalistic stance should not be overestimated because in practice there is seldom a deep empirical conflict between the two stances (Spohn 1993). Interestingly, the normative view comes very close to the diachronic perspective considering the Q and the I principle as diametrically opposed forces in language change. The diachronic perspective was clearly expressed in Horn (1984). Similarly, in the framework of optimality theoretic pragmatics it is very natural to take weak bidirectionality as expressing a basic principle of natural language change. As a consequence, bidirectional optimization has nothing to do with online processes that run during normal language interpretation/production. Rather, the results of bidirectional optimization are routinized or fossilized – a phenomenon that takes place on an evolutionary time scale. Hendriks, Hoop, Krämer, Swart and Zwarts (2010) put this point as follows:

> On Blutner and Zeevat's evolutionary view of bidirectionality, form-meaning pairs that have been determined by bidirectional optimization constitute fixed relations to a learner who sets out acquiring the language. No learner, indeed no user of the language, needs to perform a bidirectional computation for any form-meaning pair she encounters.

In contrast to this view there are representatives of optimality theoretic pragmatics who suggest a procedural formulation of week bidirectionality and propose it as a realistic model of natural language interpretation and/or natural language production (e.g. Zeevat 2000; Jäger 2002; Beaver and Lee 2004; Hendriks and Spenader 2005/2006). This position is also taken in Hendriks, Hoop, Krämer, Swart and Zwarts (2010):

> However, we take the position that bidirectionality is not in the first place an evolutionary mechanism. Some form-meaning pairings have not been fossilized or automatized, but must be computed anew in a given situation. This view of bidirectionality raises the question of whether bidirectionality is a property of an individual's linguistic performance from the onset of language acquisition, or whether it is acquired or instantiated at some later time. We believe that the latter is the case. Whenever a bidirectional pair has to be computed online in a given situation, it is necessary for the hearer to realize which options were available to the speaker, and also to realize that the speaker's eventual choice is codetermined by the speaker's assumption that the hearer is able to share his perspective. It is to be expected that such online computation requires considerable cognitive resources.

In section 5 we will try to decide the issue by discussing recent empirical studies that relate to the two different positions.

3.5. Relations between the three frameworks

In Figure 2, I have illustrated two ways of describing Horn's division of pragmatic labor: (a) by assuming the two dominant linking constraints F→M and *F→*M; (b) by assuming the markedness constraints F and M. In the first case unidirectional optimization gives already the intended solution (both in the interpretation perspective and the production perspective). In the second case it requires weak bidirectional optimization to get the intended solution, and this requires much more computational power than the unidirectional case. The significant computational complexity is compensated by the simplicity of the involved knowledge base since only markedness constraints are involved here. In the first case, contrastingly, the computational simplicity is compensated by the more complex system of linking constraints. Interestingly, there is a general way to transform the (b)-system into a (a)-system, and I have introduced the term *fossilization* for describing the relevant transfer. The corresponding mechanism of evolutionary learning will be discussed in the following section.

Taken the example from Figure 2, Levinson's (2000) formulation corresponds to the (a)-system and Horn's (1984) formulation corresponds to the (b)-system. Correspondingly, we can see Levinson's system as a *fossilization* of Horn's neo-Gricean system. Hence, both systems are compatible if we take the different perspectives into account: the synchronic perspective for the (a)-system and the diachronic perspective for the (b) system.

Though relevance theory takes presumably another system of constraints than Levinson's, the relevance theoretic system can likewise be seen as a fossilized processing architecture where no explicit mind reading capacities are required. Fossilization or routinization does not necessarily result in automatic processing (in contrast to Levinson's suggestion). I have discussed previously why the controlled character of processing assumed in relevance theory is fully compatible with the neuronal embodiment of optimality theoretic pragmatics.

Given the existence of fossilization and the corresponding transfers, is can be concluded that the three discussed variations on Grice are much more closely related than the occasional polemics let us expect. Despite of their similarities there are also important differences, mostly relating to different assumptions concerning the nature of natural language processing.

4. Fossilization as a phenomenon at the semantics–pragmatics interface

The essence of the fossilization view concerns the observation that the borderline between semantics and pragmatics is transparent in at least one direction: tendencies predicted from pragmatics (conversational implicatures) may become *frozen* in the semantic part of knowledge representation. Hence, fossilization is a phenomenon at the semantics–pragmatics interface. Interestingly, the framework of optimality theoretic pragmatics provides a theoretical instrument to account for this phenomenon.

The idea of fossilization was introduced in Morgan's (1978) paper about *short-circuited implicatures* as a mechanism of conventionalization for implicatures. Leaning on this idea, Horn and Bayer (1984) propose an elegant account of so-called neg-raising, "the availability (with certain predicates) of lower clause understandings for higher clause negations" (p. 397). There is a principal difficulty for nonsyntactic treatments of these neg-raising interpretations. The difficulty has to do with the existence of lexical exceptions to neg-raising, i.e. we find pairs of virtual synonyms of which one member allows the lower clause understanding and the other blocks it.[9] Horn and Bayer (1984) argue that conversational implicatures may become conventionalized ("pragmatic conventions") and this conventionalization sanctions neg-raising. The short-circuiting of implicatures as a matter of convention has important empirical consequences, some of them we will discuss in the following section.[10]

In an early paper, Cole (1975) investigates similar phenomena in the lexical realm. Calling the conventionalization phenomenon "lexicalization of contextual meaning" he makes quite clear that the relevant conventions are built on the basis of particularized conversational implicatures (i.e. what Levinson (2000) calls *utterance token meanings*). Further, he proposes a diagnostics for discriminating between implicatures proper and their lexicalized counterpart. This may help to clarify the synchronic/diachronic status of conversational implicatures.

Traugott and her colleagues (e.g. Traugott 1989; Traugott and Dasher 2005) applied the idea of fossilization to explain language change. According to this model innovation may arise in the individual and spread or propagate through the community. In their *invited inferencing theory of semantic change*, Traugott and co. postulate a cycle starting with coded meaning, exploiting particularized conversational implicatures, transforming these implicatures into generalized conversational implicatures (= conventionalization), and finally resulting in new coded meanings (cf. Traugott and Dasher 2005). Figure 3 shows a simplified picture of this model.

---

9 One of Horn and Bayer's (1984) examples concerns opinion verbs. For instance, Hebrew *xogev* 'think' permits NR readings while *maamin* 'believe' does not. Interestingly, the opposite pattern obtains in Malagasy. In French *souhaiter* 'hope, wish' exhibites neg-raising, but its near-synonym *espdrer* does not – although it's Latin etymon *sperare* did. (cited after Horn and Bayer 1984: 400).

10 For example, we expect to find differences between speakers and between languages as to just which conventions of usage are operative. And exactly this happens as it is pointed out in Horn and Bayer (1984).

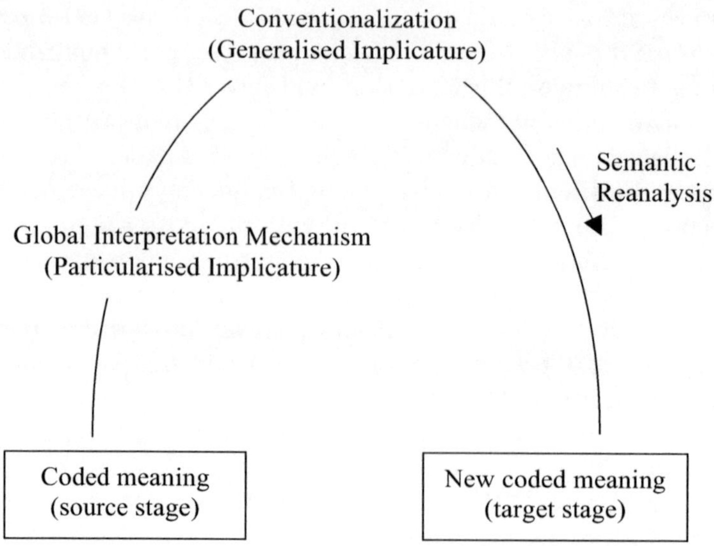

Figure 3. Simplified representation of the *invited inferencing theory of semantic change* (see Traugott and Dasher 2005: 38)

In the domain of syntax, Levinson (2000) and Mattausch (2004) used very the same idea for explaining the development of binding principles.

I will use the term *fossilization* here in a very broad sense that covers the whole spectrum of the mentioned phenomena. It stands for processes of *individual fossilization* (sometimes called *routinization*) that take place in individual language acquisition, i.e. on a time scale of seconds, hours and months. What is more it stands for social processes of *cultural fossilization* that take place in language change on a historical time scale of years up to centuries; the relevant mechanism is iterated learning/cultural evolution.

In optimality theoretic pragmatics, fossilization relates to a transformation of knowledge systems. As we have seen (Figure 2) it is possible to describe the same solution space in two different ways. In the first case (Figure 2a) unidirectional optimization (either hearer or speaker perspective) is sufficient to calculate the solution pairs. It is plausible to assume that this kind of optimality theoretic systems can be used to construct cognitively realistic models of online, incremental interpretation (see Blutner 2006, 2007). The second case (Figure 2b) is using the recursion of weak bidirectionality (super-optimality) and has a completely different status. Because of its strictly non-local nature the proposed algorithms that calculate the super-optimal solutions do not even fit the simplest requirements of psychologically realistic models of online, incremental interpretation (Zeevat 2000; Beaver and Lee 2004).

The proper understanding of weak bidirectionality and super-optimality relates best to an off-line mechanism that is based on bidirectional learning (Lentz and Blutner 2009; Benz 2003; Van Rooy 2004; Benz 2006). In these approaches the solution concept of weak bidirectionality is considered as a principle describing the results of language change: super-optimal pairs emerge over time in language change. This relates to the view of Horn (1984) who considers the Q and the I principle as diametrically opposed forces in language change, and it conforms to the good old idea that synchronic structure is significantly informed by diachronic forces.

For the sake of illustration let us go back to our example illustrated in Figure 2. Let us assume a population of agents who realize speaker- and hearer strategies based exclusively on the markedness constraints F and M. In this population, each content is expressed in the simplest way (f_1) and each expression is understood in the simplest way (m_1). Let us assume further that these agents communicate with each other. When agent x is in the speaker role and intends to express m_1, then expressive optimization yields f_1. Agent y is a hearer who receives f_1 and, according to interpretive optimization, he gets the interpretation m_1 – hence the hearer understands what the speaker intends: successful communication. Now assume the speaker wants to express m_2. With the same logic of optimization he will produce f_1 and the agent y interprets it as m_1. In this case, obviously, the communication is not successful. Now assume some kind of adaptation either by iterated learning or by some mutations of the ranked constraint system (including the linking constraints). According to this adaptation mechanism the *expected utility* (how well they understand each other in the statistical mean) can improve in time. In that way a system that is evolving in time can be described including its special attractor dynamics. In each case there is a stabilizing final state that corresponds to the system of Figure 2a where the two Levinsonian (2000) constraints I = [F→M] and M = [*F→*M] outrank the rest of the constraints. It is precisely this system that reflects Horn's division of pragmatic labor. The only condition we have to assume is that the marked contents are less frequently expressed than the unmarked contents.[11]

---

[11] For more discussion of the role of frequencies in an evolutionary setting cf. Stalnaker (2006). The general conclusion is that the solution concept of weak bidirection can be seen as a rough first approximation to the more adequate solution concepts of evolutionary game theory that describe the results of language change.

Hence, the important insight is that a system that is exclusively based on markedness constraints such as in Figure 2b is evolutionary related to a system based on highly ranked linking constraints such as in Figure 2a. It is opportune to present some more details at this point. Our own simulation studies (Lentz and Blutner 2009) have provided the following results assuming the three different strategies illustrated in Figure 4. Here the Horn-strategy describes the famous pattern of iconicity (Horn's division of pragmatic labor). The anti-Horn-strategy describes a kind of anti-iconicity, and the Smolensky-strategy describes the presumed initial state of a learner where unmarked forms and unmarked meanings are preferred simultaneously.

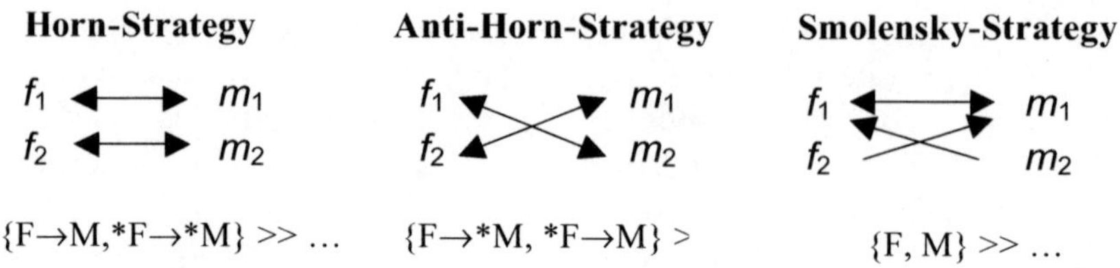

Figure 4. Three different strategies – based on the indicated three different rankings of the constraints

- Horn- und anti-Horn-strategies are the only evolutionary stable strategies.
- If the initial state represents a uniform Smolensky-population, then the system develops into
  - a pure Horn-population, assumed the frequency of the realization of m_1 is higher than that of m_2: $P(m_1) > P(m_2)$.
  - a pure anti-Horn-population, assumed the frequency of the realization of m_2 is higher than that of m_1: $P(m_2) > P(m_1)$.
- The corresponding proposition is true if the initial state represents a mixed population.

Hence, the probabilities for the situations that are described, i.e. $P(m_1)$, $P(m_2)$, are decisive for the result. The classical pattern of iconicity is predicted only in cases where the unmarked situation has the highest probability. McCawley (1978) has listed numerous cases of constructional iconicity in the lexicon. Krifka (2007) has observed that the phenomenon is the decisive factor in determining the precise/vague interpretation of measure expressions.

Interestingly, there are also examples of anti-iconicity. They are found in connection with semantic broadening where the initial meaning is described as that of an ideal shape, figure or state. A good example can be found in Dutch, where besides the preposition *om* (= Engl. *round;* German *um*) the expressions *rond* and *rondom* are in use. The expression *rond* is a word borrowed from French. It refers to the ideal shape of a circle. Starting with its appearance it comes in competition with the original (and *unmarked*) expression *om*. The results is a division of labor as demonstrated in the following examples (cf. Zwarts 2003, 2006):

(4) a. *Ze zaten rond (?om) de televisie.*
They sat rond the television
'They sat round the television.'

b. *Een man stak zijn hoofd om (?rond, ?rondom) de deur.*
A man put his head round the door
'A man put his head round the door.'

c. *De auto reed om (?rond, ?rondom) het obstakel heen.*
The car drove round the obstacle
'The car drove round the obstacle.'

d. *het gebied rondom (?om) het stadje.*
the area round the little town
'the area round the little town.'

According to the principle of iconicity we would expect that the unmarked form (*om*) is paired with the ideal of the circle shape and the marked form (*rond*) with the detour interpretation.[12] However, the opposite is true. I think there is a simple explanation for this fact: ideal shapes/situations are much less frequent then non-ideal situations; hence, since $P(m_1) < P(m_2)$, the present evolutionary approach predicts anti-iconicity.

I think these examples and many other examples in the area of lexical pragmatics (e.g. Blutner 1998; Wilson 2003) strongly suggest the reality of fossilization. Accepting that both possibilities are real to some extent – the online calculation of implicatures and the access of their fossilized counterparts, the question concerns the distribution of labor between online pro-

[12] The assumption that the ideal path description (circle) is realizing the unmarked interpretation and the detour interpretation is realizing the marked interpretation is justified by independent thoughts about the preference of the logically strongest interpretation (e.g. Dalrymple, Kanazawa, Kim, Mchombo and Peters 1998).

cesses (calculating optimal outcomes) and offline processing (fossilization processes). We can ask this question for standard scalar implicatures, as well as for other types of pragmatic inferences. In the next section I will review some experiments that are claimed to decide the issue. These experiments are closely related to the issue of asymmetries between comprehension and production processes.

5. The role of experimental data: Asymmetries between natural language comprehension and production

It is a common observation that we often are not able to produce what we can understand. The opposite situation where we are able to produce a certain expression but unable to understand is observed much less often. The phenomenon of aphasia gives a feasible illustration of the existence of both kinds of asymmetries (e.g. Jakobson 1941/1968). Likewise, in the domain of language acquisition both sides of the phenomenon can be detected. It is well known that children's ability in production lags dramatically behind their ability in comprehension (e.g. Benedict 1979; Clark 1993). It was only recently that attention was devoted to the opposite case where children's comprehension performance lags years behind their ability of production (cf. Hendriks and Spenader 2005/2006).

Theoretically, there are three different ways to deal with these observations. The first approach is to assume dissociation between a comprehension grammar and a production grammar (Larsen-Freeman 2002). Unfortunately, this account requires some ad hoc stipulations which conflict with general assumptions of parsimony.

The second approach is to assume different processing restrictions for production and comprehension. Joshi (1987) was possibly the first who discussed the asymmetry issue from the viewpoint of artificial intelligence:

> Comprehension and generation, when viewed as functions mapping from utterances to meanings and intentions and vice versa, can certainly be regarded as inverses of each other. However, these functions are enormously complex and therefore, although at the global level they are inverses of each other, the inverse transformation (i.e., computation of one function from the other) is not likely to be so direct. So, in this sense, there may be an asymmetry between comprehension and generation even at the theoretical level. (Joshi 1987: 183)

Joshi further suggests (p. 184) that the human generation mechanism involves some monitoring of the output, presumably by the comprehension mechanism. A corresponding monitoring (by generation) is not assumed for the human comprehension mechanism.

The third way of dealing with the asymmetry follows from an optimization approach. This was first demonstrated by Smolensky (1996). As we have seen in the previous sections, natural language production in optimality theory goes from a given interpretation to an optimal expression and natural language comprehension goes from a given expression to an optimal interpretation. It is these different directions of optimization which impose different boundary conditions on the process of optimization. As a result, the same system of constraints and the same constraint hierarchy can account for the observed asymmetry, without taking recourse to multiple grammars or different processing restrictions for production and comprehension.

In this section, I will discuss asymmetries between comprehension and production in the context of recent experimentation. The natural language expressions investigated are pronouns, reflexives, referential and quantifying expressions – the latter in connection with scalar implicatures. The fundamental questions asked are twofold:

(i) How to explain the observed differences between comprehension and production in a certain stage of development?
(ii) What is the mechanism that handles how to overcome the gap between comprehension and production during natural language acquisition?

OT has a very simple answer to the question (i). In order to account for the usual observation that comprehension can be perfect while production is not, Smolensky (1996) assumes two kinds of constraints: (a) markedness constraints for forms and (b) linking (faithfulness) constraints – linking forms and meanings in an adequate way. Further, he assumes that the markedness constraints initially dominate the linking constraints. It is exactly under these conditions that we get the expected pattern. If correct, then we can conclude that the cognitive architecture assumed by optimality theory fits to a great extent with the empirical requirements in the domain of comprehension/production asymmetries.

For sake of illustration, let us go back to the earlier example with two forms and two meanings. We assume the markedness constraint for forms F and the two linking constraints $F \rightarrow M$ and $*F \rightarrow *M$ (see Table 1). If $\{F\} >> \{F \rightarrow M, *F \rightarrow *M\}$ then comprehension is always correct (interpreting f_1 as m_1 and f_2 as m_2). However, the production perspective sometimes gives the wrong result. This is because of the dominance of the markedness constraint F, and it gives the result that all meanings m_i (i = 1,2) are expressed by the simpler form f_1.

Interestingly, the opposite pattern of delayed comprehension is also possible. In this case we have to assume an incomplete system of linking constraints that outranks the system of markedness constraints. A very simple example is {F→M} >> {F}. In this case m_1 produces f_1 and m_2 produces f_2. However, while f_1 is always interpreted correctly as m_1 the form f_2 comes out as ambiguous. It can be interpreted both as m_1 and m_2, and this constitutes a case of delayed comprehension.

The research question (ii) addresses the problem of language acquisition. It is much more difficult to answer than the first question. The difficulty arises from the fact that there is not only one potential mechanism to overcome the gap between comprehension and production. There are at least two such mechanisms, and I will consider them in correspondence with the two ways of viewing bidirectionality discussed earlier. The first mechanism is based on an optimality theoretic learning mechanism that re-ranks the involved constraints. That is exactly Smolensky's view as taken in Smolensky (1996). The second mechanism is a mechanism of maturation resulting in a processing system that integrates the comprehension and the production perspective. The resulting integrated system can be either the symmetric system of bidirectional optimality theory or an asymmetric version such as proposed by Joshi and worked out by Zeevat (2000).

In a slightly different formulation, the first mechanism is realizing the diachronic view of bidirectionality where bidirectional optimization takes place offline (during language acquisition) and leads to some kind of fossilizing optimal form-meaning pairs. In contrast, the second mechanism presumes bidirectional optimization as a psychologically realistic online mechanism. According to this online/synchronic view, speakers (hearers) optimize bidirectionally and take into account hearers (speakers) when selecting (interpreting) a referring expression. In the following I will consider some experimental investigations that shed a light on the empirical adequacy of these two positions.

5.1. The pronoun interpretation problem

In a recent research article, Hendriks and Spenader (2005/2006) give a new interpretation of children's delay of the comprehension of pronouns (see also Hendriks, Rijn and Valkenier 2007). I discuss the validity of their interpretation and present an alternative account in terms of iterated learning.

A series of experiments has shown that children make errors in interpreting pronouns as late as age 6;6, yet correctly comprehend reflexives from the age of 3;0 (e.g. Chien and Wexler 1990; McKee 1992; Koster 1993; Spenader, Smits and Hendriks 2007). For example, children were confronted with a context where two boys, Bert and Paul, are introduced, and the following sentences were given:

(5) a. *Bert is washing himself.*
 b. *Bert is washing him.*

Sentences like (5a) are correctly understood from a young age (95% of the time according to some studies). However, children misinterpret the pronoun in (5b) as coreferring with the subject about half the time. Hence, it seems that children did not yet realize that the coreferring reading of (5b) must be blocked given the existence of the sentence (5a) which clearly has the coreferring reading.

Contrasting with the comprehension data, language production experiments consistently have shown that children do not have problems in producing reflexives or pronouns correctly. For example, Bloom, Barss, Nicol and Conway (1994) demonstrated that even in the youngest age groups investigated (ranging from 2;3 to 3;10), the children consistently used the pronoun to express a disjoint meaning, while they used the reflexive to express a coreferential interpretation. It can be concluded from the production data that children have competence of binding principles. Why they do not use this knowledge in comprehension?

I cannot go into all the different theoretical proposals concerning the pronoun interpretation problem. Instead, I will be mainly concentrated on the possibilities opened by optimality theoretic pragmatics. Recently, several authors have argued that the observed delay in comprehension can be explained by assuming that children are only able to consider their own perspective, whereas adult hearers are able to simultaneously take into account the perspective of the speaker (deHoop and Krämer 2005, Hendriks and Spenader 2005/2006, Hendriks, Rijn and Valkenier 2007).

As explained at the beginning of this section it is possible to account for the delay of comprehension by assuming an incomplete system of linking constraints that outranks the system of markedness constraints for forms, for instance the system {F→M} >> {F}. In the concrete case of pronoun/reflexive interpretation f_1 stands for the reflexive, f_2 for the pronoun, m_1 for the coreferential interpretation and m_2 for the disjoint interpretation. The markedness constraint F prefers he reflexive over the pronoun and can be read as "referential ecomomy" (see Burzio 1998). The linking constrain F→M excludes the reflexive from the disjoint interpretation – that is just the binding principle A (a reflexive must be bound locally) expressed as a violable constraint. Figure 5 shows the preferences between the four possible form meaning pairs arising from the system.

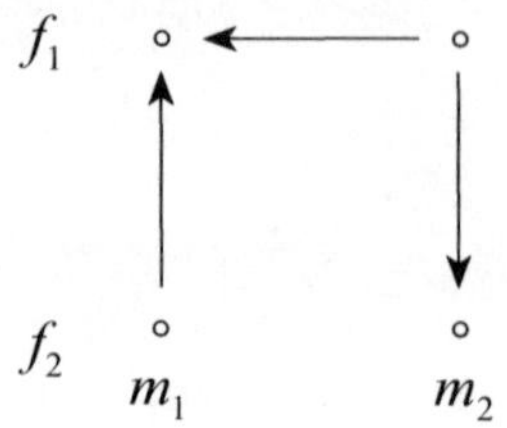

Figure 5. Diagram illustrating the pronoun interpretation problem. It shows the preferences between the four form-interpretation pairs based on the system {F→M} >> {F} of ranked constraints

Assume now that children begin with unidirectional optimization. In the case of production everything goes right: the meanings m_1 and m_2 are expressed by f_1 and f_2, respectively. However, in case of comprehension the form f_2 (the pronoun) exhibits an ambiguity: both he interpretation m_1 and m_2 are optimal taken the interpretive perspective for optimization. And that is exactly the expression of the pronoun interpretation problem.

Optimizing bidirectionally inherently involves reasoning about alternatives not present in the current situation. In the present case, a child who is hearing f_2 (a pronoun) must reason what other non-expressed forms the speaker could have used. The child can realize then that a coreferential meaning m_1 is better expressed with f_1 (a reflexive). Then, by a process of elimination, the child must realize the pronoun should be interpreted as disjoint meaning m_2 and this resolves the ambiguity. Since the ability to optimize bidirectionally may be a skill acquired relatively late, this idea gives a plausible explanation of the lag in acquisition.

Summarizing, the online processing account of Hendriks and Spenader (2005/2006) provides a new way to explain children's delay of the comprehension of pronouns. What is essential for this solution is the hypothesis that the hearer has to take a potential speaker into account. Thus, the authors are able to derive principle B effects (pronouns are free) from principle A alone, through bidirectional optimization. The approach nicely combines a pragmatic explanation with a processing account (lack of processing recourses). Besides the stipulation of the constraints and their ranking no other stipulations are required.

However, there are also some arguments that challenge the discussed view. First at all there is the question of constraint grounding. Other systems of constraints are conceivable and successfully used in the literature (see, e.g., Levinson 2000, Mattausch 2004). Further, there is no answer on the question why the particular ranking {F→M} >> {F} is assumed. Another problem has to do with children's abilities for mind reading ("theory of mind") that is explicitly assumed in Hendriks' and Spenader's approach. The assumption of mind reading as a prerequisite for making the transition to bidirectional reasoning has the consequence that there should be strict correlations between the behavior in standard tests of theories of mind (see Perner, Leekam and Wimmer 1987) and the behavior in tasks involving bidirectionality (such as pronoun interpretation). Unfortunately, such strict correlations never were found (Flobbe, Verbrugge, Hendriks and Krämer 2007). Further, mind reading requires awareness of other conversation participant's choices. Hence, it is based on controlled rather than automatic processing. However, pronoun processing appears to be automatic rather than controlled. There is no explicit hint for mind reading capacities in such tasks.

In the following subsection, I will propose an alternative account that can describe the same kind of data and in addition has some conceptual advantages. The main advantage is that it goes without stipulating a change of the cognitive architecture at some age (using bidirectional optimization instead of unidirectional one).

5.2. Pronoun interpretation and related task: individual fossilization

In section 4 I described an approach to fossilization and I made a distinction between individual and cultural fossilization. Cultural fossilization was successfully used by Mattausch and Jäger (Jäger 2004, Mattausch 2004). I will consider now individual fossilization in connection with the pronoun interpretation problem.

In the informal description given here the focus is on pointing out the differences to the processing account provided by Hendriks and co. Let us start with Hendrik's initial system {F→M} >> {F}. In order to apply optimality theoretic learning mechanisms we assume that a complete system of constrains is present in a background of equally ranked constraints. The following system which is functionally equivalent with the system described before is used: {F→M} >> {F} >> {F→*M, *F→M *F→*M}. The learning rule then says: promote constraints that favor wanted behavior over unwanted, demote constraints that favor unwanted behavior over wanted. If a competent adult acts as speaker and the child as hearer, then this learning rules lead to the promotion of *F→*M (principle B). Figure 6 illustrates the transfer between the two systems.[13]

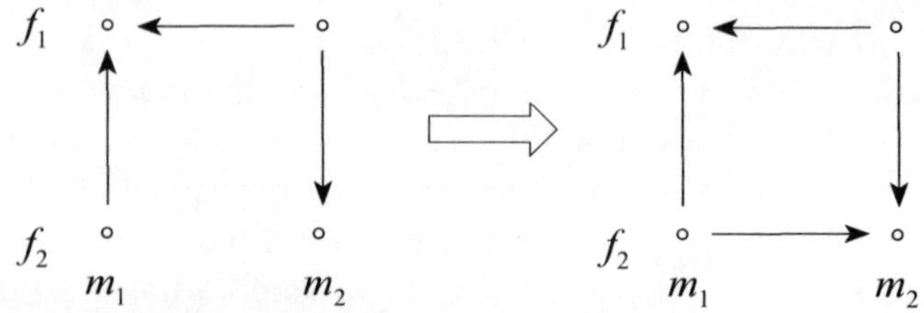

Figure 6. Transformation between two systems of ranked constraints provided by individual fossilization

It is obvious that this transfer is dependent of parameters of use. Hence, we expect frequency effects when the fossilization mechanism is at work. Further, we would expect no significant differences between the comprehension of pronouns and the comprehension of reflexives. The reason is that their processing loads are not significantly different. Hendriks' online view of processing (involving bidirectionality) conflicts with both hypotheses. It suggests a domain-independent transition from the unidirectional to the bidirectional case. Consequently, we should not expect significant effects of use (frequency effects). Further, for adult subjects we should expect significant differences in processing between pronouns and reflexives, since the pronoun requires bidirectional processing but the reflexive does not.

I think both hypotheses supporting the fossilization view can be confirmed. Though there is no direct verification of the second hypothesis at the moment, I think in the light of the eye tracking investigations of Karabanov, Bosch and König (2007) it is not probable that the comprehension of pronouns takes significantly more time than the comprehension of reflexives assuming comparable conditions. For the first hypothesis, it is

[13] Alternatively, we could start with the system {*F, *M} >> {F→M, F→*M, *F→M, *F→*M}. The two dominating constraint *F and *M express that f_2 (pronoun) is the preferred form and that m_2 (disjoint interpretation) is the preferred interpretation. The linking constraints cancel each other. Then it can be shown that iterated learning leads to different stages of development. First the principle A is evolving if the plausible stipulation is made that $P(m_2) > P(m_1)$. Hence we have a motivation why the system of preferences as given on the left hand site of Figure 6 appears – it reflects delayed comprehension – instead of a system exhibiting delayed production. Only later the principle B becomes dominant, giving the preferences shown on the right hand site of Figure 6.

important to see that there are some other domains which realize the same structural relations as exhibited in the case of pronoun interpretation exhibited in Figure 5. Consider first the domain of natural language quantifiers and consider dual quantifiers such as *some(A)* and *all(A)*, where A stand for a certain restrictive term. Logically, *all(A)(B)* has the set inclusion interpretation stating $A \subseteq B$, and *some(A)(B)* has an interpretation expressing nonempty intersection $A \cap B \neq \emptyset$. Of course, this interpretation does not exclude the set inclusion reading. It is the scalar implicature that excludes this interpretation – leading to a *some_but_not_all* interpretation. The ordering of all form interpretation pairs given in Figure 5 can be applied to the quantifier case when we assume that f_1 stands for *all*, f_2 for *some*, m_1 for the set inclusion interpretation, and m_2 for the *some_but_not_all* reading. The markedness constraint F now prefers *all* over *some.* We can see that as a realization of the strongest meaning hypothesis (Dalrymple, Kanazawa, Kim, Mchombo and Peters 1998). Further, the dominating constraint F→M expresses the meaning postulate for *all*, and the potential constraint *F→*M expresses the scalar implicature for *some.*

The first systematic investigation of the acquisition of scalar implicature can be attributed to Noveck (2001). From his experiments it can be concluded that young children initially treat a relatively weak term logically before becoming aware of its pragmatic potential, and that, in this respect, "children are more logical than adults" (Noveck 2001: 165). Concluding, we can speak of delayed comprehension of the pragmatic potential of the weak quantifier.

Another domain where we find similar effects is the interpretation of indefinite expressions. In several languages it has been observed that indefinite noun phrases such as *a boy* take on different interpretations depending on whether they appear in a scrambled or unscrambled word ordering (e.g. de Hoop and Krämer 2005; Unsworth 2005). Adults interpret unscrambled indefinites (f_1) as *non-specific* (m_1) whereas they interpret scrambled indefinites (f_2) as *specific* (m_2). Again we find a delayed comprehension effect: children interpret scrambled indefinites in both ways. Only later they realize that the *specific* interpretation is the proper one.

In a recent article Hendriks, Rijn and Valkenier (2007) discuss the results of diverse experiments in different domains and conclude that children seem to differ in the ages at which they provide adult-like responses for particular linguistic forms.

> Whereas from the age of 6 or 7 on children start to interpret pronouns correctly, children until roughly 11 years old select a non-adult meaning for indefinite objects (Unsworth 2005), and many 10- and 11-year-olds do not draw a scalar implicature where most adults would (Noveck 2001). This

> suggests that bi-directional optimization is not a general strategy that has to be learned by children in one step, but rather that the possibility of bi-directional optimization is dependent on the frequency of use of the relevant production rules. (Hendriks, Rijn and Valkenier 2007: 1893)

Hence, the first hypothesis suggested above – predicting a domain-independent transition from the unidirectional to the bidirectional view – seems to be falsified. And this might be a powerful argument supporting the fossilization view.

Thought the domain independence of he transfer from unidirectional to bidirectional processing is a natural consequence of the online processing view, it is not a necessary consequence. Hendriks, Rijn and Valkenier (2007) provide an improvement of their online processing view in order to describe the empirically found domain dependency. This improvement is formulated in terms of the ACT-R[14] model (Anderson and Lebiere 1998).

ACT-R understands itself as an integrated theory of the mind. Different from Smolensky's (Smolensky and Legendre 2006) theory of *harmonic mind* which sees the symbolic part (i.e., OT) as a high-level description of the neural realm, ACT-R is a *hybrid* theory that relates different symbolic modules with certain subsymbolic processes. These subsymbolic processes serve to guide the selection of rules to fire as well as the internal operations of modules and much of learning.

Hendriks, van Rijn and Valkenier (2007) model unidirectional and bidirectional optimality theory in terms of the ACT-R model. In this model bidirectional optimization is described as the serial application of two unidirectional processes of optimization. A crucial property of ACT-R is the assumption that actions take time to perform and that performance is limited by the serial processing bottleneck. Since bidirectional optimization needs much more processing resources than unidirectional optimization does, a process of production compilation[15] comes in increasing the processing efficiency. The result of production compilation conforms to an *instance based* kind of automatization (Logan 1988). I think what is described here comes very close to the idea of fossilization. Whereas fossilization leads to the introduction of new linking constraints product compilation leads to the generation of new productions who describe the results of certain bidirectional actions.

---

[14] ACT-R stands for *Adaptive Control of Thought-Rational.*

[15] In production compilation, two existing production rules are integrated into one new production rule. Production compilation occurs when two existing production rules are repetitively executed in sequence.

5.3. Choosing the right referring expression

The standard case of production/comprehension asymmetries is delayed production. Comprehension can be perfect while production is not. A good example is given by production and understanding of nominal descriptions and pronouns as illustrated in (6).

(6) Discourse context: A woman is waiting at the corner. Her girl is eating an ice cream cone.
  a. *She wears a red shirt.*
  b. *The woman wears a red shirt.*

The interpretation of the pronoun in (6a) clearly refers to the discourse topic (*the girl*). If we want to express the alternative meaning as in (6b) we cannot use the pronoun. Interestingly, young children very often produce such subject pronouns when intending to refer to non-topics. Karmiloff-Smith (1985) found this pattern of production in children until the age of 6.

I have already mentioned that the phenomenon can be modeled by assuming markedness conventions that initially dominate linking constraints. Figure 7 shows the corresponding diagram. Hereby, f_1 stands for the pronoun and f_2 for a nominal description. Further, m_1 is the interpretation referring to the topicalized discourse referent while m_2 refers to the non-topicalized one. F can be seen as referential economy (preferring pronouns to nominal descriptions) and F→M expresses the preference for pronouns to be interpreted as the topic of the discourse.

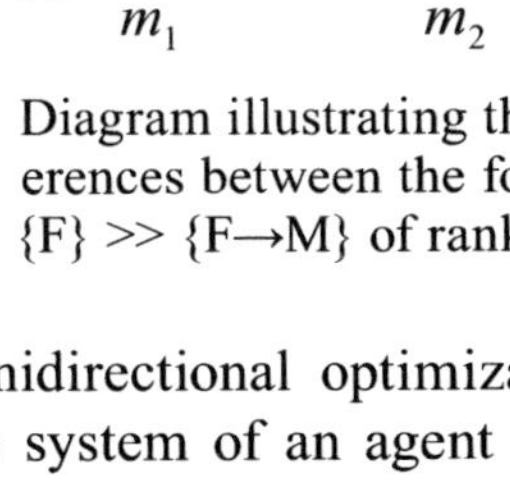

Figure 7. Diagram illustrating the pronoun production problem. It shows the preferences between the four form-interpretation pairs based on the system {F} >> {F→M} of ranked constraints

Using unidirectional optimization, the diagram describes the optimality theoretic system of an agent who can properly understand pronouns and nominal descriptions but who overuse pronouns when intending to refer to non-topics.

The two considered models now make different assumptions for describing the transfer from the child system to the adult system. The online processing model handles the production problem by assuming that the producer takes the hearer into account and begins to reason bidirectionally at some point of development. In contrast, the fossilization view says that unidirectional optimization is sufficient if it is assumed that the relevant information has been fossilized at some part of the human development.

In a recent research article, Hendriks, Englert, Wubs and Hoeks (2007) argue that the investigation of elderly adults could decide between the two models. Elderly adults possess the required pragmatic and grammatical knowledge to select and interpret referring. However, their linguistic performance can be defective, due to a decreasing working memory capacity. And indeed, the authors found that elderly adults produce non-recoverable pronouns significantly more often than young adults when referring to the old topic in the presence of a new topic. With respect to the comprehension task, no significant differences were found between elderly and young adults.

Obviously, this experimental outcome seems to be a problem for the fossilization view, since a stipulation of a mechanism of *de-fossilization* does not make any sense in the present context. However, as Biro has shown recently, it is possible to explain such performance effects by using unidirectional optimization and a mechanism of simulated annealing (Biro 2009).

On the other hand, there is a big problem for the bidirectional processing view. It says that both the speaker takes the hearer into account and, vice versa, the hearer takes the speaker into account. If that is right, then the same argumentation that is given in the paper by Hendriks, Englert, Wubs and Hoeks (2007) can be applied for the delayed comprehension experiments discussed in the previous subsections. Thought I do not know of any experiments with elderly people concerning the delayed comprehension task, I bet more than my finger that the behavior of elderly people does not go down to that of young children in the relevant respects. Hence, the idea of fossilization is needed in order to account for the delayed comprehension data.

Finally, the role of experimental data in deciding between the two rivaling theories – the bidirectional processing view and the fossilization view – should be highlighted. Introspection and intuition, which are central for validating many linguistic conjectures, are of no value in the present case for reasons that have to do with the nature of processing as an unconscious or preconscious concept. For that reason experimental psychological data are *a conditio sine qua non* for deciding between the two processing hypotheses.

6. Conclusions

The main methodological aim of this article was to argue for optimality theory as a conceptual framework that can help to close the gap between experimental pragmatics and neo-Gricean theories of pragmatics. Further, I have argued that optimality theoretic pragmatics has the potential to account both for the synchronic and the diachronic perspective in pragmatics.

In discussing modern pragmatic theories, I have shown that relevance theory and Levinson's theory of presumptive meanings account for the resolution of the conflict between effort minimization and effect maximization in different ways. In a certain sense, the crux of both approaches can be translated in optimality theoretic pragmatics by making use of particular linking constraints. This translation makes the advantage of both approaches visible: both conform to the incremental, online character of natural language interpretation.[16]

Another important methodological issue concerns the proper interpretation of bidirectional optimality theory, either as a psychologically realistic online mechanism or as an offline phenomenon that relates to the fossilization of certain pragmatic effects. Accepting that both possibilities are real to some extent the impending question concerns the distribution of labor between online processes (calculating optimal outcomes) and offline processing (fossilization processes). This question is asked for standard scalar implicatures, as well as for other types of pragmatic inferences such as semantic broadening, certain types of manner-implicatures, and inferences in connection with pronoun/reflexives interpretation.

Concerning the role of data at the semantics–pragmatics interface, I have discussed recent work about the phenomenon of delayed comprehension and delayed production. This is a phenomenon which was not discussed within experimental pragmatics so far, though the importance of the problem was clearly recognized within optimality theoretic pragmatics. A

[16] In discussing processing characteristics, incrementality and automaticity of processing have to be discriminated. Whereas automaticity of processing implicates the incremental character of processing the opposite is not true: incrementality does not implicate automatic processing. Relevance theory explains the incremental character of processing and has good reasons for assuming controlled processing in order to account for the processing of conversational implicatures. That's different from Levinson's account which assumes automatic processing for generalized conversational implicatures. It seems that relevance theory is better justified on empirical grounds (cf. Noveck and Sperber 2005).

careful discussion of this problem is required in order to discriminate between the two central models: the online processing model and the fossilization account. Although I have argued in favor of the fossilization view, it needs further experimentation in order to reach a definite decision.

The essence of the fossilization view concerns the observation that the borderline between semantics and pragmatics is transparent in at least one direction: tendencies predicted from pragmatics (conversational implicatures) may become *frozen* in the semantic part of knowledge representation. This directly affects the nature of the semantics–pragmatics interface. I have demonstrated that psycholinguistic data are required to test hypotheses about the underlying cognitive architecture. It has been pointed out that the concept of fossilization can help to understand the idea of naturalization and (cultural) embodiment in the context of natural language interpretation.

Regarding the theoretical status of fossilization, there are important open questions. In a by now classical paper Cole (1975) considered the following example of a true conversational implicature, where a girl called Pamela upon being asked (7) might reply (8):

(7) *How are you doing in your new position at San Andreas Fault University?*

(8) *Well, I haven't been fired yet.*

Although the logical content of (8) is roughly that of the proposition that Pamela has not yet lost her job, more than that is implicated, namely that Pamela is not doing well. In this example, the implicature is really novel. There is no construction involved whose frequent use could lead to the fossilization phenomenon (Cole's term is *lexicalization*). Hence, this implicature is different from many other cases where a certain amount of fossilization is plausible. The important question is how to discriminate between offline implicatures that are not fossilized and their fossilized counterparts. Where is the boundary between aspects of interpretations that are truly conversational and aspects which have become lexically (or syntactically) encoded? We think the former aspect of interpretation can require some real mind reading capacities, requires conscious reflections and proceeds offline. So far we can see none of the discussed pragmatic theories has an interesting answer for this long-standing and intriguing question.

Earlier investigations have convincingly demonstrated that the evaluation of linguistic theories depends heavily on the kind of data that can be regarded as evidence for or against their hypothesis (see Kertész and Rákosi 2008). The present paper has contributed the view that optimality theoretic pragmatics in particular and optimality theoretic linguistics in general seriously acknowledges psycholinguistic data as evidence.

Acknowledgements

I thank Enikő Németh T., Károly Bibok and an anonymous referee for helpful comments and critical reading of the manuscript. I further acknowledge valuable discussions with Anton Benz, Stefan Blutner, Paul Boersma, Helen de Hoop, Michael Franke, Petra Hendriks, Jason Mattausch, Paul Smolensky, and Henk Zeevat.

References

Aissen, Judith
2003 Differential Object Marking: Iconicity vs. Economy. *Natural Language and Linguistic Theory* 21: 435–483.

Anderson, John R. and Christian Lebiere
1998 *The Atomic Components of Thought*. Mahwah, NJ: Erlbaum.

Anderson, Michael L.
2003 Embodied Cognition: A field guide. *Artificial Intelligence* 149: 91–130.

Atlas, Jay David
2005 *Logic, Meaning, and Conversation: Semantical Underdeterminacy, Implicature, and Their Interface*. Oxford: Oxford University Press.

Atlas, Jay David and Stephen C. Levinson
1981 It-clefts, informativeness and logical form. In *Radical Pragmatics*, Peter Cole (ed.), 1–61. New York: Academic Press.

Axelrod, Robert
1984 *The evolution of co-operation*. London: Penguin.

Bach, Kent
1994 Conversational impliciture. *Mind and Language* 9: 124–162.

Beaver, David and Hanjung Lee
2004 Input-output mismatches in OT. In *Optimality Theory and Pragmatics*, Reinhard Blutner and Henk Zeevat (eds.), 112–153. Houndmills / Basingstoke / Hampshire: Palgrave / Macmillan

Benedict, Helen
1979 Early Lexical Development: Comprehension and Production. *Journal of Child Language* 6: 183–200.

Benz, Anton
2003 Partial Blocking, associative learning, and the principle of weak optimality. In *Proceedings of the Stockholm Workshop on Variation within Optimality Theory*, Jennifer Spenader, Anders Eriksson and Östen Dahl (eds.), 150–159. Stockholm.

Benz, Anton
2006 Partial blocking and associative learning. *Linguistics and Philosophy* 29: 587–615.
Bezuidenhout, Anne
2002 Generalized conversational implicatures and default pragmatic inferences. In *Meaning and Truth: Investigations in Philosophical Semantics*, Joseph K. Campbell, Michael O'Rourke and David Shier (eds.), 257–283. New York: Seven Bridges.
Bezuidenhout, Anne and J. Cooper Cutting
2002 Literal meaning, minimal propositions, and pragmatic processing. *Journal of Pragmatics* 34 (4): 433–456.
Biro, Tamás
2009 Elephants and Optimality Again: SA-OT accounts for pronoun resolution in child language, *Selected papers from Computational Linguistics in the Netherlands 19 (Groningen)*; see also ROA-1038.
Bloom, Paul, Andrew Barss, Janet Nicol and Laura Conway
1994 Children's knowledge of binding and coreference: Evidence from spontaneous speech. *Language* 70 (1): 53–71.
Blutner, Reinhard
1998 Lexical pragmatics. *Journal of Semantics* 15: 115–162.
Blutner, Reinhard
2000 Some aspects of optimality in natural language interpretation. *Journal of Semantics* 17: 189–216.
Blutner, Reinhard
2004 Nonmonotonic inferences and neural networks. *Synthese (Special issue on Knowledge, Rationality and Action)* 142 (2): 143–174.
Blutner, Reinhard
2006 Embedded implicatures and optimality theoretic pragmatics. In *A Festschrift for Kjell Johan Sæbø: In partial fulfilment of the requirements for the celebration of his 50th birthday*, Torgim Solstad, Atle Grønn and Dag Haug (eds.). Oslo.
Blutner, Reinhard
2007 Optimality Theoretic Pragmatics and the Explicature/Implicature Distinction. In *Pragmatics*, Noel Burton-Roberts (ed.), 67–89. Houndmills / Basingstoke / Hampshire: Palgrave / MacMillan.
Blutner, Reinhard, Helen de Hoop and Petra Hendriks
2005 *Optimal Communication*. Stanford: CSLI Publications.
Blutner, Reinhard and Henk Zeevat (eds.)
2004 *Optimality Theory and Pragmatics*. Houndmills / Basingstoke / Hampshire: Palgrave / MacMillan.
Boersma, Paul and Bruce Hayes
2001 Empirical tests of the gradual learning algorithm. *Linguistic Inquiry* 32: 45–86.

Burzio, Luigo
1998 Anaphora and soft constraints. In *Is the best good enough?* Pilar Barbosa, Danny Fox, Paul Hagstrom, Martha McGinnis and David Pesetsky (eds.), Cambridge, MA: The MIT Press.

Carston, Robyn
2002 *Thoughts and Utterances: The Pragmatics of Explicit Communication*. Oxford: Blackwell.

Carston, Robyn
2005 Relevance Theory, Grice and the neo-Griceans: a response to Laurence Horn's 'Current issues in neo-Gricean pragmatics'. *Intercultural Pragmatics* 2 (3): 303–319.

Chien, Yu-Chin and Kenneth Wexler
1990 Children's knowledge of locality conditions on binding as evidence for the modularity of syntax and pragmatics. *Language Acquisition* 13: 225–295.

Chierchia, Gennaro
2004 Scalar implicatures, polarity phenomena, and the syntax/pragmatics interface. In *Structures and Beyond*, Adrian Belletti (ed.), 39–103. Oxford: Oxford University Press.

Clark, Eve V.
1993 *The Lexicon in Acquisition*. Cambridge: Cambridge University Press.

Cole, Peter
1975 The synchronic and diachronic status of conversational implicature. In *Syntax and Semantics, Volume 3: Speach Acts*, Peter Cole and Jerry L. Morgan (eds.), 257–288. San Diego, CA: Academic Press.

Dalrymple, Mary, Makoto Kanazawa, Yookyung Kim, Sam Mchombo and Stanley Peters
1998 Reciprocal expressions and the concept of reciprocity. *Linguistics and Philosophy* 21: 159–210.

de Hoop, Helen and Henriette de Swart
2000 Temporal adjunct clauses in optimality theory. *Rivista di Linguistica* 12 (1): 107–127.

de Hoop, Helen and Irene Krämer
2005 Children's optimal interpretations of indefinite subjects and objects. *Language Acquisition* 13: 103–123.

Dekker, Paul and Robert van Rooy
2000 Bi-directional optimality theory: An application of game theory. *Journal of Semantics* 17: 217–242.

Flobbe, Liesbeth, Rineke Verbrugge, Petra Hendriks and Irene Krämer
2007 *Children's application of Theory of Mind in reasoning and language*. Unpublished ms., University of Groningen and Radboud University Nijmegen.

Fodor, Jerry
1975 *The Language of Thought*. New York: Thomas Crowell.

Garrett, Merrill and Robert M. Harnish
2007 Experimental pragmatics: Testing for implicitures. *Pragmatics and Cognition* 15: 65–90.
Gazdar, Gerald
1979 *Pragmatics*. New York: Academic Press.
Harnad, Stevan
1990 The symbolic grounding problem. *Physica D* 42: 335–346.
Heim, Irene
1982 *The semantics of definite and indefinite noun phrases*. Unpublished PhD dissertation, University of Massachusetts at Amherst.
Hendriks, Petra and Helen de Hoop
2001 Optimality theoretic semantics. *Linguistics and Philosophy* 24: 1–32.
Hendriks, Petra, Christina Englert, Ellis Wubs and John Hoeks.
2007 *Age differences in adults' use of referring expressions*. Unpublished manuscript, University of Groningen.
Hendriks, Petra, Helen de Hoop, Irene Krämer, Henriëtte de Swart and Joost Zwarts
2010 *Conflicts in Interpretation*. London: Equinox Publishing.
Hendriks, Petra, Hedderik van Rijn and Bea Valkenier
2007 Learning to reason about speakers' alternatives in sentence comprehension: A computational account. *Lingua* 117: 1879–1896.
Hendriks, Petra and Jennifer Spenader
2005/06 When production precedes comprehension: An optimization approach to the acquisition of pronouns. *Language Acquisition* 13 (4): 319–348.
Hobbs, Jerry and P. Martin
1987 Local Pragmatics, *Proceedings, International Joint Conference on Artificial Intelligence*, 520–523. Milan.
Horn, Larry
1984 Towards a new taxonomy of pragmatic inference: Q-based and R-based implicature. In *Meaning, form, and use in context: Linguistic applications*, Deborah Schiffrin (ed.), 11–42. Washington: Georgetown University Press.
Horn, Larry
1989 *A natural history of negation*. Chicago: Chicago University Press.
Horn, Larry
2004 Implicature. In *Handbook of Pragmatics*, Larry Horn and Gregory Ward (eds.), 3–28. Oxford: Blackwell.
Horn, Larry
2005 Current issues in neo-Gricean pragmatics. *Intercultural Pragmatics* 2 (2): 191–204.
Horn, Larry and Samuel Bayer
1984 Short-circuited implicature: A negative contribution. *Linguistics and Philosophy* 7: 397–414.

Jäger, Gerhard
2002 Some notes on the formal properties of bidirectional optimality theory. *Journal of Logic, Language and Information* 11: 427–451.
Jäger, Gerhard
2004 Learning constraint sub-hierarchies. The bidirectional gradual learning Algorithm. In *Pragmatics and Optimality Theory*, Reinhard Blutner and Henk Zeevat (eds.). Houndmills / Basingstoke / Hampshire: Palgrave / Macmillan.
Jakobson, Roman
1941/68 *Child Language, Aphasia and Phonological Universals*. The Hague: Mouton.
Jaszczolt, Katarzyna M.
to appear Semantics and pragmatics: the boundary issue. In *Semantics: An International Handbook of Natural Language Meaning*, Claudia Maienborn, Klaus von Heusinger and Paul Portner (eds.). Berlin / New York: Mouton de Gruyter.
Joshi, Aravind K.
1987 Generation – a new frontier of natural language processing? *Theoretical Issues in Natural Language Processing* 3: 181–184.
Karabanov, Anke, Peter Bosch and Peter König
2007 Eye tracking as a tool for investigating the comprehension of referential expressions. In *Roots: Linguistics in search of its evidential base*, Sam Featherston and Wolfgang Sternefeld (eds.), 207–226. Berlin / New York: Mouton de Gruyter.
Karmiloff-Smith, Annette
1985 Language and cognitive processes from a developmental perspective. *Language and Cognitive Processes* 1 (1): 61–85.
Kertész, András and Csilla Rákosi (eds.)
2008 *New Approaches to Linguistic Evidence. Pilot Studies*, Vol. 22. Frankfurt: Lang.
Koster, Charlotte
1993 *Errors in Anaphora Acquisition.* Unpublished PhD dissertation, Utrecht University.
Krifka, Manfred
1995 The semantics and pragmatics of polarity items. *Linguistic Analysis* 25: 209–257.
Krifka, Manfred
2007 Approximate interpretation of number words: A case for strategic communication. In *Cognitive foundations of interpretation*, Gerlof Bouma, Irene Krämer and Joost Zwarts (eds.), 111–126. Amsterdam: Koninklijke Nederlandse Akademie van Wetenschapen.
Larsen-Freeman, Diane
2002 Making sense of frequency. *Studies in Second Language Acquisition* 24 (2): 275–285.

Lentz, Tom and Reinhard Blutner
2009 Signalling games: evolutionary convergence on optimality. In *Papers on Pragmasemantics. ZASPIL*, Vol. 51, 95–110. Berlin: Zentrum für allgemeine Sprachwissenschaft.

Levinson, Stephen
2000 *Presumptive meaning: The theory of generalized conversational implicature.* Cambridge, MA: MIT Press.

Logan, Gordon D.
1988 Toward an instance theory of automatization. *Psychological Review* 95: 492–527.

Mattausch, Jason
2004 *On the Optimization and Grammaticalization of Anaphora.* Unpublished PhD thesis, Humboldt University, Berlin.

McCawley, James D.
1978 Conversational implicature and the lexicon. In *Syntax and Semantics 9: Pragmatics*, Peter Cole (ed.), 245–259. New York: Academic Press.

McKee, Cecile
1992 A Comparison of pronouns and anaphors in Italian and English acquisition. *Language Acquisition* 2: 21–54.

Morgan, Jerry L.
1978 Two types of convention in indirect speech acts. In *Pragmatics* (*Syntax and Semantics* 9), Peter Cole (ed.), 261–280. New York: Academic Press.

Noveck, Ira
2001 When children are more logical than adults. *Cognition* 78: 165–188.

Noveck, Ira A. and Daniel Sperber (eds.)
2005 *Experimental Pragmatics.* Houndmills / Basingstoke / Hampshire: Palgrave / MacMillan.

Perner, Josef, Sue R. Leekam and Heinz Wimmer
1987 Three-year olds' difficulty with false belief: the case for a conceptual deficit. *British Journal of Developmental Psychology* 5: 125–137.

Prince, Alan and Paul Smolensky
1991 Notes on Connectionism and Harmony Theory in Linguistics, *Technical Report*: Department of Computer Science, University of Colorado, Boulder.

Russell, Benjamin
2006 Against grammatical computation of scalar implicatures. *Journal of Semantics* 23: 361–382.

Sæbø, Kjell Johan
2004 Optimal interpretations of permission sentences. In *Proceedings of the 5th Tbilisi Symposium on Language, Logic and Computation*, Dick de Jongh and Paul Dekker (eds.), 137–144). Amsterdam and Tbilisi.

Sandt, Rob van der
1992 Presupposition projection as anaphora resolution. *Journal of Semantics* 9: 333–377.
Sauerland, Ulli
2004 Scalar implicatures in complex sentences. *Linguistics and Philosophy* 27: 367–391.
Schneider, Walter and Richard M. Shiffrin
1977 Controlled and automatic human information processing. *Psychological Review* 84 (1): 1–66.
Smolensky, Paul
1996 On the comprehension/production dilemma in child language. *Linguistic Inquiry* 27: 720–731.
Smolensky, Paul and Géraldine Legendre
2006 *The Harmonic Mind: From neural computation to optimality-theoretic grammar.* Cambridge, MA: MIT Press.
Soames, Scott
1982 How presuppositions are inherited: A solution to the projection problem. *Linguistic Inquiry* 13: 483–545.
Spenader, Jennifer, Erik-Jan Smits and Petra Hendriks.
2007 *Coherent discourse solves the Pronoun Interpretation Problem.* Unpublished manuscript, University of Groningen.
Sperber, Dan, Francisco Cara and Vittorio Girotto
1995 Relevance theory explains the selection task. *Cognition* 57: 31–95.
Sperber, Dan and Deirdre Wilson
1986/95 *Relevance.* Oxford: Basil Blackwell.
Spohn, Wolfgang
1993 Wie kann die Theorie der Rationalität normativ und empirisch zugleich sein? In *Ethik und Empirie. Zum Zusammenspiel von begrifflicher Analyse und erfahrungswissenschaftlicher Forschung in der Ethik*, Lutz Eckensberger and Ulli Gähde (eds.), 151–196. Frankfurt a.M.: Suhrkamp.
Stalnaker, Robert
2006 Saying and meaning, cheap talk and credibility. In *Game Theory and Pragmatics*, Anton Benz, Gerhard Jäger and Robert Van Rooij (eds.), 82–101. Houndmills/Basingstoke/Hampshire: Palgrave/Macmillan.
Traugott, Elisabeth
1989 On the Rise of Epistemic Meanings in English: An Example of Subjectification in Semantic Change. *Language* 65 (1): 31–55.
Traugott, Elisabeth and Richard B. Dasher
2005 *Regularity in Semantic Change.* Cambridge: Cambridge University Press.
Unsworth, Sharon
2005 *Child L2, Adult L2, Child L1: Differences and Similarities.* Unpublished PhD Dissertation, Utrecht University.

Van Rooy, Robert
2004 Signalling games select Horn strategies. *Linguistics and Philosophy* 27: 493–527.

Wilson, Deidre
2003 Relevance and Lexical Pragmatics. *Italian Journal of Linguistics/ Rivista di Linguistica* 15 (2): 273–291.

Wilson, Deirdre and Tomoko Matsui
1998 Recent approaches to bridging: Truth, coherence, relevance. *UCL Working Papers in Linguistics* 10: 173–200.

Zeevat, Henk
1999 Explaining presupposition triggers. *Proceedings of the 12th Amsterdam Colloquium, ILLC, Amsterdam*, 19–24.

Zeevat, Henk
2000 The asymmetry of optimality theoretic syntax and semantics. *Journal of Semantics* 17: 243–262.

Zeevat, Henk
2002 Explaining presupposition triggers. In *Information Sharing*, Kees van Deemter and Rodger Kibble (eds.), 61–87. Stanford: CSLI Publications.

Zeevat, Henk
2007 *Optimal Interpretation as an Alternative to Gricean Pragmatics* Unpublished manuscript, Universiteit van Amsterdam.

Zwarts, Joost
2003 Lexical Competition: 'Round' in English and Dutch. In *Proceedings of the Fourteenth Amsterdam Colloquium*, Paul Dekker and Robert van Rooy (eds.), 229–234). Amsterdam: ILLC.

Zwarts, Joost
2006 Om en rond: Een semantische vergelijking. *Nederlandse Taalkunde,* 11 (2): 101–123.

Part Three

Pragmatic ways from words to constructions and utterances

The cognitive background of grammaticalization

Katalin Nagy C.

1. Introduction

1.1. Background

Semantic change in grammaticalization has been the topic of several studies in historical pragmatics (cf. Hopper and Traugott 1993; Traugott 1999; Bybee 2002; Traugott and Dasher [2002] 2004; Fortson 2003; Heine 2003). On the basis of historical data, various "cognitive paths" have been identified along which meanings evolve in different languages of the world (cf. Bybee et al. 1994; Heine and Kuteva 2002; Traugott and Dasher 2004). It is well known, for instance, that future markers frequently develop from lexical items originally meaning 'motion' or 'intention' (cf. Bybee 2002: 181; Bybee et al. 1994: 243–280). It seems to be obvious that the process whereby a certain lexical unit or construction undergoes grammaticalization presupposes some reorganization in its semantic structure. One of the main tasks of historical pragmatics is to examine the dynamism of such a process.

Semantic change in grammaticalization is an authentic semantics–pragmatics interface phenomenon. Various historical pragmaticians (Hopper and Traugott 1993; Traugott 1999; Diewald 2002; Heine 2002; Bybee 2003; Detges 2004; Traugott and Dasher 2004) agree that it is a pragmatically motivated process. Semantic and contextual information interact in the composition of utterance meaning, and due to its dynamism, contents which are originally context-dependent, become context-free. That is, from a historical pragmatics point of view, semantic change in grammaticalization develops at the semantics–pragmatics interface inasmuch as originally pragmatic contents become semantic, that is, coded contents. Investigating such a phenomenon can also provide us with useful pieces of information about the nature of this interface. If we accept the gradualness of semantic change in grammaticalization (cf. Bybee et al. 1994: 106; Bybee 2007), we have to reject the idea that there would be a sharp distinction between semantics and pragmatics.

The context of use is a major factor in the process of how the coded meaning of lexical items and constructions changes over time, and various authors have argued that semantic change in grammaticalization involves a process of conventionalization of particularized conversational implicatures emerging in contexts where the lexical item undergoing grammaticalization is frequently used (Hopper and Traugott 1993; Traugott 1999; Levinson 2000; Kearns 2002; Traugott and Dasher 2004). Traugott's (1999; cf. also Traugott and Dasher 2004: 38) "invited inferencing model" describes how particularized conversational implicatures (in her term: *invited inferences*), arising in particular contexts become part of the coded meaning of a lexeme.[1] Let us see the initial and the final stage of the model:

$$\begin{array}{lll} \text{Initial stage:} & \qquad & \text{Final stage:} \\ \text{lexeme} \rightarrow \text{meaning}_1 & & \text{lexeme} \rightarrow \text{meaning}_1 + \text{meaning}_2 \\ \qquad\qquad \updownarrow & & \qquad\qquad \updownarrow \qquad\qquad \updownarrow \\ \qquad\qquad C_a & & \qquad\qquad C_a \qquad\qquad C_b \end{array}$$

As Traugott describes, at the initial stage the coded meaning of a lexeme is linked to a conceptual structure (C). The original meaning can disappear or survive, and the old and new meanings can coexist side by side (*layering*). The emergence of new meanings presupposes that somehow and somewhere changes should have taken place in the conceptual structure of the lexeme. The model describes pragmatic inferencing in particular contexts as the driving force of such a process. During the process of semantic change, invited inferences conventionalize as generalized invited inferences (at the level of utterance-type meaning) and, finally, enter the coded meaning. According to Traugott's view, one of the main driving forces of semantic change is pragmatic inferencing (cf. Hopper and Traugott 1993; Traugott 1999; Kearns 2002). In a recent work (Nagy C. 2010) I have discussed two ways of how new abstract meanings can emerge in grammaticalization:

---

1 "The prime objective of IITSC [= Invited Inferencing Theory of Semantic Change] is to account for the conventionalizing of pragmatic meanings and their reanalysis as semantic meanings. Differently put, historically there is a path from coded meanings to utterance-token meanings to utterance-type, pragmatically polysemous meanings to new semantically polysemous (coded) meanings." (Traugott and Dasher 2004: 35)

(i) through the conventionalization of semantic content originating in the context as particularized conversational implicature and,
(ii) as part of the process where a certain semantic component within the semantic structure of a lexical item becomes salient compared to the others.

As I have mentioned above, the first way is widely discussed in historical pragmatics literature. However, the new meaning cannot always be traced back to implicatures that arise in a particular context. As the second way indicates, the salience of a certain semantic component within the semantic structure of a lexical item also influences the way in which abstract meanings emerge. This occurs when the semantic component in question originally forms part of the semantic structure of the lexeme which undergo grammaticalization, and it becomes salient in certain contexts of use due to the implicatures which arise in that context. That is, the salience of a certain element and the reorganization of semantic structure are influenced by pragmatic inferencing in particular contexts as well. In other words, beyond the fact that implicatures can become part of the semantic meaning of a certain form they can also promote the salience of a certain meaning component within the meaning of a lexeme and influence its conceptual reorganization.

To sum up, linguistic units under grammaticalization gain new meanings and become compatible with several new pragmatic functions (*pragmatic strengthening*). The cognitive background of these new pragmatic functions should be the reorganization in the semantic structure of the grammaticalizing item. Without any changes in its semantic structure, it would not be possible that a particular linguistic unit fulfills new functions and its use extends to new contexts. However, we need a methodology to trace how these processes presumably take place. However, this is far from being simple. Do we have the appropriate means to reconstruct the cognitive background of semantic change in grammaticalization? Historical pragmatics, which aims to learn of hardly accessible aspects of meaning, has to face the data problem which consists in how to obtain enough and reliable data. Methodological questions are present in every area of current linguistics, and current metalinguistic discussion also addresses issues concerning data, evidence, methods and argumentation in linguistic research (cf. Kepser and Reis 2005; Penke and Rosenbach 2007; Kertész and Rákosi 2008). Methodological considerations have been dealt with in historical pragmatics from the beginning (cf. Jacobs and Jucker 1995; Jucker 1994) and Fitzmaurice and Taavitsainen (2007) also regard the future of historical pragmatics as determined by methodological issues. They believe that

> "a step forward can be taken by raising the level of awareness of methodological problems. This can be done by explicit discussions on what and how methods are applied, what their limitations are, and what can be done in the future. We can learn more about data, be more systematic in contextual analysis, ask questions about the reliability of our sources and consider their special restrictions". (Fitzmaurice and Taavitsainen 2007: 29)

The research question and the perspective of the study determine what types of data historical pragmaticians use. Semantic change in grammaticalization can be viewed from two perspectives. First, the "beginning" of semantic change, that is, the innovation can only be imagined in particular pragmatic circumstances where conversational implicatures arise according to speakers' intentions. Second, the "expansion" of the innovation can last centuries and is influenced by cognitive factors which are independent of individual speakers' intentions. A comparison of developments of lexemes with similar meanings in different languages of the world outlines several "cognitive paths" along which meanings usually evolve. Both innovation and the expansion of the innovative use offer perspectives on the cognitive background of semantic change. On the one hand, since semantic change in grammaticalization requires specific contexts to take place, cognitive factors can be studied through the examination of contexts in which pragmatic meanings emerge. At an early stage, constructions undergoing grammaticalization may induce associations and inferences which later attach to them in a context in which they are frequently used (Hopper and Traugott 1993: 75–77; Traugott 2003: 634–635). Studies which deal with this aspect of semantic change use data from different historical states of a certain language with the aim of determining when and how the innovation occurred, and of observing how the meaning of the grammaticalizing item changes during the course of centuries. On the other hand, if we want to account for mechanisms of semantic change, we need to look for its cognitive basis and reveal the interrelations between different conceptual domains form the point of view of language history. Studies with this perspective use data from different languages, comparing paths of semantic change in them in order to find common features of semantic development, which are assigned to the nature of the human cognitive system. Data for the study of a particular linguistic change can also come from the comparison of similar historical processes that have taken place in other languages, that is, the cognitive paths of semantic change can provide data for the investigation of other grammaticalization processes (cf. Heine 2003: 580, 585).

1.2. The aims and structure of the paper

Providing a historical pragmatics study, the present paper has a dual aim: on the one hand, it intends to reconstruct a part of the history of the Catalan "*anar* 'go' + infinitive" construction. On the other hand, it discusses methodological issues of historical pragmatics research concerning the role of context. The first aim of the paper is realized through the comparison of the use of formally and functionally similar periphrases in their broad contexts in medieval Spanish and Catalan. In doing so, we have to deal with methodological problems concerning the data we can use for assigning meanings in historical texts. Therefore, as an additional goal, the present paper intends to examine the role of context in studying the cognitive background of semantic change in grammaticalization, regarding contextual analysis the most important device of historical pragmatics methodology.

The organization of the paper is as follows. After the present Introduction, section 2 deals with methodological issues, with special attention to the role of context in grammaticalization and contextual analysis. Section 3 introduces a study at the semantics–pragmatics interface, namely, the grammaticalization of the Catalan "*anar* 'go' + infinitive". The occurrences of "*anar* 'go' + infinitive" will be compared with occurrences of a medieval Spanish GO-construction and other, functionally similar medieval periphrases ("THINK OF + infinitive" and "BEGIN TO/OF + infinitive"), in order to obtain additional data about its semantic development. Section 4 discusses some relevant linguistic clues which can help us to assign meaning to historical occurrences. Section 5 offers a comparison of the use of the three periphrases considered, providing further evidence of the conceptual affinity of "GO + infinitive" and "THINK OF + infinitive". Section 6 summarizes the conclusions of the paper.

2. The role of context in grammaticalization research

2.1. Contextual analysis as a method in historical pragmatics

Historical pragmatics research on changes in semantic structures raises the methodological question of how we can reveal the dynamism of the process. From a methodological point of view, the two aspects of semantic change, that is, the innovation and the change itself can hardly be separated. This is due to the fact that, in practice, we have only one method to investigate changes in earlier periods: examining the particular written utterances as they occur in historical texts. First, we have to explore meaning nuances in historical texts considering several historical occurrences, and, then, to draw conclusions concerning where they come from. However, in order to reveal semantic nuances we need a sensitive contextual analysis. Only contextual analysis can shed light on changes in semantic structure. The description of changes in the semantic structure is closely linked to the description of contexts in which the grammaticalizing linguistic item is used (cf. Heine's (2002) "switch context", which he considers to be "an interaction of context and conceptualization", see before). In order to capture the innovation phase of semantic change, we have to examine historical utterances in context in order to reveal pragmatic inferencing and find out where the new meaning could come from. Universal tendencies of meaning developments in languages of the world can be explored by checking the meanings of a certain lexeme and of its later corresponding forms in several different stages of the history of the language. However, this method also presupposes a previous micro-analysis of the meanings in particular contexts of each language state. Therefore, we should conclude that the investigation of contexts is a prerequisite for any kind of historical pragmatics investigation.

2.2. Contexts of semantic change in grammaticalization

Semantic change can be conceived of as a change of contexts in which a certain linguistic construction can be used. Context has a dual character from the point of view of historical pragmatics. On the one hand, both coded and contextual information is involved in the composition of utterance meaning, and in this sense context triggers semantic change: the meaning of linguistic constructions changes in and due to ordinary language use in context. On the other hand, the occurrence or non-occurrence of a certain linguistic construction in a certain context in historical documents can provide data about the process of semantic change. In other words, historical occurrences in certain types of context can evidence a previous semantic change. The nature of contexts in which particular stages of semantic change processes can be detected has been the topic of some papers on grammaticalization (Diewald 2002; Heine 2002). Context is conceived of in Heine's (2002: 87) work as "the crucial factor in shaping new grammatical meanings". Some general pathways of meaning change in grammaticalization are widely known and accepted in historical pragmatics. However, the need for investigating the intermediate stages is also recognized. Heine (2002: 83) emphasizes that "without a more comprehensive understanding of the nature of these intermediate stages, generalizations on the overall process must remain preliminary".

Heine (2002) provides a scenario of grammaticalization, distinguishing between three different kinds of context. The first stage in Heine's scenario is "bridging context", which triggers an inferential mechanism to the effect that a new, more plausible interpretation is possible, different from the old, lexical meaning. However, this new meaning is still cancelable, and the old meaning can also be assigned. The following stage is the "switch context stage". Switch contexts are incompatible with some salient property of the source meaning, and the new meaning is the only possible interpretation in them. The third stage is conventionalization, when the new meaning no longer needs to be supported by context. At this stage, the grammaticalizing item can be used in new contexts, which are different from the bridging and switch contexts. "Conventionalization contexts can contradict or violate the source semantics" (Heine 2002: 85). Heine discusses the process of conventionalization of implicatures from the point of view of contexts, intending to reveal what types of contexts can be associated with what stage of this process. Cancelability shows whether the meaning is context-dependent or already independent of context. Heine focuses especially on switch contexts because he considers them to be responsible for the process of meaning change in grammaticalization. At this stage, the rise of a new grammatical meaning is due to an interaction of context and conceptualization. Heine regards switch context as "a filtering device that rules out the source meaning" (Heine 2002: 86).

Diewald (2002) also deals with contexts in grammaticalization, and her model is based on morphological and structural factors more strongly than Heine's (2002) model. She also proposes three successive stages in grammaticalization that are associated with three different types of contexts. First, a lexical unit gets to be used in contexts where it has not been used before. These are called "untypical contexts" in Diewald's model, and in them the new meaning may arise as a conversational implicature. The second type, the "critical context" is characterized by multiple semantic and structural ambiguities, and the new meaning presents itself in it as a possible interpretation among others. Critical context triggers inferencing procedures, because "there is no way to process this structure in a routinized way" (Diewald 2002: 112), that is, conversational implicatures are needed to create a meaningful utterance. Third, the new meaning is isolated as a separate meaning in what is called "isolating contexts" that favor one reading to the exclusion of the other. Isolating contexts exist for each competing interpretation in a certain language state. In these contexts the semanticization of these meanings can be said to have been completed.

Two points should be underlined. First, we can distinguish between two main types of contexts. The first group contains Heine's bridging context and Diewald's untypical and critical contexts. These contexts trigger grammaticalization, because the old meaning is only one of the possible interpretations in them and a new meaning can also be assigned. Ambiguity is always a necessary stage of meaning change if we investigate it in concrete contexts. The other type includes Heine's switch and conventionalization contexts and some of Diewald's isolating contexts, which favor the new reading and exclude the old, lexical meaning. These are more important from a methodological point of view, because they can serve as evidence of a previous meaning change. In other words, their existence presupposes a previous reorganization of the semantic structure of the grammaticalizing lexical item. To put it differently, although Heine and Diewald consider the use of lexical items in contexts as a triggering device in grammaticalization, there are types of context which provide a methodological clue as well: if we find an occurrence in a certain type of context (Heine's switch and conventionalization contexts and Diewald's isolation context if it isolates the new meaning), we can conclude at which stage of development the grammaticalizing unit may be. We have to base our analysis on contexts which favor or disregard one meaning in opposition with another one.

Second, in order to investigate semantic change in historical context, we should be able to assign meanings to historical occurrences and to determine what kind of context we have. For example, Heine's switch context is incompatible with some salient property of the source meaning, and the conventionalization context contradicts or violates the source semantics. However, in order to reveal such incompatibilities and contradictions, we have to know what the meaning of the lexical items is in that context. That is, in any case, the analysis of semantic change presupposes the researcher's knowledge of the semantics of the linguistic units which are present in the historical contexts. We have to check (i) whether the new interpretation is possible or not, (ii) whether it is the only possible reading or one possible interpretation, and (iii) whether the new meaning is context dependent, i.e. arising as a conversational implicature or already independent of context. We should minimize the subjectivity in assigning meanings and base our analysis on possible linguistic clues (see below in section 4).

How do we know what interpretations of a construction are possible in a certain language state and whether there are context dependent or coded meanings? The methods applied in Diewald (2002) offer a possible answer. Examining the development of German modal verbs, Diewald (2002) analyzes the interpretation of what she considers a highly ambiguous construction, because if the wider linguistic context is disregarded, it can be interpreted in at least three ways. How does Diewald know that these three readings are actually accessible at the language state under study? She argues that "this can be concluded from the fact that there are instances of the critical context in Middle High German where, due to contextual disambiguation, only one of the three alternative interpretations is possible, while the other two are excluded" (Diewald 2002: 110). She also maintains that if there are disambiguating contexts for various possible readings, it is justified to regard the construction as an ambiguous structure in the sense defined with these possible readings. The wider context, which provides further information, disambiguates the construction. But how can we determine which one is the default (or preferred) reading? Default interpretations are those that we assign for lack of wider context, that is, further contextual clues. In order to determine it, Diewald intends to reconstruct chains of pragmatic inferences which result in a certain reading. She considers the preferred reading as one which is accessible through more than one chain of inferences with different starting points, and she also uses data about the further development of the construction. Diewald's method highlights the fact that it is not enough to consider only one context, but several contexts have to be taken into account together in which the construction under investigation can occur at a certain language state.

2.3. Conceptions of context

Only a deep analysis of contexts can highlight the particular steps in meaning change processes. But what do we mean by contextual analysis? Context can be conceived of in several ways. Let us examine the definition of "critical context" in Diewald (2002). As I have mentioned above, Diewald's critical context is characterized by multiple semantic and structural ambiguities, and the new meaning presents itself in it as one of the possible interpretations. But how do we know what reading has to be preferred in critical contexts? Diewald characterizes the attribution of meanings in the following way: "A reading (…) is excluded not because the critical context would not allow it, but because of further contextual factors" (Diewald 2002: 111). According to this wording, critical context only includes a narrow passage, perhaps the clause which contains the morphological construction itself, but "further contextual factors", which presumably are clues capable of disambiguating the meaning, do not belong to it. Consequently, Diewald's wording implies two types of contexts: a narrow context ("critical context") and a wider one ("further contextual factors").

Another narrow conception of context appears when we examine what types of verbs can occur in a certain construction (cf. Bybee 2003). In the grammaticalization process whereby new, abstract meanings evolve, it can be observed that the grammaticalizing unit gradually extends to be used with more and more types of verbs and subjects. The final stage of this process is when all types of verbs or subjects can enter the construction, without any constraint. There is no doubt about the importance of considering the combinational possibilities of the grammaticalizing item, since quantitative data concerning these aspects of the process inform us about semantic development, and frequency analyses are indispensable in historical pragmatics (cf. Bybee 2003, 2005). It is reasonable to apply this method working with a large corpus, when it is not possible to check the larger context of each example. However, it is not sufficient to take into account only the narrow context, because it does not provide enough information to determine what meaning a certain lexical unit expresses. Furthermore, the exclusive use of quantitative data is likely to result in a misguided analysis of semantic change in grammaticalization. Consequently, we have to use further data and to examine historical occurrences in their broad contexts. Navarro (2008: 14–16) points out that, in historical pragmatics, quantitative analysis should be complemented with qualitative research, and considers the "quali-quantitative" method, that is, one which combines qualitative and quantitative approaches, the most appropriate method, with more reliable results. The quantitative method helps us to avoid the problems which subjectivity and introspection cause, and, at the same time, with the qualitative method we can learn about those aspects of meaning which are hardly accessible on the basis of quantitative data.

I have discussed above (in section 2.2) Diewald's (2002) method, which takes into account several contexts together in which the construction under investigation can occur at a certain language state. This method implies a broad conception of context: we consider each example in the broad perspective of the whole language state and consider more occurrences together. Traugott and Dasher (2004) also try to determine what inferencing mechanisms may be supposed to be at work at a certain historical period. They investigate how we know when an invited inference (IIN = conversational implicature) is beginning to be exploited.

> "This must always be a matter of interpretation, on the assumption that IINs are cross-linguistic. Sometimes an IIN may be inferred because the later history by hypothesis requires an earlier stage in which the IIN has operated, but we must always exercise utmost care in projecting such IINs on the textual data. As a working principle, as long as the original coded

> meaning is accessible, we should assume that the invited inference is just that, a meaning derivable from the semantics in combination with the discourse context. In written records, clear evidence of semanticization of a polysemy typically comes from the appearance of an item in a "new" context in which the earlier meaning(s) of the item would not make sense. At a later time the older meaning may or may not disappear; if it does, this is further confirmation of the earlier coding of the former pragmatically invited inference." (Traugott and Dasher 2004: 44)

Traugott and Dasher's (2004) method requires an even broader context for the investigation of historical occurrences: the context of the further history of a construction can weaken hypotheses about earlier stages of development or make them more plausible.

In the present paper I distinguish between two types of contexts: narrow and broad contexts. Narrow and broad conceptions of context are not unknown in pragmatic research. Inspired by Relevance Theory, Bibok and Németh T. (2001) also establish two types of contexts: *immediate context* and *extended context*. By the immediate context of a word they mean the remaining part of the utterance under investigation, that is, the utterance itself in which the lexical item under study occurs (Bibok and Németh T. 2001: 307; cf. also Bibok 2004: 300). The utterance context can be extended with the help of three types of information: (i) with information from the immediately observable physical environment, (ii) with information from preceding discourse, and (iii) by adding encyclopedic information (Bibok and Németh T. 2001: 300). Determining the utterance borders is not easy in synchronic pragmatics (cf. Németh T. 1994), but in historical studies it is even more difficult because of the absence of punctuation in early texts. Therefore, in historical research, a slightly different conception of contexts is necessary. Because of this I use the terms narrow context and broad context in this paper. In this historical study, a narrow context must be defined grammatically, as a part of the text which corresponds to a sentence or a clause, containing one finite verb, that is, it can be shorter than an utterance.[2] A narrow context shows which infinitives can co-occur in the construction with the grammaticalizing item, but it can also contain other lexemes (e.g. nouns or adverbs) which help to assign meaning to the utterance. To sum up, the main difference between Bibok and Németh T.'s (2001) immediate context and narrow context is that narrow context is grammatically defined and can be shorter than an utterance.

2 In the present investigation this finite verb is the finite verb form of the lexeme under study. In other studies another conception of narrow context would be necessary, which also allows for contexts which do not contain a finite verb.

The concept of the broad context mainly coincides with that of extended context in Bibok and Németh T. (2001). However, a broad context adds information to a narrow context not only from preceding discourse, but also from subsequent utterances. This is possible because the present definitions of contexts do not only want to serve for describing the composition of utterance meaning, but also for contextual analysis as an investigation method in historical pragmatics. Therefore, from the point of view of the content I define the broad context as a coherent passage of the historical text. Its length can vary at different occasions. The broad context includes sentences or clauses which precede or follow the occurrence of the lexical unit under investigation, and also contain information from the physical environment and the encyclopedic information of concepts and inferences present in the context. The term *context* does not refer exclusively to textual circumstances. The physical context cannot be reconstructed, but we have encyclopedic information about the circumstances of the production of historical texts. Furthermore, taking into account the broad context, we can infer the presence of pragmatic inferences which form part of the cognitive context.

The question arises to what extent the context should be broadened. The consideration of a broadened context can override our preliminary assumptions about the meaning of a certain construction, formed on the basis of its narrow context. In some cases, it already occurs with the inclusion of only one further utterance. In other cases, the interpretation survives in the broad context and remains the same as was in the narrow context. It is not worth broadening further the context when a new, independent passage begins which is not supposed to modify the interpretation. That is, this method is based on semantic factors, and the evaluation of the particular cases requires a qualitative analysis and the subjective judgment of the researcher. The consideration of broad contexts can serve as a basis to determine the meaning, the most plausible reading of a historical occurrence, and it can also change the previous interpretation and influence how we conceptualize the event described in the utterance.

3. A study at the interface of semantics and pragmatics

3.1. Universal tendencies of development of GO-constructions: the Catalan "*anar* 'go' + infinitive" and the Spanish "*ir (a)*[3] 'go (to)' + infinitive"

In the following sections I illustrate the above considerations through a historical case study concerning the initial stage of the grammaticalization of the Catalan "*anar* 'go' + infinitive" (*infinitive* hereafter abbreviated as

Inf) construction, comparing it with a similar GO-construction in medieval Spanish, namely, "*ir (a)* + Inf". The Catalan verb *anar* and the Spanish *ir* encode the same concept 'go'. The formal difference of the infinitives *anar* and *ir* is due to the peculiar history of these Romance verbs. Both are suppletive verbs whose different forms derive from several distinct Latin verbs. In the paradigm of the Catalan *anar* 'go', the stems *va-* (< VADERE) and *an-* (< *ANDARE) can be traced, although in some archaic and dialectal future and conditional forms the stem *ir-* (< IRE) also appears. The paradigm of the Spanish *ir* 'go' contains forms based on three different verbal stems: *i-* (< IRE), *va-* (< VADERE) and *fu-* (< ESSE) (for more details, see Juge 1999 and Moll 2006: 224–225). As a result, the paradigms of the modern Catalan and Spanish verbs meaning 'go' show some formal differences, however, most of the present indicative forms of the full verb and those of the auxiliary are based on the verbal stem *va-* (< VADERE) in both languages, as Table 1 shows:

Table 1. Paradigms of the Catalan *anar* and Spanish *ir*

the Catalan auxiliary *anar* and full verb *anar* 'go'		the Spanish auxiliary *ir* and full verb *ir* 'go'
preterit auxiliary	'go'	
1SG *vaig (vàreig)*	1SG *vaig*	1SG *voy*
2SG *vas (vares)*	2SG *vas*	2SG *vas*
3SG *va*	3SG *va*	3SG *va*
1PL *vam (vàrem/vem)*	1PL *anem*	1PL *vamos*
2PL *vau (vàreu/veu)*	2PL *aneu*	2PL *vais*
3PL *van (varen)*	3PL *van*	3PL *van*

[3] The use of the preposition *a* 'to' was optional in the medieval Spanish "*ir (a)* 'go (to)' + Inf" construction, but it is obligatory in the modern Spanish immediate future "*ir a* + Inf". However, as one of the reviewers of the manuscript of the present paper has pointed out, in the modern Spanish "*ir a* + Inf" construction the preposition *a* is sometimes ommitted in colloquial use. I indicate the optionality of the preposition in the medieval Spanish construction with the use of parenthesis. In the Catalan texts there are only a few occurrences where the verb 'go' and the infinitive are linked together with the preposition *a* 'to'. However, in all of them the finite verb seems to convey its lexical meaning of motion, that is, they are not periphrastic uses.

Before presenting the historical study, let us consider some present day Spanish and Catalan data concerning the current use of these GO-constructions in the two languages. When Spanish grammars describe "*ir a* + Inf", the semantic nuance of conveying futurity is mentioned in the first place. Therefore, I follow the tradition of referring to this construction as the *immediate future*, however, it can express several other shades of meaning as well, similarly to other morphemes of future tense in languages of the world. The Spanish immediate future is formed with auxiliary forms that have the verb *ir* 'go' as a source. Currently, there are no restrictions on what verbs can appear in the construction. The construction "*ir a* + Inf" does not only have a periphrastic use of immediate future, but in some cases the verb *ir* 'go' retains its full lexical meaning of motion. In its grammaticalized use, beyond conveying futurity, the construction suggests an emotional involvement of the subject or the speaker in the event, and it is strongly linked to the situation which holds at the moment of the utterance (Matte Bon 1998; Bauhr 1989). Gómez Torrego (1988: 66–75) attributes the following values to this periphrasis: immediate future, potential modality, inchoative aspect and intentional modality. In contrast to the simple future (1), the immediate future (2) describes the event as inherent and a natural consequence of the situation which exists at the moment of the utterance.

(1) *Moriré.*
'I will die.' (some day, like everybody)

(2) *Estoy seguro de que* ***voy*** ***a morir.***
AUX.1SG.PRES[4] to die.INF
'I am sure **I am going to die**.' (soon, I feel, for instance because I am ill)

In contrast to the Spanish "*ir (a)* + Inf", the Catalan GO-construction, "*anar* 'go' + Inf", evolved into a past tense. The construction "*anar* + Inf" is used to express a perfective past meaning in modern Catalan:[5]

[4] The following abbreviations are used in the glosses throughout this paper: 1 – first person, 2 – second person, 3 – third person, AUX – auxiliary, CLIT – clitic, IMPP – imperfect past tense, INF – infinitive, NEG – negative particle, PL – plural, PRES – present tense, PERFP – perfect past tense, REFL – reflexive pronoun, SG – singular.

[5] In spoken Catalan, the simple preterit is only used in Valencia and some parts of the Baleares, while the periphrastic preterit is the preferred form in the rest of the Catalan dialects. In these dialects the simple past is reserved only for literary purposes (Badia i Margarit 1995: 546–548; cf. also Juge 2006). In the

(3) *Pere II* ***va*** ***morir*** *l'any 1285.*
AUX.3SG.PRES die.INF
'Pere II **died** in 1285.'

This Catalan periphrastic perfective past is formed with auxiliary forms that have the verb *anar* 'go' as a source. Currently, there are no restrictions on what verbs can appear in the construction.[6] The verb *anar* 'go', without infinitive, continues to be used also as a full lexical verb. Although in modern Catalan the paradigms of the full lexical verb and of the auxiliary *anar* almost coincide, they are divergent from each other in some forms.[7] In opposition with the Spanish construction, in the Catalan "*anar* + Inf" the auxiliary *anar* cannot express the full lexical meaning 'go'. In order to refer to a real motion with the aim of doing something, the preposition *a* 'to' should be used: "*anar a* 'go to' + Inf". However, in the "*anar a* 'go to' + Inf" construction the verb *anar* 'go' can only be interpreted as expressing the lexical meaning of motion, and not as referring to futurity, past or any other abstract meaning. In modern Catalan, the use of "*anar a* + Inf" in present tense, if the verb *anar* does not refer to motion but to futurity or intention, is considered a Castellanism and is disallowed in normative language use (Badia i Margarit 1995: 615).

GO-constructions are the starting points of the formation of several different abstract, grammatical meanings in the languages of the world. In them the verb meaning 'go' loses its full lexical meaning of motion and becomes an auxiliary. The *World lexicon of grammaticalization* (Heine and Kuteva 2002) lists several abstract meanings which can evolve from the meaning GO in the languages of the world. However, the different meanings evolve in different constructions. The GO-construction considered in the present study is "GO (TO) + Inf". In its origins, it is a purposive construction, which refers to a motion with the aim of carrying out a certain

Algherese, the Catalan dialect spoken in the city of *Alghero* (Sardinia, Italy), the simple past perfect has been replaced by the present perfect, instead of the periphrastic GO-perfect, possibly due to Italian influence (cf. Scala 2003: 57; Perea 2007).

6 Pérez Saldanya (1996: 101–102) claims that the modern Catalan "*anar* + Inf" construction cannot be used with the verb *deure* 'must', but Juge (2002) provides evidence to the contrary.

7 Cf. the 1Pl-*anem* and 2Pl-*aneu* of the full lexical verb *anar* 'go', the 1Pl-*vem* and 2Pl-*veu* and the *var*- forms of the auxiliary. These latter were created by analogy, modeled on the regular preterit forms of a first conjugation verb (see Table 1, cf. Juge 2006).

act. Verbs meaning 'go' in such purposive constructions are typical sources of future markers in languages of the world. The cognitive path in (4) is one of the typical developmental routes of future markers:

(4) 'the motion path': motion with the aim of doing something > intention > future (Bybee 2002: 181; cf. also Bybee et al. 1994: 266–270)

The evolution of the Spanish GO-construction fits the schema in (4), so it is a typical representative of this universal tendency. In contrast, the development of the Catalan construction did not follow the typical pathway, thus it needs further investigation. In the present study, I intend to discuss the reorganization which may have taken place in the semantic structure of the verb 'go' in the Catalan construction and explain the semantic development of the construction in which it occurs. I argue that since the verb 'go' in the Spanish GO-construction "*ir (a)* 'go (to)' + Inf" followed a typical pathway, that is, it evolved into the auxiliary of a future tense in modern Spanish, a comparison of the origins of the Catalan and Spanish GO-constructions will be useful in order to reveal the grammaticalization of the Catalan "*anar* 'go' + Inf", which does not fit the schema presented in (4).

3.2. The medieval Catalan and Spanish GO-constructions

The medieval Catalan and Spanish languages both used a construction formed with GO. Compare the following medieval Catalan (5) and Spanish (6) examples.

(5) *Sobr.assó vengren-li bé X cavalers justats e* ***anaren**-lo*
go.3PL.PERFP-CLIT
ferir.
attack.INF
'10 knights on horseback came up to him and **went to attack/attacked** him.' (Desc II 43, 28)[8]

(6) *e **fueron-se** **ferir** asi fuerte mente deste pri`mero encuentro*
go.3PL.PERFP-CLIT attack.INF
que los cauallos & los caualleros fueron en tierra`(a) todos juntos
'at their first encounter, they **went to attack/attacked** each other so ferociously that both the horses and the knights fell to the ground together' (Tris 20v)

[8] The sources of the examples are abbreviated at the end of each example, with page and/or line numbers (full details of sources can be found at the end of the paper).

Examples (5) and (6) illustrate typical uses of the medieval Spanish and Catalan GO-constructions and reveal their similarity. Descriptions of battle scenes contain most of the utterances with these GO-periphrases, where they seem to fulfill a function of dynamification, intensifying and drawing the addressees' attention to the event in the story which the speaker considers to be the most important one. *Ferir* 'attack(/hit/wound)' is the most frequent verb in the earliest occurrences of this construction both in Spanish and Catalan. The similarity of contexts, functions, semantic nuances and morphological characteristics of the Catalan and the Spanish constructions in medieval texts demonstrates that they have a common origin.

The verb 'go' appears in the medieval Spanish and Catalan texts conjugated in either past or present tense. It should be noted that this construction has a version where the purposive preposition *a* 'to' appears between the finite verb 'go' and the infinitive. This version is very rare at the beginning, but later its use extends in Spanish. The presence of this preposition may have played a decisive role in the different evolutions the Catalan and Spanish constructions underwent later. However, in the present paper I do not consider this version separately, because I aim to account only for the initial stage of the grammaticalization of these two GO-constructions. At this stage, the Spanish construction seems to have the same meaning and the same functions as the Catalan construction, and both of them use the prepositional version only in very few examples, and occurrences with and without the preposition *a* 'to' seem to convey the same meaning.

3.3. Tense and aspect in the grammaticalization of the Catalan "*anar* 'go' + Inf"

The grammaticalization of the Catalan "*anar* 'go' + Inf" is not only a question of tense but also of aspect in two senses. On the one hand, it evolved into a perfective past in Catalan, in opposition with other Romance languages which have a similar periphrasis with future meaning. On the other hand, several authors agree that at an intermediate stage of its development into a perfective past tense, the verb 'go' of this Catalan periphrasis was an "aspectual auxiliary" (Pérez Saldanya 1996; Detges 2004). Badia i Margarit (1995: 646–647) characterizes the current Catalan "*anar* + Inf" as a tense which indicates perfective aspect and describes punctual events.[9] Where

[9] These forms actually do not only express tense but also aspect and mood. Juge (2006) adopts the term *tamcat* to refer to a set of forms with a given tense/aspect/mood combination.

can this perfective meaning come from? Describing the way future markers evolve in languages of the world, Bybee et al. (1994: 268) point out that in cases when a new future marker develops, "the overt or inherent aspect of the construction is progressive, present, or imperfective". The earliest medieval Catalan "*anar* 'go' + Inf" occurrences, in which the GO-verb is in a perfective past, do not fit this schema. This fact explains why this construction did not evolve into a future tense. The aspect of the infinitives which entered the periphrasis could also have a role in the semantic development of the whole construction. The present study does not aim to discuss the role of aspect in the later development of the construction: for more details see Colon (1978a), Juge (2008) and Nagy C. (2010).

The questions to be answered here are whether the medieval "*anar* 'go' + Inf" is an aspectual periphrasis or not, and if it is, what aspect it represents. In the literature about the Catalan GO-construction we can find two hypotheses concerning its aspectual value or semantic nuances. According to the first (Colon 1978a, 1978b), already the medieval occurrences express a past tense meaning. If we accept this hypothesis, we also have to believe that the grammaticalization of "*anar* 'go' + Inf" had taken place before, at an earlier stage, from which we do not have any documented data. However, a closer look at data in medieval Catalan chronicles reveals that occurrences of "*anar* 'go' + Inf" are not fully grammaticalized forms. We can conclude this from the following findings concerning the distribution of the construction. On the one hand, in contrast with the current use of "*anar* + Inf", its medieval occurrences are restricted to a limited number of contexts. On the other hand, certain verb types are missing and others predominate in the occurrences, which means a lower frequency, while in the current language state it can be used with any verb types, without any restriction, which also suppose a higher frequency. Furthermore, in uses of "*anar* 'go' + Inf" in the two chronicles considered in the present study, we can perceive a slight difference between their degree of grammaticalization. Desclot's Chronicle is almost half a century earlier than Muntaner's Chronicle and it reflects a less advanced stage of grammaticalization of the construction. All these considerations show that the Catalan "*anar* 'go' + Inf" in the Middle Ages did not have a past tense value as its coded meaning. Of course, this allows that past tense meaning could be inferred in contexts. To sum up, the first hypothesis, which claims that the earliest documented occurrences of "*anar* 'go' + Inf" already have a past tense value can be accepted only if it is not about a semanticized "past tense value", but about a past tense meaning which is present as a contextually implicated content.

According to the second hypothesis (Detges 2004), the medieval "*anar* 'go' + Inf" is an aspectual periphrasis, expressing inchoative meaning. The inchoative hypothesis is already mentioned in Colon (1978b: 156). He presents this view as a widely accepted one, and cites Meyer-Lübke (1890–1902: 357) as its source. However, Colon does not accept it. His more convincing argument is that there are several instances (not only in Catalan, but in French too), which combine the GO-periphrasis with the inchoative verb 'begin' (Catalan "*va començar* 'began' + Inf"). This goes against the hypothesis that "*anar* 'go' + Inf" in itself would express beginning. Colon (1978b: 159) assigns to "*anar* 'go' + Inf" the function of animating the story-telling, and not that of referring to the beginning of events: "After its concrete semantic content of a verb of motion has bleached, the verb *anar*, due to its dynamic character, has the only function of animating the story(telling) and not that of indicating the beginning or the end of an action chronologically" (my translation – K. N. C.). I accept Colon's arguments, and in the present paper I provide further evidence against the inchoative account. The inchoative hypothesis re-appears in Detges (2004: 213–215), where it is claimed that the "*anar* 'go' + Inf" in Old Catalan was a periphrasis with the aspectual meaning 'abrupt start'. Detges (2004) supposes that GO-constructions in various medieval Romance languages are representatives of the inchoative aspect. He offers a very detailed analysis about the semantic development of the Catalan GO-construction analyzing the process in several steps, which he considers to be independent from each other, emphasizing the role of discursive factors in it. In his scenario, inchoative aspect is the first stage in the development of the Catalan "*anar* 'go' + Inf". It expresses the beginning of an action or process, thus it can be paraphrased as 'begin to + Inf'. Inchoative constructions are compatible with durative verbs, which denote actions or processes characterizable with a time interval. Inchoative aspect signals the left starting point of this interval (Kiefer 2006: 169–170). As Detges (2004) describes, inchoative aspect suggests cognitive relevance and its use with such an aim is very common strategy in various languages of the world. He (Detges 2004: 214) mentions several instances of development of inchoative aspect markers from verbs denoting some kind of movement.[10] Detges (2004: 213) claims

---

[10] For instance, the following: the French *se mettre à faire qc.* 'start doing sg.' < 'sit down to do sg.'; the Italian *mettersi a fare qc.* 'start doing sg.' < 'sit down to do sg.'; the Spanish *ponerse a hacer algo* 'start doing sg.' < 'put oneself in a position to do sg.'; the English *start doing sg.* < Middle English *sterten* 'jump, leap'; the Latin *incipere* 'begin' and the German *anfangen* 'begin' < 'catch, grasp' (Detges 2004: 214).

that the "*anar* 'go' + Inf" construction is appropriate to express the inchoative aspect because the end of the motion and the beginning of the act, considered to be the aim of the motion, overlap in the real world, and its use instantiates the conceptual setting from MOVEMENT to BEGINNING. Due to this overlap, motion directs the attention to the proposed action itself. As described in Detges (2004), inchoative aspect is a considerable discourse-structuring device in the world's languages. The discourse-structuring nature of the Catalan GO-construction, conceived as inchoative by Detges, is the basis of the following step in its development, inasmuch as it serves as a rhetoric tool for emphasizing dramatic moments of a story (cf. also Pérez Saldanya 1996: 76). However, the first step of the analysis is the most important one, because if this is not correct, all the analysis should be modified.

3.4. The method of the study

Data about current uses of these Romance GO-constructions reflect that the Catalan construction did not follow the universal tendency of development of purposive constructions with verbs meaning 'go'. The question arises of what kind of pathway it followed instead. I argue that a comparison with the Spanish GO-construction can help us to reveal the initial stage of the grammaticalization of the Catalan "*anar* 'go' + Inf", because the evolution of the Spanish GO-construction fits a universal tendency of development. An evolution which follows a universal pathway should be considered a very plausible one. Universal tendencies can also be used as data if we do not have enough historical data about the evolution of a construction (cf. Heine 2003). Because of this, a comparison of the Spanish and Catalan constructions can provide reliable data about the evolution of the Catalan "*anar* 'go' + Inf". I argue that such a comparison is possible and useful, because the initial stage of the development of the Catalan and the Spanish constructions seems to coincide: in the medieval texts they both convey the same semantic nuances and fulfill the same functions. I claim that all their semantic nuances are based on the meaning 'intention'. It is not surprising for the Spanish construction: expressing intentionality is a prior stage to the formation of future tenses from verbs of motion in purposive constructions (cf. [4]). I claim that the first stage of the history of the Catalan periphrastic perfective past coincides with the first stage of the above mentioned future tenses. Both emphasize the intention of the subject. In order to confirm my hypothesis and point out possible conceptual affinities I also consider further periphrases in medieval Spanish and Catalan.

As mentioned above, Detges's initial supposition consists in that the early occurrences of the Catalan "*anar* 'go' + Inf" represent inchoative aspect, and other similar medieval Romance GO-constructions do as well. If this is correct, the construction should have similar uses and it should occur in similar contexts as other inchoative constructions. I will examine whether historical texts reveal such an analogy or not. The "*començar a/de* 'begin to/of' + Inf"[11] construction is the most typical inchoative periphrasis in medieval Spanish and Catalan, therefore I will compare the use of "GO + Inf" with the use of this construction. If I find that their uses are different, this finding will weaken the hypothesis under consideration. If I find similarities in their functions, this will support it. I also examine medieval occurrences of the "*pensar de* 'think of' + Inf" in medieval Spanish and Catalan, in order to test the hypothesis that the medieval GO-constructions emphasize the intention of the subject. The "THINK OF + Inf" construction expresses the intention of the subject of doing something. If the use of "GO + Inf" turns out to be similar to the use of the THINK OF-periphrasis, they can be supposed to convey similar meanings.

To sum up, in addition to the two above mentioned GO-constructions, I include in the analysis medieval Catalan and Spanish occurrences of the periphrases "*començar a/de* 'begin to/of' + Inf" and "*pensar de* 'think of' + Inf" as well, because of the similarity of their contexts and functions in medieval texts (cf. Fischer 2007: 15). I base this method on the assumption that similar uses reflect similar conceptual contents. If two constructions can occur in similar contexts and fulfill similar functions, they presumably have some conceptual affinity. However, although the THINK OF-periphrasis has an intentional meaning and the BEGIN TO/OF-periphrasis has an inchoative meaning, both seem to be used in similar contexts. This means that both inchoative and intentional constructions seem to be able to fulfill similar functions. But with which of them does the GO-periphrasis have a conceptual affinity? In order to answer this question, we offer a more detailed analysis of the contexts in which the three periphrases of question occur and find out to what extent they are analogous.

---

[11] In the medieval Catalan and Spanish texts the construction formed with *començar* 'begin' occur either with the preposition *a* 'to' or with *de* 'of', the preposition *a* 'to' being more frequent than the preposition *de* 'of'. However, so far no differences between the meanings of these two versions have been identified. The current languages use the preposition *a* 'to'. The verb *començar* 'begin' can be found in the medieval Catalan corpus written as *començar* or *comensar*, and in Spanish as *començar, conpeçar* or *compeçar*. In order to refer to this construction in the present paper, I use the form "*començar a/de* 'begin to/of' + Inf".

On the basis of the comparison of all these periphrases in their historical contexts, I argue that despite the different endpoints of the developments of the two Romance GO-constructions under study, their histories run in parallel for a time. I argue against Detges's (2004) claim that the medieval Catalan "*anar* 'go'+ Inf" is an inchoative construction, expressing 'abrupt start'. Historical occurrences seem to confirm another hypothesis, namely, that both the Catalan "*anar* 'go'+ Inf" and the Spanish "*ir (a)* 'go (to)' + Inf" had a stage in their history when the meaning component 'intention' was salient within the semantic structure of the verb 'go'.[12] The corpus of the study contains a total of 1198 occurrences of the medieval Spanish and Catalan periphrases "GO + Inf", "THINK OF + Inf" and "BEGIN TO/OF + Inf", whose distribution is shown in Table 2.

Table 2. Distribution of the occurrences of "GO + Inf", "THINK OF + Inf" and "BEGIN TO/OF + Inf" in the corpus

		"GO+Inf"	"THINK OF+Inf"[14]	"BEGIN TO/OF+Inf"	*total*
Spanish	Tris	86	19	257	*362*
	Cid	57	42	11	110
Catalan	Munt	254	205	43	*502*
	Desc	123	58	43	*224*
total		*520*	*324*	*354*	*1198*

Although strictly speaking they fall outside the topic of this paper, it is worth adding some morphological remarks. The finite verbs of the periphrases in the contexts discussed here mostly occur in the perfective past. However, the periphrases formed with 'go' and 'think' have some occurrences which show the finite verb in the imperfective past. Occurrences of the THINK

[12] As one of the reviewers of the manuscript of the present paper has pointed out, the notions inchoative and intentional are closely related in the sense that intentional meanings frequently develop from inchoative meanings. Thus, it would seem that Detges' (2004) hypotheses and the one I argue for in the present paper are not incompatible, they just focus on different stages of the semantic development of "GO + Inf". However, both Detges and I use data from the same language state, and not from subsequent languages states. In other words, I argue against the hypothesis that the GO-periphrasis in medieval Catalan would represent inchoative aspect, but I do not refute the idea that the construction would have been an inchoative periphrasis before, in a former language state. However, this hypothesis could be hardly proved, since we do not have documented data from earlier language states.

OF-periphrasis with the finite verb in imperfective seem to refer to a performed action, similarly to its perfective past occurrences. In contrast, the verb 'go' in the GO-periphrasis, when conjugated in the imperfective past, seems to retain its original motion meaning in narrative texts, that is, these contexts are not relevant in the present discussion.[13] The verb 'begin' of the BEGIN TO/OF-periphrasis does not occur in the imperfective past in the present corpus.

The GO-periphrasis has occurrences with the verb 'go' in present tense too. It can be argued that these versions represent a more advanced stage of grammaticalization, while the earliest occurrences of the GO-construction have the verb *anar* 'go' in the preterit (see Juge 2006, 2008). Juge (2006) claims that the apparently present tense forms in the current paradigm of the Catalan perfective past "*anar* + Inf" resulted from analogy, and this process only took place later when the past meaning of the whole construction had already consolidated. The syncretism of the most current forms of past vs. present of *anar* 'go' (*anam* 'we go/we are going/we went' and the second person plural *anats*) made it possible to reanalyse the periphrasis as a construction with a present tense auxiliary. As a consequence, the use of the present tense auxiliaries extended to the rest of the paradigm. Finally, the Spanish text *Cuento de Tristan de Leonis* [The story of Tristan of Leonis] shows the finite verb of the GO-periphrasis conjugated in either present or perfective past tense, similarly to the Catalan texts. However, in the *Cantar de mio Cid* [Song of my Cid], which is an example of medieval Spanish epic style, the verb 'go' appears in the periphrasis conjugated in different verb tenses, as usual in this genre (cf. Szertics 1981).

The description of the uses of these three periphrases leads to a terminological question. The constructions discussed in the present paper all are periphrases in the sense that they express a unified notion by the combination of a finite verb and an infinitive. Romance languages use several combinations of a finite verb and a second main verb in the infinitival, gerundive, or participial forms. Some of them are complex verb tenses, in which the finite component has a mere grammatical meaning (indicating number, person, tense and mood), others express aspectual or modal meanings, and in yet others the two verbal forms both express independent notions. Relevant literature uses several criteria to determine whether these constructions are periphrases or not, that is, whether the finite element of

[13] As Pérez Saldanya (1996: 89) points out, the verb 'go' conjugated in imperfective past suggests that the subject did not manage to perform the act described in the infinitive.

such combinations is an auxiliary or not, however, neither of them is valid in itself. A typical auxiliary does not have a full lexical meaning and carries only grammatical information. Desemanticization is sometimes regarded as the main criterion of auxiliarity. For instance, Gili Gaya (1961: 109, cited in Martínez Gómez 2004) claims that in the BEGIN TO/OF-periphrasis in current Spanish, the finite verb is not an auxiliary, because its inchoative character is due to the meaning of the finite verb, and not to the new result of the verbal phrase. Others conceive of auxiliarity as a gradual notion and accept forms which do retain their lexical meaning as auxiliaries (Gómez 2004; cf. also Olbertz's 1998 terms: *lexical verb, semi-auxiliary* and *auxiliary*).

Auxiliaries and the finite verb of aspectual and modal constructions have some characteristics in common, for instance, in them the two verbal elements have a closer relationship in the sense that they express a unified notion, while in other constructions where a main verb takes a verbal complement, the verbal elements express independent notions. In Neves' (2000: 25–65, cited in Wachowicz 2007: 226–227) categorization modalizers, aspectual verbs and auxiliaries all belong to the category of verbs that do not predicate (cf. also Wachowicz 2007: 233). In this sense, the verbs discussed in the present paper all belong to the same category.

The three cases of periphrasis discussed in the present paper correspond to the three categories proposed by Gómez (2004), who makes a distinction between fully grammaticalized auxiliaries ('go' in some contexts), partially grammaticalized or desemanticized auxiliaries ('think', and 'go' in some contexts), and slightly desemanticized auxiliaries ('begin'). However, the verb 'go' shows the heterogeneous behavior usual in the case of auxiliary verbs as pointed out by Wachowicz (2007: 226): "in some contexts they recover the sense of full verbs: the process of grammaticalization may exhibit different stages in one and the same synchronic cut, whereas the same does not occur with aspectualizers". This phenomenon can be observed in the GO-periphrasis, which shows different degrees of grammaticalization in different contexts in the language state under study. The verb 'go' in some contexts retains its original lexical meaning (that is, it is not about a periphrastic use in them), in some contexts it seems to express intentional modality, while in others it seems to be a "true auxiliary" (that is, the whole construction expresses a past tense value). The BEGIN TO/OF- and THINK OF-constructions seem to express aspectual and modal values. The verb 'begin' differs from 'go' in the sense that it retains its original, lexical meaning in all contexts, while the verb THINK conveys the meaning 'intention' in periphrastic uses. To sum up, the periphrases discussed in the present paper seem to be constructions possessing aspectual or modal values, although the verb 'go' seems to be a true auxiliary in some contexts. Because of the terminological problems discussed above, I avoid the use of the term *auxiliary* throughout the present paper when referring to the finite verbal element of the "GO + Inf", "THINK OF + Inf" and "BEGIN TO/OF + Inf" periphrases.

3.5. The periphrases in their narrow and broad contexts

Before discussing the use of the three periphrases one by one, let us examine the distribution of infinitives in them. Table 3 provides a summary of the infinitive types which enter the periphrases under study.

Table 3. Distribution of infinitive types in the periphrases formed with *començar a/de* 'begin to/of', *ir/anar* 'go' and *pensar de* 'think of'

	ir (a)/anar 'go' (n=520)	*pensar de* 'think of' (n=324)	*començar a/de* 'begin to/of' (n=354)
verbs of communication	3.46%	0.62%	32%
verbs of mental/ emotional state/act	—	0.62%	22%
dynamic verbs (including verbs of motion)	65.20%	83.20%	31%
verbs of durative events	31.34%	15.74%	15%

Table 3 shows that the periphrases "GO + Inf" and "THINK OF + Inf" are somewhat more similar to each other with respect to the infinitive types used in them, and "BEGIN TO/OF + Inf" is slightly different from both. The main difference lies in the frequent occurrences of "BEGIN TO/OF + Inf" with verbs of communication (e.g. the Spanish *fablar* 'speak', *dezir* 'say', or the Catalan *parlar* 'speak' and *cridar* 'shout, cry') and with those of mental/emotional state/act (e.g. the Spanish *pensar* 'think', *rreyr* 'laugh', or the Catalan *plorar* 'cry' and *riure* 'laugh'). However, dynamic verbs and verbs of durative events enter all three periphrases. Most of the dynamic verbs (e.g. the Spanish *ferir* 'attack, hit, wound', *conbatir* 'combat', or the Catalan *ferir* 'attack, hit, wound') are from descriptions of battle scenes. Verbs of motion (e.g. the Spanish *foyr* 'escape' and *ir* 'go', or the Catalan *fugir* 'escape' and *exir* 'go out') form a subgroup of dynamic verbs. It is exactly on the basis of the uses of "BEGIN TO/OF + Inf" and "GO + Inf" with dynamic verbs that Detges (2004) supposes that "GO + Inf" is a representative of inchoative aspect. Therefore, these are the contexts which should be examined with more attention. All three periphrases can be used with the same motion – and other dynamic – verbs, that is these occurrences are which show the highest degree of similarity. A qualitative analysis and a closer look at their uses will be necessary in order to compare these constructions in these contexts. The contexts in which 'go', 'think' and 'begin' are combined with an infinitive of the other three types can be excluded from the analysis for the following reasons. When verbs of prolonged events appear in these constructions, the verbs 'go', 'think' and 'begin' seem to convey their literal meaning, that is, it is not about a periphrastic use. These occurrences seem to be not grammaticalized at all.

It is worth noting that verbs of communication and mental state/act are typical in the BEGIN TO/OF-periphrasis, but in a few examples they also occur with the verbs 'go' and 'think'. Consider the Spanish (7) and the Catalan (8) examples.

(7) *E el rrey le* ***començo*** ***a*** ***demandar*** *cauallero*
begin.3SG.PERFP to ask.INF
donde soys o de qua`l parte venjades.
'The king **began to ask** him: knight, where are you from or where did you come from.' (Tris 6v)

(8) *E tuit* ***començaren*** ***a*** ***cridar****: – Ben diu l'almirall!*
begin.3PL.PERFP to cry.INF
'And all **began to cry**: "The admiral says well." ' (Munt I 127, 36–38)

Examples (7) and (8) show typical uses of "*començar a/de* 'begin to/of' + Inf", where the finite verb 'begin' is combined with a verb of communication and the occurrence of the periphrasis is followed by a more detailed description of the content of the communication in a direct quotation form. In examples (7) and (8), the lexemes *demandar* 'ask' and *cridar* 'cry' could also represent a single, perfective event. However, in this context, as they appear in the inchoative periphrasis, they gain a repetitive character in accordance with which (7) and (8) can be interpreted as describing repeated questions and cries, respectively (cf. also examples 16 and 17 in section 3.5.3).

It seems to be reasonable to suppose that the function of the periphrasis consists in addressing the attention to the content of the utterance which follows the periphrasis. That is, inchoative aspect serves as a tool for organizing the discourse, by means of indicating the beginning of an act of communication. But it is not the beginning which is important but the continuation, that is, the content of the communicative act.

Similarly to the "BEGIN TO/OF + Inf" construction, verbs of communication also occur in the GO-construction, as in the Catalan example (9).

(9) *l'endemà* ***anà*** ***parlar*** *ab l'emperador* (Desc II 50, 16–17)
go.3SG.PERFP talk.INF
'the next day he **went to talk** to the emperor' (= he went and talked to him)

The occurrence in (9) refers to motion in space with the aim of talking to somebody. Although this use may seem to be similar to the use of *començar* 'begin' with verbs of communication regarding the verb type, they are quite different in other respects. In the case of "*ir/anar* 'go' + Inf" the occurrence is not followed by a more detailed description of the content of the communication. In this type of occurrences the verb *ir/anar* 'go' seems to retain its lexical meaning, it does not seem to be grammaticalized, thus the construction is not a periphrasis. Since the occurrences of "GO + Inf" which are relevant for us are examples where it functions as a periphrasis and does not refer to motion in space, below I will consider only occurrences of the three periphrases with dynamic verbs.

3.5.1. "Ir/anar *'go' + Inf"*

Table 4 shows the distribution of dynamic verbs which occur in the GO-periphrases in the four medieval texts.

Table 4. The distribution of dynamic verbs in the periphrasis "*ir (a)/anar* 'go' + Inf"

	"*ir (a)* + Inf" (Spanish)		"*anar* + Inf" (Catalan)		
"GO + Inf"	Tris	Cid	Munt	Desc	*total*
verbs of motion	6	8	39	10	*63*
other dynamic verbs	43	21	162	50	*276*
total	*49*	*29*	*201*	*60*	*339*

In what contexts can we find the medieval GO-construction? The Catalan (10) and Spanish (11) examples show a typical use of "GO + Inf" with the dynamic verb *ferir* 'attack'.

(10) *E quant fo defora, puyí lo cavayl dels esperons e* ***anà***
go.3SG.PERFP
ferir *entre.ls sarraÿns, sí que.l primer colp n'abaté, ab lo pits del*
attack.INF
caval seu, .IIII. a terra. (Desc III 93, 23–26)
'And when he was outside, he dug his spurs into his horse and **went to attack/attacked** the Saracens, so that at first he threw four of them to the ground with the breast of his horse.'

(11) *E el torno contra el &* ***fue****-le* ***ferir*** *que le passo el*
go.3SG.PERFP-CLIT attack.INF
escudo & la loriga & metiol la lança por la carne (Tris 11r)
'And he turned toward him and **went to attack/attacked** him (in such a way) that he stabbed his shield and his coat of mail through and pierced him through with his lance.'

In examples (10) and (11) the "*ir/anar* 'go' + Inf" periphrasis is used with thoroughly completed actions. The "GO + Inf" construction presents the event in question in its entirety, as a completed action, which takes place as a whole, without being interrupted. Accordingly, the subsequent utterances describe the consequences of the action described in the infinitive. The act of attacking described in (10) caused the death of four Saracens and that in (11) had the consequence that the enemy's shield and coat of mail were pierced and he was killed. Although examples (10) and (11) allow the motion-then-action reading, too, the GO-construction seems to direct the attention to the very event described in the infinitive, which is presented in the context as an act charged with consequences. The contexts show that it does not only express motion, but, in its more grammaticalized versions, also emotional charge and dynamism inasmuch as it appears in the most tense and interesting moments of the story.

3.5.2. "Pensar de *'think of' + Inf*"

The construction "*pensar de* 'think of' + Inf" also appears frequently with dynamic verbs. Table 5 shows their proportions in this periphrasis in the different texts of the corpus.

Table 5. The distribution of the periphrasis "*pensar de* 'think of' + Inf" with dynamic verbs

"THINK OF + Inf"	"*pensar de* 'think of' + Inf" (Spanish)		"*pensar de* 'think of' + Inf" (Catalan)		
	Tris	Cid	Munt	Desc	*total*
verbs of motion	4	33	106	25	168
other dynamic verbs	10	3	65	23	101
total	*14*	*36*	*171*	*48*	*269*

The following examples show occurrences of *pensar* 'think' with dynamic verbs in medieval Catalan (12), (13) and Spanish (14).

(12) *E* ***pensaren*** ***de fugir*** *ab tota lur roba; sí que quant*
think.3PL.PERFP of get.away.INF
la host del rey hy fo junta, trobaren la vila desemparada.
'And they **thought of getting away (= got away)** with all the booty; so that when the king's troops arrived there, they found the city abandoned.' (Desc III 69, 16–18)

(13) *e los turcs, qui veeren que els muntaven darrera,* ***pensaren***
think.3PL.PERFP
ab les sagetes ***de trer,*** *e per desastre una sageta va ferir En*
of take.out.INF
Corberan, qui s'hac desarmat lo cap per calor, per lo pols. E aquí ell morí. (Munt II 76, 44–46 – 77, 1–5)
'But the Turks, seeing them come up after them, **thought of taking out (=took out)** their arrows. And, unfortunately, an arrow hit Corberan, who had taken off his iron cap because of the heat and dust, and there he died.'

(14) *Tres dias e dos noches* ***penssaron*** ***de andar***
think.3PL.PERFP of walk.INF
Alcançaron a myo çid en teuar e el pinar (Cid 970–971)
'Three days and two nights they **thought of going (= went)** and they caught up with my Cid in the pine wood of Tevar'

According to the literal meaning of *pensar de* 'think of', this verbal construction literally means that the subject has a thought about carrying an act out, in other words, he has the intention of doing something. However, on the basis of the narrow context we are not able to determine exactly what semantic nuance the construction represents. In any case, we can say that the types of verbs which enter the construction and the type of contexts in which it appears (battle scenes, emotionally charged scenes) show a similarity with the uses of the GO-construction presented above. Examples (12)–(14) reveal that the occurrences of "*pensar de* 'think of' + Inf", with the finite verb in perfective past tense, refer to a completed, perfective event. By means of the use of this construction, the speaker describes the event as connected with a previous intention of the subject, and one which is worth attracting the listener's attention. Due to the fact that the intention is expressed in a perfective tense, an inference arises to the effect that the action described in the infinitive was a fully performed action, that is was actually carried out. This inference is supported by information from the broad context. All the three examples are similar to the uses of the "*ir/anar* 'go' + Inf" construction, inasmuch as the occurrence of the periphrasis is followed by the description of the consequences of the action. On the basis of the fact that the utterance continues with the description of the consequence(s) of the action, we can infer that the act was actually performed. In example (12) they did not only think of escaping, but they actually escaped, because, as a consequence, the king's host found the city abandoned. Similarly, in (13) the Turks did not only think of taking out their arrows but they actually took them out. This is clear from the consequence: an arrow hit a knight called Corberan. Furthermore, as a consequence of the riding described in (14), they caught up with Cid. The construction "*pensar de* 'think of' + Inf" is similar to the construction "*ir/anar* 'go' + Inf" not only when they are compared in their narrow contexts but also when we compare them in their broad contexts. They both present the event in the infinitive as a completed, thoroughly performed action, which has considerable consequences and, as such, is worthy of the listeners' attention.

3.5.3. "Començar a/de *'begin to/of' + Inf*"

The "*començar a/de* 'begin to/of' + Inf" is a typical, widely used inchoative periphrasis in medieval Catalan and Spanish. Its use seems to fulfill a strategy of attracting the listener's attention, similarly to other inchoative constructions described in Detges (2004) (cf. section 3.2). Table 6 shows the proportions of dynamic verbs in the construction "*començar a/de* 'begin to/of' + Inf" in medieval Spanish and Catalan.

Table 6. The distribution of dynamic verbs in the periphrasis "*començar a/de* 'begin to/of' + Inf"

"BEGIN TO/OF + Inf"	"*començar a/de* 'begin to/of' + Inf" (Spanish)		"*començar a/de* 'begin to/of' + Inf" (Catalan)		
	Tris	Cid	Munt	Desc	*total*
verbs of motion	20	0	8	25	*53*
other dynamic verbs	44	1	6	4	*55*
total	*64*	*1*	*14*	*29*	*108*

Verbs of motion, which form a subgroup of dynamic verbs, enter all three periphrases. However, these events can be represented in different ways. Consider the Catalan example (15).

(15) *E el rey, qui assò hac entès, va pendre ses armes, e muntà a caval e*
comensà ***a*** ***córrer*** *aprés d'éls; e no foren pus de .XX.*
begin.3SG.PERFP to run.INF

cavalers ab él, que.ls altres no eren tantost aparelats. El rey era molt bon cavaler e coratgós e era molt bé encavalquat, sí que.ls altres cavalers no podien tant córrer com él; sí que.l rey fo molt a davant de tota sa companya e conseguia en aquels qui se'n fugien, sí que.ls fo molt prop, e regiraren-se e conegren que aquest era.l rey. (Desc II 43, 5–15)

'And the king, who got to know that, took his arms, and mounted his horse and **began to ride** at full speed after them; there were no more than 20 knights with him, because the others could not get ready soon enough. The king was a very good knight and courageous and could ride very well. So the other knights could not ride so fast as him; so that he rode quite ahead of all his companions and was about to catch up with those who were escaping. So he was close to them and they turned round and recognized that he was the king.'

The Catalan example (15) shows an occurrence of "*començar a/de* 'begin to/of' + Inf" with a verb of motion. The event described in the infinitive is extended in time: the act of the king's riding is presented as prolonged in time. However, the broad context shows the king's riding on his horse as "frozen", because the story teller stops and describes how it was performed, what the circumstances were, what events occurred during that, etc. The event wedged in is a very considerable one: the enemy recognizes the king's person. This recognition is considered to be of great significance by the story teller, who wants to emphasize it by means of "preparing" it through the use of the inchoative periphrasis.

To sum up, the investigation of occurrences of "*començar a/de* 'begin to/of' + Inf" in their broad contexts sheds light on the fact that this construction serves as a tool of emphasizing the subsequent events. In order to make possible the wedging in these more important events, the representation of the events in the infinitive is in the inchoative periphrasis. The event described in lexically perfective infinitives entering the construction will be reinterpreted as extended in time, and in this way they can be interrupted by another event. With such a technique the story teller manages to highlight the events which are embedded, and relegate the event described in the infinitive of the BEGIN TO/OF-construction to the background. By means of freezing the picture of the event at its beginning, the story teller directs the audience's attention to the subsequent part of the story.

Let us examine some examples in their broad contexts in order to illustrate the function of describing other dynamic actions.

(16) *[el rey] fuese contra los escuderos & **començo** los **de ferir***
start.3SG.PERFP of attack.INF
& la donzella que auja traydo a tri`stan / vio commo la falsa donzella se acogia & començo a dar bozes contra tri`stan & a dezjr Señor catad que non se vaya la mala muger ca por ventura otro tal faria ella otra vegada tri`stan ferio el cauallo contra el castillo & ante que ella entrase tomola por los cabellos & pusola en poder del Rey & tornose contra los escuderos. (Tris 131v)
'[the king] went to the squires and **began to attack** them. And the girl who had taken Tristan there saw that the false girl was about to go away and began to shout to Tristan and to say: Sir, look out! Don't let this bad woman escape, because maybe she would act in the same way again. Tristan spurred his horse and went toward the castle and before she was able to enter, he took her by the hair and handed her over to the king. Then he turned toward the squires.'

(17) *lançarote **començo** **de saltar** al deredor dela tienda E commo*
start.3SG.PERFP of jump.INF
brangel vio que saltauan en derredor / dela tienda ella salio fuera & dixo Señor cauallero amj paresçe agora que uos non sodes cortes commo yo vi de otros asaz que vos andades saltando aqui` çerca do duerme otro cauallero que por ventura`(a) ualle tanto commo vos & asy dios me de bien que yo creo que vos andades buscando rruydo & bien lo podredes fallar. (Tris 108v)

> 'Lancelot **began to** [**make** his horse] **jump** around the tent. When Brangel saw that somebody was making [his horse] jump around the tent, he went out and said: "dear knight, it seems to me that you are not as polite as I saw others to be, that you are making [your horse] jump here, where another knight is sleeping, who may be worth so much than you. And on my honor, I think that you are looking for trouble and certainly you will find it".'

In the Spanish examples (16) and (17) the BEGIN TO/OF-periphrases refer to the beginning of the actions. At the same time, we should also realize that they will continue and are not yet completed. As mentioned above (section 3.3) inchoative constructions are compatible with durative verbs, which denote actions or processes characterizable with a time interval, whose left starting point is signaled (Kiefer 2006: 169–170). However, both *ferir* 'attack' and *saltar* 'jump' refer to punctual, lexically perfective actions. Therefore, in order to make sense of the utterances, in (16) we have to represent the act of attacking as divided in several sub-acts, and in (17) the act of jumping as an act repeated several times.

Ferir 'attack, hit, wound' is one of the verbs which can enter all three periphrases and with the verb GO it forms a typical phrase. It is the verb which occurs in this construction with the highest frequency. Therefore, its occurrences in the three periphrases are worth comparing. The act of attacking in itself is a punctual, perfective event. However, as it occurs in the inchoative periphrasis, we have to change the representation of the event of attacking: instead of a momentary, punctual event, we will represent it as a durative one. The broad context of (16) highlights that it is interrupted by another, unexpected event. From the attack of the squires, the attention is directed toward this new event: a false person, who was the cause of various troubles before, is about to escape. Keeping her back from escaping is more urgent than disarming the squires, which is delayed. The event itself which is described in the infinitive is presented as one which was begun but was not completely performed, and the inchoative aspect in this example seems to fulfill the function of directing the attention to the part of the story which follows the "BEGIN TO/OF + Inf" periphrasis. That is, it is not the event described in the infinitive which the speaker seems to highlight but the subsequent event which is wedged in.

Similarly, making a horse jump is in itself a perfective, punctual event too, but as the inchoative periphrasis in (17) represents it as one characterizable with a time interval. This prolonged nature in the case of punctual events can be imagined as repetition. Sometimes the context gives a reiterative or durative interpretation to this type of verbs, and thus they can appear with the verb *començar*. This reading makes (17) acceptable: it gains a repetitive character, because, if it is extended in time, we can imagine the act of jumping only in such a way. This iterated act of jumping is interrupted by another event which is considered more important by the speaker, because it describes a potential conflict between the participants.

On the basis of the observation of occurrences of "GO + Inf", "THINK OF + Inf" and "BEGIN TO/OF + Inf", we can draw the conclusion that although all the three periphrases accept dynamic infinitives, they attract the listeners' attention to a different part of the text. "BEGIN TO/OF + Inf" represents a true inchoative periphrasis, which seems to suggest cognitive relevance, as Detges (2004) describes it. He denominates it 'abrupt start' (Detges 2004: 213) and assigns a similar function to the medieval occurrences of the Catalan "*anar* 'go' + Inf". The speaker emphasizes the beginning of the event in order to indicate that it will be worth watching all the development of the event, and the other ones which interrupt it. The use of the BEGIN TO/OF-periphrasis emphasize these wedged in actions. As to the THINK OF- and GO-periphrases, the consideration of broad contexts highlights that, in opposition with Detges' (2004) claim, the occurrences of "*anar* 'go' + Inf" are not representatives of inchoative aspect. They emphasize the action in the infinitive, by presenting it as a completely performed, perfective action, which has considerable consequences. At the same time, they highlight that this action was not performed in a common way but with more dynamism and with the subject's volitional involvement. This semantic nuance should come from the semantic components 'dynamism' and 'intention' inherently present in the meaning 'go'.

4. Methodological issues of assigning meaning in historical research

4.1. Linguistic clues in the contexts of historical occurrences

In order to avoid interpretations based on our subjective linguistic intuitions and our knowledge about the current language state, we should find some linguistic clues which may help us to reveal what shades of meaning historical occurrences express. Below, I examine some linguistic elements which suggest that the verbs GO and THINK do not retain their lexical meanings of motion and thought, respectively, but their coded meanings are changing or have already changed. In this sense, such elements reveal undergoing grammaticalization processes, and in the case of the BEGIN TO/OF-periphrasis they help to reveal what function this periphrasis has in narrative contexts. This summary highlights the double role context has. On the one hand, certain contexts do not suggest an obvious interpretation, but allow more readings, thus they induce inferences and trigger grammaticalization (cf. Heine's (2002) bridging context and Diewald's (2002) untypical and critical contexts, in section 2.2). Contexts which leave open several possible interpretations do not reveal what meaning the speaker actually intended. Other contexts, however, disambiguate the interpretation (cf. Heine's (2002) switch and conventionalization contexts and Diewald's (2002) isolating context, in section 2.2). Their existence presupposes a previous reorganization of the semantic structure of the lexical item in question and they serve as evidence of the presence of a new meaning. Occurrences of a linguistic unit in disambiguating contexts suggest that it has developed a new meaning compatible with those contexts. That is, the occurrence of the grammaticalizing item in different contexts serves us as evidence in the identification of different stages of grammaticalization. Let us consider some possible linguistic clues which can provide information about possible semantic nuances in historical documents. Obviously, not each linguistic clue presented below occurs in each context, and some contexts may contain more of them, while others neither of them. If nothing in the context contradicts it, we should attribute the original lexical meaning (cf. Traugott and Dasher 2004: 44 in section 2.3). If the lexical meaning of the finite verb must be excluded due to a linguistic clue, we should find a reading acceptable in that context.

4.2. Linguistic clues in the narrow context

Linguistic clues which serve as points of orientation in assigning meanings may occur already in the narrow context. Sometimes the infinitive itself and the nouns which appear with it are semantically irreconcilable with the literal meaning of the finite verb. In these cases some pieces of encyclopedic information are activated, which influence the interpretation of the construction, excluding the lexical meaning. Consider the Catalan example (18).

(18) ***va*** ***avallar*** *del cavall* (Munt II 176, 29)
go.3SG.PRES get.off.INF
'(he) **got off** his horse'

Example (18) literally means that 'he goes to get off the horse'. But we should realize that the lexical meaning 'go' of *anar* had already disappeared here, the verb cannot retain its literal meaning *va avallar* 'goes to get off', because one does not need to go to get off the horse.[14]

Similarly, in the case of the periphrasis "BEGIN TO/OF + Inf", some infinitives and nouns per se, due to their meaning, can help define the function of the construction, inasmuch as they refer to the durative nature of the event. Observe the following Catalan examples.

(19) ***començà*** ***a*** ***fer*** *lo major hivern del món, e de pluja,*
begin.3SG.PERFP to do.INF the most severe winter
e de neu, e de fred e de mal temps; sí que les flumaires vengren tan grans, que null hom no les pogra pasar. E així hac son consell que eixhivernàs en aquell lloc de l'Artaqui. (Munt II 73, 35–39)
'there **began to set in** the most severe winter of the world, with rain and snow and cold and bad weather, so that the rivers became so large that no man could cross them. And so he decided to winter in this place, Artaqui.'

(20) *e con* ***començaren*** ***cantar*** *„Salve regina", l'home gità un gran crit,*
begin.3PL.PERFP sing.INF
e los membres, tots quants n'havia, eixiren de llurs llocs, sí que ben sis preveres l'havien a tenir (Munt II 28, 12–14)
'and when they **began to sing** the Salve Regina, the man gave a great cry and all his limbs were convulsed, so that fully six priests had to hold him'

The expressions *set in the winter* and *sing* refer to a state and an event, respectively, which are extended in time and serve as a background for other events. In example (19), the season name *hivern* 'winter' appears. The description of seasons typically serves as a background in story telling. Winter in itself is prolonged in time, and it is described in details through mentioning the rain, the snow, the bad weather and the rivers swelling. In this example the story teller seems to refer to the real beginning of the season which will serve as a background of further events. In (20) the singing serves as a background of an unexpected event, interrupting the song. In this way, these infinitives per se, due to their meaning, underlie the backgrounding function of the BEGIN TO/OF-periphrasis.

[14] One of the anonymous reviewers commented that this example (and also example [29]) can be considered as an instance of bridging context in the sense that although the verb *anar* does not retain the original meaning of displacement from one place to another, but could indicate the movement of part(s) of the body.

Adverbs which semantically can be linked to the event in the infinitive can also be useful linguistic clues. These adverbs foreground the semantic content of the infinitive, instead of that of the finite verb. Consider the Catalan example (21).

(21) *e los altres* ***van*** ***ferir*** *en la llur peonada tan fortment que*
go.3PL.PRES attack.INF so vigorously
ab los dards ne mès cascun un en terra (Munt II 177, 18–20)
'and the others **attacked** the foot soldiers so vigorously that each one threw one down with his dart'

In example (21) the construction *van ferir* literally means '(they) are going/ go to attack'. However, the adverb *fortment* 'vigorously, hard' likely describes the way of attacking and not the way of going, and thus it foregrounds the meaning of the infinitive. This linguistic judgment is based on a kind of semantic compatibility: normally, the event of attacking can be conceptualized as realized vigorously more easily than the event of going, that is, it is a more typical phrase, which describes a more typical situation. The use of such adverbs draws the attention to the event described in the infinitive, triggering the "semantic bleaching" of the main verb, which moves to the background. Similarly, some adverbs which occur with the periphrasis "*pensar de* 'think of' + Inf" seem to modify the infinitive and not the verb *pensar* 'think', and, in this way, they foreground the action described in the infinitive.

(22) *E* ***pensaren*** *molt* ***vigorosament de combatre****, e nós* ***a defendre****.*
think.3PL.PERFP vigorously of combat.INF to defend.INF
'And they **thought of combating (=combated)** very **vigorously** and we **(thought) of defending (=defended)** ourselves.' (Munt II 101, 27–28)

In example (22), the adverb *vigorosament* 'vigorously' seems to modify the verb *combatre* 'combat' and not the verb *pensar* 'think'. The phrase 'combat vigorously' describes a typical situation, while 'think vigorously' would be hard to conceptualize. Thus, this adverb foregrounds the act of combating and backgrounds the literal meaning of *pensar* 'think'. The semantic content of the second infinitive *defendre* 'defend' also supports the reading according to which we are not dealing only with a thought, because they actually had to defend themselves. Furthermore, if the enemy had only thought of attacking, the others would not have had to defend themselves. In other words, the literal meaning of *pensar* 'think' is relegated to the background.

The periphrasis fulfills a pragmatic function, which consists in the dynamicization of the story telling, by referring to intentionality, i.e. the subject's volitional involvement in the action.

4.3. Linguistic clues in the broad context

In other cases, we have to broaden the context in order to be able to find the most plausible reading of a historical occurrence. The content of preceding or following clauses or sentences can make the literal meaning of GO and THINK unlikely to be assigned. For instance, if the sentence which contains the construction in question is followed by another sentence which describes the consequences of the event, we can suppose that the periphrasis represents a completed action and not only the motion with the aim of carrying out that action.

(23) *e* ***anà*** ***ferir*** *lo cavall per la testera, e* ***el cavall estec***
go.3SG.PERFP wound.INF
estabornit (Munt I 198, 6–7)
'and she **went to wound/wounded** the horse in the head, and **the horse was stunned**'

In the Catalan example (23) the construction *anà ferir* must convey the meaning 'wounded', because the following clause describes the consequence of the action of wounding. If we interpret *anà ferir* as "went to hit", the information that the horse was stunned would seem the consequence of the motion and not of the attack, which would not make sense, or the motion in the first clause and the stunning in the second one would appear as two events independent from each other, which would break the coherence of the story. This utterance reveals the presence of an inferencing procedure. However, we do not know whether the information that the action described in the infinitive was actually performed is present as an inference or forms part of the coded meaning of the periphrasis. But in any case, it must be present in the context: the event in the infinitive is foregrounded and, if there is a motion meaning at all, it remains in the background. The Catalan example (24) is similar to (23), but in it the following clause describes an event, which is not a consequence of the action in the infinitive but presupposes its performance.

(24) *Mas los almugàvers* ***anaren*** ***trencar*** *les lisses e el mur de la vila,*
go.3PL.PERFP break.INF
e entraren dins *e los cavalers ab eyls* (Desc III 146, 13–16)
'But the Almugavars **went to break/broke** the entrenchment and the wall of the city, and **entered** and the knights with them as well'

In (24) we have the information that the Almugavars entered, thus, we can infer that *anaren trencar* 'they went to break' does not refer to the motion with the aim of breaking the wall of the city but to the breaking itself, because in the Middle Ages this act was necessary for the enemy to enter into the city. Although we know that the breaking of the city wall was actually performed, we cannot be sure that this information comes from the coded meaning of the periphrasis, it can also be present only as an inference in the medieval language state.

Similarly, also in some occurrences of the THINK OF-periphrasis the content of the subsequent sentence suggests an inference to the effect that the action has been actually performed.

(25) ***pensaren-se*** ***d' armar****.* *E jo guardé, e viu lluir los capells*
think.3PL.PERFP-REFL of arm.INF
de ferre e les ascones munteres (Munt II 119, 25–26)
'(they) **thought of arming (=armed)**. And I looked and saw the iron caps and hunting spears shine'

In the Catalan example (25) the inference that they did not only think of arming but actually armed can be drawn on the basis of the information provided by the following clause, which says that the story teller looked and saw "the iron caps and hunting spears shine". Since these events form part of the act of arming, a part-whole inference can be drawn to the effect that the story teller saw them arm.

The periphrasis with the verb *començar* 'begin' presents the event as a one prolonged in time, or as one that has begun but has not finished. We can sometimes infer this from the fact that the sentence which contains the periphrasis with *començar* 'begin' is followed by another one which describes an event interrupting the one described in the infinitive. The prolonged nature of the event can also be emphasized by describing the subparts or circumstances of that event. The following clauses explain acts which can be considered as such parts of the event described in the infinitive. These durative events seem to serve as a background for other, more important events.

(26) *E con ells foren asseguts,* ***començaren*** ***a menjar****, e aquell pres son*
begin.3PL.PERFP to eat.INF
quarter de moltó, e va'l-se posar davant, e tallà de la carn, e dix: - Jo vull menjar d'esta carn, a deshonor de la festa que anuit és e demà serà. (Munt II 27, 26–31)
'And when they had sat down and **began to eat**, he took his quarter of mutton and set it down in front of himself and cut off a piece of meat and said: "I wish to eat of this meat to disgrace the feast of tonight and tomorrow".'

Example (26) is a passage of a story which recounts a great miracle which happened to an Almugavar who was punished because he had eaten meat on Christmas Eve. The story teller seems to emphasize all details, raising the listeners' curiosity. Taking the meat, setting it in front of oneself and cutting off a piece of it can be considered as sub-events of eating. In such a way, the prolonged nature of the event of eating is emphasized and this strategy awakes the audience's expectation that something must happen which interrupts that event. Finally, in some occurrences a subsequent clause reveals that "*començar a/de* 'begin to/of' + Inf" expresses that the event began but was not completed.

(27) *& el commo los vio* ***començo*** ***a poner*** *su escudo delante &*
begin.3SG.PERFP to put.INF
aparejar-se *para la justa mas commo fue çerça dellos luego*
prepare.INF-REFL
conosçio al rrey & descendio del cauallo & fue le a besar la mano
'and when he saw them, he **began to put** his shield in front of himself and **to prepare** himself for battle. But when he got near them, he recognized the king and he got off his horse and went to kiss/went and kissed/kissed his hand' (Tris 78v)

In the Spanish example (27), taking the shield and preparing for battle were interrupted and were not completed, because the knight realized that the other person, who he was going to attack, was the king himself, and he changed his mind. He renounced combating and, instead, decided to kiss his hand. By the use of "*començar a/de* 'begin to/of' + Inf" the wedged in event, i.e. the recognition of the king is emphasized.

Concerning the GO-periphrasis, consider the Catalan occurrence (28) where the content of the clause which precedes the one containing the periphrasis refers to a location renders the motion meaning implausible to be assigned.

(28) *E **con foren al peu de l'escala**, madona la reina e sa germana*
anaren-se **abraçar**
go.3PL.PERFP-CLIT embrace.INF (Munt I 181, 31–33)
'And when they came down the ladder, **at the foot of it**, my Lady the Queen and her sister **embraced/(went to embrace) each other**'

In example (28) the first clause provides the information that the participants were already there where the event described in the infinitive took place (at the foot of the ladder), that is, they presumably did not have to go anywhere. The very action of embracing each other seems to be emphasized by the use of the periphrasis and, the 'motion' meaning is unlikely to be relevant. By the use of the GO-periphrasis, the speaker highlights the non-ordinary nature of performance of the action in the infinitive, by referring to the intentional world of the subjects. This is possible because 'intention' and 'dynamism' are inherent components of the meaning 'go'.

(29) *e **va** **trer** lo bordó **que portava cint*** (Munt II 176, 25–26)
go.3SG.PRES take.INF
'he **took** the bordon [a kind of sword] **he was wearing in a belt**'

In example (29), *va trer* lierally means '(he) is going/goes in order to take'. The infinitive *trer* 'take' in itself does not exclude the motion meaning of *va*: it is the content of the following clause which does not allow it. The meaning 'he **goes to take** the bordon he wore in a belt' cannot be assigned because the thing the agent took was something on his own body. In other words, the utterance in (29) cannot mean that 'he goes to himself to take his bordon', instead we can assign to the construction the meaning of a completed action or a past tense value. This reading is confirmed by the verb tense of the verb in the subsequent clause. The verbal form *portava* 'was wearing' is in the imperfect past tense. It is a descriptive past tense, which (among other uses) refers to an action or a condition as coincidental with another action. Since the concordance of tenses is obligatory in Catalan, the form *va trer* also must have a past tense value. That is, the verb tense in the subsequent clause shows that this occurrence is a fully grammaticalized form (cf. the discussion of occurrences of the GO-periphrasis with the verb 'go' in present tense in section 3.4).

The temporal relations between adjoining clauses and its verb tense can also help us infer contents which are not explicitly expressed. Consider the Catalan example (30).

(30) *E així los missatgers* ***pensaren*** ***de tornar*** *en Palerm al*
think.3PL.PERFP of return.INF
senyor rei. E con lo rei hac entesa la resposta del rei Carles...
'And so the messengers **thought of returning (= returned)** to Palermo, to the Lord King. And when the Lord King had heard the answer of King Charles...' (Munt I 96, 41–43)

In example (30) we have the form *hac entesa* 'had heard'. This past tense is a perfect tense, which expresses an action, state or event that was already completed before the start of another past action. Thus, the grammatical form *hac entesa* 'had heard' informs us that the king did hear the answer of King Charles carried by messengers. On the basis of this information we can infer that the messengers did not only think of returning to the king, but they actually did, and they gave him the message.

The use of verbal mood also can provide useful pieces of information. In the Catalan example (31), the indicative mood[15] of the form *passà* 'passed' in the subordinate clause instead of subjunctive mood, which would be used if the form *anà* preserved its original 'motion' meaning, signals that the verb *anar* does not retain its lexical meaning 'go' in that context.

(31) *mès-se la lansa denant, e* ***anà*** ***ferir*** *lo cavaler alamayn*
go.3SG.PERFP attack.INF
de tal vertut que la lança li ***passà*** *de l'altra part per mig lo cors*
'[he] held the lance out and **went to attack/attacked** the German knight in such a way that the lance **passed** right through him in the middle of his body' (Desc II 55, 25–27)

In example (31), if the periphrasis referred to the motion with the intention of attacking, the following clause would have the verb in subjunctive mood. Indicative mood suggests that action described in the subsequent clause was not the aim but the consequence of the action in the GO-periphrasis. And it can be a more likely consequence of the act of attacking than that of going. In other words, that he did actually attack the German knight and the lance did actually pass through him. This grammatical feature serves as evidence

[15] Unless otherwise noted, verbal forms are in the indicative.

of a previous semantic change and reveals that the verb *anar* does not retain its lexical meaning 'go'. Similarly to the case of 'go', in the broad context of "*pensar de* 'think of' + Inf" clauses sometimes occur which contain the verb in indicative, suggesting a meaning different from 'think'.

To sum up section 4, context may contain several linguistic clues which direct us in assigning meaning to utterances in historical documents. The majority of them are based on the meaning of some elements either in the narrow or in the broad context (infinitives entering the periphrasis, nouns, adverbs, preceding or subsequent clauses etc.). However, there are some grammatical characteristics as well which can help us, for instance, verb tense or verbal mood. The narrow context is often not enough for assigning meaning, and the broad context should also be taken into account.

5. A comparison of the three periphrases

In historical occurrences, the lexical meaning of the elements of the Catalan and Spanish GO-constructions and the context construct the meaning together. The very question is what semantic nuance is provided by the finite verb of the construction. Historical data reflect a similarity between the contexts and functions of the GO- and THINK OF-constructions. They both differ from the use of the inchoative BEGIN TO/OF-construction. Since the "THINK OF + Inf" refers to the intention of doing something, the similarity in the use of the periphrases "THINK OF + Inf" and "GO + Inf" suggests that this latter periphrasis may have a stage in its development when the meaning component 'intention' was salient within the semantic structure of GO.

The analysis of historical occurrences in section 4 has led to the finding that the "*començar a/de* 'begin to/of' + Inf", "*pensar de* 'think of' + Inf" and the "*ir/anar* 'go' + Inf" are all appropriate to realize a strategy which aims to attract the listener's attention. However, they do so in different ways. While the former arouses the expectation of an important, embedded event, described later in contexts, the latter two highlight the event described in the infinitive. The inchoative "BEGIN TO/OF + Inf" describes the action or event as extended in time and through the reference to its beginning draws the listener's attention to the event(s) which interrupt(s) it. In contrast, "GO + Inf" and "THINK OF + Inf" characterize the action or event as a whole, without extension in time, and emphasize the action itself, mentioning its consequences. Figure 1 summarizes how the speaker tries to capture the addressee's attention through the use of "BEGIN TO/OF + Inf", "THINK OF + Inf" or "GO + Inf".

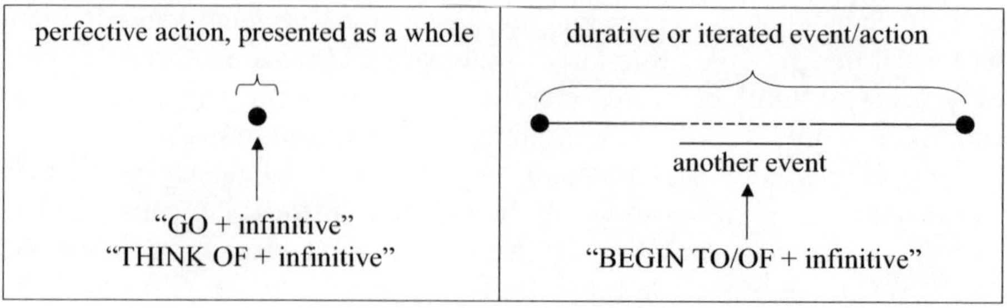

Figure 1. Strategies of capturing the listener's attention with the use of "BEGIN TO/OF + Inf", "GO + Inf" and "THINK OF + Inf"

The verbs *començar* 'begin', *pensar* 'think' and *ir/anar* 'go' all occur with similar types of verbs, but they add different nuances to the description of the event. In the cases of the GO- and THINK OF-periphrases the event described in the infinitive is highlighted, which is referred to as a whole, a completed event with considerable consequences. In the case of the BEGIN TO/OF-construction the event in the infinitive is described as a durative one, but which is interrupted as soon as it has begun. With this strategy the subsequent wedged in events are emphasized.

The completed actions in the periphrases formed with GO and THINK are characterized as born out of a strong determination of the subject. These two periphrases present the action in the infinitive connecting it with the subjects' volitional world and emphasizing the dynamism in its performance. The emphasis on the intention of the subject assigns a semantic nuance to these two periphrases, which makes them appropriate to describe non-ordinary events, like battle scenes and emotionally charged scenes. These are the contexts in which these periphrases occur most frequently. In the same contexts the construction formed with *començar* 'begin' has only a "preparatory role": the most exciting moments follow later.

The comparison of these three medieval periphrases in Catalan and Spanish has revealed a similarity between the uses of "*ir/anar* 'go' + Inf" and "*pensar de* 'think of' + Inf", and a difference of both from the use of "*començar a/de* 'begin to/of' + Inf". On the basis of these observations we can conclude that at a certain stage of its grammaticalization, "GO + Inf" had a conceptual affinity with "THINK OF + Inf", which can be attributed to the salience of the meaning element 'intention' in the semantic structure of GO. At this stage the construction expressed the intention of the subject and not an 'abrupt start' (i.e. inchoative aspect, the adjective *abrupt* is added by Detges 2004). Additional evidence comes from the finding that in medieval Spanish and Catalan the "*ir/anar* 'go' + Inf" construction often contains verbs which refer to emotional events, like *abraçar* 'embrace' or *besar* 'kiss'. The hypothesis of 'abrupt start' does not fit with these occurrences. They are not characterized by abruptness, neither do they direct the attention to the subsequent utterances. Rather, they are emotionally charged scenes, which suggest the subjects' active involvement. Compare the following examples from medieval Catalan (32) and Spanish (33).

<table>
<tr><td>(32)</td><td>Madona la reina e sa germana</td><td>anaren-se</td><td>abraçar;</td></tr>
<tr><td></td><td></td><td>go.3PL.PERFP-CLIT</td><td>embrace.INF</td></tr>
</table>

e estegren així abraçades, e besant e plorant, que null hom no les podia partir. (Munt I 181, 32–34)

'My Lady the Queen and her sister **went to embrace/embraced each other** and remained thus embracing and kissing each other and weeping much, so that no one could part them.'

<table>
<tr><td>(33)</td><td>El Çid a doña Ximena</td><td>íva-la</td><td>abraçar,</td><td>doña Ximena</td></tr>
<tr><td></td><td></td><td>go.3SG.IMPP-CLIT</td><td>embrace.INF</td><td></td></tr>
<tr><td></td><td>al Çid la mánol'</td><td>va</td><td>besar,</td><td>llorando de los ojos, que non</td></tr>
<tr><td></td><td></td><td>go.3SG.PRES</td><td>kiss.INF</td><td></td></tr>
</table>

sabe qué se far (Cid 368–370)

'Cid **was going to embrace / was embracing / embraced** doña Ximena, doña Ximena **goes / is going to kiss / kissed** his hand weeping from her eyes, she does not know what to do'

Examples (32) and (33) represent emotionally charged scenes, as confirmed also by their broad contexts. We can suppose that such a meaning nuance of the subject's emotional involvement can be derived from 'intention', because the semantic component 'intention' emphasizes a relationship with the "internal", emotional and intentional world of the person who carries out the action (the subject). Instead of conveying the motion meaning with the use of "*ir* + Inf", the speaker seems to emphasize that the action described in the infinitive was performed in a non-ordinary way: it was a more dynamic, more voluntary and more intended action than our actions usually are.

There is another pragmatic function of the GO-construction which can be derived from the meaning 'intention'. In the Catalan example (34) the periphrasis is used in order to give an emotional force to the utterance.

(34) *Barons, ¿no sabets vosaltres que el rei de França és nostre cosí germà, e misser Carles atretal? Doncs, ¿con podets consellar que jo* ***vaja pendre*** *misser Carles?* (Munt II 65, 8–10)

'Barons, do you not know that the King of France is Our cousin-german, and Sir Charles as well? Then, how can you advise me **to go and seize** Sir Charles?'

The utterance in (34), without any doubt, can also refer to a motion. In order to seize Charles, the king would have to move in space. The speech act verb *consellar* 'advise' signals a directive speech act. But the advice likely refers to taking and not to moving. The act of taking Charles seems to be more important and the verbal form in subjunctive *vaja* 'that I go' seems to have an emphasizing function. The utterance apparently has the semantic nuance of indignation. This reading is also confirmed by the question form *¿con podets...?* 'how can you…?', which is a conventional form to express indignation. The content of the preceding utterance, which is in close relationship with the utterance containing the GO-construction, describes the circumstance which explains the king's indignation. Both clauses are connected with the particle *doncs* 'then'. The king becomes indignant not at the motion but at its aim: he does not want to catch his own relative. This pragmatic function is very similar to the following example, which reflects a current Spanish use of the GO-construction: it can express surprise in relation with a suggested proposition. Consider (35).

(35) *¿Te acuerdas de tus sueños? – ¿No* ***me voy a acordar****?*
NEG REFL AUX.1SG.PRES to remember.INF
'Do you remember your dreams? – **Of course I do**!'

In example (35) the sense of futurity is eclipsed and the emotional function of the GO-construction gains ground. Example (35) shows such a use of the modern Spanish "*ir a* + Inf" in which surprise and indignation are expressed at a proposition which has been suggested before (that the hearer does not remember their dreams) and which the subject believes to be false. Thus, with the use of this construction in a negative question form, the speaker indirectly expresses their surprise and indignation, and, at the same time, denies the suggested proposition. The similarity of the Catalan examples like (34) and the current Spanish function of the periphrasis provides a further evidence in favor of their common origin, because it shows that in their origins, both Romance GO-periphrasis had the same functions. Some of them survived in Spanish (intentional modality, emotional charge), some of them in Catalan (completedness of the action, past tense value).

To sum up, on the basis of the above considerations, we can hypothesize that the evolution of the Catalan GO-construction also reflects a universal tendency, inasmuch as it followed the pathway presented in (4) (in section 3.1), repeated here for convenience, until the stage "intention".

(4) 'the motion path': motion with the aim of doing something > intention > (future)

The Catalan and the Spanish medieval GO-constructions both instantiate the grammaticalization of a motion verb into a marker of intention. At this stage of their evolution they both seem to instantiate the same construction, and their later semantic divergence, namely, in Spanish to a future and in Catalan to a past tense, can be attributed to the tense and aspect of the verb 'go' in the most frequent contexts of use, which induced different inferences (see Nagy C. 2010 for more details, cf. also Pérez Saldanya 1996).

6. Conclusions

In the present paper I have presented how contextual analysis can be applied in historical pragmatics research in order to reveal the cognitive background of semantic change in grammaticalization. Cognitive development of lexical units undergoing grammaticalization should be revealed in historical pragmatics by means of a detailed contextual analysis, for which we need a clear conception of context. Context can be conceived of in several ways, and both narrow and broad conceptions of context can be found in the literature. An important distinction can be observed in works on semantic change in grammaticalization (cf. Diewald 2002; Heine 2002) between two types of contexts: those which offer ambiguity and thus trigger grammaticalization, and those which exclude the original lexical meaning of the grammaticalizing item and thus serve as evidence of a previous semantic change. From a methodological point of view, in the present paper I have distinguished between narrow context, which I have defined grammatically, and broad context, which does not only refer to textual circumstances but also includes encyclopedic information and inferences in context.

The study reported on in the present paper has yielded findings concerning the early stage of the history of the Catalan "*anar* 'go' + Inf" periphrasis. In order to determine what conceptual content the medieval Catalan GO-construction has I have relied on the following: (i) a similar construction, namely, the Spanish "*ir (a)* 'go (to)' + Inf", whose history is better known and fits the universal tendency of the development of GO verbs in languages of the world, (ii) other medieval Catalan and Spanish constructions which show similarity in their functions and contexts, (iii) linguistic clues which help assign meaning to historical occurrences. I have emphasized that data originating from the investigation of occurrences in their broad contexts can override previous claims about meanings, formulated on the basis of the exclusive analysis of narrow contexts. The cognitive basis of semantic change can be identified only if we manage to find reliable contextual, linguistic clues which can reveal something about the meaning of lexical units or constructions. The present paper has presented some of these.

The result throws a different light on the history of the Catalan GO-construction under study, and relates its origins to the salience of the meaning component 'intention', suggesting that Detges's (2004) inchoative aspect hypothesis concerning the origin of the Catalan GO-past is mistaken. Historical data suggest that occurrences of the Catalan "*anar* 'go' + Inf" refer to completed actions and not to their beginning. "GO + Inf" in medieval texts describes the action as a whole, and the occurrences often are followed by a description of the consequences. The use of this periphrasis suggests that the action had been completely performed and that the performance of the action was more dynamic and intentional than usually. This hypothesis seems to be confirmed by the conceptual affinity of "GO + Inf" and "THINK OF + Inf", which both contrast to "BEGIN TO/OF + Inf".

Acknowledgements

Work on the present paper was supported by the Research Group for Theoretical Linguistics of the Hungarian Academy of Sciences at the Universities of Debrecen, Pécs and Szeged. I would like to express my gratitude to Enikő Németh T. and Károly Bibok for their constructive advice and valuable discussions about several topics which are touched upon in this paper. I am grateful to Anna Fenyvesi for improving my English. Finally, I thank the anonymous reviewers for their comments which helped to improve the paper. I alone am responsible for any remaining errors.

Historical sources

Spanish

Cid: *Cantar de mio Cid* [Song of my Cid]. Anonym author, 12th cent. Madrid: Espasa–Calpe. 1976.

Tris: *Cuento de Tristan de Leonis* [The Story of Tristan of Leonis]. Anonym author, about 1390–1410. In: ADMYTE (Archivo Digital de Manuscritos y Textos Españoles). CNUM 389. BOOST3 2676.

Catalan

Desc: Desclot, Bernat – *Crònica* [Chronicle]. 1283–88. Barcelona: Edicions 62. 1990.

Munt: Muntaner, Ramón – *Crònica* [Chronicle]. About 1325. Barcelona: Edicions 62. 1991. For the English translation of the examples taken from the Chronicle of Muntaner I have mainly relied on the following work: Goodenough, Lady *The Chronicle of Muntaner.* Available at www.yorku.ca/inpar/muntaner_goodenough.pdf. Date of access: December 12th, 2009.

References

Badia i Margarit, Antonio M.
1995 *Gramàtica de la llengua catalana: Descriptiva, normativa, diatòpica, diastràtica* [A Descriptive, Normative, Diatopic and Diastratic Grammar of the Catalan Language]. Barcelona: Edicions Proa.

Bauhr, Gerard
1989 *El futuro en -RÉ e 'IR' A + infinitivo en español peninsular moderno.* Goterna: Kungälv.

Bibok, Károly
2004 Word meaning and lexical pragmatics. *Acta Linguistica Hungarica* 51: 265–308.

Bibok, Károly and Enikő Németh T.
2001 How the lexicon and context interact in the meaning construction of utterances. In *Pragmatics and the Flexibility of Word Meaning*, (Current Research in the Semantics/Pragmatics Interface 8), Enikő Németh T. and Károly Bibok (eds.), 289–320. Amsterdam/London/etc.: Elsevier.

Bybee, Joan L.
2007 Diachronic linguistics. In *The Oxford Handbook of Cognitive Linguistics*, Dirk Geeraerts and Hubert Cuyckens (eds.), 945–987. Oxford: Oxford University Press.

Bybee, Joan L.
2005 From usage to grammar: The mind's response to repetition. LSA Presidential Address, January 8, 2005. Available at: http://www2.sfs.uni-tuebingen.de/~gerhard/lehre/ss08/exemplarBased/Bybee05.pdf. Date of access: October 7th, 2010.

Bybee, Joan L.
2003 Mechanisms of change in grammaticization: The role of frequency. In *The Handbook of Historical Linguistics*, Brian D. Joseph and Richard D. Janda (eds.), 602–623. Oxford: Blackwell.

Bybee, Joan L.
2002 Cognitive processes in grammaticalization. In *The New Psychology of Language*, Michael Tomasello (ed.), Volume 2, 145–167. Hillsdale, NJ: Lawrence Erlbaum.

Bybee, Joan, Revere Perkins and William Pagliuca
1994 *The Evolution of Grammar: Tense, Aspect, and Modality in the Languages of the World.* Chicago/London: The University of Chicago Press.

Colon, Germà
1978a El perfet perifràstic català "va + infinitiu" [The Catalan periphrastic perfect "*va* + infinitive"]. In *La llengua catalana en els seus textos* [The Catalan Language of Texts], Germà Colon (ed.), Volume 2, 119–130. Barcelona: Curial.

Colon, Germà
1978b Sobre el perfet perifràstic 'vado + infinitiu', en català, en provençal i en francès [On the periphrastic perfect '*vado* + infinitive' in Catalan, Provençal and, French]. In *La llengua catalana en els seus textos* [The Catalan Language of Texts], Germà Colon (ed.), Volume 2, 131–174. Barcelona: Curial.

Detges, Ulrich
2004 How cognitive is grammaticalization? The history of the Catalan *perfet perifràstic*. In *Up and Down the Cline: The Nature of Grammaticalization*, Olga Fischer, Muriel Norde and Harry Perridon (eds.), 211–227. Amsterdam: Benjamins.

Diewald, Gabriele
2002 A model for relevant types of contexts in grammaticalization. In *New Reflections on Grammaticalization*, Ilse Wischer and Gabriele Diewald (eds.), 103–120. Amsterdam: Benjamins.

Fischer, Olga
2007 *Morphosyntactic Change: Functional and Formal Perspectives.* Oxford: Oxford University Press.

Fitzmaurice, Susan and Irma Taavitsainen
2007 Historical pragmatics: What it is and how to do it. In *Methods in Historical Pragmatics*, (Topics in English Linguistics 52.), Susan M. Fitzmaurice and Irma Taavitsainen (eds.), 11–36. Berlin/New York: Mouton de Gruyter.

Fortson Iv, Benjamin W.
2003 An approach to semantic change. In *The Handbook of Historical Linguistics*, Brian D. Joseph and Richard D. Janda (eds.), 648–666. Oxford: Blackwell.

Gili Gaya, Samuel
1961 *Curso superior de sintaxis española*. Barcelona: Biblograf.
Gómez Torrego, Leonardo
1988 *Perífrasis verbales: Sintaxis, semántica y estilística*. Madrid: Arco/ Libros.
Heine, Bernd
2002 On the role of context in grammaticalization. In *New Reflections on Grammaticalization*, Ilse Wischer and Gabriele Diewald (eds.), 83–102. Amsterdam: Benjamins.
Heine, Bernd
2003 Grammaticalization. In *The Handbook of Historical Linguistics*, Brian D. Joseph and Richard D. Janda (eds.), 575–601. Oxford: Blackwell.
Heine, Bernd and Tania Kuteva
2002 *World Lexicon of Grammaticalization*. Cambridge: Cambridge University Press.
Hopper, Paul J. and Elizabeth C. Traugott
1993 *Grammaticalization*. Cambridge: Cambridge University Press.
Jacobs, Andreas and Andreas H. Jucker
1995 The historical perspective in pragmatics. In *Historical Pragmatics*, Andreas H. Jucker (ed.), 3–27. Amsterdam/Philadelphia: Benjamins.
Jucker, Andreas H.
1994 The feasibility of historical pragmatics. *Journal of Pragmatics* 22: 533–535.
Juge, Matthew L.
1999 On the rise of suppletion in verbal paradigm. In *Proceedings of the twenty-fifth annual meeting of the Berkeley Linguistics Society*, Steve S. Chang, Lily Liaw and Josef Ruppenhofer (eds.), 183–194. Berkeley: Berkeley Linguistics Society.
Juge, Matthew L.
2002 *Tense and aspect in periphrastic pasts: evidence from Iberian Romance*. PhD dissertation, University of California-Berkeley.
Juge, Matthew L.
2006 Morphological factors in the grammaticalization of the Catalan "go" past. *Diachronica* 23: 313–339.
Juge, Matthew L.
2008 Narrative and the Catalan GO-past. *Folia Linguistica historica* 29: 27–56.
Kearns, Kate
2002 Implicature and language change. In *Handbook of Pragmatics*, Jef Verschueren, Jan-Ola Östman, Jan Blommaert and Chris Bulcaen (comps.), 1–22. Amsterdam: Benjamins.
Kepser, Stephan and Marga Reis (eds.)
2005 *Linguistic Evidence: Empirical, Theoretical and Computational Perspectives*. Berlin/New York: Mouton de Gruyter.

Kertész, András and Csilla Rákosi
2008 Introduction: The problem of data and evidence in theoretical linguistics. In *Neue Ansätze zu linguistischer Evidenz: Pilotstudien* [New Approaches to Linguistic Evidence: Pilot Studies], András Kertész and Csilla Rákosi (eds.), 9–19. Frankfurt am Main/Bern/etc.: Lang.

Kiefer, Ferenc
2006 *Aspektus és akcióminőség – különös tekintettel a magyar nyelvre* [Aspect and Aktionsart with Special Regard to Hungarian]. Budapest: Akadémiai Kiadó.

Levinson, Stephen C.
2000 *Presumptive meanings: The theory of generalized conversational implicature.* Cambridge, MA: The MIT Press.

Martínez Gómez, Esther
2004 Las perífrasis verbales en español. *Revista electrónica de estudios filológicos* 7. Available at: www.um.es/tonosdigital/znum7/estudios/kdelasperifrasis.htm. Date of access: October 7th, 2010.

Matte Bon, Francisco
1998 *Gramática comunicativa del español*, Volume 1. Madrid: Edelsa.

Meyer-Lübke, Wilhelm
1902 [1890] *Grammatik der romanischen Sprachen.* Leipzig: Fues's Verlag.

Moll, Fransesc de B.
2006 [1991] Gramàtica històrica catalana. (Biblioteca Lingüística Catalana 31.) València: Universitat de València.

Nagy C., Katalin
2010 The pragmatics of grammaticalization: The role of implicatures in semantic change. *Journal of Historical Pragmatics* 11: 67–95.

Navarro, Federico
2008 Análisis histórico del discurso: Hacia un enfoque histórico-discursivo en el estudio diacrónico de la lengua. In *El valor de la diversidad (meta)lingüística. Actas del VIII Congreso de Lingüística General.* Antonio Moreno Sandoval (ed.), Madrid: Universidad Autónoma de Madrid. Available at: http://www.lllf.uam.es/clg8/actas/pdf/paperCLG85.pdf. Date of access: October 7th, 2010.

Neves, Maria Helena de Moura
2000 *Gramática de usos do português.* São Paulo: Unesp.

Németh T., Enikő
1994 Megnyilatkozás: típus–példány [Utterance: type and token]. *Néprajz és Nyelvtudomány* 35: 69–101.

Olbertz, Hella
1998 *Verbal periphrases in a functional grammar of Spanish.* (Functional Grammar Series 22.) Berlin/New York: Mouton de Gruyter.

Penke, Martina and Anette Rosenbach (eds.)
2007 *What Counts as Evidence in Linguistics. The Case of Innateness.* (Benjamins Current Topics 7.) Amsterdam / Philadelphia: Benjamins.

Perea, Maria Pilar
2007 El perfet simple: extensió i ús a començament del segle XXI [The simple past: extension and use at the beginning of 21st century]. In *Actes del tretzè col.loqui internacional de llengua i literatura catalanes* [Actas of the 13rd international symposium on Catalan language and literature], Volume 2, Martí Sadurní (ed.), 279–296. Barcelona: Publicacions de l'Abadia de Montserrat.

Pérez Saldanya, Manuel
1996 Gramaticalització i reanàlisi: el cas del perfet perifràstic en català [Grammaticalization and reanalysis: the case of the periphrastic preterit in the Catalan]. In *Actes del desè col.loqui internacional de llengua i literatura catalanes* [Actas of the 10th international symposium on Catalan language and literature], Volume 3, Axel Schönberger and Tilbert Dídac Stegmann (eds.), 71–107. Barcelona: Publicacions de l'Abadia de Montserrat.

Scala, Luca
2003 *Català de l'Alguer: Criteris de llengua escrita* [The Catalan of Alghero: Criteria for a written language]. Barcelona: Publicacions de l'Abadia de Montserrat.

Szertics, Joseph
1981 *Tiempo y verbo en el Romancero Viejo.* Madrid: Gredos.

Traugott, Elizabeth C.
1999 The role of pragmatics in semantic change. In *Pragmatics in 1998: Selected Papers from the 6th International Pragmatics Conference,* Volume 2, Jef Verschueren (ed.), 93–102. Antwerp: International Pragmatics Association.

Traugott, Elizabeth C.
2003 Constructions in grammaticalization. In *The Handbook of Historical Linguistics,* Brian D. Joseph and Richard D. Janda (eds.), 624–647. Oxford: Blackwell.

Traugott, Elizabeth C. and Richard B. Dasher
2004 [2002] *Regularity in Semantic Change.* Cambridge: Cambridge University Press.

Wachowicz, Teresa Cristina
2007 Auxiliary and aspectualizer verbs: some syntactic and semantic distinctions. *Revista Letras* 73: 223–234.

From syntactic alternations to lexical pragmatics

Károly Bibok

1. Introduction

1.1. Background

By syntactic alternation it is generally meant that a verb occurring in a type of syntactic argument structure can be used in another one as well. As to the meanings of these syntactic structures, they are different but in a predictable way. In lexicography there is a tradition that treats occurrences of a word with different syntactic patterns as instances of polysemy if they figure separately in a dictionary. However, recent trends in theoretical linguistics attempt to exceed such an enumerative conception of the lexicon. One of these uses lexical rules or operations to derive a dictionary entry with new meaning (cf. Pinker 1989; Levin and Rappaport Hovav 1995; Rappaport Hovav and Levin 1998). In addition, narrowly defined semantic classes of verbs are established which involve only the verbs taking part in a particular syntactic alternation (Pinker 1989). Another approach to syntactic alternations is constructional. Pustejovsky's (1995) Generative Lexicon Theory assumes a linguistic device that allows for several constituents to be considered functors (predicates) in a simple construction and which, therefore, is named co-composition. So a verb has only one meaning lexically and the second meaning appears when the verb is used in the corresponding construction. According to Goldberg's (1995, 2006) Construction Grammar, both variants of an alternating verb can be accounted for constructionally by assuming a single verb meaning to be able to fuse with two distinct constructions. Although these recent trends in theoretical linguistics are important steps towards a well-founded treatment of syntactic alternations, one has to realize the significance of *both constructional and lexical factors* as well as the necessity of an improved elaboration of lexical representations.

1.2. Aims and the organization of the paper

In the present paper I have two main aims. First, I intend to set forth in detail a lexical-constructional account of syntactic alternations that eliminates the shortcomings of the lexical and constructional conceptions but exploits their advantages. In the creation of my theory I rely upon the analysis of three syntactically alternating Hungarian verb classes. They include manner-of-motion verbs, verbs of sound emission, and the class of spatial position verbs, which has not been investigated yet in the Hungarian literature at all. Establishing lexical-semantic representations of alternating and non-alternating verbs in a study at the interface of lexical semantics and lexical pragmatics, I attempt to contribute to the elaboration of the lexicon in which, on the one hand, a number of words do not encode full-fledged concepts and, on the other hand, encyclopedic information or information concerning the use of language can be fixed with lexical entries. Only such a lexicon can be considered a promising starting point for lexical pragmatics. Second, I want to consciously reflect on methodological aspects of my research, especially on the relationship between theory and data as well as the criteria of the plausibility of a theory. One of these criteria is the extendibility of the lexical-constructional approach into lexical pragmatics.

The organization of the paper is as follows. In sections 2 and 3 I thoroughly examine how lexical and constructional theories try to account for syntactic alternation. Then in section 4 I introduce my lexical-constructional approach and present the analyses of the three Hungarian verb classes. Section 5 is devoted to methodological issues emerging in connection with my examination and account of syntactic alternation. The paper ends with the concluding section 6.

2. Lexical approaches to syntactic alternation

The verbs of manner of motion in Hungarian include the following:

(1) *ballag* 'walk slowly', *biceg* 'hobble', *billeg* 'tip; walk swinging slightly from side to side', *csoszog* 'shuffle one's feet', *csúszik* 'slide', *dülöngél* 'reel', *folyik* 'flow', *forog* 'spin', *fut* 'run', *gurul* 'roll', *himbálózik* 'swing', *hömpölyög* 'surge', *imbolyog* 'totter', *kúszik* 'creep', *lebeg* 'float', *mászik* 'climb', *ömlik* 'pour', *pattan* 'bounce', *pattog* 'bounce (several times)', *pörög* 'spin', *repül* 'fly', *ring* 'swing', *rohan* 'rush', *sétál* 'walk', *sántikál* 'hobble', *siklik* 'glide', *szalad* 'run', *száll* 'fly', *szökdécsel* 'skip', *szökdel* 'skip', *szökken* 'skip (once)', *támolyog* 'stagger', *táncol* 'dance', *tántorog* 'wabble', *tipeg* 'waddle; toddle', *totyog* 'waddle; toddle', *ugrál* 'jump (several times)', *ugrik* 'jump', *úszik* 'swim; float', etc.[1]

[1] Several verbs of (1), such as *dülöngél* 'reel', *forog* 'spin', *fut* 'run', *himbálózik* 'swing', *imbolyog* 'totter', *lebeg* 'float', *pattog* 'bounce (several times)', *pörög* 'spin', *ring* 'swing', *szökdécsel* 'skip', *szökdel* 'skip', *táncol* 'dance', *ugrál* 'jump

Just like the equivalent English verbs, the Hungarian ones in (1) can take a directional phrase, denoting not a manner of motion but a directed motion in a particular manner. E.g.:

(2) a. *A gyerek úszik.*
the child.NOM[2] swims
'The child is swimming.'
b. *A gyerek a barlangba úszik.*
the child.NOM the cave.ILL swims
'The child is swimming into the cave.'

The verb *úszik* 'swim' and other similar verbs in (1) show a type of systematic and productive polysemy (Ladányi 2007: 214–215). This relation may be treated by a lexical rule according to which a verb can take a directional argument if it denotes a manner of motion (Komlósy 1992: 355). However, only some of those verbs which mean manner of motion of inanimate entities capable of moving in the presence of external effects are suitable for designating a directed motion (Komlósy 2000: 257). Compare, for instance, the verbs *pattog* 'bounce' and *inog* 'wabble' in (3) and (4), respectively.

(3) a. *A labda a fal mellett pattog.*
the ball.NOM the wall.NOM by bounces
'The ball bounces by the wall.'
b. *A labda a fal mellé pattog.*
the ball.NOM the wall.NOM to bounces
'The ball bounces to the wall.'

(several times)', *ugrik* 'jump', denote manner of motion of not only displacement but also of position change. The latter kind of motion may unequivocally be referred to by using the expression *(egy) helyben* 'in (a) place'. – For the list and description of English verbs of manner of motion, see Levin (1993: 264–267).

2 The glosses are not intended to capture all morphological properties of Hungarian words but indicate the necessary ones for the present purposes. The abbreviations used in the glosses throughout this paper are the following: 3pl = third person plural, 3SG = third person singular, ACC = accusative, ALL = allative, ELA = elative, ILL = illative, INE = inessive, INS = instrumental, NOM = nominative, POSS = possessive inflexion (of third person singular), SUB = sublative, SUP = suppressive and TEM = temporal.

(4) a. *A szék a fal mellett inog.*
the chair.NOM the wall.NOM by wabbles
'The chair wabbles by the wall.'

b. **A szék a fal mellé inog.*
the chair.NOM the wall.NOM to wabbles
'The chair wabbles to the wall.'

Similarly to verbs of manner of motion, Hungarian verbs of sound emission are also characterized by regular and productive polysemy as well as by syntactic alternation resulting in a directed motion sense (Ladányi 2007: 215–216). The verbs of sound emission in Hungarian include the following:

(5) *berreg* 'throb', *cuppog* 'squelch', *csattog* 'flap; clank', *csikorog* 'squeak', *csörömpöl* 'clank', *dübörög* 'rumble', *nyikorog* 'squeak', *pöfög* 'chuff', *süvít* 'howl', *zakatol* 'rattle', *zúg* 'hum', *zümmög* 'buzz', etc.[3]

The relevant syntactic alternation is shown in (6):

(6) a. *A fiú csattog a papucsával.*
the boy.NOM claps/flaps[4] the slippers.POSS.INS
'The boy is clapping his slippers (with his hands).'
Or: 'The boy is flapping his slippers (while walking).'

b. *A fiú a folyosóra csattog a papucsával.*
the boy.NOM the corridor.SUB flaps the slippers.POSS.INS
'The boy is flapping his slippers walking out into the corridor.'

It is worth noting that several expressions formed according to (6b) seem to be still uncommon and strange (Ladányi 2007: 215). A prefixed version of the verb is more usual. For example, the verb *csattog* 'flap' can take the preverb *ki* 'out' as in (7).

(7) *A fiú kicsattog a papucsával a folyosóra.*
the boy.NOM out.flaps the slippers.POSS.INS the corridor.SUB
'The boy is flapping his slippers walking out into the corridor.'

---

[3] The verbs *pattan* 'bounce' and *pattog* 'bounce (several times)' given among those of manner of motion in (1) also have a cracking sound emission sense. But they do not seem to belong to (5) since motion can be considered bouncing one without any concomitant cracking sound. – For the list and description of English verbs of sound emission, see Levin (1993: 234–236).

[4] The verb *csattog* also means 'clap'. However, unlike *csattog* 'flap', *csattog* 'clap' does not alternate and have a directed motion sense.

Furthermore, if a verb occurs with an agent argument and the sound is produced by the agent's sound formation organs, it cannot be interpreted as a directed motion even together with a directional phrase and preverb (Ladányi 2008: 310). Thus, neither (8b) with a directional phrase, nor (9) with a prefixed verb and directional phrase yields the intended interpretation.

(8) a. *Péter ordít.*
Péter.NOM screams
'Péter is screaming.'

b. *Péter a folyosóra ordít.*
Péter.NOM the corridor.SUB screams
*'Screaming, Péter is moving into the corridor.'

(9) *Péter kiordít a folyosóra.*
Péter.NOM out.screams the corridor.SUB
*'Screaming, Péter is moving into the corridor.'

(8b) and (9) only have a sound emission sense: 'Péter is screaming (through the door) into the corridor.'

The fact that both verbs of manner of motion and those of sound emission can belong to another semantic class of directed motion and occur with multiple argument realizations can be handled as meaning shifts which are rule-governed processes. Levin and Rappaport Hovav (1995: 20–30) assume that the verb meaning is represented in the form of a predicate composition made up of primitive predicates and what have been called constants. Constants encode the idiosyncratic elements of verb meaning, and combinations of predicates represent its grammatically relevant aspects. The latter constitute lexical-semantic templates of a language, which correspond to various ontological types of events. Pairs of verbs of manner of motion and of directed motion as well as of sound emission and of directed motion involve different lexical-semantic templates that have a shared constant and arise from a lexical rule of some sort (Levin and Rappaport Hovav 1995: 182–205). What they state in connection with English verbs is valid for Hungarian as well: these shifts are "regular and productive, although their existence and scope need to be stipulated in the lexicon of a language" (Levin and Rappaport Hovav 1996: 503). Therefore, a lexical rule amounts to a necessary condition and has to be supplemented with an enumeration of narrow semantic classes that the given lexical rule can actually be applied to (cf. Pinker 1989).

This lexical, or projectionist, approach to the type of phenomena presented above has another form which can be demonstrated by the following example (Rappaport Hovav and Levin 1998). The constant SWEEP categorized as a manner modifies an activity. Therefore, a canonical realization rule associates it with the predicate ACT in the activity event structure template, yielding the activity sense of the verb of surface contact through the motion *sweep*.

(10) a. Phil swept the floor.
b. [x $\text{ACT}_{<\mathit{SWEEP}>}$ y]

Several other meanings of *sweep* can arise via an operation called Template Augmentation, at least some applications of which must be lexical. One of these other meanings is the accomplishment sense, when *sweep* combines with a directional phrase. To account for it, the activity with the manner constant is augmented to the causative lexical-semantic template with the activity at stake as a cause and the achieved location caused by that activity.

(11) a. Phil swept the crumbs onto the floor.
b. [[x $\text{ACT}_{<\mathit{SWEEP}>}$ y] CAUSE [BECOME [z <*PLACE*>]]]

However, as Rappaport Hovav and Levin (1998: 121) acknowledge in a footnote, this account of the accomplishment use of verbs of surface contact through motion may not be extended to verbs of manner of motion. Although the directed motion use of manner-of-motion verbs (see (2b) above) also involves an activity-to-accomplishment shift, a causative analysis is not appropriate for such derived accomplishments. In another work by the same authors (Levin and Rappaport Hovav 1998: 259), a distinct primitive predicate for accomplishments other than CAUSE, namely GO, is introduced. The authors take the association of a constant with this accomplishment lexical-semantic template to be effected by a rule not formulated there.[5] To illustrate this, I present their example of accomplishment *walk* in the original form of notation.

5 An anonymous reviewer of this paper remarks that the lexical template approach is clearly constructional in spirit. However, there is no direct evidence for that. Rather, the authors in question admit the lexical character of the Template Augmentation operation (see above) and their commitment to lexical approach (e.g. Levin and Rappaport Hovav 1995: 29), while generally using lexical templates in meaning representations. Moreover, although they abstract away as much as possible from the projectionist–constructional debate in their recent book (Levin and Rappaport Hovav 2005: 193), they do not mention themselves when they list works of the constructional approach (p. 191, cf. also p. 207).

(12) GO (x, y)
|
$[\text{WALK}]_{\text{MANNER}}$

In such a theory, however, there is nothing but the manner constant WALK, which relates the activity *walk* to the accomplishment one in (12). At the same time, more is characteristic of both meanings of verbs under investigation even if one only takes strictly their common paraphrases such as 'manner of motion' and 'directed motion'. The paraphrases indicate a possibility to include into their representations a predicate shared by the two senses, namely, MOVE. This is supported by the fact that among the verbs of manner of motion there are those which have or can have inanimate subjects. Besides the verbs *pattog* 'bounce' and *inog* 'wabble' in (3) and (4) with intrinsically inanimate subjects, consider the verb *úszik* 'float' in (13), which is an inanimate subject variant of the same verb *úszik* 'swim' in (2).[6]

(13) a. *Az üveg úszik.*
the bottle.NOM floats
'The bottle is floating.'
b. *Az üveg a barlangba úszik.*
the bottle.NOM the cave.ILL floats
'The bottle is floating into the cave.'

From the present point of view it is not important whether a verb of manner of motion occurs with a directional phrase or not, but none of the verbs in (3), (4) and (13) have agentive arguments and, therefore, the activity lexical-semantic template, i.e. the predicate ACT, either, in their representations. It means that there would be no predicate which the corresponding constant of manner could be connected to. For such a predicate, MOVE is a promising candidate. Perhaps further research into the nature of MOVE will result in lexical-semantic representations which more clearly express the relationship between manner of motion and directed motion. Indeed, this idea will be clarified in the subsequent sections of the paper.

[6] English verbs of manner of motion also have such a special subgroup (cf. Levin 1993: 264–267). As to mapping the non-agentive verbs of manner of motion onto the agentive verbs of manner of motion, or vice versa, there is no need to posit a lexical rule because this variable behavior is "simply the result of the existence of a lexical semantic constant that, by virtue of its nature, is basically compatible with more than one lexical semantic template" (Levin and Rappaport Hovav 1995: 211).

A third group of Hungarian verbs seems to be relevant to the meaning shift under investigation. Consider (14).

(14) *áll* 'stand', *fekszik* 'lie', *guggol* 'crouch', *hasal* 'lie on one's stomach', *hever* 'lie around', *könyököl* 'lean on one's elbow', *támaszkodik* 'lean on', *térdel* 'kneel', *ül* 'sit', etc.

These verbs can also take a directional phrase as in (15).

(15) a. *Péter áll.*
Péter.NOM stands.
'Péter is standing.'

b. *Péter a szőnyegre áll.*
Péter.NOM the carpet.SUB stands
'Péter steps onto the carpet.'

In (15a) the verb specifies being in a particular spatial configuration, while in (15b), assuming a spatial position through displacement. However, displacement is not necessary, the change of spatial configuration can also be carried out when one remains in place (cf., e.g., *guggol* 'crouch', *hasal* 'lie on one's stomach').

Like the two other classes of verbs in (1) and (5) above, besides the alternating verbs there are non-alternating verbs denoting being in particular spatial configurations. Consider (16) and (17).

(16) a. *A fiú a bordásfalon függ.*
the boy.NOM the wall.bars.SUP hangs
'The boy is hanging on the wall-bars.'

b. **A fiú a bordásfalra függ.*
the boy.NOM the wall.bars.SUB hangs
'The boy hangs onto the wall-bars.'

(17) a. *A fiú az ágyon heverészik.*
the boy.NOM the bed.SUP lies.around
'The boy is lying around on the bed.'

b. **A fiú az ágyra heverészik.*
the boy.NOM the bed.SUB lies.around
'The boy lies around onto the bed.'

What is more, the Hungarian verb *heveredik* 'lie down at full length' behaves the opposite way than *heverészik* 'lie around'. It takes a directional phrase but does not appear without it. Cf.:

(18) a. **A fiú az ágyon heveredik.*
the boy.NOM the bed.SUP lies.down.at.full.length
'The boy is lying down at full length on the bed.'

b. *A fiú az ágyra heveredik.*
the boy.NOM the bed.SUB lies.down.at.full.length
'The boy lies down at full length onto the bed.'

To the best of my knowledge, there is no analysis offered in the literature to account for the syntactic alternation and meaning shift of verbs in (14) as well as the non-alternating cases in (16)–(18).[7]

Although different kinds of lexical rules and operations have been mentioned above in connection with syntactic alternations and meaning shifts, they all pertain to a lexical, or a projectionist, model, in which verbs with multiple meanings have multiple lexical-semantic representations, and these meanings determine the various syntactic structures that verbs can occur in. In spite of the fact that in this model much attention is paid to testing meaning shifts by syntactic criteria and to linking rules connecting semantic structure constituents with syntactic ones, the meaning brought about by a meaning shift is grasped as a lexical phenomenon but not as a meaning occurring in a particular syntactic structure. Meaning shifts and syntactic alternations are approached by constructional conceptions from such a point of view.

---

7 Both *heveredik* 'lie down at full length' and *heverészik* 'lie around' contain as a stem the verb *hever* 'lie around' from (14). However, the durative and inchoative meanings ascribed to suffixes *-ész-* and *-ed-* (Tompa 1961: 348, 354), respectively, do not seem to explain their different behavior of non-alternation. Nevertheless, if the corresponding word-formation structure determined their non-alternation, this would only mean that the behavior at stake is connected to morphologically complex, and not simple, lexical-semantic representations. – English verbs, equivalent to Hungarian ones in (14) and occurring with different argument structures similarly to (15), are separately given in Levin (1993: 255–256, 262; see classes 47.6 and 50, respectively). In other words, taking a directional argument is not a property of verbs of being in a particular spatial configuration, unlike verbs of manner of motion and sound emission. According to Jackendoff (1990: 91–95), the verb *stand* also has an inchoative reading, which is expressed by a function INCH, mapping a state of being at some place into an event whose termination is this particular state. One should realize that the appearance of the directional phrase is not motivated at all because a locative phrase with a state of being remains unchanged in the representation of the inchoative meaning.

3. Constructional approaches to syntactic alternation

Pustejovsky's (1995: 125–126) could be considered a version of the constructional approach, relying on which one may explain the systematic polysemy 'manner of motion' → 'directed motion' in the following way. Consider (2) and (13) again, which, for the sake of convenience, are repeated here as (19) and (20).

(19) a. *A gyerek úszik.*
the child.NOM swims
'The child is swimming.'

b. *A gyerek a barlangba úszik.*
the child.NOM the cave.ILL swims
'The child is swimming into the cave.'

(20) a. *Az üveg úszik.*
the bottle.NOM floats
'The bottle is floating.'

b. *Az üveg a barlangba úszik.*
the bottle.NOM the cave.ILL floats
'The bottle is floating into the cave.'

The verb *úszik* 'swim; float' has only one meaning in the lexicon, which expresses the manner of motion (see the (a) examples above). The meaning 'to move in some direction in some manner' appearing in the (b) examples above does not belong to the verb *úszik* 'swim; float' itself, but to the phrase consisting of this verb and the inflected noun. This second, more complex meaning associated with a transition from an initial point to an end cannot be derived from the constituent parts, i.e. the verb and inflected noun, by means of a standard rule of composition. One has to assume that the inflected noun also behaves like a functor (predicate) in respect to *úszik* 'swim; float'. Consequently, the meaning of the phrase *a barlangba úszik* 'is swimming/floating into the cave' is constructed by the mechanism which allows for several constituents to be considered functors in a simple construction and which, therefore, is called co-composition in Pustejovsky's (1995) Generative Lexicon Theory.[8]

[8] An anonymous reviewer of this paper objects that Pustejovsky's theory is characterized as constructional. My intention is only to indicate that his co-composition is constructional in the sense that one of the meanings of the verb *úszik* 'swim; float' appears in a *construction consisting of this verb and the inflected*

A constructional analysis becomes a full-fledged one in Goldberg's (1995, 2006) Construction Grammar. According to Construction Grammar, constructions are form–meaning pairs. Distinct constructions are defined constructions some of whose properties are unpredictable from knowledge of other constructions. They exist independently of particular verbs and determine syntactic structures. There is no strict division between syntactic constructions and lexical entries. The latter are also considered constructions. The two types of constructions only differ in internal complexity and in the extent to which phonological form is specified.[9]

In each construction, the meaning of the verb is fused with that of the construction. In general, representations of word meanings can be conceived of in regard to Fillmorian frames (or Langackerian background, or Lakoffian idealized cognitive models). However, when verbs are integrated into constructions, one part of their representations plays a crucial role, namely, participant roles. They are frame-specific roles which have to be distinguished from more general argument roles, figuring in the semantic part of constructions, such as agent, patient or goal.

The fusion of a lexical entry with a construction is constrained by several factors. A semantic generalization can apply to a particular construction and, in turn, this semantic generalization is sensitive to contextual information and world knowledge. If causation typically implies some incidental motion, this motion may be specified by a directional phrase in the caused-motion construction. For example, salami normally falls down from the slicer, and cheese from the grater. That is why one can use the verbs *slice* and *grate* in the caused-motion construction. Cf.:

(21) The salesman sliced the salami onto the wax paper.

(22) The mother grated the cheese onto the macaroni.

Notice that slicing and grating in the described way relate to the given verbs only in a neutral context, and this depends on our world knowledge. One can imagine a salami slicer which slices salami put into a container which does not allow the salami to move after being sliced. It is obvious that such a slicing cannot be expressed by a caused-motion construction as in (21).

---

noun and is not fixed in the lexicon. This statement does not at all intend to posit Pustejovsky among constructionists.

[9] In the rest of this paper, however, the term *construction* is used instead of *syntactic construction* because *lexical entry* more often figures in the terminology of Construction Grammar than *lexical construction*.

Among constraints of integration of lexical entries into constructions there are two other factors, also known in lexical theories: narrow semantic classes and idiosyncratic properties of lexical entries.

Applying the machinery of Construction Grammar to syntactic alternations, I first cite Goldberg's (1995: 176–177) own example. The lexical-semantic representation of the verb *slather* contains the following participant roles:

(23) *slather* <slatherer, thick-mass, target>

The three participant roles of *slather* are compatible with the argument roles of both the caused-motion construction and the causative-plus-*with*-adjunct construction. The first construction has three argument roles: a cause, a theme and a goal (directional). The two kinds of role sets can be fused with each other because the slatherer is semantically construable as a cause, thick-mass as a theme since it undergoes a change of location, and the target as a directional. Cf.:

(24) Sam slathered shaving cream onto his face.

Fusing the slatherer with the first argument of the other construction is the same as above. The target can be construed not only as a directional (see above) but also as a patient in that the entity which is slathered on is affected. Since the third participant role of *slather* requires that it be expressed, a *with*-phrase emerges even though in the framework of Construction Grammar it is an adjunct of the corresponding construction. Cf.:

(25) Sam slathered his face with shaving cream.

Thus, if the participant roles of a verb are compatible with the argument structure of two constructions, this verb occurs in syntactically alternating structures.

Applying Goldberg's (1995, 2006) Construction Grammar to syntactic alternations, I also attempt to re-analyze (19) and (20) with *úszik* 'swim; float'. While in Pustejovsky's version of the analysis only the occurrence of the verb with a directional phrase is considered a constructional meaning, according to Construction Grammar, both uses of the verb, i.e. with and without a directional phrase, are analyzable in constructional terms. In the case without a directional phrase, the verb is integrated into a kind of simple intransitive construction, and in the case with a directional phrase into the intransitive motion construction. The verb can be associated with the latter construction and given a directed motion interpretation (in accordance with the semantic generalization concerning the caused-motion construction) even if no participant role is fixed with the verb which corresponds to the directional role. The directional role belongs to an argument which the intransitive motion construction itself owns, independently of whether the verb has a participant role corresponding semantically to a directional role.

What is crucially important in connection with the constructional analysis of the syntactic alternation characteristic of *úszik* 'swim; float', is that, according to Construction Grammar, the first argument role of the intransitive motion construction, i.e. of the predicate MOVE, is nothing but a theme, similarly to the second argument role of the caused-motion construction. Thus, the intransitive motion construction (and, consequently, the simple intransitive construction) accounts for the use of *úszik* 'swim; float' only with a theme subject as in (20). Therefore, another construction has to be assumed to handle sentences with agentive subjects as in (19b), provided that the child actually acts and he/she is not interpreted as the inanimate subject of (20b) is.

In doing so, besides the predicate MOVE, one needs another predicate which takes an agent. CAUSE is usually held to be such a predicate (cf. Goldberg 1995: 165; Pinker 1989: 73). Notice, however, that the first argument of CAUSE, i.e. the cause, is not simply an agent. In fact, an activity, i.e. ACT, serves as an actual cause. So, the agent is nothing other than the first argument of ACT.[10] Consequently: [[x ACT] : [x MOVE]], which can be paraphrased as follows: 'x acts so that x moves'. In accordance with this, one assumes the intransitive activity-motion construction (and, perhaps, for lack of motion, the intransitive activity construction).

Nevertheless, this duplication of constructions does not necessarily imply the lexical proliferation of the Hungarian verb *úszik* 'swim; float'. In constructional terms, one can offer that the single participant role of the verb at stake is construable either as a theme, or as an agent in both the directed motion sense, i.e. in the intransitive motion and activity-motion constructions with the directional argument role, and in the manner of motion sense, i.e. in the simple intransitive and intransitive activity constructions without the directional argument role. Then the question of what the double construal depends on arises. The answer should be postponed till the following section, where a detailed analysis of meaning structures of verbs in (1) will be carried out.

---

[10] For the logical types and thematic roles of the arguments of CAUSE, see also Komlósy (2000: 249–250); Levin and Rappaport Hovav 1995: 83–84); Tenny and Pustejovsky (2000: 7–15).

Recall that a verb of manner of motion may be fused with the intransitive motion construction and – it can already be added – with the intransitive activity-motion construction. It may also be given a directed motion sense if it does not have such a participant role which semantically corresponds to the directional argument role of those constructions. Now, one can realize that what has been stated about verbs of manner of motion is effective for other classes of verbs, namely, those of sound emission and those of being in a particular spatial configuration, although this is not explicitly formulated in Goldberg's (1995, 2006) Construction Grammar. This means that in the constructional framework all three syntactic alternations under investigation can be captured in the same way. If so, one cannot avoid the question concerning the motivation of occurrence of a directional in the intransitive activity-motion construction. An attentive reader certainly remembers that according to a semantic generalization sensitive to contextual information and world knowledge, the caused-motion construction is possible if an event of causation of change of state involves some incidental but predictable motion (see (21) and (22)). Let us suppose that the directional role of the intransitive activity-motion construction can also be motivated semantically if it is about an event of motion since, as our world knowledge dictates, a direction inherently belongs not only to directed motion but also to any motion activity (see (19a) and (20a)), or if sound emission is a concomitant of motion (see the second interpretation of (6a), namely 'The boy is flapping his slippers while walking'). However, in case of (15a), i.e. *Péter áll* 'Péter is standing', one cannot refer to any motion which would motivate the directional role in (15b), i.e. *Péter a szőnyegre áll* 'Péter steps onto the carpet'. A solution would consist in the indication of the agentive role since the agent's intention to act includes the possibility of moving. Notice that according to Goldberg's (1995, 2006) Construction Grammar, the agentive role is an argument role which is connected to a construction (in the present case, to the intransitive activity-motion construction). Thus, we once again face the difficulty of the double, theme or agent, construal of a participant role, which has already been mentioned in connection with the (single) participant role of *úszik* 'swim; float' and for which a solution was then postponed to the subsequent section.

Now what about the cases when particular verbs do not alternate? Besides their corresponding idiosyncratic properties, can one postulate some semantic generalizations? Consider once again such exceptions as (4) and (16) mentioned above and repeated here for the sake of convenience as (26) and (27).

(26) a. *A szék a fal mellett inog.*
the chair.NOM the wall.NOM by wabbles
'The chair wabbles by the wall.'

b. **A szék a fal mellé inog.*
the chair.NOM the wall.NOM to wabbles
'The chair wabbles to the wall.'

(27) a. *A fiú a bordásfalon függ.*
the boy.NOM the wall.bars.SUP hangs
'The boy is hanging on the wall-bars.'

b. **A fiú a bordásfalra függ.*
the boy.NOM the wall.bars.SUB hangs
'The boy hangs onto the wall-bars.'

Let us start out from the Komlósy's (2000: 257) statement cited in section 2. According to it, of the verbs which denote the manner of motion of inanimate things that are able to move in consequence of external effects, only a small group is suitable for expressing directed (proceeding) motion. The point of this statement is that the group of verbs under discussion does not behave homogeneously. For example, the verb *inog* 'wabble' does not take any arguments referring to an end point (see (26b)) but the verb *pattog* 'bounce' does (see (3b) above, i.e. *A labda a fal mellé pattog* 'The ball bounces to the wall'). However, among the verbs enumerated by Komlósy, there are verbs which only appear with theme subject (the two verbs just mentioned, *inog* 'wabble' and *pattog* 'bounce') while others occur with both theme subjects and agentive subjects (e.g. *billeg* 'tip; walk swinging slightly from side to side' and *csúszik* 'slide'). Consider the following examples with *csúszik* 'slide'.

(28) a. *A szánkó a jégen csúszik.*
the sled.NOM the ice.SUP slides
'The sled is sliding on ice.'

b. *A szánkó az árokba csúszik.*
the sled.NOM the ditch.ILL slides
'The sled is sliding into the ditch.'

(29) a. *A fiú a jégen csúszik.*
the boy.NOM the ice.SUP slides
'The boy is sliding on ice.'

b. *A fiú a lányhoz csúszik (a jégen).*
the boy.NOM the girl.ALL slides the ice.SUP
'The boy is sliding to the girl (on the ice).'

Unlike (28), (29) can actually be interpreted as the boy's intended activities when, e.g., he and his friends are playing on a lake frozen up in the winter.

Considering the ability of verbs at stake to take subjects with different argument roles and recognizing that the occurrence in a construction with an agent is especially important to account for the directed motion sense in cases such as (15b), i.e. *Péter a szőnyegre áll* 'Péter steps onto the carpet' (see also (31b) below), one can re-formulate Komlósy's statement in the following way. If a verb, e.g. *inog* 'wabble', cannot occur in a construction with an agentive role, it cannot be integrated into the intransitive motion construction either (cf. (26b)), exclusive of exceptions, e.g. *pattog* 'bounce' (cf. (3b)). If a verb occurs in a construction with an agentive role, the intransitive activity-motion construction can also take place (see (19b), i.e. *A gyerek a barlangba úszik* 'The boy is swimming into the cave' as well as (15b), i.e. *Péter a szőnyegre áll* 'Péter steps onto the carpet'), again not counting possible exceptions.

Furthermore, depending on whether the meaning of a verb contains a motion element, the intransitive motion construction is also possible. In other words, a verb referring to some motion inherently occurs with theme subject while a verb not having an inherent relation to motion does not. Cf. *úszik* 'swim; float' in (20), repeated here as (30), where it occurs with a theme subject and in the float sense, and *áll* 'stand' in (31), which is a theme variant of (15).

(30) a. *Az üveg úszik.*
the bottle.NOM floats
'The bottle is floating.'

b. *Az üveg a barlangba úszik.*
the bottle.NOM the cave.ILL floats
'The bottle is floating into the cave.'

(31) a. *A váza az asztalon áll.*
the vase.NOM the table.SUP stands.
'The vase is on the table.'

b. **A váza az asztalra áll.*
the vase.NOM the table.SUB stands.
'The vase steps onto the table.'

Nevertheless, it is the third occasion that we are faced with the issue of the double theme–agent construal of a participant role. At this point, in the next section, I will propose my solution to this issue in particular and to syntactic alternations in general.

4. A study at the interface of lexical semantics and lexical pragmatics

4.1. The overall characterization of the lexical-constructional approach

In the preceding sections we have seen that both lexical and constructional factors play a role in syntactic alternations. That is why I offer a lexical-constructional explanation, which will be elaborated in two steps. The first step is that conditions of the fusion of verbs with constructions are not restricted to the indication of a single constituent in lexical-semantic representations, namely, to participant roles, but enriched meaning representations should be introduced for verbs. Thus, this would be in accordance with general ideas concerning word meaning representations in Pustejovsky's (1995) Generative Lexicon Theory, and, in addition, possibilities involved originally in Goldberg's (1995, 2006) Construction Grammar and provided by frame semantics could be exploited. In the present case, the enriched meaning structure only requires that – besides the meaning without the activity element – another meaning be supposed, which includes this element.

However, it is only the first step, and we need a second one. We cannot be satisfied with proposing another meaning since it would be equivalent to an enumerative type of the lexicon in which alternating verbs occur twice according to their meanings. At the same time, we could come to a contradiction with different fundamental efforts of both lexical and constructional theories attempting to go beyond the simple multiplication of meanings in the lexicon. Recall that lexical rules or operations as well as a generative mechanism of co-composition or various constructions are assumed in order to account for contextually evoked senses. However, because of the troubles clarified in the above critical evaluation of lexical and constructional theories, one should propose a different solution to handling alternating verbs. Bearing permanently in mind the requirement of lexical economy (cf. also Bierwisch 1997), I offer such a general meaning representation of a verb which is semantically and pragmatically rich enough to serve as a basis for both constructional meanings coming about in syntactic alternation (and, of course, for double construals of participant roles). Thus, constructional meanings of a verb are condensed into one lexical meaning. In other words, in the lexicon, verbs have underspecified representations with optional components relevant to one or another constructional meaning and not representations that are as specific as constructional meanings. It is worth noting that while lexical representations are underspecified they should also be more detailed than in approaches criticized above, which is in full harmony with a statement demonstrated by Croft (2003: 61): "closer examination of the linguistic facts almost always reveals idiosyncrasies that show that more specific representations are required than is usually thought".

The conception outlined in the preceding paragraph and essential parts of which can be found in my earlier work (Bibok and Németh T. 2001; Bibok 2004) can be called lexical-constructional.[11]

Now, from the point of view of syntactic alternations it can be stated that verbs take part in them if they have a general meaning which is compatible with all meanings occurring in alternations. If a verb does not have a lexical representation that can result in different interpretations, that is, if a verb is lexically more specific, it cannot alternate syntactically. It is important to note that lexically specified verbs can appear in both (a)-lines and (b)-lines of above examples (see especially (16a) and (18b), i.e. *A fiú a bordásfalon függ* 'The boy is hanging on the wall-bars' and *A fiú az ágyra heveredik* 'The boy lies down at full length onto the bed'), which also requires an underspecified type of representations for the alternating verbs.

Moreover, my lexical-constructional account of syntactic alternations has some important consequences for the notion of polysemy. First, there is no need to consider one of the constructional meanings of a verb which is basic or primary with respect to others. One can consider the underspecified lexical meaning primary and all the constructional meanings non-primary. In addition, the latter are not to be derived from the former but compatible with the underspecified lexical meaning according to the non-derivational character of Construction Grammar. Second, the occurrence of a lexical item in different constructions can be regarded as the sufficient condition of its polysemy, but the necessary condition is the occurrence in different contexts (see below in 5.2).

---

[11] The lexical-constructional conception presented here has some common features with Iwata's (2002, 2005) but also differs from it in the details of the characteristics of both lexical and constructional meanings. A comparison between them would deserve a separate paper.

4.2. A lexical-constructional treatment of alternations with a directed motion sense

4.2.1. Alternation in manner-of-motion verbs

Consider the familiar examples *úszik* 'swim; float' once again.

(32) a. *A gyerek úszik.*
the child.NOM swims
'The child is swimming.'

b. *A gyerek a barlangba úszik.*
the child.NOM the cave.ILL swims
'The child is swimming into the cave.'

(33) a. *Az üveg úszik.*
the bottle.NOM floats
'The bottle is floating.'

b. *Az üveg a barlangba úszik.*
the bottle.NOM the cave.ILL floats
'The bottle is floating into the cave.'

As one can remember from section 3, the difference between (32a) and (33a) has been attributed to the presence or absence of the component ACT. The meaning of the verb *úszik* 'swim' in (32a) can be paraphrased as follows: 'x acts so that x moves in a particular manner'. The meaning of *úszik* 'float' in (33a) does not contain the component ACT, i.e.: 'x moves in a particular manner'. For these two meanings of *úszik* 'swim; float' to be condensed at the lexical level it is necessary to assume such an underspecified meaning which serves as a starting point of both occurrences of *úszik* 'swim; float' in (32a) and (33a). If one puts round brackets around the part of the two paraphrases which is only relevant to (32a), one can get the required formula:

(34) '(x acts so that) x moves in a particular manner'.

Thus, the round brackets in (34) indicate the optionality of the fragment 'x acts so that', which is not shared by both paraphrases.

Let us turn to the relationship between (32a) and (32b) as well as between (33a) and (33b). In accordance with a substantial idea of my lexical-constructional approach, some kind of underspecification would be appropriate in this case as well. To establish it we should examine once again the argument structure of *úszik* 'swim; float' in the (a) examples. Instead of (32) and (33), consider (35) and (36).

(35) a. *A gyerek a barlangban úszik.*
the child.NOM the cave.INE swims
'The child is swimming in the cave.'
b. *A gyerek a barlangba úszik.*
the child.NOM the cave.ILL swims
'The child is swimming into the cave.'

(36) a. *Az üveg a barlangban úszik.*
the bottle.NOM the cave.INE floats
'The bottle is floating in the cave.'
b. *Az üveg a barlangba úszik.*
the bottle.NOM the cave.ILL floats
'The bottle is floating into the cave.'

Despite the common view that verbs of manner of motion take only one argument semantically, there are some reasons to assume that they have another semantic argument, namely, a locative one. The verb *úszik* 'swim; float' and the other verbs in (1), such as *ballag* 'walk slowly', *biceg* 'hobble', *billeg* 'tip; walk swinging slightly from side to side', *csoszog* 'shuffle one's feet', *csúszik* 'slide', *dülöngél* 'reel', *folyik* 'flow', *forog* 'spin', *fut* 'run', *gurul* 'roll', etc., mean being in motion in some manner, which necessarily implies the occupation of some space. Therefore, the description of events denoted by these verbs needs the locative argument whereby the verbs at stake should be considered to have two arguments. If such a verb occurs in an utterance without a lexical realization of the locative argument, its omission only concerns the syntactic structure, but the number of arguments does not decrease on the level of meaning representation.

The appropriateness of treating verbs of manner of motion as two-argument predicates is further confirmed if they are compared with the verb *áll* 'stand' and the other verbs in (14), such as *fekszik* 'lie', *guggol* 'crouch', *hasal* 'lie on one's stomach', *hever* 'lie around', *könyököl* 'lean on one's elbow', *támaszkodik* 'lean on', etc. Since the latter mean being in a particular spatial configuration, i.e. the occupation of some space in a spatial position, it is more obvious that the localization is inevitable in the given situations. In addition, in case of a non-agentive subject, a locative constituent is syntactically necessary not only with verbs of being in a particular spatial configuration but also with verbs of manner of motion. See (31a), i.e. *A váza az asztalon áll* 'The vase is on the table'), except when the verb is stressed and focused: *A váza áll* with a meaning 'The vase is not overturned, it does not lie but stands'. Similarly, *A folyó a völgyben folyik* 'The river flows in the valley'; *A folyó folyik* is acceptable if it means something like 'The river is not frozen up'.

A third reason for postulating a locative argument in the meaning representation of *úszik* 'swim; float' and similar verbs comes from examples such as (37).

(37) *A traktor a szántóföldön berreg.*
the tractor.NOM the field.SUP throbs
'The tractor is throbbing in the field.'

Depending on whether the phrase with the inflected noun *a szántóföldön* 'in the field' counts as an adjunct or argument, one can interpret (37) in two ways. If (37) has an adjunct, the verb *berreg* 'throb' only expresses sound emission when the tractor stands in place, while (37) with a locative argument denotes a motion someplace in some manner accompanied with sound emission.

Another issue also needs to be discussed in connection with the locative argument which has been argued to pertain semantically to a motion in some manner. In footnote 1 it was mentioned that several verbs of (1), such as *dülöngél* 'reel', *forog* 'spin', *fut* 'run', *himbálózik* 'swing', *imbolyog* 'totter', *lebeg* 'float', *pattog* 'bounce (several times)', *pörög* 'spin', *ring* 'swing', *szökdécsel* 'skip', *szökdel* 'skip', *táncol* 'dance', *ugrál* 'jump (several times)', *ugrik* 'jump', denote not only a manner of displacement but also that of physical position change. At the same time, the paraphrase 'being in motion in some manner' was attributed to the verb *úszik* 'swim; float' and the other verbs in (1) in discussion of their argument structure. Labeling the two distinct kinds of motion as simply motion is in accordance with a view that since motion is not always a displacement but also a change of spatial position, a generalized meaning component MOVE which indicates both motion types is appropriate for semantic representations.[12]

Now we can turn to explicating the relationship between locative and directional semantic arguments. First of all, I mean to make unmistakably clear that displaying an additional locative role with a verb cannot be treated by Goldberg's (1995, 2006) version of Construction Grammar since it is not obvious what happens to this syntactically optional role when this verb integrates into the intransitive activity-motion construction containing a directional role. Of course, if the lexical-semantic representation of the verb implied both the locative and the directional roles, no difficulty would

[12] For such a treatment of MOVE, see Wierzbicka (1996: 82–83).

emerge. Such a solution is offered by my lexical-constructional conception as follows. The place of an individual or thing, swimming/floating, in general, moving, has an 'in' relation (expressed by the inflection *-ban* in (35a) and (36a)) to the place of the reference entity denoted by the inflected noun *barlangban* 'in cave'. By comparison to this, the end point of a swimming/floating individual or thing is nothing other than the end of the path of swimming/floating, i.e. the place which the individual or thing occupies moving throughout the path of swimming/floating and which has an 'in' relation (expressed by the inflection *-ban*) to the place of the reference entity. However, directed motion is not limited to reaching the end of a path. There are two deviations from this most typical case. First, the path followed by an agent or a theme may have its final part (or goal) outside the path. Cf.: *a barlang felé úszik* 'swim/float toward the cave'. Second, the reference entity equals no end point included or not included in the path but indicates the location of the whole path. Cf.: *a folyó mentében úszik* 'swim/float along the river'. Nevertheless, all the three cases of motion are connected to a path having some direction but its final part is not focused. As to the meanings of the locative and directional arguments, they share a common part, namely, the relation of the place occupied by the agent or theme to another place. At the same time, their difference can also be grasped easily. The directional role contains something more, namely, that the place of the agent or theme, in some way or other, belongs to a path with a particular direction.

Let us reword swimming/floating as moving in a particular manner and symbolize generally the relation between places of the agent/theme and reference entity as α. Then one can substitute (38a) for (34), and (38b) is a formalization of (38a):

(38) a. '(x acts so that) x moves in a particular manner so that x's place (which belongs to a path with a particular direction) has relation α to the place of reference entity marked by r';

b. [([x ACT] :) [[x $MOVE_m$] : [(DIR) [x LOC] α r LOC]]], where m = a particular manner of motion.

The underspecified meaning representation in (38) – through the components in round brackets – accounts for the alternation not only between agentive and theme subjects but also between locative and directional arguments. Similarly to how the facultative predicate ACT is activated in one of the constructional meanings, i.e. in the agentive meaning, the component DIR also plays a role in one of the constructional meanings, namely, in the directed motion sense, which requires a directional argument. So, only those manner-of-motion verbs occur with directional phrases whose meanings have a kind of underspecified representation as in (38) containing the optional DIR. If one or another verb does not have such an underspecified meaning representation, it does not alternate in the way discussed. The meaning representation of the verb *inog* 'wabble' is more specified because – like the optional component ACT of (38) – the optional component DIR of (38) does not figure in it. Cf. (26a) and (26b), i.e. *A szék a fal mellett inog* 'The chair wabbles by the wall' and **A szék a fal mellé inog* 'The chair wabbles to the wall'. The sentence *Péter inog* 'Péter wabbles' does not denote Péter's volitional motion, except for marked cases when, for instance, he wabbles following stage directions. The verb *pattog* 'bounce', which does not also occur with an agentive subject, has a special property that it can take a directional phrase. Cf. (3a) and (3b), i.e. *A labda a fal mellett pattog* 'The ball bounces by the wall' and *A labda a fal mellé pattog* 'The ball bounces to the wall'. Therefore, the meaning representations of *pattog* 'bounce' is underspecified with regard to DIR, but not underspecified with regard to ACT.

What has been said above can be recapitulated in Table 1.

4.2.2. Alternation in sound emission verbs

First, let us return to (8) and (9), repeated here as (39) and (40).

(39) a. *Péter ordít.*
Péter.NOM screams
'Péter is screaming.

b. *Péter a folyosóra ordít.*
Péter.NOM the corridor.SUB screams
*'Screaming, Péter is moving into the corridor.'

(40) *Péter kiordít a folyosóra.*
Péter.NOM out.scream the corridor.SUB
*'Screaming, Péter is moving into the corridor.'

As mentioned above, (39b) and (40) only have a sound emission sense: 'Péter is screaming (through the door) into the corridor.' If a verb occurs with an agent argument and the sound is produced by the agent's sound formation organs, it cannot be interpreted as a directed motion even with a directional phrase and preverb together (Ladányi 2008: 310). Thus, neither (39b) with a directional phrase, nor (40) with a prefixed verb and directional phrase yields the directed motion interpretation.

Table 1. Meaning representations of alternating and non-alternating manner-of-motion verbs

	underspecified lexical meaning	specific lexical meaning	constructional meaning	example
úszik 'swim; float'	[([x ACT] :) [[x MOVE$_m$] : [(DIR) [x LOC] α r LOC]]] (= (38b))		[[**x ACT**] : [[x MOVE$_m$] : [x LOC α r LOC]]]	*A gyerek a barlangban úszik* 'The boy is swimming in the cave' (= (35a))
			[[**x ACT**] : [[x MOVE$_m$] : [**DIR** [x LOC] α r LOC]]]	*A gyerek a barlangba úszik* 'The boy is swimming into the cave' (= (35b))
			[[x MOVE$_m$] : [x LOC α r LOC]]	*Az üveg a barlangban úszik* 'The bottle is floating in the cave' (= (36a))
			[[x MOVE$_m$] : [**DIR** [x LOC] α r LOC v]]	*Az üveg a barlangba úszik* 'The bottle is floating into the cave' (= (36b))
inog 'wabble'		[[x MOVE$_m$] : [x LOC α r LOC]]		*A szék a fal mellett inog* 'The chair wabbles by the wall' (= (26a))
pattog 'bounce'	[[x MOVE$_m$] : [(DIR) [x LOC] α r LOC]]		[[x MOVE$_m$] : [x LOC α r LOC]]	*A labda a fal mellett pattog* 'The ball bounces by the wall' (= (3a))
			[[x MOVE$_m$] : [**DIR** [x LOC] α r LOC]]	*A labda a fal mellé pattog* 'The ball bounces to the wall' (= (3b))

However, a directed motion sense is not excluded even in the presence of an agentive subject. Recall our example with the verb *csattog* 'clap; flap', repeated here as (41).

(41) a. *A fiú csattog a papucsával.*
the boy.NOM claps/flaps the slippers.POSS.INS
'The boy is clapping his slippers (with his hands).'
Or: 'The boy is flapping his slippers (while walking).'

b. *A fiú a folyosóra csattog a papucsával.*
the boy.NOM the corridor.SUB flaps the slippers.POSS.INS
'The boy is flapping his slippers walking out into the corridor.'

Moreover, the verb *csattog* 'flap; clank' shows the alternation and meaning shift at stake not only with agentive subjects but also with non-agentive ones, e.g. with an instrument which can move, according to our encyclopedic or world knowledge. Consider (42).

(42) a. *A Dózsa György utca zajos, ott csattog a troli.*[13]
the Dózsa György street.NOM noisy there clanks the trolley.bus.NOM
'Dózsa György street is noisy, the trolley bus clanks down it.'

b. *A troli a Dózsa György utcába csattog.*
the trolley.bus.NOM the Dózsa György street.ILL clanks
'The trolley bus is clanking into Dózsa György street (e.g. because there is a stop).'

Before an analysis of the alternation under discussion in lexical-constructional terms, we should deal with the fact mentioned in section 2 that, contrary to prefixed version in (7), the occurrence of unprefixed sound emission verbs with directional phrases may be still uncommon (Ladányi 2007: 215). Despite the lexically strange character and potential occurrence of several expressions formed as (41b), the meaning shift pattern is considered productive (Ladányi 2007: 215). This is fully enough for my lexical-constructional approach, which does not have to assume a full-fledged lexical meaning for the verb in (41b) but only an underspecified lexical meaning that underlies specific – perhaps uncommon – constructional meanings, among others, the directed motion meaning. In other words, the lexical-constructional analysis does not suppose a lexicalized proceeding motion sense.

---

[13] This example is cited from a Hungarian regional daily newspaper: *Délmagyarország* Jan 7, 2006, p. 3.

At the same time, one should accurately characterize the condition in the presence of which the directed motion sense constructionally emerges with a verb of sound emission – at least potentially. By contrast, if such a condition is absent, the meaning at stake does not arise, for example, verbs denoting the sound emission by agents' sound formation organs are excluded from the present alternation. But what is that condition? To answer this question, I examine in detail the idea appeared in Levin and Rappaport Hovav (1995: 191) as well as in Ladányi (2007: 215, 2008: 310), namely, that a verb occurs with a directional phrase or role if sound emission is a concomitant of motion. First of all, what one has to realize is that sound emission is not a consequence of motion. To put it differently, sound must be brought about simultaneously with motion. That is why verbs of sound emission produced as a consequence of the motion of sound formation organs are not suitable for the alternation discussed (Gecső 2003: 74). Second, one has to take into consideration that the verb *csattog* 'flap; clank' and the others in (5), such as *berreg* 'throb', *cuppog* 'squelch', *csikorog* 'squeak', *csörömpöl* 'clank', *dübörög* 'rumble' and *nyikorog* 'squeak', do not necessarily denote sound emission coming into being together with a proceeding motion. The boy can emit sound when the slippers do not move to an end point, for example, when the boy walks about in his slippers. Without doubt, the sense 'motion accompanied with sound emission' connected to (41b) can only come into existence in case of sound emission during *directed, or proceeding,* motion of the boy wearing the slippers. Third, although the sounds are actually emitted by the slippers (cf. Levin and Rappaport Hovav 1995: 190–191), sound emission is predicated of the boy wearing them and moving in a particular direction. The slippers can also produce sound when the boy claps them. But in this case motion precedes sound emission. Moreover, this sound emission is not connected to the boy's directed motion. Similarly, sound produced by the vocal tract is not a consequence of motion only, it is not even caused by an agent's proceeding motion. Fourth, as the above discussion indicates, there is another possible meaning which has not been identified in the literature so far and which relates to sound emission during motion *in some manner* (e.g., the boy walks about in his slippers). Cf. also the second interpretation of the verb *berreg* 'throb' in (37) *A traktor a szántóföldön berreg*, i.e. 'motion someplace in some manner accompanied with sound emission'.

Being in possession of all the necessary information, we can establish the meaning representations of alternating verbs given in (5). My proposal consists of the following essential aspects, illustrated through the example of *csattog* 'clap; flap; clank'. Its underspecified representation includes the component ACT in round brackets because the event may be carried out either by agents or non-agents. Furthermore, it needs MOVE and the related LOC but again in round brackets because agents or non-agents do not move necessarily. Since the corresponding sound may be evoked not only together with directed motion, DIR referring to path is also involved optionally. If there is a motion event, it can be connected to the event of sound emission by the predicate CAUSE. Now, one can depict the underspecified representation of the verb *csattog* 'clap; flap; clank' as follows.

(43) a. 'the event "(x acts so that) (x moves in a particular manner so that x's place (which belongs to a path with a particular direction) has relation α to the place of reference entity marked by r"
causes)
the event "x emits some particular sound"';

b. [[([x ACT] :) ([[x $MOVE_m$] : [(DIR) [x LOC] α r LOC]]] CAUSE) [x $EMIT\_SOUND_s$]], where m = a particular manner of motion and s = a particular sound.

Thus, one can state that the verb *csattog* 'clap; flap; clank' alternates as in (41b) because having added to LOC the optional DIR makes accessible the sense 'sound emission during directed motion'.

As for the verbs *ordít* 'scream' and *kiordít* 'scream out' in (39b) and (40), respectively, they could not alternate because sound emission is only the consequence of motion of sound formation organs and, moreover, this sound emission is not connected to the agent's directed motion. In terms of their meaning representations, unlike (43), they are not underspecified in respect to ACT, which is obligatory for them, as well as to MOVE and the related components, which, in turn, are missing. Thus, *ordít* 'scream' and *kiordít* 'scream out' express sound emission but not directed motion together with sound emission. Consequently, the meaning representation of *ordít* 'scream' and *kiordít* 'scream out' can be depicted as in (44).[14]

(44) a. 'x acts so that x emits some particular sound';

b. [[x ACT] : [x $EMIT\_SOUND_s$]], where s = a particular sound.

What has been said in section 4.2.2 is recapitulated in Table 2.

---

[14] For the sake of simplicity the additional meaning supplied by the preverb *ki* 'out' is left out of consideration.

Table 2. Meaning representations of alternating and non-alternating sound emission verbs

	underspecified lexical meaning	specific lexical meaning	constructional meaning	example
csattog 'clap; flap; clank'	[[([x ACT] :) ([[x MOVE$_m$] : [(DIR) [x LOC] α r LOC]]] CAUSE) [x EMIT_SOUND$_s$]] (= (43b))		[[[**x ACT**] : [[**x MOVE$_m$**] : [**x LOC α r LOC**]]] **CAUSE** [x EMIT_SOUND$_s$]]	*A fiú csattog a papucsával* 'The boy is flapping his slippers (while walking)' (= (41a))
			[[[**x ACT**] : [[**x MOVE$_m$**] : [**DIR** [**x LOC**] **α r LOC**]]] **CAUSE** [x EMIT_SOUND$_s$]]	*A fiú a folyosóra csattog a papucsával* 'The boy is flapping his slippers walking into the corridor' (= (41b))
			[[[**x MOVE$_m$**] : [**x LOC α r LOC**]] **CAUSE** [x EMIT_SOUND$_s$]]	*… ott csattog a troli* '… the trolley bus clanks down it' (= (42a))
			[[[**x MOVE$_m$**] : [**DIR** [**x LOC**] **α r LOC**]] **CAUSE** [x EMIT_SOUND$_s$]]	*A troli a Dózsa György utcába csattog* 'The trolley bus is clanking into Dózsa György street' (= (42b))
			[[**x ACT**] : [x EMIT_SOUND$_s$]]	*A fiú csattog a papucsával* 'The boy is clapping his slippers (with his hands)' (= (41a))[15]
ordít 'sream'		[[**x ACT**] : [x EMIT_SOUND$_s$]] (= (44b))		*Péter a folyosóra ordít* 'Péter is screaming (through the door) into the corridor' (= (39b))

[15] Even in this case there is a non-agent variant, not mentioned above (cf. *A papucs csattog* 'The slippers are clapping'). It is obvious that such an example easily finds its place in my analysis.

4.2.3. Alternation in verbs denoting being in a particular spatial configuration

Let us turn to the lexical-constructional account of the third case of alternations in examples such as (15), which is given now as (45).

(45) a. *Péter* *áll.*
Péter.NOM stands.
'Péter is standing.'

b. *Péter* *a* *szőnyegre* *áll.*
Péter.NOM the carpet.SUB stands
'Péter steps onto the carpet.'

As a starting point one can think of verbs in (14), e.g. *áll* 'stand', *fekszik* 'lie', *guggol* 'crouch', *hasal* 'lie on one's stomach', *hever* 'lie around', *könyököl* 'lean on one's elbow', that their meaning indicates the non-dynamic and locative component BE_p, where p = a particular position. Now one faces an issue whether it is possible to find an underspecified meaning representation, and if so, how it can be motivated, which, besides the non-dynamic and locative BE_p, also contains the component MOVE. Recall that in section 3 I offered to link the possibility of motion with the presence of an agent. Consequently, the lexical representation of verbs at stake includes the component ACT but optionally because these verbs can occur with theme subjects (cf. (31a), i.e. *A váza az asztalon áll* 'The vase is on the table'). What is more important at present is that, as our world knowledge dictates, x can typically occupy some place if x carries out some activity which – typically again – is nothing other than x's motion to an end point. Actually, it is more specific motion than in case of the alternation of manner-of-motion and sound emission verbs because it is not only a path that is necessary, but also its distinguished part, i.e. the end point, has to appear in the lexical representation of verbs under investigation. Cf. *a szőnyeg felé áll*, which is an expression with a directional phrase not indicating the final part of a path and which is ungrammatical with the intended meaning 'step toward the carpet'. Therefore, MOVE and FIN are optional elements of verbs' meaning representation not simply because the verbs denoting being in a particular spatial configuration can occur with theme subjects, but also because those components become constituents, although optional, of a meaning representation on the basis of our world knowledge. Thus, the following meaning representation is offered for the verb *áll* 'stand':

(46) a. '(x acts (so that x moves in a particular manner so that x's place which is the end point of a path has relation α to the place of reference entity marked by r) so that)
x is in a particular spatial position so that x's place has relation α to the place of reference entity marked by r';

b. [(([[x ACT] (: [[x $MOVE_m$] : [FIN [x LOC] α r LOC]])] :) [[x BE_p] : [x LOC α r LOC]]], where m = a particular manner of motion, p = a particular spatial position.

Unlike the underspecified lexical-semantic representations of *úszik* 'swim; float' and *csattog* 'clap, flap; clank' in (38) and (43), respectively, the formula (46) contains MOVE and its argument in round brackets inside round brackets. It is in accordance with the double optional character of the motion which was indicated above. Thus, (46) correctly predicts the behavior of *áll* 'stand' with regard to alternation. The involvement of typically extant directed motion into the meaning representation provides enough motivation for the verb to express not only being in a spatial configuration but also assuming such a position through motion to an end point.[16] It is worth noticing that since the bracketed components of directed motion figure in a wider scope of other brackets, the former can play a role together with the latter. Thus, (46) allows appearance of the directed motion sense only in the presence of an agentive subject activated by that very component ACT. Therefore, in case of a theme subject, the meaning of directed motion is excluded on the basis of (46), which is attested by (31b), i.e. **A váza az asztalra áll* 'The vase steps onto the table'. Consequently, (46) embraces all three of the senses of verbs of spatial configuration which are mentioned by Levin and Rappaport Hovav (1995: 127), namely those of maintain position, assume position and simple position. Moreover, (46) expresses their connections and the relation between locative and directional phrases, which are not explicitly indicated by Levin and Rappaport Hovav (1995).

If verbs have lexically more specific meanings, the alternation does not take place at all. The verbs *függ* 'hang' and *heverészik* 'lie around' in (16) and (17), respectively, are more specific because typical directed motion is not connected to being in a particular spatial configuration. Cf. (16b) and (17b), i.e. **A fiú a bordásfalra függ* 'The boy hangs onto the wall-bars'

[16] The occurrence of verbs *szeletel* 'slice' and *reszel* 'grate' with directional phrases in (21) and (22) can be accounted for in a similar way: the change of state *typically* implies that some parts of an entity *move to an end point.*

and **A fiú az ágyra heverészik* 'The boy lies around onto the bed'. For that reason no directional argument is possible. By contrast, the verb *heveredik* 'lie down at full length' in (18) is specific in the opposite way, namely, directed motion is obligatorily characteristic of it. Cf. (18b): *A fiú az ágyra heveredik* 'The boy lies down at full length onto the bed'. In other words, that sense does not alternate with being in a spatial position. Nevertheless, with respect to theme subjects the three verbs also behave differently. While the verb *függ* 'hang' can occur with that type of subjects (cf. *A kép az óra mellett függ* 'The picture hangs beside the clock', the two others cannot (cf. **A kép az asztalon heverészik* 'The picture is lying around on the table' and **A kép az asztalra heveredik* 'The picture lies down at full length onto the table'). So, the first verb has a representation with an optional, i.e. bracketed, ACT, but the others have it obligatorily.

Consider Table 3 where you can find a summary of what has been said in the present section.

To conclude section 4 regarding all three kinds of alternations, I want to make the following statement. Not only does the formulation of conditions of alternations, namely, the possibility of motion along a path, or sometimes – as a more specific subcase – even to an end point, connect constructional meanings to the corresponding underspecified meanings but also the same fragment of underspecified meanings naturally motivates the constructional meaning 'directed motion' in all three cases of alternations. Thus, one can account for the change of *three kinds of syntactic alternations* with the help of *a single meaning scheme.* In view of the totality of alternating verbs discussed, the part of underspecified representations, necessary for the identification of the relevant semantic class of verbs and for the appearance of the directed motion sense, can be depicted as (47):

(47) a. 'x moves in a particular manner so that x's place, which belongs to a path with a particular direction or which is the end point of a path, has relation α to the place of reference entity marked by r';

b. [[x MOVE$_m$] : [DIR/FIN [x LOC] α r LOC]], where m = a particular manner of motion.

Table 3.
Meaning representations of alternating and non-alternating verbs of being in or assuming a particular spatial configuration

	underspecified lexical meaning	specific lexical meaning	constructional meaning	example
áll 'stand'	[(([x ACT] (: [[x MOVE$_m$] : [FIN [x LOC] α r LOC]]]) :) [[x BE$_p$] : [x LOC α r LOC]]] (= (46b))		[[**x ACT**] : [[x BE$_p$] : [x LOC α r LOC]]]	*Péter áll* 'Péter is standing' (= (45a))
			[[[**x ACT**] : [[**x MOVE$_m$**] : [**FIN** [**x LOC**] **α r LOC**]]] : [[x BE$_p$] : [x LOC α r LOC]]]	*Péter a szőnyegre áll* 'Péter steps onto the carpet' (= (45b))
			[[x BE$_p$] : [x LOC α r LOC]]	*A váza az asztalon áll* 'The vase is on the table' (= (31a))
függ 'hang'	[(([x ACT] :) [[x BE$_p$] : [x LOC α r LOC]]] [17]		[[**x ACT**] : [[x BE$_p$] : [x LOC α r LOC]]]	*A fiú a bordásfalon függ* 'The boy is hanging on the wall-bars' (= (16a))
			[[x BE$_p$] : [x LOC α r LOC]]	*A kép az óra mellett függ* 'The picture hangs beside the clock'
heverészik 'lie around'		[[**x ACT**] : [[x BE$_p$] : [x LOC α r LOC]]]		*A fiú az ágyon heverészik* 'The boy is lying around on the bed' (= (17a))
heveredik 'lie down at full length'		[[**x ACT**] : [[**x MOVE$_m$**] : [**FIN** [**x LOC**] **α r LOC**]]]		*A fiú az ágyra heveredik* 'The boy is lying down at full length onto the bed' (= (18b))

[17] In accordance with the above discussion, this representation is not underspecified in respect to being in or assuming a spatial position but in respect to agentive or theme subjects

5. The lexical-constructional approach from a metatheoretical point of view

5.1. From data to theory and vice versa

First, I claim that although in the preceding section there is not a large amount of data and it mainly consists of examples available from previous literature, including dictionaries, and my introspection (but cf. (42a)), the data used is sufficient and suitable to fulfill my purposes to critically evaluate theories concerning syntactic alternations and to propose a more reliable one.

First of all, if one had taken into consideration some simple examples, they should have improved their theory. For example, such pairs of simple examples which include agentive and theme subjects (cf. (32) vs. (33), (35) vs. (36), (41) vs. (42) and (45) vs. (31)) have turned out to be important to test the capacity of a theory. Furthermore, my investigation involves a semantic class of verbs no account of which can be found in previous Hungarian literature on alternations, namely, verbs of being in and assuming a spatial position.

Second, there can always be uncertain judgments concerning the acceptability of particular linguistic expressions, including syntactic alternations. Recall that verbs of sound emission with directional phrases can sometimes be considered uncommon and strange. It is worth realizing, however, that introspection is unavoidable even in connection with using corpus data. Introspection is necessary to recognize not only obvious mistakes in text corpora but also figurative speech or innovative expressions. Furthermore, if examples such as (37) and (41a), or similar examples from a corpus, can be interpreted (pragmatically or contextually) in different ways, the various possible interpretations are always shown through making use of speakers' language knowledge, that of linguists, among them. Nevertheless, there cannot be any doubt about the general possibility of the syntactic pattern change (or about the impossibility of such a change with some verbs of the same semantic class). Then it seems to be a safe statement that one cannot avoid the problem of explaining the possibility of using words with various syntactic structures.

Therefore, I offer a solution for this problem that divides into two parts and uses the well-known type–token distinction for metatheoretical (metalinguistic) purposes. On the level of theory construction, one should critically assess how one's own and others' theories cope with data considered a set, or a type, of data which only in their totality count as evidence (i.e. as a crucial empirical basis). On the level of data analysis, one deals with data as separate tokens even though one carries out one's research in the framework of a theory. Consequently, ignorance or false judgments and analyses of data as separate tokens do not destroy a theory.

Furthermore, third, theory and data are mutually connected to each other. Not only does a theory depend on a type (or several types) of data but also what counts as data is theory-dependent as well (cf. Lehmann 2004). On the basis of the present paper, I can state that the lexical-constructional approach to syntactic alternations determines what kind of examples one should take into consideration as data for what kind of word meanings, and how meanings in (explanatory) dictionaries can be used as data (cf. also Weigand 2005). Since examples from the real use of language are always bound to corresponding situations, they cannot be related immediately to underspecified meanings. What they have a direct connection to is constructional meanings. One should bear in one's mind that things are often like this if one turns to the meaning descriptions of dictionaries (cf. Bibok 2008).

5.2. Extending the lexical-constructional approach into lexical pragmatics

In section 4 I have argued for a single lexical-constructional account of syntactic alternations of three Hungarian verb classes against some lexical and constructional theories. This argumentation can be held to be a plausible one in the Kertész and Rákosi's (2008) sense, which does not lead to a thoroughgoing certainty but has some degree of it. At the same time, the plausibility of a theory can be tested by its theoretical extendibility. For this reason and in order to explicate the pragmatic character of my analysis presented in the previous section, I briefly outline in two steps how the lexical-constructional approach to syntactic alternations naturally extends into lexical pragmatics.

First, I indicate that the lexical-constructional approach can be applied well to other types of alternations, e.g. such as in (48):

(48) a. *A gyerek kenyeret eszik.*
the child.NOM bread.ACC eats
'The child is eating bread.'

b. *A gyerek eszik.*
the child.NOM eats
'The child is eating.'

Independently of the lexical realization, the verb *eszik* 'eat' always has two arguments on the semantic level because the activity denoted by that verb is logically inconceivable without a second argument. Furthermore, its lexical-semantic representation contains a selection restriction put on the second argument: it has to be of type FOOD. Since this selection restriction constrains the information about the type of possible objects, in case of a typical food the second argument can be omitted syntactically. However, it only happens semantically that this object is not in the focus of attention but the information concerning the type of the required object is accessible as background information. Thus, the lexical-semantic representation of the verb *eszik* 'eat' can be seen as underspecified because it gives two interpretations: either the object is focused (together with the verb), or it is only in the background (for further details, see Bibok 2008 and Németh T. 2008).[18] So, a hearer can try to interpret (48b) without any specific context. In decoding the verb *eszik* 'eat', they arrive at more specific information than 'eat something'. It is enough for them to rely on the selection restriction of that verb to get a relevant interpretation: 'The child is eating something that can be eaten (i.e. food).'

Now consider (49) answering the question *Mit csinál a felesége?* 'What is his wife doing?'

(49) *A felesége fogta a tányért és a kanalat, és eszik.*
the wife.POSS.NOM took.3SG the bowl.ACC and the spoon.ACC and eats
'His wife took the bowl and spoon and is eating.'

Let us try to interpret (49) without any specific context external to that utterance. In (49) the lexical-semantic representation of the verb *eszik* 'eat' including the appropriate selection restriction alone does not yield a relevant interpretation. We have to take into account the rest of the utterance, i.e. the immediate context, to identify the lexically unexpressed direct object argument. The encyclopedic information stored with lexical items of the utterance makes accessible an assumption like the following: Adult people typically eat liquid food, e.g. soup or a vegetable stew, out of a bowl and with a spoon. Naturally, a little child may eat other food with a spoon too, but this reading cannot come into one's mind without specific indication because, according to our encyclopedic knowledge, the lexeme *feleség* 'wife' typically denotes an adult human being. Hence the relevant interpretation of (49) may be that 'his wife took the bowl and spoon and she is eating soup, a vegetable stew or something similar out of the bowl with a spoon'.

[18] In this respect the representation of *eszik* 'eat' is similar to that of verbs undergoing the locative alternation. It contains two events either of which is highlighted by two alternating syntactic structures (cf. Iwata 2002, 2005).

However, the verb *eszik* 'eat' can also occur with implicit arguments in a third manner. In this case the identification of a lexically unrealized argument is made by extending the immediate context as in (50).

(50) A: *Mi* *történt* *a* *csokoládéval?*
what.NOM happened.3SG the chocolate.INS
B: *A* *gyerekek* *ettek* *a* *szobában.*
the children ate.3PL the room.INE
'A: What happened to the chocolate?
B: The children were eating in the room.'

The implicit direct object argument in the second utterance can be identified by extending the immediate context with information from the preceding utterance. Thus, it turns out to be coreferential with the noun *csokoládé* 'chocolate', which is of a type FOOD.[19]

Second, and, more importantly, closer to lexical pragmatics, the lexical-constructional approach can also be applied to such cases where the problem concerning the change of syntactic argument structure does not appear (cf. Bibok and Németh T. 2001). Consider (51).

(51) a. *Péter* *kilépett* *az* *egyházból.*
Péter.NOM left.3SG the church.institution.ELA
'Péter left [=quit religious affiliation] the church [=the institution].'
b. *Péter* *kilépett* *a* *templomból.*
Péter.NOM left.3SG the church.building.ELA
'Péter left [= changed place] the church [= the building].'

However, the underdetermined representation of the verb *kilép* 'leave' is not captured by means of putting optional parts into round brackets, as above. Rather, the component MOVE figures in a very abstract sense, which only refers to a concrete one, depending on the directional (source) arguments *egyházból* and *templomból* with lexically fixed meanings 'church as institution' and 'church as building', respectively. This specified constructional sense refers either to the "social motion" (change in affiliation), or the physical motion. So, in both cases the verb meaning is affected by the lexically fixed meaning of arguments of the same type, i.e. of source arguments.

Consider (52), in which the noun *iskola* 'school' is substituted for *egyház* 'church as institution' and *templom* 'church as building'.

[19] The interpretation possibilities of Hungarian verbs with implicit arguments are found in Németh T. (2001, 2008 and this volume).

(52) *Péter elment az iskolából.*
Péter.NOM left.3SG the school.ELA
'Péter left [= quit affiliation] the school [= the institution].'
'Péter left [= changed place] the school [= the building].'

Since the noun *iskola* 'school' can be interpreted as both 'institution' and 'building', the specification of the verb *elmegy* 'leave' with an abstract motion meaning indicating neither physical, nor social change of location depends on the disambiguation of this noun. In the case of the institution sense the verb means a quitting of affiliation, while in the case of the building sense a change of place. Moreover, if one also assumes an underspecified meaning representation for the noun *iskola* 'school', i.e. it is not specified in the lexicon whether an institution or a building has the goal to provide for teaching/learning processes, [20] the ambiguity of (52) can only be resolved by means of information evoked by immediate or extended contexts. For the former type of contexts, consider (53), in which time adverbials are added to (52) (cf. Németh T. and Bibok 2010).

(53) a. *2009-ben Péter elment az iskolából.*
2009.INE Péter.NOM left.3SG the school.ELA
'In 2009 Péter left [= quit affiliation] the school [= the institution].'

b. *Délelőtt tíz órakor Péter elment az iskolából.*
morning ten o'clock.TEM Péter.NOM left.3SG the school.ELA
'At 10 a.m. Péter left [= changed place] the school [= the building].'

In the context of the time adverbial *2009-ben* 'in 2009' in (53a), the noun *iskola* 'school' most likely refers to an institution and, accordingly, the verb *elmegy* 'leave' is interpreted as quitting of affiliation. In the context of the time adverbial *délelőtt tíz órakor* 'at 10 a.m.' in (53b), *iskola* 'school' typically refers to a building and *elmegy* 'leave' is interpreted as a change of place. Thus, depending on the time adverbial phrases, the meanings of *iskola* 'school' and *elmegy* 'leave' are coordinated.

---

[20] As can be seen from the proposed lexical representations, the underspecification may take several forms: starting from the bracketing of the optional parts through the double interpretation to components abstracted from concrete instantiations and the use of variables or to other procedures which were unnecessary for the representations of words analyzed in the present paper. For types and motivations of lexical underspecification, see Bibok (2004). Cf. also Bierwisch (1997: 238–244), where the similarity of underspecification in semantics to that in phonology is stressed.

Disambiguation of (52) can be done not only by completing it with time adverbials but also by context extension, e.g. through such pieces of information from previous utterances of the discourse or the physical environment of the discourse which are deductible from the time adverbial phrases of (53).

The interpretations with (53) seem to be only typical ones because they can be overridden in extended contexts (cf. Németh T. and Bibok 2010). It is sufficient if the broad or narrow range of time indications typically expressed by time adverbials can be interpreted the opposite way on the basis of extended contexts. For instance, if we get knowledge from previous discourse or from the physical environment of the discourse that Péter's change of place was very slow and difficult, and, in addition, he had to overcome a relatively long distance, then the time adverbial *2009-ben* 'in 2009' in (53a) does not induce Péter's quitting of affiliation. If one is informed in the morning of a particular day that Péter had a serious clash with the principal or he managed to find a new job at eleven a.m., then these pieces of knowledge serve as adequate motivations for an interpretation of the time adverbial *délelőtt tíz órakor* 'at 10 a.m.' in (53b), which is opposite to its typical one. Thus, *délelőtt tíz órakor* 'at 10 a.m.' can provide information about the time of Péter's quitting of affiliation.

Since research into word meanings should pay special attention to the necessary *interaction of lexicon and contexts*, as the above discussion clearly indicates, a conception of *lexical pragmatics* can be proposed, which takes the contextualist stance in the debate on the semantics–pragmatics boundary (cf. Jaszczolt in press) and has the following main theses.

First, lexical pragmatics accepts – as a starting point of the construction of word meanings in utterances – lexical-semantic representations which can be radically underspecified because a number of words do not encode full-fledged concepts and allow for other methods of meaning description than componential analysis. In the latter respect, a significant role can be given to prototype semantics usable for grasping encyclopedic information or typical pieces of world knowledge referred to several times above in connection with lexical representations of verbs.

Second, lexical pragmatics is of the opinion that as words have underspecified, although semantically and pragmatically enriched (see section 4.1), meaning representations, they reach their full meanings in corresponding contexts through considerable pragmatic inference. However, unlike in Grice (1975) and in neo-Gricean pragmatics (e.g. Levinson 2000), inferential processes are considered necessary not only to establish (conversational) implicatures via the Co-operative Principle and its maxims. Constructing propositions expressed by utterances also requires the execution of some inferences, because – as post-Gricean Relevance Theory (Sperber and Wilson 1986/1995) propagates – the linguistically encoded information is not sufficient for that. Thus, the distinction between semantics and pragmatics is not correlated with the distinction of propositional meaning and implicatures. Rather, the research into semantic and pragmatic meanings can be separated alongside with decoding and inference (cf., e.g., Carston 2002).

Third, inspired also by Relevance Theory (Sperber and Wilson 1986/1995), lexical pragmatics distinguishes between immediate and extended contexts. However, in lexical pragmatics they are meant as contexts inside and outside utterances, respectively, that words under interpretation can have.

Fourth, lexical pragmatics claims that utterance meaning can be construed in three different ways: by means of lexical-semantic representations, immediate and extended contexts.

Fifth, in the view of lexical pragmatics, the Cognitive Principle of Relevance (Sperber and Wilson 1986/1995) regulates the construction of utterance meaning in one of three ways, the hierarchy of which is also influenced by the same principle.[21]

In a recent paper (Németh T. and Bibok 2010), the interaction of the lexicon and contexts is further extended into the interaction of grammar and pragmatics, which is basically considered a co-operation of two separate components of the theory of language in contexts of language use. At the same time, it is also accepted that detached from its contexts, some contextual information becomes not only context-independent, i.e. general pragmatic information, but also such encyclopedic information or information concerning the use of language can be fixed in semantic representations of lexical entries as integral parts.

The plausibility of the lexical-constructional approach converted into a full-fledged lexical pragmatic theory can also be increased by considering the claim that human and machine disambiguation or semantic annotation of words in corpora cannot be solved on the basis of the traditional dictionary model of meaning representation (Fellbaum et al. 2005). What is offered for this task is very much in accordance with the tenets of my lexical pragmatic conception. Cf.: "Annotators and automatic systems need the option to select either a cluster of specific senses or a single, broader sense, where specific meaning nuances are contained but hidden" (Fellbaum et al.

---

[21] For the motivation of these theses of lexical pragmatics in full detail, see Bibok (2004).

2005: 37). Thus, the next question, which goes beyond the aims of the present paper and has to be addressed by further research, can also be formulated: How can one establish the empirically and theoretically adequate measure of generality or underspecificity of meaning representations in the lexicon?

6. Conclusions

Considering the two main aims of the research in the present paper, I have two final conclusions. First, the lexical-constructional approach to syntactic alternations proposes underspecified but encyclopedically and pragmatically enriched meaning representations containing explicitly such information that causes syntactic pattern change of whole verb classes. In comparison with rival lexical and constructional conceptions, the lexical-constructional treatment of syntactic alternations has more predictive force and gives a more general explanation in the sense that it provides a clearer motivation of alternating syntactic structures.

As to the application of the lexical-constructional theory to Hungarian verb classes, its results include the following:

1. underspecified meaning representations predict constructional meanings appearing due to syntactic alternations,
2. the lack of alternations can be explained by specific meanings which verbs have because of idiosyncratic lexicalizations,
3. the analysis of some verb classes handled separately in previous research can be generalized further: they can be collectively referred to as one group through a meaning scheme (template) containing the shared properties of the verb classes.

Second, the relationship between theory construction and data analysis should be regarded mutual: a theory could be attested not only by data considered as a type and not as tokens, but it should also be compared to a larger body of theoretical and practical issues to reach a more plausible theory. On the basis of the results of my object theoretical investigations, I hope both the lexical-constructional explanation of syntactic alternations and the construction of contextual meanings in a framework of lexical pragmatics seem to be plausible enough to be subjected to further testing.

Acknowledgements

The research reported on in the present paper was supported by the Research Group for Theoretical Linguistics at the Universities of Debrecen, Pécs and Szeged, Hungary. I would like to express my gratitude to the anonymous reviewer for his criticisms and suggestions, which helped me to improve the paper.

References

Bibok, Károly
2004 Word meaning and lexical pragmatics. *Acta Linguistica Hungarica* 51: 265–308.

Bibok, Károly
2008 Az igék szemantikája és a szintaktikai alternáció [The semantics of verbs and syntactic alternation]. In *Strukturális magyar nyelvtan 4: A szótár szerkezete* [A Structural Grammar of Hungarian, vol. 4: The Structure of the Lexicon], Ferenc Kiefer (ed.), 23–70. Budapest: Akadémiai Kiadó.

Bibok, Károly and Enikő Németh T.
2001 How the lexicon and context interact in the meaning construction of utterances. In *Pragmatics and the Flexibility of Word Meaning*, Enikő Németh T. and Károly Bibok (eds.), 291–320. Amsterdam: Elsevier.

Bierwisch, Manfred
1997 Lexical information from a minimalist point of view. In *The Role of Economy Principles in Linguistic Theory*, Chris Wilder, Hans-Martin Gärtner and Manfred Bierwisch (eds.), 227–266. (Studia Grammatica 40.) Berlin: Akademie Verlag.

Carston, Robyn
2002 *Thoughts and Utterances: The Pragmatics of Explicit Communication.* Oxford: Blackwell.

Croft, William
2003 Lexical rules vs. constructions: A false dichotomy. In *Motivation in Language: Studies in Honor of Günter Radden*, Hubert Cuyckens, Thomas Berg, René Dirven and Klaus-Uwe Panther (eds.), 49–68. Amsterdam: Benjamins.

Fellbaum, Christiane, Lauren Delfs, Susanne Wolff and Martha Palmer
2005 Word meaning in dictionaries, corpora and the speaker's mind. In *Meaningful Texts: The Extraction of Semantic Information from Monolingual and Multilingual Corpora*, Geoff Barnbrook, Pernilla Danielsson and Michaela Mahlberg (eds.), 31–38. London: Continuum.

Gecső, Tamás
2003 *A nyelvleírás lehetőségei és határai* [The Possibilities and Limitations of Language Description]. Budapest: Tinta Könyvkiadó.

Goldberg, Adele E.
1995 *Constructions: A Construction Grammar Approach to Argument Structure.* Chicago, IL: University Press of Chicago.

Goldberg, Adele E.
2006 *Constructions at Work: The Nature of Generalization in Language.* Oxford: Oxford University Press.

Grice, H. Paul
1975 Logic and conversation. In *Syntax and Semantics 3: Speech Acts*, Peter Cole and Jerry Morgan (eds.), 41–58. New York: Academic Press.

Iwata, Seizi
2002 Does MANNER count or not? Manner-of-motion verbs revisited. *Linguistics* 40: 61–110.

Iwata, Seizi
2005 Locative alternation and two levels of meaning. *Cognitive Linguistics* 16: 355–407.

Jackendoff, Ray
1990 *Semantic Structures.* Cambridge, MA: MIT Press.

Jaszczolt, Katarzyna M.
in press Semantics and pragmatics: The boundary issue. In *Semantics: An International Handbook of Natural Language Meaning*, Klaus von Heusinger, Paul Portner and Claudia Maienborn (eds.). Berlin/New York: Mouton de Gruyter.

Kertész, András and Csilla Rákosi
2008 Introduction: The problem of data and evidence in theoretical linguistics. In *New Approaches to Linguistic Evidence: Pilot Studies*, András Kertész and Csilla Rákosi (eds.), 9–18. Frankfurt am Main: Lang.

Komlósy, András
1992 Régensek és vonzatok [Regents and complements]. In *Strukturális magyar nyelvtan 1: Mondattan* [A Structural Grammar of Hungarian, vol. 1: Syntax], Ferenc Kiefer (ed.), 299–527. Budapest: Akadémiai Kiadó.

Komlósy, András
2000 A műveltetés [Causativization]. In *Strukturális magyar nyelvtan 3: Morfológia* [A Structural Grammar of Hungarian, vol. 3: Morphology], Ferenc Kiefer (ed.), 215–292. Budapest: Akadémiai Kiadó.

Ladányi, Mária
2007 Systematic polysemy of verbs. In *The Cognitive Basis of Polysemy: New Sources of Evidence for Theories of Word Meaning*, Marina

Rakova, Gergely Pethő and Csilla Rákosi (eds.), 189–220. Frankfurt am Main: Lang.

Ladányi, Mária
2008 Rendszeres igei poliszémia [Systematic polysemy of verbs]. In *Strukturális magyar nyelvtan 4: A szótár szerkezete* [A Structural Grammar of Hungarian, vol. 4: The Structure of the Lexicon], Ferenc Kiefer (ed.), 269–321. Budapest: Akadémiai Kiadó.

Lehmann, Christian
2004 Data in linguistics. *The Linguistic Review* 21: 175–210.

Levin, Beth
1993 *English Verb Classes and Alternations: A Preliminary Investigation.* Chicago, IL: University Press of Chicago.

Levin, Beth and Malka Rappaport Hovav
1995 *Unaccusativity: At the Syntax–Lexical Semantics Interface.* Cambridge, MA: MIT Press.

Levin, Beth and Malka Rappaport Hovav
1996 Lexical semantics and syntactic structure. In *The Handbook of Contemporary Semantic Theory*, Shalom Lappin (ed.), 487–507. Oxford: Blackwell.

Levin, Beth and Malka Rappaport Hovav
1998 Morphology and lexical semantics. In *The Handbook of Morphology*, Andrew Spencer and Arnold M. Zwicky (eds.), 248–271. Oxford: Blackwell.

Levin, Beth and Malka Rappaport Hovav
2005 *Argument Realization.* Cambridge: Cambridge University Press.

Levinson, Stephen C.
2000 *Presumptive Meanings: The Theory of Generalized Conversational Implicature.* Cambridge, MA: MIT Press.

Németh T., Enikő
2001 Implicit arguments in Hungarian. In *Argument Structure in Hungarian*, István Kenesei (ed.), 113–156. Budapest: Akadémiai Kiadó.

Németh T., Enikő
2008 Az implicit alanyi és tárgyi igei argumentumok előfordulásának lexikai-szemantikai jellemzői [The lexical-semantic properties of the occurrence of implicit subject and direct object arguments]. In *Strukturális magyar nyelvtan 4: A szótár szerkezete* [A Structural Grammar of Hungarian, vol. 4: The Structure of the Lexicon], Ferenc Kiefer (ed.), 71–128. Budapest: Akadémiai Kiadó.

Németh T., Enikő
this vol. How lexical-semantic factors influence the verbs' occurrence with implicit direct object arguments in Hungarian.

Németh T., Enikő and Károly Bibok
2010 Interaction between grammar and pragmatics: The case of implicit arguments, implicit predicates and co-composition in Hungarian. *Journal of Pragmatics* 42: 501–524.

Pinker, Steven
1989 *Learnability and Cognition: The Acquisition of Argument Structure.* Cambridge, MA: MIT Press.
Pustejovsky, James
1995 *The Generative Lexicon.* Cambridge, MA: MIT Press.
Rappaport Hovav, Malka and Beth Levin
1998 Building verb meanings. In *The Projection of Arguments: Lexical and Compositional Factors*, Miriam Butt and Wilhelm Geuder (eds.), 97–134. Stanford: Center for the Study of Language and Information.
Sperber, Dan and Deirdre Wilson
1986/95 *Relevance: Communication and Cognition.* Oxford: Blackwell, First/ second edition.
Tenny, Carol and James Pustejovsky
2000 A history of events in linguistic theory. In *Events as Grammatical Objects: The Converging Perspectives of Lexical Semantics and Syntax*, Carol Tenny and James Pustejovsky (eds.), 3–37. Stanford: Center for the Study of Language and Information.
Tompa, József (ed.)
1961 *A mai magyar nyelv rendszere. Leíró nyelvtan 1: Bevezetés. Hangtan. Szótan* [The Structure of the Modern Hungarian Language. A Descriptive Grammar, vol. 1: Introduction. Phonetics. Lexicology]. Budapest: Akadémiai Kiadó.
Weigand, Edda
2005 The role of lexical data in pragmatics. In *Lexicology: An International Handbook on the Nature and Structure of Words and Vocabularies, vol. 2*, D. Alan Cruse, Franz Hundsnurscher, Michael Job and Peter Rolf Lutzeier (eds.), 1696–1702. Berlin/New York: Mouton de Gruyter.
Wierzbicka, Anna
1996 *Semantics: Primes and Universals.* Oxford: Oxford University Press.

How lexical-semantic factors influence the verbs' occurrence with implicit direct object arguments in Hungarian

Enikő Németh T.

1. Introduction

1.1. Background: previous results on implicit arguments in Hungarian

Previous research into implicit arguments in Hungarian (cf. e.g. Kiefer 1990–1991; Komlósy 1994; Pléh 1994; Németh T. 2000, 2001, 2008; Bibok and Németh T. 2001; Németh T. and Bibok 2001, 2010; Pethő and Kardos 2009) has led to a conclusion that the occurrence and interpretation of implicit arguments in Hungarian are guided by lexical-semantic, grammatical, discourse structural and pragmatic factors together. In accordance with this conclusion implicit arguments can be defined as arguments involved in the lexical-semantic representations of verbs but which are lexically unrealized, and whose implicit presence in utterances is attested by lexical-semantic, grammatical (phonological, morphological, syntactic and semantic), discourse, and/or pragmatic evidence (cf. e.g. Németh T. 2000, 2001, 2008; Bibok and Németh T. 2001; Németh T. and Bibok 2010). Such evidence demonstrates the implicit presence of an argument and attests that the particular utterance does not have a performance error. This definition makes it possible to consider phonetically not realized, empty or covert pronouns (*pro* and even PRO) as implicit arguments. But, unlike the other types of implicit arguments which are not represented in the syntactic structure of sentences, pronouns without overt phonetic form have an own well-defined position in the syntactic structure. So, this conception of implicit arguments obviously differs from the definition widely accepted in the generative grammatical tradition (cf. Radford 1997).

Another conclusion of the previous investigations on implicit arguments is that in Hungarian as in other *pro*-drop languages verbs can occur with implicit arguments more frequently and in ways controlled differently than in languages without *pro*-drop phenomena (Németh T. 2000, 2001; Bibok and Németh T. 2001; Németh T. and Bibok 2010). In Hungarian, verbs do not vary as to whether they can occur with implicit arguments at all, but they vary as to in what manners or in what contexts they occur. Thus, in Hungarian there are various types of implicit arguments and their occurrence in utterances is licensed by various factors. The separate mention of these various factors in the above mentioned definition of implicit arguments indicates the diverse character of the different types of implicit arguments. However, although the possibilities of the occurrence of implicit arguments in Hungarian can be explained by various factors, their intensive interaction should be emphasized. An argument can be left implicit in Hungarian in the following three cases (Németh T. 2000, 2001, 2008; Bibok and Németh T. 2001; Németh T. and Bibok 2010):

(A) If some element of the lexical-semantic representation of a verb licenses the lexically unrealized occurrence of an argument involved in it, according to the principle of relevance (cf. *Rita eszik* 'Rita is eating').
(B) If the rest of the utterance, i.e. immediate context in which the argument occurs provides a relevant, typical interpretation (cf. *Ági adott a koldusnak* 'Ági gave [money] to the beggar').
(C) If extending the immediate context of the argument results in an interpretation consistent with the principle of relevance (cf. *Látod?* 'Can you see [that]?').

Four remarks seem to be in order in connection with these three possibilities. First, it is obvious that these generalizations are formed on the basis of the kind and "size" of the context in which the verb with an implicit argument occurs. In the case A, the possibility for the use with a lexically unrealized argument is built into the lexical-semantic representation of the particular verb. However, this does not mean that the utterance context and grammatical requirements including grammatical morphemes do not influence the occurrence of verbs with implicit arguments in the case A. In the case B, in addition to the lexical-semantic and grammatical information, general pragmatic and encyclopedic pieces of information stored under the conceptual addresses of the lexemes in the utterances in which the implicit arguments occur should be considered. And, in the case C, the immediate context should be extended with information from the previous discourse or from the physical environment or with further pieces of encyclopedic knowledge. Taking into account of the kinds of information which should be considered in cases A–C, it is also obvious that implicit arguments are phenomena situated not only at the semantics–pragmatics interface, but, from a wider perspective, at the grammar–pragmatics interface.

Second, the definition of implicit arguments itself and the formulation of the three cases above are suitable for describing of possibilities both how a Hungarian verb can occur with implicit arguments and how implicit arguments can be interpreted.

The third remark is that these three possibilities neither predict that every verb can be used with implicit arguments only in one manner or that every verb can be used in all three manners, nor restrict which argument of a verb can be left lexically unrealized. According to the manners of their occurrences with implicit arguments Hungarian verbs can be classified into three groups, as it was outlined in Németh T. 2001, 2008; Bibok and Németh T. 2001.

Verbs in the first group can be used with implicit arguments in all three manners. The verbs of this type are e.g. *eszik* 'eat', *etet* 'feed', *megetet* 'pvb.[1]feed', *fal* 'devour', *zabál* 'devour/gobble', *rág* 'chew', *iszik* 'drink', *itat* 'make drink', *megitat* 'make drink', *vedel* 'swill', *lát* 'see', *bámul* 'gaze', *hall* 'hear', *olvas* 'read', *ír* 'write', *rajzol* 'draw', *fest* 'paint', *főz* 'cook', *süt* 'bake', *mos* 'wash', *vasal* 'iron', *mosogat* 'do dishes', *takarít* 'clean', *varr* 'sew', *kapál* 'hoe', *locsol* 'water', *szánt* 'plow', *vet* 'sow', *kaszál* 'scythe', *arat* 'harvest', *épít* 'build', *fúr* 'drill', *farag* 'carve', *foltoz* 'patch', *stoppol* 'darn', *tereget* 'hang up [to dry]', *szárogat* 'dry', *szemetel* 'trash', *vág* 'cut' etc.

The second group contains verbs which can occur with implicit arguments in the second and the third manner. This group can be illustrated by verbs like *ad* 'give', *adományoz* 'donate', *ajándékoz* 'give a present', *teleszór* 'pvb. scatter', *megjavít* 'pvb.repair', *megjavíttat* 'pvb.make repair', *kijavít* 'pvb. mend', *kijavíttat* 'pvb.make mend', *megcsinál* 'pvb.repair/mend', *megcsináltat* 'pvb.have repaired/mended', *megszerel* 'pvb.repair', *megszereltet* 'pvb.have repaired' *szerepel* 'play a role', *győz* 'win', *nyer* 'win', *veszt* 'lose', *veszít* 'lose', *kap* 'get', *cserél* 'change, trade', *büntet* 'punish', *gyűjt* 'collect', *oszt* 'distribute', *juttat* 'distribute', *vesz* 'buy', *vásárol* 'buy' etc.

Verbs in the third group can only occur with implicit arguments in the third manner, by means of the extension of their immediate context. The verbs belonging to this type are e.g. *elmélyül* 'pvb.become absorbed', *átfut* 'pvb.sweep over', *elrepül* 'pvb.fly away', *felpróbál* 'pvb.try on', *lök* 'push', *beüt* 'pvb.punch in', *tologat* 'push', *tesz* 'put', *bánik* 'deal with', *lakik* 'dwell', *elolvas* 'pvb.read', *tűnik* 'seem', *bízik* 'trust', *elfelejt* 'pvb.forget', *otthagy* 'pvb.leave', *beletanul* 'pvb.learn' etc.

An interesting implication which follows is that if a verb can be used with an implicit argument in the first manner then it can also occur with

[1] The abbreviation *pvb* is used for the term *preverb.*

it in the second manner, and – since an implicit argument of a verb of the second type can also be identified in the third manner – in this latter manner as well, i.e. A⇒B⇒C. Although there are verbs which can be used with implicit arguments only in the third manner, this is the one which is suitable for every Hungarian verb to be used with lexically unrealized arguments.

The lexical-semantic representation of the verbs in the first group is rich enough to license implicit arguments. These verbs put strict constraints on the type or properties of their arguments by means of selection restrictions, lexical stereotype, and prototypical structure. The lexical-semantic representation of the verbs in the second group is poorer, i.e. less specific and that of the verbs in the third group is even poorer, i.e. even less specific. The relevant interpretation of utterances containing verbs with implicit arguments can be reached by taking into consideration larger and larger contexts moving from the first group to the third one.

On the basis of this order of interpretation it can be predicted that if the lexical-semantic representation of a verb in the second or third group becomes rich, i.e. specific enough to identify the lexically unrealized argument by itself, the verb may move to the first group. The enrichment of the lexical-semantic representation of a verb can happen by means of conceptualization and grammaticalization of some elements of the context.

And finally, the fourth remark concerns the role of the principle of relevance in the use and interpretation of implicit arguments. The cognitive principle of relevance forms a generalization according to which human cognition tends to be geared towards the maximization of relevance (Sperber and Wilson 1986/1995: 260), i.e. to achieve more cognitive effects with less processing effort. This principle motivates the occurrence of implicit arguments and also helps to identify them. If an argument can be used in the above mentioned three manners, it should be left lexically unrealized, because its implicit use can reach the same effects as the use of its overt form but with less processing effort. The cognitive principle of relevance also guides the interpretation of implicit arguments. To avoid unnecessary processing effort, the adequate interpretation can be formed, first, through the lexical-semantic representation (case A). If this does not result in a relevant interpretation, then, second, the immediate utterance context with its encyclopedic and grammatical information should also be considered (case B). If this does not lead to an adequate interpretation either, then, third, the immediate utterance context should be extended (case C). It must be emphasized that this order of interpretation mechanisms also involves important implications: ~A⇒B, ~B⇒C. These implications indicate that the use and interpretation of implicit arguments are under the control of an economy balance, i.e. they are guided by the requirement to take into account lexical-semantic, grammatical and contextual information only to a necessary extent.

1.2. Aims and organization of the paper

In the present study I investigate in detail the first one of the above mentioned possibilities, case A. I have two main aims. First, I intend to examine what lexical-semantic factors influence the occurrence of verbs with implicit direct object arguments in Hungarian and how they do that. However, in the course of the investigation I concentrate not only on lexical-semantic properties of verbs but take into consideration grammatical (morphosyntactic) and pragmatic (contextual) factors to a necessary extent as well.

My second aim in the present paper is to consciously reflect on methodological aspects of my research. Researchers have to decide very carefully what kinds of data they use and in what functions in their studies. On the one hand, mostly relying on the notion of data as defined by Kertész and Rákosi (2009) and on the functions of linguistic data established by Lehmann (2004: 191–195), I attempt to analyze what kind of data and in what functions occur in different phases of my research and theory construction, and also in reporting on the research and theory formation. On the other hand, by means of this analysis I want to highlight how theory formation influences the use of data in the research and how data influences the theory formation without the process becoming circular.

The organization of the paper is as follows. In section 2, I will briefly overview some typical kinds of explanation suggested by the literature to account for the occurrence of verbs with implicit direct object arguments. I will give a fairly detailed treatment to proposals which emphasize the role of lexical-semantic factors and, since I will argue for a need for a complex approach, also to some recent complex theories. In section 3, I will investigate which lexical-semantic factors in a complex approach influence the use of verbs with implicit direct object arguments in Hungarian and how they do so in accordance with grammatical (morphosyntactic) and pragmatic (contextual) information. I will discuss in detail how selection restrictions, lexical stereotype, prototypical structure of objects and also indefinite/definite conjugations constrain verbs' occurrences with implicit direct object arguments. In section 4, I will turn to the methodological issues concerning the relationship between theory construction and data handling in my research. And, finally, in section 5, I will summarize the results.

2. Explanations of the occurrence of verbs with implicit direct object arguments

2.1. Purely syntactic explanations

Cote (1996) overviews the large literature concerning zero object arguments in various languages and demonstrates rather convincingly why purely syntactic explanations are inadequate in themselves. In purely syntactic explanations, the zero objects are represented in the syntactic structures of sentences and they can be accessed through binding principles. This kind of explanation cannot be accepted at least for three reasons. First, sometimes the zero object is not represented in the syntactic structure of the sentence, e.g. the verbs that can be used with indefinite null objects show different behavior in the occurrences with implicit objects and overt pronominal objects (cf. *Joyce ate this afternoon because the turkey was ready* vs. **Joyce ate it*$_i$ *this afternoon because the turkey*$_i$ *was ready*).

Second, it is inconsistent with a syntactic analysis that verbs with indefinite null objects do not allow their zero objects to have an antecedent which violates the binding principles (cf. Chomsky 1981). It may be a solution that one assumes a special empty category which differs from the zero pronominal, but this proposal also raises some further questions. Third, in a purely syntactic analysis it is not possible to make a distinction between the verbs with definite null objects and the otherwise similar verbs which give thematic roles only to overt objects (cf. *John entered* vs. **John penetrated*).

In the past two decades various versions of the argument realization principle (according to which there must be one argument XP in the syntax to identify each subevent in the event structure template) have been put forward by a number of researchers (cf. eg. Grimshaw and Vikner 1993; Kaufmann and Wunderlich 1998; Rappaport Hovav and Levin 2001) in order to describe general tendencies in argument realization in languages like English. Goldberg (2005a) demonstrates, however, that these have not solved the above mentioned problems and fail to account for open-ended classes of counterexamples. The syntactic analyses underestimate the role of other factors such as constructions, lexical semantics and discourse constraints and some of them even ignore them.

2.2. Purely pragmatic approach

Pragmatic explanations relying only on conversational implicatures through Gricean maxims are also insufficient to account for verbs' behavior with implicit arguments in different languages (Cote 1996: 123). Pragmatic explanations state that verbs can optionally have lexically unrealized objects and assume a true intransitive–transitive alternation. If it is possible to clearly account for the occurrences of zero objects pragmatically, then, on the one hand, there should not be any evidence for the presence of null objects in the syntax. On the other hand, the occurrences of zero objects should never be lexically or grammatically determined, but all information concerning them must be pragmatically inferred. However, both verbs with indefinite and definite implicit objects show certain lexical alternations independently of the pragmatic factors (cf. section 2.3) Further, it is allowed to refer to the zero objects of these verbs later in discourse with overt forms that are grammatically constrained and not characteristic of pragmatic inferences.

2.3. Purely lexical-semantic approaches

In the literature on implicit arguments in different languages a hypothesis that lexical-semantic properties of verbs can determine their various occurrences with lexically unrealized arguments has also been formulated. However, there is no consensus among the various proposals whether the occurrence with an implicit argument is an idiosyncratic property of the verb in question or a predictable (lexical-)semantic property.

In Fillmore's (1986) approach the omissibility of an argument is defined by the particular, unique lexical-semantic features of verbs. It is marked in the lexical-semantic representation of the verbs what argument can be left implicit. According to this view, in English there are verbs whose lexical-semantic features license the use of verbs with implicit arguments, and there are verbs whose lexical-semantic features do not. Fillmore divides the verbs which license implicit arguments at all into three groups regarding the indefiniteness/definiteness of their omitted complements. Verbs in the first group can occur with indefinite null complements (INC), e.g. *eat, drink, read, sew, sing, cook,* and *bake.* The reference of the null complement is unknown or the speaker does not consider essential to identify it exactly, thus INC is obligatorily disjoint in reference with anything saliently present in the context. The second group contains verbs which can be used with definite null complements (DNC), e.g. *accept, object, wait, win, lose,* and *insist.* These verbs can occur with null complements only if the missing information can be immediately retrieved from the context. The reference of the null complement can be identified with a saliently present entity of the context unambiguously, i.e. the null complement has a definite reading. Verbs in the third group may have both indefinite and definite omissible complements, e.g. *contribute* and *give* 'donate'. In the lexical-semantic representations of verbs it is marked not only that a verb can occur with null complements at all, but if yes, it is also marked what kind of reading, i.e. indefinite or definite, the null complement can have.

However, the markedness regarding the occurrence with an indefinite or definite complements in the lexical-semantic representation of verbs does not always make the right predictions about the behavior of verbs in different contexts (Groefsema 1995: 141–142). On the one hand, the references of null complements of INC verbs do not differ very often from all entries saliently presented in the context. To identify the reference of the missing complement the context involves the necessary information. On the other hand, definite null complements do not always have a discourse antecedent. Consider Groefsema's examples in (1)–(2).

(1) *John brought the sandwiches and Ann ate.*

(2) *Martina Navratilova has won again.*

Since Fillmore states that the reference of an INC must differ from everything in the context, (1) is expected to have an interpretation like 'John brought the sandwiches and Ann ate something other than sandwiches'. However, English native speakers interpret (1) something like 'Ann ate of the sandwiches that John brought', although this leaves unspecified how many of them Ann ate. So, the null complement does not necessarily refer to all the sandwiches that John brought, neither is it disjoint in reference with the sandwiches that John brought. The null complement of *eat* in (1) refers to the sandwiches cumulatively (i.e. there is no quantitative restriction on how many objects are denoted by it), similarly to the reference of bare common nouns (Maleczki 1994), or the appropriate cases of noun incorporation (Kiefer 1990–1991),[2] while Hale and Keyser (2002) as well as Cummins and Roberge (2005) propose that implicit direct objects are represented by null bare nouns. Similarly to the verbs *lose, wait, accept, object* and *insist* the verb *win* in (2) licenses a definite null complement in Fillmore's classification, and the null complement should have a discourse antecedent. Analyzing the behavior of *win* and *lose*, Fillmore argues that these verbs can only occur with implicit direct object arguments if there is a concrete competition in the context of which the subject is the winner or the loser. This claim is too strong in Groefsema's opinion (1995: 144), because

[2] For a more detailed explanation see Németh T. (2001), and also consider Scott (2006).

there is no need to mention a particular competition in the context in the case of famous sports people. Thus, in (2), if the speaker/hearer knows who Navratilova is and what she is famous for, a contextually given competition is not necessary to access the interpretation 'Martina Navratilova has won the competition in which she took part'.

Furthermore, it can also happen that the same verb behaves differently with regard to INC-DNC-phenomena in its different occurrences. Consider Groefsema's (1995: 142–143) examples again.

(3) Ann: *I don't know how to finish this letter.*
Sue: *Why don't you put 'yours sincerely'?*

(4) ? *Mary walked to the table with a book in her hand. She put the book.*

(5) (John, Bruce and Mary were playing a game which involved putting something on the table.)
John put his book, Bruce put his pipe, and Mary her glasses.

The locative argument of *put* can be left implicit in (3), but it cannot be lexically unrealized in (4) in spite of the fact that there is an antecedent immediately recoverable from the context. It may be an acceptable solution that *put* is used in two different meanings in (3) and (4). However, this does not explain why (5) is more acceptable than (4).

Saeboe (1996) agrees with Filmore (1986) that the omissibility of an argument is an idiosyncratic lexical-semantic feature of verbs. It is not possible to predict semantically when an argument can be optional at all. The omissibility of an argument varies across languages, even among such closely related languages as English, German and Norwegian. Many English verbs which allow their definite direct object arguments to be phonetically unrealized correspond to verbs requiring overt anaphors in German or Norwegian (Saeboe 1996: 193). Saeboe enumerates three possibilities with respect to the realization of an argument. First, an argument is obligatory, it can never be omitted; second, an argument can be left implicit with definite, anaphoric interpretation, and third, an argument can have a zero form with indefinite, non-anaphoric interpretation. A fourth possibility can be added to these three cases in terms of Fillmore's argumentation. There are some verbs which can occur with both definite, anaphoric and indefinite, non-anaphoric null complements, cf. *contribute, give* 'donate'. The borderlines between the first and second or first and third possibilities may be partly syntactically based, subject to parametric variation across languages, and partly arbitrary. In Saeboe's opinion it is for the borderline between the second and third kind of cases that one can provide a semantic account which predicts that the anaphoricity of zero arguments cannot vary across languages. This means that it should not be possible to find two otherwise synonymous verbs where an argument of one language can be left implicit with definite reading but the same argument of the other language can be left implicit with indefinite interpretation.

Saeboe connects the anaphoricity of zero arguments to presuppositions. A zero argument is anaphoric if it is involved in a presupposition triggered by the verb and is recovered in the same process in which the presupposition is verified. Thus, the context dependence of the missing complement can be described as a presuppositional effect. The relevant referent is introduced in the presupposition and the substituted referent is extended to the assertion in an update process. The difference between indefinite/definite implicit arguments surfaces where the referent is introduced: in the case of indefinite implicit arguments the referent is introduced in the universe of the assertion, but in the case of definite implicit arguments the referent is introduced in the presupposition. If a predicate with an optional argument triggers a presupposition involving the argument, the presupposition itself becomes anaphoric as soon as the argument is omitted. Consider Saeboe's example.

(6) *Susan dissuades John.*

(6) asserts that Susan dissuades John from P and triggers the presupposition that John plans P. On the basis of the anaphoric notion of the presupposition, P must be anchored to some familiar action Q in the context: John plans Q, and once it is, Q substitutes P in the assertion. Thus, zero anaphors are not really anaphors. There is no need to distinguish between definite/indefinite implicit arguments in any other way than through the presence of a presupposition. For example, the occurrences of the verbs triggering reactions (*agree, disagree, refuse, accept*), factive predicates (*remember, remind, forget, notice, aware*) and state transition predicates (*recover, return*) with zero arguments can be considered anaphoric. The triggering of a presupposition must be involved in the lexical-semantic representations of verbs and it must be marked in the lexicon.

However, Saeboe's proposal raises some further questions. First, if a verb does not trigger a presupposition involving the lexically unrealized argument then the zero occurrence of this argument can be anaphoric. Consider (7a–c). [3]

[3] (7a, b) are Saeboe's examples, but my explanations of them differ from his.

(7) a. *Sue had not heard from Joe for months when, suddenly, she received a letter.*
b. 'Sue had not heard from Joe for month when, suddenly, she received a letter from him.'
c. 'Sue had not heard from Joe for month when, suddenly, she received a letter from somebody about him.'

(7a) is an utterance with a zero argument, (7b–c) demonstrate its possible interpretations. As we have seen above, the anaphoricity of a zero argument in Saeboe's proposal can be explained by the introduction in the presupposition. The verb *receive* in (7a) does not trigger such a presupposition which involves the zero argument *from x*, so in (7a) the assertion structure of *Sue received a letter* contains the variable *from x,* it does not occur in a presupposition, so it cannot get an anaphoric interpretation through the presupposition. However, native speakers prefer (7b) out of the possible interpretations, and it is quite natural for them that Sue received the letter from Joe. (7c) can also be a possible interpretation but is not preferred. In (7b), the zero argument is also anaphoric, but its anaphoricity is not caused by the presupposition triggered by the verb *receive.* This zero complement gets its anaphoricity through a pragmatically driven inference process. Relevance considerations lead to the identification of the lexically unrealized argument with a known entity of the context, independently of the semantic presupposition. Thus, (7b) demonstrates that a zero argument also can have an anaphoric reading even if it is not involved in a presupposition triggered by the verb. In this case the anaphoricity of the null argument can be explained by other lexical-semantic features or non-lexical-semantic properties.

Second, it may also happen that a zero argument involved in a presupposition is not anaphoric. This case can be well illustrated by the occurrences of the German verb *erkränken* 'become sick' with zero arguments.[4] Some occurrences of the English verbs *eat* and *drink* also may be problematic in this respect, depending on the definition of presupposition. The third problem is that sometimes it is very difficult to verify the anaphoricity of a zero argument because the presupposition triggered by the verb is vague, as, for example, in the case of *come* and *go.*[5] There is a fourth problem with Saeboe's proposal. He states that the anaphoricity of zero arguments does not vary across languages. If one takes into consideration not

[4] Saeboe (1996: 204–205) analyzes the use of *erkränken* 'become sick' with implicit arguments in much detail.

[5] These three problems are also discussed by Saeboe (1996).

only the languages closely related to English but also *pro*-drop languages, which allow their arguments to be left implicit far more freely than English does, it is not certain that Saebo's claim can be maintained. For example, in Hungarian most of the transitive verbs can occur both with indefinite and definite zero arguments following from the special morphosyntactic properties of Hungarian, namely, from the indefinite and definite conjugations, i.e. in addition to subject *pro*-drop in Hungarian, object *pro*-drop is also possible (cf. Bartos 1997; É. Kiss 2002). So, one can easily find two otherwise synonymous English, German, or Norwegian verbs, on the one hand, and Hungarian verbs, on the other hand, where an argument in a language of the first group can be left implicit with a definite reading, but the same argument in Hungarian can be left implicit, not only with a definite but also with an indefinite interpretation.

2.4. Complex approaches: interaction between lexical-semantic, grammatical and pragmatic factors

To avoid the insufficiency of purely syntactic, pragmatic or lexical-semantic explanations, recent proposals assume an interaction between lexical-semantic, grammatical and pragmatic factors in the licensing of the occurrence of verbs with implicit arguments and also in their interpretation processes (cf. Groefsema 1995; Cote 1996; Cummins and Roberge 2005; Goldberg 2005a, b; Iten et al. 2005; Scott 2006; Bibok 2008; Pethő and Kardos 2009; Németh T. 2008; Németh T. and Bibok 2010). Although these different proposals in diverse theories emphasize the role of various factors to a different extent, they share the view that implicit arguments can be adequately accounted for only by assuming an interaction between the various factors.[6] For example, in addition to the lexical-semantic features of a verb, the encyclopedic pieces of information under the conceptual addresses of lexemes in the utterance in which the verb with an implicit argument occurs should also be taken into account (Groefsema 1995). Consider (8a–c).

(8) a. *Paul gave to Amnesty International.*
b. ?*Paul gave to Ann.*
c. *I always give books on birthdays.*

The direct object argument of *give* is left implicit in (8a). The omissibility of this argument is permitted because of the fact that the interpretation of

[6] I do not aim to overview all recent complex approaches to implicit arguments, instead, I will only refer to some elements which I will use in my explanation.

give and *Amnesty International* make immediately accessible the assumption that people donate money to Amnesty International. So, from this the hearer can infer that what Paul gave to Amnesty International was some money. The acceptability of (8b) is questionable, because the missing direct object argument does not become immediately accessible by the interpretation of *Paul, give* and *Ann*. In (8c) *give* and *birthdays* make immediately accessible the information that friends and relatives give presents to each other on birthdays. Using this assumption one can infer that the reference of the implicit argument in (8c) is the people to whom the speaker gives presents on their birthdays.

Various discourse factors can also influence the occurrence of implicit arguments (Cote 1996). If a speaker does not realize verbal arguments lexically, he/she considers these arguments to be in the center of the hearer's attention. The interpretations of the previous utterances and the organization of the discourse or the situation and also encyclopedic knowledge make it possible to access these arguments very easily without any explicit mention.[7]

Among the latest approaches to lexically unrealized arguments functional discourse grammar (García Velasco and Portero Muñoz 2002) claims that the licensing of the occurrence of an implicit direct object argument with an indefinite reading is basically determined by lexical-semantic factors, i.e. it depends on the semantic class which the verb at stake belongs to and also on the type of the direct object argument. But implicit arguments with a definite interpretation are licensed by lexical-semantic, structural and pragmatic factors cooperatively. In both cases the starting point is the abstract meaning definition of verbs which determines the necessary number of participants. Then the predicate frames provide the syntactic environments which the lexical entries can enter according to the linking rules. The same lexical entry can join more than one predicate frame, which results in a syntactic alternation. For example, in the abstract meaning definition of the verb *eat*, two participants are involved. If *eat* enters a transitive predicate frame, then both participants in its abstract meaning definition are projected into the syntactic structure. In this case the second participant is also expressed explicitly as the syntactic object. The speaker wants to emphasize the object of the eating activity. If the speaker wants to transfer the focus of attention from the object of eating activity to the eating activity itself, then the abstract meaning definition of the verb *eat* joins an intransitive predicate frame which does not contain a direct object position to be

7 Similar claims are made by Ariel (1991).

filled in. However, a selection restriction in the abstract meaning definition of *eat* makes it possible to interpret the direct object argument omitted in this way with an indefinite reading as a kind of food. In the case of the occurrence of verbs with definite implicit arguments the speaker intends to identify the reference of lexically unrealized arguments from the preceding discourse or from the physical environment.

However, it must be noted that the definite implicit arguments can be identified not only with the help of information from the preceding discourse and physical environment, but also by considering some pieces of encyclopedic information. Furthermore, it can also happen that an indefinite implicit argument has an antecedent in the preceding discourse. In this case the indefinite implicit argument is not only lexically determined as García Velasco and Portero Muñoz (2002) suggest.

In construction grammar the explicit or implicit realization of arguments are determined by two interacting factors, i.e. by lexical semantics and constructions (Goldberg 2005b). The lexical-semantic representations of individual verbs involve frame-specific participant roles, while constructions, i.e. the conventional pairings of form and meaning which are independent of individual verbs, have general argument roles capturing generalizations over individual verbs' participant roles. Not all of the participant roles of individual verbs and argument roles of constructions are profiled. To be lexically profiled is a stable aspect of lexemes. Profiled participant roles usually are obligatorily expressed or receive a definite interpretation in a language like English. The profiled argument roles usually appear syntactically as subject, object or the second object of ditransitives, and there are also certain types of arguments roles, e.g. animate roles which are inherently profiled more likely than others and, therefore, are obligatorily expressed. A participant role of an individual verb must be fused with an argument role of a construction in order to be explicitly realized. The possibility of this fusion is constrained by the semantic coherence principle and the correspondence principle. The semantic coherence principle predicts that the participation role of the verb and the argument role of the construction to be fused must be semantically compatible. The correspondence principle requires that lexically profiled participant roles will be fused with profiled argument roles. An exception arises if a verb has three profiled participant roles and one of them can be fused with an unprofiled argument role. The correspondence principle is a default principle which can be overridden by specifications of particular constructions. Taking into account all these requirements, in construction grammar verbs can occur with implicit arguments in the following two manners. First, there are constructions which override the correspondence principle and deemphasize a normally profiled participant role. In English such constructions are, for example, the implicit theme construction and the deprofiled object construction. Verbs of bodily emission, e.g. *sneeze, blow, cry, spit, ejaculate, piss,* and *vomit*, and verbs of donation, e.g. *contribute, donate,* and *give* 'donate' can be fused with the implicit theme construction. In the deprofiled object construction the patient argument normally explicitly expressed as a syntactic object loses its emphasized status, it becomes deemphasized instead of the action itself becoming particularly emphasized, e.g. *Pat gave and gave, but Chris just took and took. Owls only kill at night.* (cf. also García Velasco and Portero Muñoz 2002). Second, a non-profiled participant role is omitted in the intransitive use of transitive verbs, e.g. *drink, eat, sing, dance* and *smoke.* In both manners the lexical-semantic properties of individual verbs are crucial to determine whether a verb can be fused with a construction licensing an implicit argument, i.e. a profiled participant role can be deemphasized or a non-profiled participant role can be omitted. The issue of what these lexical-semantic properties are exactly and which semantic classes of verbs can take a part in the occurrence with implicit arguments require further empirical research.

The lexical-constructional approach treats the occurrence of verbs with explicit vs. implicit direct object arguments as a syntactic alternation which can only be explained by considering both lexical-semantic and constructional factors (Bibok 2008). This approach assumes such a general meaning representation of syntactically alternating verbs which is encyclopedically and pragmatically rich enough to serve as a basis for constructional meanings coming about when these verbs change their patterns of syntactic government. Thus, constructional meanings of a verb are condensed into one lexical meaning. In other words, in the lexicon, verbs have underspecified representations and not those that are as specific as constructional meanings. From the point of view of syntactic alternations it can be stated that verbs take part in them if they have a general meaning which is compatible with all meanings occurring in alternations. The verbs' occurrence with implicit arguments originates in this encyclopedically and pragmatically rich general meaning. The lexical-semantic representation of verbs which can occur with implicit direct object arguments can be interpreted in two ways. Either only the physical activity denoted by the verbs is in the focus of attention (cf. *A gyerek iszik* 'The kid is drinking') or their object as well (cf. *A gyerek tejet iszik* 'The kid is drinking milk'). When only the physical activity is in the focus of attention, the direct object arguments can be left lexically unrealized (cf. also García Velasco and Portero-Muñoz

2002; Goldberg 2005b), but this argument remains available as background information in the lexical-semantic representation. And, if the direct object argument is also in the focus of attention the direct object arguments must be explicitly expressed.

2.5. Internal summary

On the basis of 2.1–2.4 it can be concluded that the lexical-semantic properties of verbs have a very important, but not exclusive role in the licensing and interpretation of implicit arguments. It is not sufficient to consider an idiosyncratic lexical property of the individual verbs for them to occur with lexically unrealized arguments. In addition to the lexical-semantic factors one also has to take into account certain grammatical/constructional and pragmatic (contextual) factors, and even their interaction. The proposals briefly overviewed in section 2.4 attest that the lexical-semantic properties which license the occurrence with implicit arguments in the first, A, manner can be grasped and formulated in various theories, and these explanations can be compatible.

In the subsequent sections I want to examine which elements of the lexical-semantic representation of verbs license their occurrence with implicit direct object arguments in Hungarian and how they do that. However, since the lexical-semantic properties are not sufficient conditions of licensing lexically unrealized arguments, I will also take into account the other constraints involved in the definition of implicit arguments (cf. 1.1) such as grammatical and pragmatic (contextual and encyclopedic) factors. Consequently, assuming an intensive interaction between lexical semantics, grammar and pragmatics in licensing and identifying implicit arguments, I consider the occurrence and interpretation of lexically unrealized arguments phenomena to be situated and studied at the semantics–pragmatics interface and, even more, at the grammar–pragmatics interface.[8]

---

[8] The interaction between grammar and pragmatics has been studied by Ariel (2008) as well as Németh T. and Bibok (2010).

3. A study at the grammar/semantics–pragmatics interface: implicit direct objects in Hungarian

3.1. Observations concerning the objectless use of Hungarian transitive verbs

The qualifications *with an object* and *without an object* in the verbal entries of explanatory dictionaries of Hungarian mirror the observation that there are verbs which can occur with an object and verbs which can be used without any object. In the Hungarian grammatical tradition it is well known that this observation grasp not only the difference between the transitive vs. intransitive verbs, but it refers to the phenomena that transitive verbs can also occur without a direct object argument. For example, it is not necessary to add the object *étel* 'dish' to the verb *főz* 'cook', because it is involved in the meaning of the verb as the object of the action denoted by the verb. However, if we want to use such a verb with a more specific direct object argument, then it must be explicitly realized, cf. (9a–b).

(9) a. *A nagymama főz.*
the grandmother.NOM[9] cooks.INDEF
'The grandmother is cooking.'

b. *A nagymama vacsorát főz.*
the grandmother.NOM dinner.ACC cooks.INDEF
'The grandmother is cooking dinner.'

In order to explain the relation between the transitive verbs' occurrences with and without direct object arguments, two different questions should be answered: (i) what kind of lexical-semantic representation of verbs can be assumed underlying the alternative use, and, (ii) what kind of syntactic structures can be rendered to the sentences in which transitive verbs occur with explicit direct objects or without them. Given the aims of the present paper, I will concentrate only on the first question.

In the Hungarian grammatical tradition there is an observation that direct object arguments can be absent not only in cases when the transitive verbs are inflected for the indefinite conjugation but also when transitive verbs are inflected for the definite conjugation.[10] The suitable form of the

[9] The abbreviations used in the glosses throughout this paper are the following: 1 – first person, 2 – second person, 3 – third person, SG – singular, PL – plural, NOM – nominative, ACC – accusative, INDEF – indefinite (conjugation), and DEF – definite (conjugation).

[10] In Hungarian there are two types of conjugations, namely, what is called the indefinite and definite conjugations. Transitive verbs can be inflected for both

definite conjugation is used when the personal pronoun is not explicitly expressed but can be understood, and the sentence itself can be accounted for as elliptical, requiring a context (H. Molnár 1962: 158). Consider (10).

(10) "*Olvassa Éva a Népszabadságot?*"
reads.DEF Éva the Népszabadság.ACC
"*Nem olvassa.*"
not reads.DEF
'Does Éva read the Népszabadság?'
'She does not read [it].'

In (10) the answer should not be necessarily considered an elliptical utterance. The verb form inflected for the definite conjugation has a direct object as it has a subject as well. The 3SG form direct object is a phonetically empty pronoun, i.e. *pro* (Bartos 2000: 740), thus the use of the lexically unrealized direct object argument comes from the *pro*-drop characteristics of Hungarian. If the direct object inflected for the 3SG form gets into the focus position, then it must be lexically realized, i.e. an overt pronoun must be used, cf. (11).

(11) "*Olvassa Éva a Népszabadságot?*"
reads.DEF Éva the Népszabadság.ACC
"*Azt nem olvassa.*"
it not reads.DEF
'Does Éva read the Népszabadság?'
'She does not read it.'

It is also worth examining the 1SG verb form with *-lak/-lek* inflection. This form traditionally belongs to the definite conjugation but recently it

---

conjugations, but intransitive verbs only for the indefinite conjugation. The use of the indefinite/definite conjugations is determined by mostly semantic (pragmatic) and (morpho)syntactic criteria. Intransitive verbs do not have an object argument in their lexical-semantic representation, therefore they cannot be used with an object and can only be inflected for the indefinite conjugation. Transitive verbs have an object argument in their lexical-semantic representation and if they are used with an indefinite object, they need to be inflected for the indefinite conjugation. If they are used with a definite object, then they need to be inflected for the definite conjugation. For a discussion of the problems with the accounts for the indefinite/definite conjugations, see Németh T. and Bibok (2001).

has been considered a form in indefinite conjugation. The specificity of the *-lak/-lek* is that a verb inflected for it can only occur with a 2SG direct object. In accordance with the previous observations, the 2SG objects can be omitted if a verb is inflected for the *-lak/-lek* form, cf. (12).

(12) *Látlak* *és* *irigyellek.*
see.INDEF.1SG and envy.INDEF.1SG
'I can see [you] and envy [you].'

The implicit object of the verbs *lát* 'see' and *irigyel* 'envy' has a 2SG interpretation, which refers to the communicative partner. The implicit object can be identified as a 2SG object with the help of the information stored in the meaning representation of the morpheme *-lak/-lek* without a context. Thus, the implicit object argument is interpreted in the first (A) manner, but not on the basis of the lexical-semantic representation of the verbs *lát* 'see' and *irigyel* 'envy', instead, by means of the information in the representation of the inflection morpheme.

However, the object of the verbs conjugated for the *-lak/-lek* form can be 2PL object as well. According to the Hungarian grammatical tradition, 2PL objects always have to be explicitly expressed with *-lak/-lek*. Cf. (13).

(13) (The children are shouting at their father in the playground.)
"Apa, *figyelj* *csak* *ide?* *Látsz* *minket?"*
daddy.NOM look.INDEF.IMP.2SG just here see.INDEF.2SG us
"Látlak."
see.1SG
'Daddy, look here. Can you see us?'
'I can see [you].'

In the father's answer the verb *látlak* has a 2PL implicit direct object. This 2PL implicit direct object can be identified with the help of the pieces of information from the physical environment and the preceding discourse: you, the shouting kids. Thus, it can be concluded that the verbs conjugated for the *-lak/-lek* form can occur with both singular and plural 2nd person implicit direct object. But while the singular 2nd person direct object can be left implicit in the first (A) manner, the plural 2nd person direct object argument can be left implicit in the third (C) manner.

After the brief overview of the observations concerning the objectless use of Hungarian transitive verbs let us turn to the question of what kind of lexical-semantic representation of verbs can be assumed to underlie the verbs' use with and without a direct object argument.

3.2. The role of selection restrictions in the verbs' occurrence with implicit direct object arguments

Let us start out from the meaning representations of the verb *iszik* 'drink' constructed by Bibok's (2008: 61) lexical-constructional approach (cf. (14)).

(14) iszik 'drink': 'x's action causes that y which is liquid goes into the mouth of x'
[[ACT x] CAUSE [[GO y] : [[LIQUID y] & [FIN [LOC y] $\subset$ LOC x's MOUTH]]]]

In (14) the verb *iszik* 'drink' has two arguments, it is a transitive verb. The type of its second argument is constrained by a selection restriction: it must be the type of LIQUID. The lexical-semantic representation of *iszik* can be interpreted in two ways. In the first case, only the activity of drinking itself is in the focus of attention, but the information which is involved in the selection restriction – to be the type of LIQUID – can also be accessed as background information. The verb *iszik* can occur with an implicit direct object argument in the sentence *János iszik* 'János is drinking' by means of this background information provided by the selection restriction. In the second case, the second argument is also in the focus of attention, the speaker wants to indicate the particular object of drinking as a specific token of the type of LIQUID, so it must be explicitly expressed, cf. (15).

(15) *János* *málnaszörpöt* *iszik.*
János.NOM raspberry juice.ACC drinks.INDEF
'János is drinking raspberry juice.'

If the object of drinking is not a typical liquid for living beings, then it must also be lexicalized in the lack of a specific context as in (16).

(16) *János* *fagyállót* *iszik.*
János.NOM antifreeze.ACC drinks.INDEF
'János is drinking antifreeze liquid.'

The occurrences of the verb *iszik* with and without a direct object can be considered syntactic alternation in which the number of arguments decreases (Bibok 2008).

Similarly, the verbs *eszik* 'eat', *lát* 'see', *hall* 'hear, listen', *olvas* 'read', and *főz* 'cook' etc. also have two arguments in their lexical-semantic representation, and they put a selection restriction on their second argument. The verb *eszik* 'eat' predicts that its second argument must be a type of FOOD, the verb *lát* 'see' predicts the type of VISUALLY PERCEPTIBLE, the verb *hall* 'hear, listen' predicts the type of AUDITORY PERCEPTIBLE, the verb *olvas* 'read' predicts the type of SYMBOLIC REPRESENTATION for the second argument. The verb *főz* 'cook' predicts that its second argument must be a token of the type FOOD, i.e. it must be a DISH. These verbs can be used with implicit direct object arguments in the same manner as the verb *iszik* 'drink', i.e. by means of their selection restriction. In (17) there are Hungarian verbs which put a selection restriction – to be of a type, to be a token of a type, to have a particular property or a unique selection – on their second argument:

(17) *eszik* 'eat', *etet* 'make eat', *fal* 'devour', *zabál* 'devour/gobble', *rág* 'chew', *nyel* 'swallow', *iszik* 'drink', *itat* 'make drink', *vedel* 'swill', *bámul* 'gaze', *ír* 'write', *rajzol* 'draw', f*est* 'paint', *süt* 'bake', *mos* 'wash', *áztat* 'soak', *öblít* 'rinse', *vasal* 'iron', *mosogat* 'do dishes', *takarít* 'clean', *törölget* 'dry, dust', *varr* 'sew', *ás* 'dig', *gyomlál* 'weed', *permetez* 'spray', *kapál* 'hoe', *locsol* 'water', *szánt* 'plow', *vet* 'sow', *kaszál* 'scythe', *arat* 'harvest', *fej* 'milk', *épít* 'build', *fúr* 'drill', *farag* 'carve', *foltoz* 'patch', *stoppol* 'darn', *tereget* 'hang up [to dry]', *szárogat* 'dry', *fon* 'spin', *kö*t 'knit', *sző* 'weave', *vásárol* 'shop', *kézbesít* 'deliver', *gyógyít* 'cure', *operál* 'operate on', *tanít* 'teach', *gyón* 'confess' etc.

Verbs in (17) always have a second, *y* argument in their lexical-semantic representation which can be realized as syntactic object. Therefore, these verbs really differ from verbs such as *szuszog* 'pant', *bőg* 'cry', *elsápad* 'become pale', *leizzad* 'get sweaty' etc. which have only one *x* argument in their lexical-semantic representation, i.e. intransitive verbs which can take a syntactic object only in marked, specific context only in a highly constrained way. The lexical-semantic representation of verbs in (17) can be interpreted in two ways. First, when the action denoted by the verbs alone is in the focus of attention then these verbs occur with implicit indefinite second arguments with the help of selection restrictions they put on their second argument. The implicit direct object arguments can be identified with the information involved in the selection restriction concerning the type of the *y* argument as in the case of the verb *iszik* 'drink' or the token of a type as in the case of *főz* 'cook' or a unique selection as in the case of *gyón* 'confess'. In other words: if these verbs occur without an explicit direct object argument, the implicit direct object argument refers to the type or token of a type or a unique object predicted by the selection restriction.

It can also happen that two different selection restrictions on the second argument are involved in the lexical-semantic representation of a verb such as in the case of *itat* 'make drink' and *etet* 'feed'. The verbs *itat* and *etet* predict that their direct object argument must be the type of ANIMAL or HUMAN. These verbs constrain their adverbial argument as well, it must be the type of LIQUID and the type of FOOD, respectively, cf. (18a–b).

(18) a. *itat* 'make drink': 'x's action causes that y which is liquid goes into the mouth of z which is animal or human'
[[ACT x] CAUSE [[GO y] : [[LIQUID y] & [FIN [LOC z] ⊂ LOC z's MOUTH] : {ANIMAL, HUMAN}]]]
b. *etet* 'feed': 'x's action causes that y which is food goes into the mouth of z which is animal or human'
[[ACT x] CAUSE [[GO y] : [[FOOD y] & [FIN [LOC z] ⊂ LOC z's MOUTH] : {ANIMAL, HUMAN}]]]

Particular contexts in which the verbs *itat* and *etet* occur decide what selection restriction constrains the type of the direct object argument. Consider (19).

(19) *Reggelente*	*először*	*itatok/*	*etetek.*
in the morning	first	make drink.INDEF.1SG	feed.INDEF.1SG

'In the morning first I make [ANIMAL or HUMAN] drink/feed [ANIMAL or HUMAN].'

If (19) is uttered in a conversation on farm life, the context makes the selection restriction ANIMAL active, thus, the lexically unrealized direct object argument cannot be human. The active ANIMAL selection restriction and the context provide a relevant interpretation: in the morning the speaker, first, makes the farm animals drink/feed them. The implicit direct object argument of *itat* and *etet* can be identified with the farm animals. Let us imagine now that the speaker works as a nurse at a daycare, an old people's home, or a hospital. There are people in these institutions who need feeding. In this context, the selection restriction HUMAN becomes active. Thus, the implicit direct object arguments of *itat* and *etet* in (19) can be identified with babies/children, old people etc. who have to be fed. In both cases one has to rely on the interaction between the verbs' lexical-semantic representations and context to construct the relevant utterance meanings.

It is worth mentioning that the verbs *itat* 'make drink', *etet* 'feed' and their perfective forms *megitat* 'pvb.make drink' and *megetet* 'pvb.feed' can also be used with implicit adverbial arguments by means of the same selection restriction to be of type of LIQUID and FOOD, respectively, which is involved in the lexical-semantic representation of the verbs *iszik* 'drink' and *eszik* 'eat'. In (19) both the direct object argument and the adverbial argument of the verbs *itat* and *etet* are left implicit. Furthermore, if the direct object argument of *itat* is an adult person the implicit adverbial argument of *itat* refers to alcohol in the same way as the direct object argument of *iszik* 'drink' does in a habitual reading without a specific context, cf. (20a–b).

(20) a. *Az anya itatja a kislányát.*
the mother.NOM makes drink.DEF the her daughter.ACC
'The mother makes her daughter drink.'

b. *A férj itatja a sógorát.*
the husband makes drink.DEF the his brother in law.ACC
'The husband makes his brother-in-law drink.'

A further remark seems to be in order in connection with the verbs in (17). Alsina (1992: 524) assumes that those verbs can be used without non-specific objects which denote an unbounded process, i.e. an event that takes place over time and is not inherently delimited. However, this assumption cannot be applied to Hungarian entirely. In spite of the fact that the verbs *megetet* 'pvb.feed', *megitat* 'pvb.make drink', *megfőz* 'pvb.cook', *kimos* 'pvb.wash', *kivasal* 'pvb.iron', *elmosogat* 'pvb.do dishes', *eltörölget* 'pvb. dry dishes', *kitakarít* 'pvb.clean', *meglocsol* 'pvb.water' *learat* 'pvb.harvest', *elvet* 'pvb.sow', *kitereget* 'pvb.hang up [to dry]' describe a bounded process, they can also occur with implicit unspecified direct object arguments. At the same time, not all verbs which have an end point because of their preverbs can occur with implicit direct object arguments in a sentence environment, cf. **Az apa megeszik/megépít* 'The father pvb.eats/builds'. Therefore, the lexical-constructional approach (Bibok 2008: 63) emphasizes that selection restrictions are only necessary but not sufficient conditions to use verbs without direct object arguments. This approach proposes that it must be marked in the lexical-semantic representation of verbs individually if a participant can be syntactically unrealized. Kiefer (2006: 46–47) also reminds that not all of the transitive preverb verbs can occur without a direct object argument, e.g. *elénekel* 'pvb.sing', *megír* 'pvb.write', *eljátszik* 'pvb. play', *elolvas* 'pvb.read', *elbírál* 'pvb.judge', *kigombol* 'unbutton', *megszerel* 'pvb.mend'. In accordance with Kiefer's opinion the institutionalization has an important role in the possibility to use these verbs with implicit direct object arguments, cf. *megetet* 'pvb.feed', *meggyón* 'pvb.confess', *megfej* 'pvb.milk', *megöntöz* 'pvb.water', *kimeszel* 'pvb.whitewash', but the institutionalization is also only a necessary but not a sufficient condition.

Scrutinizing the verbs in (17), they can be classified into narrower semantic classes (cf. Pinker 1989: 126–127; Goldberg 2005b; Bibok 2008: 30): verbs of eating, drinking, work, housekeeping, agriculture etc. The lexical-semantic representations of these verbs do not involve the same kind of selection restrictions. While the verbs of eating and drinking constrain the type of their direct object arguments, they must be of type of FOOD and LIQUID, respectively, the verbs of work, housekeeping and agriculture predict that their direct object argument must be of a particular type of work, housekeeping and agriculture or a token of these particular types. Finally, there are verbs such as *gyón* 'confess' which put a unique selection restriction on their direct object argument. The kind of selection restrictions also influences the occurrences of the transitive preverb verbs with and without direct object arguments. If we derive the perfective preverbed forms of the verbs in question, their direct object arguments also become the focus of attention. If a transitive perfective preverb verb constrains the type of its direct object argument by means of a selection restriction, it must be lexicalized. The perfective reading requires the identification of the direct object argument which cannot be provided by the selection restriction on type alone, cf. *megeszik* 'pvb.eat', *megiszik* 'pvb.drink', *elolvas* 'pvb.read', *megír* 'pvb.write', *meglát* 'pvb.see' etc. If a transitive perfective preverb verb puts a selection restriction on a token of a particular type or a unique selection restriction it can be used with an implicit direct object argument. The selection restriction on a token of a type and the unique selection restriction themselves provide the necessary and sufficient information to identify the direct object arguments, which are also in the focus of attention because of the perfectivization, cf. *learat* 'pvb.harvest', *kimos* 'pvb. wash', *meggyón* 'pvb.confess', *megszoptat* 'pvb.breastfeed'. The interaction between the different kinds of the selection restrictions and the aspectual properties of perfective preverb forms of the transitive verbs make a prediction whether a transitive perfective preverb verb can occur with implicit direct object argument in a sentence environment without any specific context, i.e. in the first (A) manner.[11]

[11] For the interaction between the verbs' lexical-semantic representations and the aspectual properties cf. Pustejovsky (1995); García Velasco and Portero Muñoz (2002) and Goldberg (2005b).

3.3. The characteristic manner of action

Several verbs in (17) can occur with implicit arguments not only with the help of a selection restriction but also through information on the characteristic manner (or goal) of the action. Let us examine the verbs *eszik* 'eat', *zabál* 'devour, gobble' *iszik* 'drink' and *vedel* 'swill' from this perspective. It is not sufficient that the lexical-semantic representations of these verbs contain only selection restriction on the direct object argument to be of type of FOOD and LIQUID, respectively, at least for two reasons (Bibok and Németh T. 2001: 295–296). On the one hand, there is a sharp difference in the characteristic manner of the denoted activities between the verbs *eszik* 'eat', *zabál* 'devour, gobble' and the verbs *iszik* 'drink', *vedel* 'swill'. On the other hand, the verbs *eszik* 'eat' and *zabál* 'devour, gobble', as well as *iszik* 'drink' and *vedel* 'swill' also differ from each other in the characteristic manner of the actions expressed. Consider Bibok and Németh T.'s (2001: 295) examples.

(21) a. *Péter eszi a levest/ joghurtot/ kakaót/*
Péter.NOM eats.DEF the soup.ACC yogurt.ACC hot.chocolate.ACC
bólét.
punch.ACC
'Péter is eating the soup/yogurt/hot chocolate/punch.'

b. *Péter zabálja a levest/ joghurtot/*
Péter.nom devours.DEF the soup.ACC yogurt.ACC
kakaót/ bólét.
hot chocolate.ACC punch.ACC
'Péter is devouring the soup/yogurt/hot chocolate/punch'.

c. *Péter issza a levest/ joghurtot/*
Péter.NOM drinks.DEF the soup.ACC yogurt.ACC
kakaót/ bólét.
hot chocolate.ACC punch.ACC
'Péter is drinking the soup/yogurt/hot chocolate/punch.'

d. *Péter vedeli a levest/ joghurtot/*
Péter.NOM swills.DEF the soup.ACC yogurt.ACC
kakaót/ bólét.
hot chocolate.ACC punch.ACC
'Péter is swilling the soup/yogurt/hot chocolate/punch.'

Soup, yogurt, hot chocolate and punch can be both eaten/devoured and drunk/swilled, since they are FOOD and LIQUID at the same time.

However, there is a difference, on the one hand, between eating and drinking, as well as between devouring and swilling. On the other hand, eating and devouring, as well as drinking and swilling also can be distinguished. The differences between these verbs concern not only the quantity of FOOD and LIQUID but also the characteristic manner of the actions expressed, i.e. eating, devouring, drinking and swilling. The lexical-semantic representations of verbs have to be extended with the pieces of information concerning the characteristic manner (or goal) of actions or events (cf. Jackendoff 1990; Pustejovsky 1995, 1998) or this kind of information has to be connected to the verbs' lexical-semantic representations by means of lexical stereotypes (cf. Bierwisch 1983, 1996; Bibok 1996, 2000) or an intensive interaction between the verbs' lexical-semantic representations and the cognitive level involving the encyclopedic kind of information has to be assumed (cf. Sperber and Wilson 1986/1995; García Velasco and Portero Muñoz 2002). Any of these solutions are selected, information on the characteristic manner of eating, devouring, drinking, and swilling has to be added to the lexical information involved in the lexical-semantic representations of the verbs in the course of use and interpretation.[12]

3.4. The prototypical structure of implicit arguments

In addition to selection restrictions and information on the characteristic manner (or goal) of action the typical properties of the object types also influence the verbs' occurrence with implicit direct object arguments (Bibok and Németh T. 2001; García Velasco and Portero Muñoz 2002; Goldberg 2005b; Bibok 2008). In the case of *eszik* 'eat' / *zabál* 'devour' and *iszik* 'drink' / *vedel* 'swill' it also has to be taken into account what prototypical structure the categories FOOD and LIQUID have. Consider (22) answering the question *Mit csinál Sándor?* 'What is Sándor doing?'.

---

12 One of the referees has drawn my attention to the phenomena that verbs with manner components resist *wh*-extraction of a constituent from the object position precisely because the manner of action focalizes the verbs and it is difficult to focalize the *wh*-element at the same time. This can be explained by Grice's (1975) maxim of relation or by Sperber and Wilson's (1986/1995) principle of relevance. If a speaker uses a manner of action verb, it is expected that he/she wishes to direct his/her addressee's attention to the verbal action, rather then to the object or *wh*-element.

(22) *Sándor eszi/ zabálja az akácvirágot.*
Sándor.NOM eats.DEF devours.DEF the acacia flowers.ACC
'Sándor is eating/devouring acacia flowers.'

Although the flower of an acacia tree is usually not considered FOOD by people, one can conceptualize it as such. The flowers of the acacia trees have several characteristic properties of the category FOOD: they are solid, chewable, and fragrant, and have an excellent taste. On the basis of these characteristic properties of FOOD, the flowers of the acacia trees can be categorized as FOOD. However, it must be admitted that they can be categorized as non-typical instances of that category. Now consider (23).

(23) a. *Sándor eszi/ zabálja a kovászos uborka levét.*
Sándor.NOM eats.DEF devours.DEF the pickled cucumber.GEN juice.ACC
'Sándor is eating/devouring pickle juice.'

b. *Sándor issza/ vedeli a kovászos uborka levét.*
Sándor.NOM drinks.DEF swills.DEF the pickled cucumber.ACC fluid.ACC
'Sándor is drinkink/swilling pickle juice.'

Pickle juice can be categorized as atypical FOOD, and since it is liquid, also as LIQUID. If a direct object argument can be categorized as FOOD and LIQUID at the same time (cf. (21a–d)), it can be used with the verbs *eszik* 'eat', *zabál* 'devour', *iszik* 'drink and *vedel* 'swill' as well. The use of these verbs with the *kovászos uborka leve* 'pickle juice' is determined by the characteristic manner of action in the course of which pickle juice gets into one's mouth.

However, the question *Mit csinál Sándor?* 'What is Sándor doing?' can be answered with utterances including implicit direct object arguments. Cf. (24).

(24) *Sándor eszik/ zabál vs. iszik/ vedel.*
Sándor.NOM eats.INDEF devours.INDEF drinks.INDEF swills.INDEF
'Sándor is eating/devouring vs. drinking/swilling.'

Selection restrictions in the lexical-semantic representations of the verbs *eszik* 'eat' / *zabál* 'devour' and *iszik* 'drink' / *vedel* 'swill' as well as information on the characteristic manner of actions make it possible to reach relevant interpretations: Sándor is eating/devouring some FOOD and is drinking/swilling some LIQUID. The verbs in (24) mean only the physical activity of eating/devouring some FOOD and drinking/swilling some LIQUID stuff, but they do not designate exactly what the particular objects of eating/devouring and drinking/swilling are, i.e. in (24) only the activities with their characteristic manners themselves are the focus of attention. To get a relevant interpretation one also has to take into account the prototypical structure of the categories FOOD and LIQUID predicted by the selection restrictions. The speaker communicates by means of (24) that the lexically unrealized direct object is specific in some sense. It is not an atypical food or potable liquid or, in other words, the object refers to something that the hearer would not think abnormal for Sándor to eat/devour and drink/swill.[13] If Sándor is eating acacia flowers or he is drinking antifreeze or other atypical members of the categories FOOD and LIQUID, the speaker cannot communicate this by using the utterances in (24) without a specific context. The atypical members of categories cannot be left implicit without an adequate context because accessing them requires more processing effort which contradicts the relevance considerations. As Bibok and Németh T. (2001: 298) emphasize, in these cases the speaker produces utterances with corresponding explicit arguments in the same way as he/she would if he/she meant the particular (typical) stuff being eaten/devoured or drunk/swilled.

Finally, two further remarks seem to be necessary relating to *eszik* 'eat' and *iszik* 'drink'. First, there is an interesting relation between the possibility of leaving an argument implicit and noun incorporation in Hungarian. Any imperfective transitive activity verb can incorporate its (bare) direct object argument, but the semantic representation of the emerging lexical entry has to be supplemented by a conceptual constraint which accounts for the 'institutionalized' or conventionalized character of the complex activity in question (Kiefer 1990–1991). While (25a) denotes an institutionalized activity, a conventionalized form of suicide, (25b) does not.

(25)	a.	*János*	*sósavat*	*ivott.*
		János.NOM	hydrochloric acid.ACC	drank.INDEF.3SG
		'János drank hydrochloric acid [to commit suicide].'		

[13] Cote (1996: 150–151) comes to the same conclusion about the English verb *bake* used with an implicit direct object argument in the utterance like *Joe baked today.*

b. ?*János* *szappant* *evett.*
János.NOM soap.ACC ate.INDEF.3SG
'János ate soap.'

Therefore, on the one hand, no typical argument which cannot be incorporated can be left lexically unrealized, i.e. the non-typical objects (cf. 25b) for *eszik* and *iszik* cannot be left implicit or be incorporated. On the other hand, not every argument which can be incorporated can be left implicit. In (25a) the object *sósav* has been incorporated by *iszik*, but it cannot be left implicit because it is an atypical member of the category LIQUID.

Second, it is worth noting that the verb *iszik* denoting a habitual or long-lasting activity has a further specification of 'drink alcoholic beverages', which must be added to its lexical-semantic representation. If we do not want to involve this information in the lexical-semantic representation of verbs then we do not need any specific context either, e.g. discourse context to reach this interpretation. There is an alternative solution. Relying on a pragmatic division of labor, one can say that the meaning 'to drink alcohol' is a typical extension of the meaning of the verb *iszik* 'drink' by an informativity implicature (Horn 1984; Levinson 2000: 138). Informativity implicatures (henceforth I-implicatures) belonging to the group of generalized conversational implicatures are pragmatic inferences induced by typical pieces of background information. With the help of I-implicatures speakers can achieve their communicative goals producing minimal linguistic information without any special context, and hearers can enrich the informational content of the utterances by achieving the most specific interpretation relying on common world knowledge. A thorough analysis of I-implicatures can shed light on an interesting and important opposition between implicit and explicit forms (Levinson 2000: 146–149). Implicit forms are open to induce I-implicatures, they enrich the interpretation with typical situations, related events and participants. However, the typical interpretation can be deleted if the utterances involve explicit forms instead of implicit ones. The informativity principle as the principle of the typical interpretation provides rich, relevant interpretations of utterances by combining the underspecified linguistic meanings originating in the minimal linguistic forms and the communicative partners' shared knowledge concerning regularities in the world.

Let us take another verb from (17), namely, *épít* 'build' and consider (26).[14]

---

[14] The verb *épít* 'build' was also analyzed in Németh T. (2001). This section offers an improved version of that analysis relying on some new aspects.

(26) "*Mit csinál Gergő?*"
what does Gergő.NOM
"*Gergő épít.*"
Gergő.NOM builds.INDEF
'What does Gergő do?'
'Gergő builds.'

The verb *épít* 'build' puts a selection restriction on the implicit direct object argument so that it is of a particular type, namely, of the type BUILDING. The category BUILDING includes all things that can be built: house, castle, bridge, channel, as well as theory, plan, future. If the question in (26) inquires about Gergő's occupation, then the reply names Gergő's usual activity, i.e. the activity determined by the particular job is in the focus of attention.[15] It is unimportant what Gergő actually builds. In the lexical-semantic representation of *épít*, the selection restriction on the direct object argument of BUILDING type is accessible. Similarly to the categories FOOD and LIQUID, the category BUILDING has a prototypical structure. Since in our culture a house can be considered as the prototype of BUILDING – or at least a very typical member of BUILDING – the reply *Gergő épít* may be equivalent, for example, to the utterance *Gergő házakat épít* 'Gergő builds houses'. In the case of *épít* the direct object argument can be incorporated into the verb and it can also be omitted (cf. the first remark to the verbs of *iszik* 'drink' above). If the question in (26) refers to the actual present then also the activity is in the focus of attention and the direct object argument also is accessible as background information involved in the selection restriction. However, in this reading there is no possibility for the verb *épít* to incorporate its direct object argument because of the lack of the condition of conventionalization or institutionalization, but it can be omitted because the speaker does not want to name what is the particular object which Gergő is building.

Making the analysis more precise, it can be established that the category BUILDING can have two prototypical structures. If the subject of the action is an adult, BUILDING has the same prototypical structure as above. But if the subject of the action is a child, the prototype of BUILDING may be a block/Lego structure/sand castle. Two kinds of analysis can be done on the basis of the two prototypical structures.[16] If *Gergő* is an adult, the same

---

[15] The present tense is also relevant here, because it is associated with a regular, habitual activity.

[16] Of course, this does not mean that the lexicon should contain two lexical entries for the verb *épít* 'build'.

explanation can be given as in the case of usual action related to the profession or actual present action. If *Gergő* is a child, then the other prototypical structure of BUILDING becomes active and the implicit argument in the utterance *Gergő épít* 'Gergő is building [something]' may refer to a block/Lego structure/sand castle. What kind of reading takes place is determined by the interaction between the lexical-semantic representation of *épít* 'build' and the particular context. If it is important what particular type or what particular entity within the type of building is being built by Gergő, then this particular type or entity should be lexically realized in the answer (cf. *Gergő hidat/csatornát/tornyot épít* 'Gergő builds bridges/canals/towers').

Finally, a further remark on the verb *épít* 'build' seems to be in order. In 3.2, analyzing the verbs perfectivized with the help of a preverb, we have mentioned the verb *megépít* 'pvb.build' in addition to the verb *megeszik* 'pvb.eat' which cannot occur without a direct object argument. This behavior cannot be considered an idiosyncratic feature of the verb *megépít*, instead it can be derived from the property of the base verb – *épít* 'build' – that it constrains the type of its direct object argument by means of a selection restriction. The perfectivized version of the base verb inherits this selection restriction. In the case of the perfectivized version of *épít* 'build', i.e. *megépít* 'pvb.build' the direct object argument is also in the focus of attention because of the perfectivization. Since the selection restriction on the type of the direct object argument cannot provide the necessary information to identify the direct object argument in the focus of attention, the perfective verb *megépít* 'pvb.build' requires that its direct object argument must be lexicalized. If a verb wich can be perfectivized with the help of a preverb and has an endpoint such as *gyón* 'confess' puts a unique selection restriction on its direct object argument (y: sin) then the preverb, perfectivized version of the base verb (*meggyón* 'pvb.confess') also inherits the unique selection restriction. In accordance with the perfectivization the direct object argument also comes into the focus of attention and since it can exactly be identified with the help of information provided by the unique selection restriction, there is no need to lexicalize it.

3.5. The influence of the indefinite/definite conjugations

The indefinite/definite conjugations also have some influence on the occurrences of Hungarian verbs with implicit direct object arguments. If a verb is conjugated for the indefinite form it can be used with implicit direct object arguments not in the same manners as if it is conjugated for the definite form. From the point of view of the interpretation we can say that the indefinite vs.

definite forms indicate what manner of the verbs' occurrence with implicit arguments can be taken into consideration to identify the lexically unrealized direct object argument. In principle, the indefinite conjugation allows transitive verbs to occur with implicit arguments in all three manners (cf. 1.1). Of course, real occurrences depend on which group a verb belongs to (cf. 1.1). The definite conjugation requires the salient presence of an entity in the context, i.e. verbs conjugated for the definite form can occur with implicit direct object arguments only in the third manner independently of which group verbs at stake belong to.

The verbs in (17) conjugated for the indefinite form can occur with implicit direct object argument with an indefinite reading relying on information provided by the selection restrictions in their lexical-semantic representations, information on the characteristic manner of actions and the prototypical structure of the predicted object categories in the first (A) manner. However, if the verbs in (17) are conjugated for the definite form, information involved in or related to their lexical-semantic representation cannot give the necessary information to identify the implicit direct object arguments, their immediate context must be extended, i.e. the implicit direct object arguments with definite readings can only be interpreted in the third (C) manner.

If a verb is inflected for the indefinite conjugation then we try to find the necessary information to construct the relevant interpretation, first, in the lexical-semantic representation of the verb, second, in its immediate context, and, third, in its extended context. If a verb is inflected for the definite conjugation then its implicit direct object argument can only be identified in the third manner with the help of the extended context.[17]

To summarize: this section of the study has revealed that in Hungarian the lexical-semantic properties of verbs such as selection restrictions, lexical stereotypes (characteristic manners of actions), the prototypical structure of objects, and aspectual factors interact with grammatical (morphosyntactic) requirements such as indefinite/definite conjugations as well as pragmatic (contextual) information in the licensing and identifying implicit direct object arguments in the first (A) manner. Consequently, the investigation of implicit direct object arguments in Hungarian really requires a complex approach. Now, let us turn to the methodological issues of my research. In the next section I want to examine what kinds of analysis of what kinds of data

---

[17] Németh T. and Bibok (2001) is devoted to the detailed analysis of the influence of these morphosyntactic features in Hungarian on the verbs' occurrence with implicit direct object arguments.

and in what functions have led to my conclusions in order to shed some light on the relation between theory construction and data handling.

4. The role of data: the relationship between the theory and data

As to the users of linguistic data, Lehmann (2004: 191–195) distinguishes between the researcher who takes linguistic data for granted and the addressee of the research. For a researcher it is his/her epistemic interest that triggers the research including the supply of data. From the point of view of a researcher linguistic data can be used (i) as the basis of an inductive construction of a hypothesis, (ii) as a test of theorems that were deduced, and (iii) they can play the argumentative role of evidence for a theory (Lehmann 2004: 191). The first two functions can be grasped in the course of the research, but the third function operates in reporting on the research. Examining these three functions of linguistic data, Kertész and Rákosi (2008: 390–392) criticize Lehmann's approach. In their opinion Lehmann does not clarify what relationship can be assumed between these three functions of data, which raises some problems. According to Kertész and Rákosi, the reasons for these problems are as follows. Lehmann (2004: 208) emphasizes that, on the one hand, linguistic data in the first function are theory and problem dependent, and, on the other hand, linguistic data are suitable to fulfill the second function only if they are independent of any theory and problem which is principally characteristic for raw data. Raw data which represent the whole speech situation are the most ideal type of data recorded in the form of a non-symbolic representation (Lehmann 2004: 183, 205–208). They are the kind of data which mostly fulfill the expectation that data should be outside of and independent of the researcher (Lehmann 2004: 181). The third function of linguistic data, i.e. the functioning as arguments for a theory in a particular argumentative process of the reporting on research is absolutely theory dependent. Kertész and Rákosi (2008: 390–392) consider these statements controversial, because they point in the opposite direction regarding the relationship between the theory and data, more precisely, theory and problem (in)dependence. However, two remarks seem to be necessary with regard to Kertész and Rákosi's criticism. First, one has to take into account that Lehmann makes a clear, essential distinction between the roles of data in the research itself and in the reporting on the research. Second, if one does not assume that data can fulfill Lehmann's three functions at the same time simultaneously, which is not possible without resulting in circularity, instead, if one examines the role of data in the course of the whole research, it can be established that various kinds of data from different sources have different functions according to the particular phases of the research (cf. Nagy C. 2008). Data used in the research have different functions than data used in the presentation of the results of the research. On the basis of these two remarks, it is not necessary to consider Lehmann's functions of linguistic data problematic, because it is not the case that one and the same piece of data is theory and problem dependent as well as theory and problem independent at the same time. However, it must be admitted that there is no such ideal case, not even raw data, when there is no some influence of the researcher on data, i.e. between the researcher and data there are always some theoretical considerations (cf. Nagy C. 2008).

From the point of view of the addressee of some scientific report, linguistic data also have various functions (Lehmann 2004: 194). First, if the addressee is more interested in the theoretical achievements than in the linguistic data underlying them, then he/she can join the author of the report in taking the data for granted. In this case, the addressee's consideration of data depends on the confidence that he/she has for the author and his/her sources of data. Second, if the addressee is more interested in linguistic data than in the theoretical results, then he/she may want to check the author's data because either he/she mistrusts the author or he/she develops an interest in data that goes beyond the function that the author had destined for them (Lehmann 2004: 194). However, a remark seems to be in order in connection with these two functions of linguistic data. These two functions can be mixed for the addressee. It can happen that the addressee has an additional spectrum of data which does not seem to support the theoretical results based on the author's data. In this case, he/she may want to check the author's data as well as the theoretical achievements based on them and to reformulate theoretical hypothesis also considering his/her own additional data.

According to Lehmann (2004: 194), there is a third function of linguistic data for the addressee, namely, they may also fulfill the function of illustration. In this expository function, data serve as examples in the presentation of the research in order to play the argumentative role of evidence for the author's theoretical results and persuade the addressee.

On the basis of Lehmann's treatment of linguistic data and the remarks added to them above, one can conclude, first, that linguistic data can have various functions both from the point of view of the researcher and the addressee, second, these functions can be mixed, third, there is an apparent relationship between the functions of data for the researcher and the addressee, and, fourth, the researcher and the addressee always, but not to the same extent, have influence on the status of linguistic phenomena to serve as data or not.

After clarifying the above mentioned functions of linguistic data theoretically, let us examine (i) what kind of data and in what functions have been used in research into lexical-semantic properties of Hungarian verbs' occurrences with implicit direct object arguments, and (ii) what relationship can be assumed between the theory and data in the research itself and the presentation of the results of the research.

The initial hypotheses of my research were, on the one hand, that lexical-semantic properties of verbs can strongly but not exclusively determine the manner of verbs' occurrences with implicit direct object arguments in Hungarian, and, on the other hand, that in addition to the lexical-semantic factors one also has to take into account certain grammatical/constructional and pragmatic (contextual) factors, and even their interaction (cf. 1.1 and 2.5). To construct this hypothesis, I relied on certain theoretical considerations, definitions, my previous results, data from various sources and data from other languages reported on in the literature. The theoretical considerations and the definition of implicit arguments have influenced my decisions concerning the selection of data. First, I decided to study the verbs' occurrence with implicit direct object arguments in utterances and not in sentences. In this way those occurrences of implicit arguments which were excluded because of their strong context-dependence by sentence-oriented approaches have also become data for the research. Second, relying on the definition of implicit arguments it was also possible to exclude those utterances which contained a performance error instead of an implicit argument. Third, in each phase of the research the selection of data was also driven by particular aims and problems. Data selected this way always influenced the actual argumentation process, which, then, influenced the subsequent data selection (cf. Kertész and Rákosi 2009).

Data selected in this manner originated in various kinds of direct sources, which eliminated the disadvantages of using only a particular kind of data and increased the plausibility of conclusions made on the basis of the analyses (cf. Kertész and Rákosi 2009). However, it must be remarked that researchers do not agree as to how to define the directness of the data sources. While Penke and Rosenbach (2004: 487–488) relate the notion of directness of data to the property how directly data mirror the knowledge of language, Kertész and Rákosi (2009) consider all kinds of data direct which come from perceptual experience, an experiment, a theory, an application of a method, a historical document etc. relying on Resher's (1976: 6) approach to plausible reasoning. Thus, while Penke and Rosenbach take into account data from various corpora and grammaticality judgments as data from direct sources and data from psycholinguistic or neurolinguistic experiments as data from indirect sources, Kertész and Rákosi evaluate all these kinds of data as coming from direct sources. Furthermore, Kertész and Rákosi (2009) propose that data can be interpreted as plausible statements originating in direct sources.[18] More precisely, data consist of an informational content and a plausibility value. The plausibility values of data are also determined by the reliability of direct sources which they come from. In my research, I relied on this latter proposal, so data were selected from the following direct sources: (a) "corpora": spoken corpora (recorded interviews) and written corpora (Hungarian National Text Database), dictionaries (definitions in Hungarian monolingual dictionaries), my former results and analyses (cf. e.g. Németh T. 2001), comparisons with other languages (cf. section 2), (b) introspection: the researcher's, i.e. my own intuition and some other informants' introspection, (c) experiments: minimal pair and thought experiments. This kind of classification of the direct sources of data is also problematic. For example, data from other researchers' experiments can be considered data from corpora for particular subsequent research, and data from minimal pair and thought experiments can be treated as introspective data as well.[19]

The selected data were systematically analyzed from the point of view of the lexical-semantic representations, grammatical properties and the contexts. The results of the analyses have supported the initial hypotheses (cf. section 3). In the course of the research, the relationship between the hypotheses, theory and data were not linear and unidirectional. The formulation of the initial assumptions can be considered hypothesis construction by means of inductive procedures. Since among the data which served as the basis for the induction there also were theoretical considerations and definitions, thus, the initial assumptions can also be evaluated as derived theoretical theses, the validity of which must be supported by data, i.e. which must be made plausible by linguistic data. However, data, even raw data, in this function are also theory and problem dependent. As we have seen above, it is always the particular requirements and steps of the research that determine the data selection. It must especially be emphasized that among

[18] According to Kertész and Rákosi (2009) indirect sources are those from which one can get plausible statements by means of inferences.

[19] This kind of classification is determined by the functions of data and the methods applied in the research. However, the problem of classification goes beyond the scope of the present paper.

the raw data there can occur utterances with various performance errors, but if not, then various utterances have no equal importance and relevance for the research. It can also happen that data used to support a hypothesis influence the theoretical considerations underlying the hypotheses at stake, which can yield the modification of the hypotheses (cf. Nagy C. 2008).

On the basis of the above mentioned considerations concerning the functions and sources of data one can conclude, first, that it is not reasonable to separate sharply the process of the hypothesis construction and the process to make a hypothesis plausible. Second, the relationship between theory and data must be thought of as cyclic, and it is always the actual argumentation process which determines what can serve as data and in what functions (cf. Kertész and Rákosi 2009).

In the course of the presentation of the results of the research, I have not relied on all data used in the research itself. Since the role of data in the reporting on the research is to serve as evidence for the theory and persuade the addressee, I have attempted to select such data from those used in the research which are most suitable to illustrate and support the theoretical theses. Data applied in this presentation of my results came from the following direct sources:

(a) corpora including recorded interviews, Hungarian National Text Database, Hungarian Concise Explanatory Dictionary, and data reported on in the literature: e.g. (1)–(7a,b), (8a–c), (10), (17), (21a–d), (22)–(25a,b),
(b) introspection including my own introspection and some other informants': e.g. (7c,d), (12), (13), (15), (16), (17)
(c) experiments including minimal pair and thought experiments: e.g. (20), (9a,b), (10)–(11), (19), (26).[20]

One of the methodological requirements of partly pragmatically oriented research is that it also relies on raw data. However, applying raw data has several problems as well. First, raw data in spoken or written corpora have to be analyzed very carefully from the point of view of the context in order to construct those explicit and implicit meanings of utterances which the speakers want to convey. Second, even if we analyze very carefully the spontaneous use of language in a particular context, we cannot be quite sure whether the speakers have the same intentions, attitudes, thoughts, beliefs, background knowledge which we as researchers attribute to them, i.e. we can never know whether the researchers' meaning construction of the

[20] As I have mentioned above, data from the minimal pair and thought experiments can also be considered as introspective data.

speakers' utterances is correct. Third, even if we have very large corpora consisting of more than several hundred million words we cannot extract from them the various, systematically changing interpretation possibilities of utterances. And, fourth, it can also happen that raw data do not involve utterances which demonstrate the phenomena studied in the research in a suitable amount. Because of these problems, it can be fruitful to use minimal pair experiments usually applied in sentence-oriented research, and thought experiments in pragmatically oriented research as well. In a thought experiment we fix the contextual factors in all phases of the experiment including the mental states of the language users, then we change one factor as it is widely accepted in the minimal pair experiments (cf. (19), (26)). In this way we can construct all principally possible interpretation variations and evaluate them. By applying this method, we can study interpretation possibilities which do not occur among raw data as well. Thought experiments have a further advantage in reporting on pragmatically oriented research, they are extremely illustrative, i.e. they can contribute to the effectiveness of the researchers' efforts to persuade the addressee.

5. Conclusions

Considering the two main aims of the research (cf. section 1.2), I have two final conclusions. First, the verbs studied in my research have rich lexical-semantic representations, they constrain their arguments by means of selection restrictions, lexical stereotypes, prototypical structures of the categories very strongly. Their lexical-semantic representations can be interpreted in two ways. This twofold interpretability makes it possible for them to occur with implicit arguments in the first (A) manner. If only the actions or events designated by the verbs are in the focus of attention, the direct object arguments can be left lexically unrealized. The information concerning the arguments at stake to be of a particular type or a token of a type or a unique token involved in the selection restrictions can also be accessed as background information. Although what particular constraint a verb imposes on its arguments can be considered an idiosyncratic lexical-semantic property of the verb, the property that a verb puts a selection restriction on its arguments predicts that the verb can be used with implicit arguments in the first (A) manner without a larger context. However, as we have seen in several cases, information stored in the lexical-semantic representations of the verbs is not sufficient to license the verbs' occurrence with implicit direct object arguments. One has to take into consideration morphosyntactic (indefinite/definite conjugations) and pragmatic (contextual) factors to a necessary extent as well assuming an interaction between the lexical-semantic representations of the verbs, grammar and contexts. On the basis of these results two further conclusions can be formulated. First, the use and identification of implicit direct objects should be conceived as a phenomenon at the semantics–pragmatics interface or even at the grammar–pragmatics interface. Second, the division of labor between lexical semantics, grammar and pragmatics in the use and interpretation of implicit arguments is under the control of an economy balance, i.e. they are guided by the cognitive principle of relevance (Sperber and Wilson 1986/1995: 260).

As to the second main aim of my research, I have distinguished between several functions and sources of data demonstrating what relationships and overlaps can be assumed between them without any inconsistency. The use of data from various direct sources has eliminated the disadvantages of the particular sources. I have also highlighted what problems arise if one applies raw data in pragmatically oriented research, and how these problems can be solved by using thought experiments in the research and presentation of the research as well. And finally, it can also be concluded that the relationship between the theory and data should be considered cyclic, and it is always the actual aims, problems and argumentation processes of the research or the presentation of the research that determine what can serve as data in what functions in a particular phase of the research and the presentation of the research.

Acknowledgements

The research reported on in the present paper was supported by the Research Group for Theoretical Linguistics of the Hungarian Academy of Sciences at the Universities of Debrecen, Pécs and Szeged, Hungary. I want to express my gratitude to the anonymous reviewers for their comments and remarks which helped me to clarify some points. And finally, I wish to thank Anna Fenyvesi for correcting my paper.

References

Alsina, Alex
1992 On the argument structure of causatives. *Linguistic Inquiry* 23: 517–555.

Ariel, Mira
1991 The function of accessability in a theory of grammar. *Journal of Pragmatics* 16: 443–463.

Ariel, Mira
2008 *Pragmatics and Grammar.* Cambridge: Cambridge University Press.

Bartos, Huba
1997 On "subjective" and "objective" agreement in Hungarian. *Acta Linguistica Hungarica* 44: 363–384.

Bartos, Huba
2000 Az inflexiós jelenségek szintaktikai háttere [The syntactic background of inflectional phenomena]. In *Stukturális magyar nyelvtan 3. Morfológia* [Structural Hungarian Grammar 3. Morphology], Ferenc Kiefer (ed.), 653–762. Budapest: Akadémiai Kiadó.

Bibok, Károly
1996 Problema konceptual'noj semantiki russkogo i vengerskogo jazykov [Conceptual semantic investigations in Russian and Hungarian]. *Voprosy Jazykoznanija* 2: 156–165.

Bibok, Károly
2000 Conceptual semantic investigations in Russian and Hungarian. In *Applied Russian Studies in Hungary*, Endre Lendvai (ed.), 15–32. Pécs: Krónika.

Bibok, Károly
2008 Az igék szemantikája és a szintaktikai alternáció [The semantics of verbs and syntactic alternation]. In *Strukturális magyar nyelvtan 4. A szótár szerkezete* [Structural Hungarian Grammar 4. Structure of the Lexicon], Ferenc Kiefer (ed.), 23–70. Budapest: Akadémiai Kiadó.

Bibok, Károly and Enikő Németh T.
2001 How the lexicon and context interact in the meaning construction of utterances. In *Pragmatics and the Flexibility of Word Meaning*, Enikő Németh T. and Károly Bibok (eds.), 289–320. Amsterdam: Elsevier.

Bierwisch, Manfred
1983 Semantische und konzeptuelle Repräsentation lexikalischer Einheiten. In *Untersuchungen zur Semantik.* (*Studia Grammatica* 22), Rudolf Růžička and Wolfgang Motsch (eds.), 61–99. Berlin: Akademie Verlag.

Bierwisch, Manfred
1996 How much space gets into language? In *Language and Space*, Paul Bloom, Mary A. Peterson, Lynn Nadel and Merrill F. Garrett (eds.) 31–76. Cambridge, MA: MIT Press.

Chomsky, Noam
1981 *Lectures on Government and Binding: The Pisa Lectures.* Dordrecht: Foris.

Cote, Sharon A.
1996 *Grammatical and discourse proporties of null arguments in English.* PhD dissertation, http://falcon.jmu.edu/~cotesa/research.html. Date of access: October 8, 2010.

Cummins, Sarah and Yves Roberge
2005 A modular account of null objects in French. *Syntax* 8: 44–64.

É. Kiss, Katalin
2002 *The Syntax of Hungarian.* Cambridge: Cambridge University Press.
Fillmore, Charles J.
1986 Pragmatically controlled zero anaphora. *Berkeley Linguistic Series* 12: 95–107.
García Velasco, Daniel and Carmen Portero Muñoz
2002 *Understood objects in functional grammar.* (*Working Papers in Functional Grammar* 76.) Amsterdam: University of Amsterdam.
Goldberg, Adele
2005a Argument realization. The role of constructions, lexical semantics and discourse factors. In *Construction Garmmars. Cognitive Grounding and Theoretical Extensions*, Jan-Ola Östman and Mirjam Fried (eds.), 17–43. Amstardam: John Benjamins.
Goldberg, Adele
2005b Constructions, lexical semantics and the correspondence principle: Accounting for generalizations and subregularities in the realization of arguments. In *The Syntax of Aspect*, Nomi Erteschik-Shir and Tova Rapoport (eds.), 215–236. Oxford: Oxford University Press.
Grice, H. Paul
1975 Logic and conversation. In *Syntax and Semantics 3: Speech Acts*, Peter Cole and Jerry L. Morgan (eds.), 41–58. New York: Academic Press.
Grimshaw, Jane and Sten Vikner
1993 Obligatory Adjuncts and the structure of events. In *Knowledge and Language II: Lexical and Conceptual Structure*, Eric J. Reuland and Werner Abraham (eds.), 143–155. Dordrecht: Kluwer Academic Publishers.
Groefsema, Marjolein
1995 Understood arguments: A semantic/pragmatic approach. *Lingua* 96: 139–161.
Hale, Ken and Samuel Jay Keyser
2002 *Prolegomena to a Theory of Argument Structure.* Cambridge, MA: MIT Press.
H. Molnár, Ilona
1962 A tárgy [Direct object]. In *A mai magyar nyelv rendszere. Leíró nyelvtan 2. Mondattan* [The Structure of the Modern Hungarian Language. A Descriptive Grammar. Vol. 2: Syntax], József Tompa (ed.), 147–161. Budapest: Akadémiai Kiadó.
Horn, Laurence R.
1984 Toward a taxonomy for pragmatic inference: Q- and R-based implicature. In *Meaning, Form, and Use in Context*, Deborah Schiffrin (ed.), 11–42. Washington: Georgetown University Press.

Iten, Corinne, Marie-Odile Junker, Aryn Pyke, Robert Stainton and Catherine Wearing
2005 Null complements: licensed by syntax or by semantics–pragmatics? *Actes du congrés de l' Association canadienne de linguistique 2004. Proceedings of the 2004 Annual Conference of the Canadian Linguistic Association*, 15 pages, http://www.eastcree.org/mojunker/ACL-CLA/pdf/Iten-Junker-Pyke-CLA-2004.pdf. Date of access: October 8, 2010.

Jackendoff, Ray
1990 *Semantic Structures.* Cambridge, MA: MIT Press.

Kaufmann, Ingrid and Dieter Wunderlich
1998 Cross-linguistic patterns of resultatives. *Working Papers SFB Theorie des Lexikons* 109. Düsseldorf: University of Düsseldorf.

Kertész, András and Csilla Rákosi
2008 Megjegyzések a nyelvészeti adatok és evidencia problémájáról folyó vita jelenlegi állásához [Remarks on the current discussion on linguistic data and evidence]. *Magyar Nyelv* 104: 274–286, 385–402.

Kertész, András and Csilla Rákosi
2009 Evidence and the argumentation structure of linguistic theories. Manuscript.

Kiefer, Ferenc
1990–91 Noun incorporation in Hungarian. *Acta Linguistica Hungarica* 40: 149–179.

Kiefer, Ferenc
2006 *Aspektus és akcióminőség. Különös tekintettel a magyar nyelvre* [Aspect and Aktionsart. With special regard to the Hungarian Language]. Budapest: Akadémiai Kiadó.

Komlósy, András
1994 Complements and adjuncts. In *Syntax and Semantics* 27, Ferenc Kiefer and Katalin É. Kiss (eds.), 91–178. New York: Academic Press.

Lehmann, Christian
2004 Data in linguistics. *The Linguistic Review* 21: 175–210.

Levinson, Stephen C.
2000 *Presumptive Meanings: The Theory of Generalized Conversational Implicatures.* Cambridge, MA: Cambridge University Press.

Maleczki, Márta
1994 Bare common nouns and their relation to the temporal constitution of events in Hungarian. In *Papers in the Theory of Grammar*, Zoltán Bánréti (ed.) 168–184. Budapest: Research Institute for Linguistics of the Hungarian Academy of Sciences.

Nagy C., Katalin
2008 Data in historical pragmatics: A case study on the Catalan periphrastic perfective past. In *New Approaches to Linguistic Evidence:*

Pilot Studies, András Kertész and Csilla Rákosi (eds.), 171–197. Frankfurt am Main: Peter Lang.

Németh T., Enikő
2000 Occurrence and identification of implicit arguments in Hungarian. *Journal of Pragmatics* 32: 1657–1683.

Németh T., Enikő
2001 Implicit arguments in Hungarian. In *Argument Structure in Hungarian*, István Kenesei (ed.), 113–156. Budapest: Akadémiai Kiadó.

Németh T., Enikő
2008 Az implicit alanyi és tárgyi argumentumok előfordulásának lexikai-szemantikai jellemzői [The lexical-semantic properties of the occurrence of implicit subject and direct object arguments. In *Strukturális magyar nyelvtan 4. A szótár szerkezete* [Structural Hungarian Grammar 4. Structure of the Lexicon], Ferenc Kiefer (ed.), 71–128. Budapest: Akadémiai Kiadó.

Németh T., Enikő and Károly Bibok
2001 Az alanyi és a tárgyas ragozás szerepe az igei tárgyi argumentumok elhagyhatóságában [The role of indefinite and definite conjugations in the omissibility of verbal directs object arguments]. In *Újabb tanulmányok a strukturális magyar nyelvtan és a nyelvtörténet köréből* [Recent Studies in Structural Hungarian Grammar and in the History of Language], Marianne Bakró-Nagy, Zoltán Bánréti and Katalin É. Kiss (eds.), 78–96. Budapest: Osiris Kiadó.

Németh T., Enikő and Károly Bibok
2010 Interaction between grammar and pragmatics: The case of implicit arguments, implicit predicates and co-composition in Hungarian. *Journal of Pragmatics* 42: 501–524.

Pethő, Gergely and Éva Kardos
2009 Cross-linguistic evidence and the licensing of implicit arguments. In *Structuring Information in Discourse: The Explicit-Implicit Dimension*, Bergljot Behrens and Chatrine Fabricius-Hansen (eds.), *Oslo Studies in Language* 1: 33–61.

Pinker, Steven
1989 *Learnibility and Cognition: The Acquisition of Argument Structure.* Cambridge, MA: MIT Press.

Pléh, Csaba
1994 Mondatközi viszonyok feldolgozása: az anafora megértése a magyarban [Processing intersentential relations: Interpreting anaphors in Hungarian]. *Magyar Pszichológiai Szemle* 50: 287–320.

Penke, Martina and Anette Rosenbach (eds.)
2004 What counts as evidence in linguistics? Special issue of *Studies in Language*.

Pustejovsky, James
1995 *The Generative Lexicon.* Cambridge, MA: Cambridge University Press.
Pustejovsky, James
1998 Generativity and explanation in semantics: A reply to Fodor and Lepore. *Linguistic Inquiry* 29: 289–311.
Radford, Andrew
1997 *Syntax: A Minimalist Introduction.* Cambridge: Cambridge University Press.
Rappaport Hovav, Malka and Beth Levin
2001 An event structure account of English resultatives. *Language* 77: 766–797.
Resher, Nicholas
1976 *Plausible Reasoning.* Assen/Amsterdam: Van Gorcum.
Saeboe, Kjell
1996 Anaphoric presupposition and zero anaphora. *Linguistics and Philosophy* 19: 187–207.
Scott, Kate
2006 When less is more: implicit arguments and relevance theory. In *UCL Working Papers in Linguistics* 18, Richard Breheny and Mary Pearce (eds.), 139–170.
Sperber, Dan and Deirdre Wilson
1986/95 *Relevance: Communication and Cognition.* Oxford: Blackwell. 1st/2nd editions.

Co-constructing what is said in interaction

Michael Haugh

1. Introduction

1.1. Background

The traditional view of the semantics–pragmatics boundary, inherited largely from the received view of Grice's (1957, 1969, 1975, 1989) work, is that semantics concerns "what is said", while pragmatics concerns "what is implicated" (Szabó 2005: 3). According to this view, it is assumed that semantics is primarily "responsible for compositionally construed sentence meaning", which involves combining "the meanings of lexical items and the structure in which they occur" (Jaszczolt 2009c: 458), since Grice only admitted inferential processes into the determination of what is said in cases where it was required by the lexico-syntax of that utterance. Yet in allowing, albeit to a limited extent, inferential processes into fixing what is said, Grice inadvertently opened the door for current boundary disputes (Jaszczolt in press: 14). These disputes were brought to the fore with the rise of the semantic underdetermination view in the 1970s (Cole 1981), where it was first argued semantic analysis that is limited to what is afforded by the lexico-syntactic structure of an utterance only takes us part of the way in determining the truth conditions of those utterances. This view later developed into various instantiations of contextualism, where it is assumed that a range of pragmatic processes enrich the logical form of an utterance in giving rise to what is said (Recanati 1989, 2001, 2004), or alternatively explicature (Carston 1988; Sperber and Wilson 1995). The rise of contextualism, however, has blurred the semantics–pragmatics boundary considerably with various debates arising as a consequence, including just how the scope of a pragmatically-enriched notion of what is said should be delimited. More recently, moreover, proponents of various forms of semantic minimalism (Bach 2004, 2006; Borg 2004; Cappelen and Lepore 2005) have advocated paring back the object of semantic theory so that pragmatic processes intrude as little as possible on a minimalist notion of what is said, creating even further debate around the semantics–pragmatics interface.[1]

[1] As pointed out by one of the anonymous reviewers, there is another key approach to semantics, namely structural semantics (Coseriu and Geckeler

Arguments about the best way to draw the boundary between semantics and pragmatics have thus splintered into two philosophically different views of meaning. On the one hand, we have those who argue that semantics should be concerned with the meanings of utterances to which speakers and addressees attend or orient to in actual interactions. This view is perhaps most well articulated in Recanati's (2004) availability based approach, and in Jaszczolt's (2005, 2009a, 2009b) Default Semantics. Jaszczolt (in press), for instance, argues that

> the speaker and the addressee attend to the meaning of the *utterance*: the real, concrete unit of meaning that carries some information content through the words used, the structure, the exact placement in the structure of the conversation, the additional senses it brings to mind in the particular context, the immersion in the overall system of gestures and other ways of conveying meaning, and so forth. (Jaszczolt in press: 5)

Recanati (2004) develops a similar philosophical stance, albeit within a different theoretical framework, in claiming that "what is said must be analysed in conformity to the intuitions shared by those who fully understand the utterance – typically the speaker and the hearer, in a normal conversational setting" (p. 14).

On the other hand, we have those who place greater importance on the formal linguistic properties of sentences, as opposed to speaker intuitions, in equating what is said with a minimally enriched linguistically encoded meaning or logical form. Bach (2002), for example, points out the dangers of drawing unreflexively upon speaker intuitions about what is said, taking Gibbs and Moise's (1997) experiments as a case in point:

> They thought they could get data about what is said, and thereby test the empirical validity of Recanati's Availability Principle, by asking people what is said by a given utterance, or by asking them whether something

1981; Lyons 1968, 1995), where a third type of basic type of language-specific meaning is postulated in addition to the truth-conditional meaning that is the focus of semantic minimalism, on the one hand, and contextual meaning which lies at the interface of semantics and pragmatics, on the other. However, since language-specific meaning, whether understood as the denotation or sense of an expression (Lyons 1995: 79–80), is uncontroversially semantic in being "wholly internal to the language-system" (Lyons 1995: 80), it arguably lies largely outside the purview of the current debate. See Kienpointner (2008: 100), however, for further discussion of the importance of this third type of meaning in constituting the semantic skeleton of a sentence.

> that is conveyed by a given utterance is implicated or merely said. Evidently they assumed that what people *say* about what is said is strongly indicative of what *is* said. In fact, what it is indicative of is how people apply the phrase "what is said" and perhaps of what they mean by the word "say." It tells us little about what is said, much less about the cognitive processes whereby people understand utterances. (Bach 2002: 27)

As Bach quite rightly points out, the problem with such experiments is that what people say about communication does not necessarily accurately reflect what actually happens in communicating (see also Carston 2007). In other words, while through such experiments we can gain insight into the way in which ordinary speakers vacillate between two senses of *say*, namely, the indirect-quotational sense (i.e., what the sentence is standardly taken to mean) and the commitment sense (i.e., what the speaker is committing him/herself to in producing the utterance) (Berg 2002: 347; Carston 2002: 169), this does little to settle debates about how to best delimit the scope of what is said. The place of speaker intuitions in delineating the semantics–pragmatics boundary thus remains hotly contested, particularly in regards to defining the scope of what is said.

However, there is another way in which analysts can access speaker intuitions about what is said, which has not been considered to any great extent thus far by those working at the semantics–pragmatics interface. Namely, through careful analysis of the ways in which participants themselves orient to the interactional achievement of meanings (and actions) in actual conversational data. A large body of work in interactional pragmatics and conversation analysis has been built around the observation that participants' display their understandings of the meaning of previous utterances through their next responses to those utterances. This "next turn proof procedure" rests on the finding that "throughout the course of a conversation or other bout of talk-in-interaction, speakers display in their sequentially 'next' turns an understanding of what the 'prior' turn was about" (Hutchby and Wooffitt 2008: 13; Sacks, Schegloff and Jefferson 1974: 729). While participants in conversations are, for the most part, orienting to actions, there are particular cases where they can be observed to be demonstrably orienting to meanings.

In this chapter, the way in which speaker intuitions about what is said can be elucidated through an analysis of a particular interactional phenomenon, the co-construction of syntactic units by two or more speakers in conversation, is explored. While co-construction has traditionally been treated as lying at the boundary of syntax and pragmatics, it is suggested here that it in fact lies at the intersection of syntax–pragmatics–semantics, and should be analysed as such. For this reason, an analysis of the co-construction of what is said provides a relatively hitherto unexplored window into the semantics–pragmatics interface. Admitting interactional data and analyses into debates at the interface of semantics–pragmatics may seem, at first glance, unnecessary or even counter-productive, particularly for those embedded in a more formal perspective on semantics. However, it is argued in this chapter that introducing this kind of interactional perspective allows us to more readily access speaker intuitions, and thereby bring to the fore tacit conceptions that underlie the semantics–pragmatics distinction (Szabó 2005: 7–8).

1.2. Aims and organization of the paper

The aims of this chapter are threefold. First, it is claimed that the semantic and pragmatic underpinnings of co-construction have been relatively neglected in research thus far. Previous work has generally treated co-construction as a syntactic phenomenon with little analysis of semantic and pragmatic contributions to the joint production of utterances. Examples from interactions illustrating both the semantic and pragmatic underpinnings of co-constructions are thus explored here. Second, it is argued that co-constructions actually constitute evidence of participants orienting to (speaker) meanings rather than just syntax in interaction. It is suggested such an analysis may support a conceptualisation of what is said that is more empirically robust than previous approaches to eliciting speaker intuitions. Third, it is argued in the subsequent section that while interactional data and analysis may seem primarily of interest to researchers in pragmatics, there is greater potential than generally accepted for semantics to be informed by such research and methods. However, as the underlying epistemological and ontological commitments of interactional methodologies such as conversation analysis and those of language philosophy are arguably different, the implications of admitting interactional data and analysis into debates about the semantics–pragmatics interface need to be first carefully considered.

2. A study at the interface of semantics and pragmatics: co-constructing what is said

2.1. Co-constructions: previous approaches

The term "co-construction" is used to denote instances where a syntactic unit (often what is loosely termed an "utterance") is uttered by two or more speakers.[2] This kind of interactional phenomenon was first noted in the seminal work of the ethnomethodologist Harvey Sacks ([1965] 1992: 144–146, [1968] 1992, Vol II: 57–60), and later expanded upon in work by researchers with an interest in interactional perspectives on grammar (Bolden 2003; Helasvuo 2004; Lerner 1991, 1996; Local 2004; Ono and Thompson 1996; Rühlemann 2007: 87–114; Szczepek 2000a, 2000b). While various terms for the phenomenon exist, including "collaboratively built sentences" (Sacks [1965] 1992, Vol. I: 144–146), "sentence-in-progress" (Lerner 1991, 1996), or "joint utterance construction" (Hayashi 2003), research in this area is unified through its focus on "practices by which a speaker produces an utterance that is designed to grammatically continue (and sometimes complete) an ongoing utterance initiated by another speaker" (Hayashi 2003: 1).

Co-construction phenomena are generally divided into two broad types: completions and expansions (Hayashi 2003: 25, 173; Ono and Thompson 1996: 72, 78; Rühlemann 2007: 100). Completion type co-constructions encompass instances where "the next speaker completes a syntactic unit that the first speaker has left incomplete" (Rühlemann 2007: 100), or more specifically, "a practice whereby a participant produces an utterance that is grammatically fitted to the ongoing trajectory of another participant's utterance-in-progress and which brings that other participant's utterance to completion" (Hayashi 2003: 25). Expansion type co-constructions, on the other hand, are defined as instances where "the first speaker articulates an utterance that is syntactically complete and the next speaker expands the first speaker's utterance into a longer syntactic unit, e.g., by adding a prepositional phrase or a dependent clause" (Rühlemann 2007: 100; Ono and Thompson 1996: 78; cf. Hayashi 2003: 173).

In the following excerpt, for instance, from a conversation in the British National Corpus (BNC) between an older married couple talking about fuchsias, both completion and expansion type co-constructions can be observed.

2 This specific linguistic sense of co-construction should be differentiated from the broader social interactional sense in which the term may also be used following Jacoby and Ochs (1995) definition of co-construction as "the joint creation of a form, interpretation, stance, action, activity, identity, institution, skill, ideology, emotion, or other culturally meaningful reality" (p. 171).

(1) BNC: KBP2506

1	Nina:	No, they die down ( )
2	Clarence:	Mm. Mm.
3	Nina:	most of the ones that we brought seem to have erm
4	Clarence:	Survived.
5	Nina:	Survived. Which I'm glad.
6	Clarence:	Mm. Mm. (adapted from Rühlemann 2007: 100)

Here, in response to Nina indicating through the hesitation token *erm* that she is struggling to find the right word (line 3), Clarence completes the clause begun by Nina in the next turn (line 4). This therefore constitutes an example of a completion co-construction. Nina then further expands upon the previously co-constructed utterance with the addition of a sentence relative *which I'm glad* (line 5), which thus constitutes an instance of an expansion co-construction. In other words, through both completion and expansion these two speakers can be seen to be co-constructing a single, complex syntactic unit (Rühlemann 2007: 101).

Much of the work on co-constructions thus far has been carried out within the methodological framework of conversation analysis (Bolden 2003; Goodwin 1979, 1981; Hayashi 1999, 2003; Hayashi and Mori 1998; Helasvuo 2004; Kim 2004; Lerner 1991, 1996, 2004; Lerner and Takagi 1999; Local 2004; Szczepek 2000a, 2000b), or discourse analysis more broadly (Ford and Thompson 1996; Fox and Thompson 1990; Geluykens 1992; Maynard 1989; Ono and Yoshida 1996; Thompson and Mulac 1991), with the bulk of this work focusing primarily on syntactic aspects of co-construction. This analytical bias towards the syntax of co-constructions follows from Sacks' ([1965] 1992, Vol I: 144–146) initial interest in "collaboratively built sentences", which he claimed to be "direct evidence of the fact that hearers are engaged in analysing *syntactically*, utterances in their course, and have that analysis available as something they can use 'immediately'" (Sacks [1967] 1992, Vol I: 654, emphasis added). Lerner's (1991, 1996) exemplary work on co-constructions, for instance, has focused on compound turn constructional units consisting of a preliminary and a final component. He argues that a subordinating conjunction such as *if*, *when* or *once* at the beginning of a clause can "provide for the *sequential possibility* of anticipatory completion" (Lerner 1991: 445, original emphasis). Conversation and discourse analysts have thus traditionally regarded co-construction as lying at the intersection of syntax, prosody, and interaction.[3]

[3] More recently there has been a move towards the analysis of co-constructions from a corpus-based perspective (Rühlemann 2007: 87–114; Suzuki and Usami

However, as Lerner (1991, 1996) himself recognises, the projected syntax of an utterance does not constitute sufficient grounds upon which to collaboratively complete utterances. Bolden (2003) expands upon this in arguing that

> the syntactic organization of the turn in progress locates a class of possible sentence 'completers' (Sacks, Jefferson and Schegloff 1974), but does not specify which member of the class will be used or would be appropriate to use in any particular interactional context. (Bolden 2003: 190)

Participants thus draw upon a variety of linguistic and non-linguistic resources to successfully collaborate in producing a single unit of talk. These resources include not only syntactic features (Lerner 1991, 1996), but also prosodic features (Local 2004; Szczepek 2000a, 2000b), non-linguistic features of the surrounding environment and the participants' bodies (Bolden 2003), and most relevant to this volume, discourse-pragmatic and semantic features (Szczepek 2000a, 2000b). In other words, while syntactic and prosodic features allow for the possibility of collaborative completions and expansions, it is suggested here that participants in fact rely primarily on semantic and pragmatic features to flesh out these projected syntactic forms. Yet in spite of their relative importance, there has been little attention paid in research thus far to semantic and pragmatic dimensions of co-constructions. Thus, insofar as co-constructions involve both semantic and pragmatic input into what is said, they provide hitherto relatively unexplored territory in which to explore the semantics–pragmatics interface.

The relevance of semantic and pragmatic perspectives on co-construction also become apparent when one considers the relatively high frequency with which "delayed completions" (Lerner 1989) and "collaborative turn sequences" (Lerner 2004) can be observed to co-occur with co-constructions. The former refers to instances where the original speaker produces "an alternative, possibly competing completion which deletes the sequential relevance of the preemptive completion" by the second speaker (Lerner 1989:

2006). While the quantification of interactional phenomena is traditionally eschewed in conversation analysis (Schegloff 1993), it is argued by Suzuki and Usami (2006) that the frequency of interactional phenomena such as co-constructions can be ascertained through corpus analysis, thereby achieving a higher level of generalizability for claims made by analysts. However, such work is presently limited to the analysis of only certain types of co-construction due to current constraints on searching large amounts of spoken data, and so this perspective is not further explored in this chapter.

175), while the latter encompasses cases where "the acceptability of the proffered completion can be implicated as a next action", thereby allowing "the original speaker to maintain his or her authority over a turn even when completed by another" (Lerner 2004: 225). In other words, while an utterance may be co-constructed by two or more speakers, by maintaining "authority" over the turn, the original speaker remains accountable for the semantic content and pragmatic implications of that collaborative construction. In that sense, then, it is also argued in this section that we have clear evidence of participants orienting primarily to *meanings*, in this case, "what is said," rather than syntax when co-constructions occur in interaction.[4]

The following analysis of co-construction is based on a data set drawing from approximately 15 hours of audio recordings of (Australian) English sourced from a number of different corpora, including the Australian Component of the International Corpus of English (ICE-AUS) (33 conversations between friends and family members, 500 minutes), the Griffith Corpus of Spoken Australian English (GCSAusE) (18 conversations, 90 minutes), and the Australians Getting Acquainted corpus (AGA) (18 conversations, 300 minutes). From this data set, 46 candidate examples of co-construction were identified through careful examination of transcripts of these conversations. These 46 putative co-constructions were then more carefully analysed through repeated listenings to the recordings and creating more detailed transcriptions according to standard conversation analytic transcription practices (Jefferson 2004). Based on this analysis, 30 of these co-constructions were classified as completions, while 16 were treated as expansions. The semantic and pragmatic underpinnings of these co-constructions were then analysed.

As the subsequent analysis builds on participant understandings, it takes the view that meaning is something towards which speakers and addressees attend or orient in actual interactions. Thus, rather than attempting to draw a clear boundary between semantics and pragmatics, a broadly contextualist perspective on the semantics–pragmatics interface is assumed. The anal-

---

4 Participants are, of course, also orienting to actions and relationships (both as affiliative/supportive and as non-affiliative/competitive) at the same time as meanings are interactionally achieved (Ferrrara 1992; Rühlemann 2007: 102; Sacks [1965] 1992, Vol I: 145; Suzuki and Usami 2006: 271; Szczepek 2000b). However, these dimensions are not discussed any further in this section, since the focus here is primarily on the semantics–pragmatics boundary, and the analysis of both actions and relationships lie, uncontroversially, within the direct purview of pragmatics.

ysis illustrates how syntactic, semantic, and pragmatic information is interweaved in complex ways in the co-construction of utterances. This finding is arguably consistent with the approach to meaning proposed in Default Semantics (Jaszczolt 2005), namely, that primary meanings involve merger representations of word meaning and sentence structure, world knowledge, situation of discourse, society and culture, and properties of the human inferential system. In the following dataset, the primary meanings to which the participants are attending are roughly equivalent to a pragmatically-enriched notion of what is said. However, since primary meanings cannot always be equated with what is said (Jaszczolt 2009b: 274), this analysis has implications for how participants co-construct primary meanings more broadly in interaction.

2.2. Semantic and pragmatic contributions to co-constructing what is said

Semantic contributions to co-constructions can be divided into at least five different types: lexical constructions, lexical constrasts, lexico-semantic fields (Lyons 1968: 443–470, 1995: 124–130; Szczepek 2000a: 10–14), alternative formulations, and formulaic/idiomatic phrases.[5] Lexical constructions contribute to co-constructions by starting a piece of information that requires completion, such as ending an utterance with *for example*, or something like *she's called* which projects a proper noun, continuing instructions and the like (Szczepek 2000a: 12). Lexical contrasts involve utterance-final conjunctive particles that project a contrast, such as *but* or *however* (Szczepek 2000a: 4; see also Haugh 2008b). Lexico-semantic fields encompass instances where the participants draw from the way in which one item can project the replication of certain qualities of the same item (Szczepek 2000a: 14). Alternative formulations involve the occurrence of (near) synonyms in the co-construction and surrounding co-text, while formulaic or idiomatic phrases afford co-constructions through shared knowledge of such phrases. Semantic co-construction thus involves participants drawing, at least in part, from shared knowledge of semantic units in order to collaboratively complete an utterance. In this data set, examples of the latter four types of semantic contributions to co-constructions were found.

---

5 The notions of lexical contrasts and lexico-semantic fields postulated by Szczepek 2000a: 10–14) are based, in turn, on work in structural semantics, in particular, the theory of semantic (or lexical) fields (Lyons 1968: 429, 443–470, 1995: 102, 124–130), and the analysis of sense relations (Lyons 1968: 427, 1995: 80).

In the following excerpt, for instance, we have an example of a completion co-construction building on lexical contrast. In the conversation so far between two females (Sally and Ildika) who have only just met, they are discussing the first name of one of the participants. She has been discussing how her name, Ildika, is a variation of a Hungarian name, Ildikó.[6]

(2) AGA: SJIK: 0:33
26 I: I have met (0.5) people who know of (.) Ildikó:s,
27 but [not many of them]
28 S: [°not many of them°]=
29 =So you're an original.
30 (0.3)
30 I: Ye:s.

Ildika goes on to say in line 26 that she knows through others of people who are named Ildikó, and after a micro-pause begins a related clause with a contrast conjunctive, namely *but* (line 27). At this point Sally chimes in to complete, at the same time as Ildika, that the latter has only heard of a few examples of Ildikós (line 27). In this sense, it constitutes an instance of completion co-construction. This latter unit is arguably inferable as a scalar quantity implicature, drawing from something like the <many, some, not many> scale (Horn 2004: 11). In making this scalar inference explicit though, it arguably constitutes part of what is said rather than being an implicature. Most importantly for the current discussion, however, is that this scalar inference is derived from the projection of a clause which contrasts semantically with that preceding the conjunction.

In the next excerpt, we can observe an instance of a failed attempt at a completion co-construction drawing from a particular lexico-semantic field, namely, the names of (European) countries. Here two middle-aged female friends (Donna and Anna) are talking about a mutual acquaintance.

6 The symbols used in these excerpts are based on the standard conversation analytic transcription system (Jefferson 2004). See the list of transcription symbols at the end of the chapter for further detail. Pseudonyms are used for all the participants.

(3) ICE-AUS: S1A-033: 8:45

227 D: Do you kno:w um (.) did I tell you you know that girlfriend
228 that lives up at- works at the um Swiss embas↑sy.
229 A: ↑Ye:s. The one who's going off to live in:[::::::
230 D: [Oh I told you
231 didn't yeah in [Romania
232 A: [Germany
233 (0.2)
234 A: R[omania]
235 D: [Romani]a.

Donna begins in lines 227–228 by reporting news about their mutual friend. She tries to fix the reference for *that girlfriend* by qualifying her as the one who works at the Swiss embassy (line 228). Anna then attempts to confirm their mutual understanding of this referent by interpolating further information about her (Heritage 2007), specifically that their friend is planning to shift to another place to live. However, she does not yet specify the place in line 229, indicating through an elongated preposition that she may be trying to recall the name of the country (Lerner 1996: 261). This possible case of word searching occasions the offering of the name of country on the part of Donna (lines 230–231). Yet echoing Donna's previous entry into her speaking turn following the preposition *in*, Anna also attempts to complete Donna's utterance (lines 230–231) by naming the country in line 232 at the same time as Donna. While Anna initially names Germany, she recasts this as Romania after hearing Donna's utterance in line 234, which is confirmed through repetition by Donna (line 235). It thus constitutes an instance of failed co-construction. In this case, in attempting to complete what Donna is saying, Anna draws from a particular lexico-semantic field of country place names, which in turn is triggered specifically by the preceding preposition and co-text. She also draws from (apparently incorrect) shared knowledge about their friend in making this inference. But, crucially, this inference is constrained and thus guided by that particular lexico-semantic field.

In the next excerpt, we find an instance of a successful completion co-construction drawing from an alternative formulation of a previously said noun phrase. In this excerpt, Ildika is talking with Natalie about an anecdote from a book written by Ben Elton that she has read.

(4) AGA: NJIK: 2:31

76 I: And he was sa:ying (.) you know (.) what is it? with Australia,
77 this country because (1.0) everything is na:med a:fter (.) you
78 know some obscure administrator in- in a- in a certain era (.)
79 like for example (0.2) uh Uluru
80 which was formerly known as Ayer's Rock.
81 (0.4)
82 N: [mm.]
83 I: [And] (.) and they- imagine (.) naming this <fantastic sacred
84 object>
85 (0.5)
86 I: af[ter]
87 N: [af]ter some public servant=
88 I: [↑Ye:ah.]
89 N: [°tch°]
90 (0.2)
91 I: From South Australia.

Ildika elaborates on her previous theme that history is dominated by discussions of men, even obscure men, by referring to Ben Elton's discussion of place names in Australia. She gives the example of Uluru in the middle of Australia, which was previously known as Ayer's Rock, as an example of an important place being named after *some obscure administrator* (lines 76–80). Ildika goes on to express incredulation that such a *fantastic sacred object* could be named after this kind of person (lines 83–84, 86). However, the utterance-medial pause in line 85 that precedes the preposition appears to occasion Natalie's attempted completion of the clause with *some public servant* in line 87. This co-construction constitutes an alternative formulation of the term *administrator* previously used by Ildika (line 78), and thus is arguably semantic in origin.

The final type of semantic co-construction to be found in the dataset arose from the participants' knowledge of idiomatic or formulaic phrases. In this conversation, two friends (Jason and Lisa) have been talking at university about the foul-tasting coffee they are drinking. In the following excerpt, knowledge of the common idiomatic expression, *lay back and think of England*, allows one friend to "finish" the other's utterance in regards to how they should respond to the coffee. In this context, it means that they will just have to suffer the bad coffee in stoical silence.

(5) ICE-AUS, S1A-020: 0:38

```
21  J:  just (.) lay back and think of
22      (0.4)
23  L:  England (0.4) as I al(hh)ways [do.
24  J:                                [(l-
25      Hhh.
26  L:  He he.
```

In line 23, we can see that Lisa completes Jason's utterance, which he started in line 21, after a brief pause (line 22). This pause indicates that perhaps Jason's attention has momentarily shifted away from what he is saying, or alternatively that he is having trouble recalling the complete idiom (Lerner 1996: 261). It appears Lisa prospectively infers that Jason could say England to complete the idiom, and so says this herself before he completes it. Importantly, this inference draws from knowledge of a particular semantic unit, in this case an idiom. That *lay back and think of England* does indeed constitute an idiomatic unit can easily be established through a broader corpus-based analysis.

Pragmatic co-construction, in contrast, is occasioned by the local sequential context, yet also draws from knowledge outside of that local context. Pragmatic contributions to co-constructions can be divided into at least four different types: world knowledge, shared knowledge, sociocultural assumptions, and conscious pragmatic inference. World knowledge involves understandings of the world around us that are commonly shared across large groups of people, while shared knowledge involves understandings of the world or a particular environment that are shared only between selected persons. Sociocultural assumptions encompass particular emic conceptualisations of values, beliefs and attitudes, social categories, emotions and the like which underlie speech practices (Goddard 2006: 2). Finally, conscious pragmatic inference involves computations across the situation of discourse, sociocultural assumptions and world knowledge (Jaszczolt 2009b: 275–276). In this data set, examples of all four types of pragmatic contributions to co-constructing what is said were found.

In the following excerpt, two sisters (Barbara and Anna) are talking about a universally shared experience, namely, feeling sleepy after lunch. There are two examples of completion co-constructions in this excerpt that arise as a direct result of this world knowledge.

(6) ICE-AUS: S1A-022: 7:07

195 B: we were having lunch (.) at the studio.
196 A: mm¿
197 B: and (.) no:rmally if you have lu:nch (.) and then you go back
198 after lunch (.) everyone fi:nds this I think (0.2)
199 [that you're too-
200 A: [that you're sleepy.
201 B: ye:ah ye:ah=°you° can't concentrate=and I thought I don't
202 want this cause I was almost falling asleep anyway co:s
203 (0.2)
204 A: a full stomach's not good for working.
205 B: ye:ah.

The first co-construction arises when Barbara begins relating the "normal" experience people have when they have lunch and go back to work (lines 197–199), namely feeling sleepy. Anna's completion of this common experience is occasioned by a brief pause on Barbara's part after which they start almost simultaneously (lines 199–200). Barbara, however, abandons her utterance leaving it to Anna to complete. A second co-construction arises when she pauses (line 203) before going on to give the reason for not being able to concentrate and *falling asleep* (lines 201–202). The reason is offered by Anna in line 204, and subsequently ratified by Barbara (line 205). In both cases, these co-constructions are possible not just because of the syntactic trajectory established by Barbara, but also due to the common knowledge that people often feel sleepy after eating lunch.

A related type of pragmatic co-construction is where shared knowledge is restricted to a particular group of people who have experiences in common. In this conversation, three students (Katherine, Mark and Peter) have been talking about their shared experiences in living away from home in university residences or colleges. In the following excerpt from that conversation, they are focusing on the difficulties that arise from what they perceive to be akin to living in two different places.

(7) ICE-AUS: S1A-029: 46–62, 1:38

46 K: It's re:ally difficult 'cos it's a inbetween time °and you've got°
47 (0.4)
48 M: And you've got ha:lf your stuff down here and ha:lf your stuff
49 at ho:me [and]
50 K: [and]
51 M: you've never quite got a complete> s(hh)et he.

52 K: And you go ho:me and you're sort of always waiting (.) to
53 [go back] and like (.)
54 M: [mm he]
55 K: you have >to sort of< get yourself packed up.
56 P: But when you're in college [you]'re waiting to go home
57 K: [bu-]
58 P: [Ha ha
59 M: [Ha ha [ha ha]
60 K: [HA ha [When] y(hh)ou're in college you're waiting to go home.
61 Exactly.

Two instances of co-constructions can be observed in this excerpt. The first arises when Mark continues on with Katherine's claim that it's *really difficult* being in this kind of *inbetween time* (line 46), by outlining one of those difficulties, namely having one's possessions spread across two separate locations (lines 48–49). This completion by Mark of Katherine's utterance appears to have been occasioned by Katherine's trailing off with a markedly softer voice and subsequent intra-turn pause (line 47). A second expansion type of co-construction occurs when Peter elaborates in line 56 on Katherine's claim in lines 52–53 that there is a second difficulty: the feeling that when they are back at home they are always waiting to go back to live in the university residence or college. This expansion is subsequently ratified by Katherine through repetition (line 60) and emphatic agreement (line 61). In both instances, the inferences underlying these co-constructions are arguably facilitated because they have shared experiences in regards to their living arrangements while studying at university.

Pragmatic contributions to co-constructions may also involve certain sociocultural assumptions. In the following excerpt, two students (Michael and Cameron) co-construct within a joking frame a somewhat cynical view of the way in which some dentists work. This jocular mockery is occasioned by Cameron's over-extolling of the skill and integrity of his dentist (Haugh 2010).

(8) (Two male students chatting) (ICE-AUS, S1A-024)

88 M: bet he gets you if he has to do any work.
89 (2.3)
90 C: ye::ah but he- (.) he's the sort of guy who w:on't do work unless
91 there's work to be done.
92 M: mm.
93 C: you know how with some they'll give you a fluori:de an[d um

94	M:	[chip your
95		teeth away (.) and then tell you they've gotta cap 'em.
96	C:	[Ha ha [ha ha ha °he he he°
97	M:	[Ha HA ha ha ha
98		(1.0)
99	C:	°he he°
100		(1.0)
101		°he he he°
102		(1.0)
103	M:	°pro[b'ly°
104	C:	[ye:ah.

Cameron has been telling Michael that his dentist is very good, to which Michael responds by teasing that Cameron is probably charged a lot for the dentist's services (line 88). Cameron counters in lines 90–91 that his dentist will not do any work unless it is really necessary. He goes on to contrast his dentist's practice with those of others in line 93, but before he has finished Michael chimes in to complete Cameron's utterance in a humorous way in lines 94–95, and both speakers then laugh (lines 96–101). While it is not clear what Cameron might have said if he had finished what he was saying in line 93, M has anticipated what *could* have been said and so co-constructs with Cameron a common stance about dentists who do unnecessary work. This common stance is explicitly endorsed by both Michael and Cameron in lines 103–104, which indicates that whether or not the anticipatory inference made by Michael was the same as what Cameron might have "intended", it was accepted by both speakers as a plausible continuation of Cameron's speaking turn. It is important to note, then, that pragmatic co-construction is not constrained to the same degree as is semantic co-construction, and so there is greater potential for different meanings to emerge and be ratified in the process of collaborative meaning making between the speakers.

The final type of pragmatic contribution to co-constructions that was found in the dataset involved conscious pragmatic inferences. In the following conversation, Emma has been talking to Kathy about the difficulties she has with Japanese, both communicating in it, and translating it into English.

(9) AGA: ERKR: 10:06

306	E:	Yeah it's really frustrating I'm not always like
307		this I've just sort of been translating a lot over
308		the break over the uni break and it- just like=
309	K:	=I'm brain dead
310	E:	Yeah
311	K:	Yep had enough

Emma begins by relating her frustration with Japanese with the translating work she has been doing over the holidays (lines 306–307). She cuts off her own utterance near the end of line 308 (*and it*) and resorts to a filler (*just like*), which occasions Kathy to attempt to explicate the feeling that Emma has when doing so much translation, namely feeling *brain dead* (line 309). This feeling is expressed in the first person by Kathy, although it is attributed to Emma. The inference underlying this completion is arguably a conscious pragmatic one similar to those underlying particularised implicatures, as it draws from both the situation of discourse (that is, Emma's troubles with Japanese), and shared knowledge (that is, translation between unrelated and structurally very different languages takes a lot of mental effort), leading to the assumption that one would feel *brain dead* (or, in other words, totally exhausted) after such work. The inferential chain leading to Kathy's candidate completion of Emma's utterance might resemble something like the following retrospectively constructed chain of inference (although this chain is not meant to represent the exact order of actual processing):

i. Emma says she feels frustrated (line 306).
ii. Emma has previously said she finds Japanese difficult (co-text).
iii. Emma feels frustrated about her Japanese (inference from i and ii).
iv. Emma says she does not always feel frustrated [about her Japanese] (lines 306–307).
v. Emma says she has been translating a lot over the break (line 307).
vi. (v) is the reason for (iii) despite (iv) (bridging inference).
vii. Emma wants to give another reason why she feels frustrated (line 308).
viii. Translation takes a lot of energy (world knowledge).
ix. Another potential reason for (iii) despite (iv) is she is exhausted from the translation work. (inference from v, vii, viii)

Whether this second reason inferred by Kathy is really what Emma "intended" remains equivocal, but since this completion is subsequently ratified by Emma through expressing agreement (line 310), it becomes, in effect, part of what is said by Emma.

The analysis thus far has demonstrated the complex interweaving of projected syntax in local sequential environments with semantic and pragmatic contributions in the co-construction of utterances by participants in interactions. Yet despite being jointly produced by two speakers, co-constructed utterances are oriented to as what is said by the first speaker rather than both speakers, as it is generally only first speakers who are ultimately held accountable for these co-constructed meanings, as is discussed next.

2.3. Participant orientations to co-constructing what is said

In the collection of 46 co-constructions analysed, first participants oriented to the meaning of the co-constructed utterance in two key ways, either by ratifying (or not) the second speaker's completion or expansion, or by implicitly rejecting (or sometimes supporting) it through a delayed completion (Lerner 1989: 175). This orienting to what is said illustrates the way in which participants assume first speakers will be held accountable for what is said despite it being co-constructed jointly with a second speaker.

Yeah ratification involves explicit expressions of agreement by the first speaker with the second speaker's completion or expansion, such as *yeah* or *yep*. These occurred relatively frequently in the dataset, as seen from the examples discussed in the previous section. In example (4), repeated here for convenience, Ildika and Natalie had been discussing how Uluru was originally named after an *obscure administrator*.

(4) AGA: NJIK: 2:31

83 I: And (.) and they- imagine (.) naming this <fantastic sacred
84 object>
85 (0.5)
86 I: af[ter]
87 N: [af]ter some public servant=
88 I: [↑Ye:ah.]
89 N: [°tch°]
90 (0.2)
91 I: From South Australia.

Ildika here responds to the completion of her utterance by Natalie with an expression of emphatic agreement (line 88). This agreement token appears to ratify Natalie's completion as part of what Ildika meant, and thus part of what is said, in addition to the role it plays in their co-constructing of a shared stance of disbelief about the motivations of those who originally gave Uluru the name Ayer's Rock.

While in many of the examples discussed above the first speaker ratifies the second speaker's completion of the first speaker's utterance, co-constructions can also be subsequently disputed by the first speaker. Non-ratification can involve, for instance, explicit expressions of disagreement by the first speaker with the second speaker's completion or expansion, such as *no* or *nah.* In the following excerpt between two friends (Dave and Alison), Dave is describing his struggle to save money.

(10) GCSAusE10: 3:40

117 D: >you get real stingy people you get really
118 flamboyant people< (1.4)
119 and so I was sorta li:ke ah: we:ll (1.7) >I was-< (.)
120 fuck it like (0.6) I'll just spend money, I don't
121 really give a fuck (1.3) and I'm just buying dinner
122 it's like (0.2) going out an' buying everybody dinner
123 and shit like that an:'
124 A: kinda: throwing your- ↑NOT throwing it
125 a[round but (.)
126 D: [>nah but like<
127 j[ust stuff that made everybody happy,
128 A: [like-

Here Dave positions himself as someone who is quite *flamboyant* with his money, buying not only himself dinner, but others as well (lines 121–122). Alison latches on to complete Dave's further description of his behaviour projected by the conjunctive *and* by positioning his behaviour as *throwing it* [money] *around*, although she abandons this completion mid-clause (line 124), and goes on to distance herself from this initial positioning (lines 124–125). Dave nevertheless explicitly rejects this attempted completion by Alison, overlapping with Alison's retraction (line 126), before going on to give an alternative completion (line 127) to the utterance projected by the conjunction at the end of line 123.

In some instances first speakers simultaneously ratify and reject the second speaker's completion or expansion of the first speaker's utterance through the seemingly contradictory discourse marker, *yeah-no*, which is said to be relatively frequent in Australian English (Burridge and Florey 2002). In the next example, Kathy is asking why Emma became an acupuncturist.

(11) AGA: ERKR: 15:55
466 K: So what made you start looking at it (0.4) in the beginning
467 E: O:h I was a whi↑mp (0.2) umm I had really (0.2) pretty poor
468 hea↑lth
469 K: Yeah?
470 E: So umm (0.9) I tried acupuncture and it actually (0.2) didn't
471 really work (0.4) but .hh reg(hh)ardless of [that=
472 K: [Hh hh
473 =you became an acupuncturist
474 E: <↑Yeah ↑no>
475 I- (0.6) it was- I- I loved i↑t

Emma first says she become interested in acupuncture because she had experienced health problems (lines 467–468), but then goes on to admit that when she tried it herself the treatment was not very successful (lines 470–471). She projects a continuation of her explanation with a contrastive conjunction on to which Kathy latches a completion (line 473), namely, that despite the lack of success Emma still became an acupuncturist. Emma responds in turn with a *yeah-no* discourse marker (line 474). It appears that Emma simultaneously expresses agreement with Kathy's completion of what is said, namely she did become an acupuncturist, and disagreement with the ironic implication that her career choice was somewhat surprising in light of her own lack of success with acupuncture treatment. The latter rejection of this apparent irony of her choice is further warranted through her claim to have *loved* the treatment despite its lack of success (line 475). In this way, *yeah-no* is used by Emma to orient both to what is said and to what is implicated through the joint production of a completion co-construction.

Delayed completion is another way in which participants may orient to what is said. It involves instances where the first speaker produces "an alternative, possibly competing completion which deletes the sequential relevance of the preemptive completion" (Lerner 1989: 175), as previously noted. In the excerpt below, for example, two friends (Susie and Jack) are talking about a mutual friend about whom Susie has related some gossip.

(12) ICE-AUS: S1A-010: 2:40
67 S: What did ↑you think (.) when I told you.
68 Were you shocked or what.
69 (0.8)
70 J: Not shocked. I mean I'm respectful of her deci:sion.

71 (0.4)
72 S: [Ye[:ah]
73 J: [She's] [a-
74 S: [But did it sur↑prise you.
75 Nah
76 (0.2)
77 Ye:s.
78 (1.0)
79 J: A a little bit I guess I mean I never really expected anyone I
80 knew to be
81 (0.4)
82 S: ga:y.
83 J: to be so inclined.
84 S: >He he he he<

Susie appears to be attempting to elicit from Jack his feelings in relation to learning that their friend is a lesbian. After prompting Jack as to whether he felt *shocked* (line 68), Susie reframes her question as to whether he felt *surprised* (line 74), in response to Jack denying he felt shocked (line 70). Jack admits in response to Susie's prompting that he felt *a bit* surprised, and then goes on to frame an account for this feeling of surprise (lines 79–80). He pauses, however, before explicitly naming what their friend's decision entails (line 81), which appears to occasion Susie's completion of his utterance with the term *gay* (line 82). Jack, however, implicitly rejects Susie's completion of his utterance in recasting with the euphemistic phrase *to be so inclined* (line 83). While the two descriptors are in some ways synonymous, the second has very particular connotations, namely, that Jack does not want to explicitly focus on their friend's sexual orientation. In other words, Jack is orienting through his recasting of Susie's completion of his utterance to the meaning, in particular, the connotations of the final part of the co-constructed utterance.

In the examples discussed so far we can observe participants orienting to first speaker *intentions* beyond a broad orientation to the intentionality of communication (Haugh 2008a, 2009). Participants oriented to the co-constructed utterance as being synonymous with what the first speaker meant in the vast majority of cases, with only 15% of first speaker responses being unmarked as to whether the participants were holding the first speaker accountable for what is said, as illustrated in Table 1 below.

Table 1. First participant responses to co-constructed utterances

	Completions	Expansions	Total
Yeah/no ratification	21	12	33
Delayed completion	5	1	6
Unmarked	4	3	7

The high proportion of explicit expressions of agreement (or disagreement) and delayed completion (85% in total) is arguably indicative of the fact the participants generally hold the first speaker, not both speakers, accountable for what is said, despite it being co-constructed by both participants. Although this trend is fairly robust in this dataset, due caution should, of course, be taken when attempting to extrapolate from it due to its relatively small size. It remains an open question whether participants always orient to co-constructed utterances as what is said by the first speaker. Nevertheless, it does illustrate how analysts can empirically demonstrate that participants do, at times, orient to the meaning of what is said through careful examination of interaction data. This approach thus offers another possible way of elucidating how ordinary speakers understand what is said.

3. The role of interactional data at the interface of semantics and pragmatics

Current debates around the semantics–pragmatics interface reflect broader ongoing debates around the role of different sources of language data and approaches to analysing that data in semantics and pragmatics. Clark and Bangerter (2004) suggest that there are essentially three ways in which language use has been investigated: intuition, experiment and observation.

> With intuitions, you imagine examples of language used in this or that situation and ask yourself whether they are grammatical or ungrammatical, natural or unnatural, appropriate or inappropriate….With experiments, you invite people into the laboratory, induce them to produce, comprehend or judge samples of language, and measure their reactions. With observations, you note what people say or write as they go about their daily business. (Clark and Bangerter 2004: 25)

Intuited data tends to be used by those using philosophical methods, elicited data is used for the most part in experimental approaches, and natural data (gained either through direct observation or recording) is generally employed by those using empirical methods. While linguists and language philosophers often claim the superiority of one kind of data and methodology over others, the question of which kind of data or approach is "best" does not have a straightforward answer. As Jucker (2009) has recently argued in relation to speech act research, it ultimately "depends on the specific research question whether one or the other of these three approaches can yield useful insights" (p.1611). It is suggested here that this pragmatic approach to linguistic data is useful to bear in mind when considering theoretical questions and debates around the semantics–pragmatics interface.

While research in semantics has traditionally drawn from intuited and elicited data, it has been implicitly proposed through the case study of co-constructions undertaken here that natural data, in particular, interactional data and analysis, may provide a complementary perspective on meaning that has yet to be fully exploited. However, such an assumption deserves further examination in light of the relative neglect of natural data in semantics to date. Some might question whether interactional data and analysis constitutes legitimate data and approaches for investigating the semantics–pragmatics interface, and, in particular, for theorizing meaning.

At first glance, any response to such a question would seem to be dependent on one's view of what semantics should be concerned with. As was previously alluded to at the beginning of this chapter, while there are various approaches to delimiting the proper scope of semantics, there are essentially two key ways in which the semantics–pragmatics boundary has been drawn (Carston 2008: 322). The first approach, advocated in various guises in semantic minimalism, is that a distinction should be drawn between context-independent linguistically encoded meaning and speaker meaning. The second approach, advocated in various ways in semantic contextualism, is that a distinction should be made between the intuitive proposition expressed versus the rest of speaker meaning.

For those who take the view that semantics ought to be concerned with logical forms (that is, a minimal notion of what is said), such data may seem, at first glance, to be of relatively little import. However, such a conclusion is only reasonable if one assumes that "minimalism can be regarded as compatible with contextualism, each of them having a distinct set of objectives and a distinct object of study" (Jaszcolt 2009c: 461), and thus that those interested in studying context-independent linguistically encoded meaning can legitimately regard interactional data and analyses as lying outside their research programme. Since there remains considerable work to be done in regards to the degree of compatibility between semantic minimalism and contextualism it might seem prudent to not reject such data too hastily. Indeed, in the case of co-constructions at least, which should be of interest even to minimalists as they involve jointly produced logical forms, it is important to remember that they cannot be readily studied through intuited data. In order to successfully identify co-constructions careful observation of natural interactional data is required. While searching corpus data may seem a more palatable form of natural data for those with a minimalist bent, since it (traditionally at least) tends to involve stripping interactions of much of its contextual information, using the syntactic properties of co-constructions to motivate search strings currently has a low degree of recall. As was previously noted (see footnote 3), corpus-based approaches are limited to investigating only certain types of co-constructions. Most of the co-constructions discussed in the analysis above could not be identified through traditional approaches to interrogating corpora.

For those who take the view that semantics ought to be concerned with the intuitive proposition expressed, on the other hand, interactional data and analysis may seem, at first glance, to be of potentially greater value. As illustrated through the analysis of co-constructions, interactional data and analysis provides a further means of accessing primary meanings. It thus allows philosophically-motivated theories of semantics, such as Default Semantics, to be tested with another form of language data in addition to intuited and experimental data (Jaszczolt 2008).

Yet while interactional data and analysis can arguably provide an alternative perspective on the semantics–pragmatics interface, which complements existing approaches, there are two possible stumbling blocks to integrating such approaches. First of all, it should not be automatically assumed that findings from one methodological approach are necessarily commensurable with findings arising from another methodology. The underlying epistemological and ontological commitments of interactional pragmatics are arguably different from those of much of philosophical semantics. Interactional pragmatics rests on the basic claim that "meaning comes into existence in and out of our engagement with the realities in our world" (Crotty 1998: 8), or what is termed constructionism. Objectivism, in contrast, rests on the claim that "meaning and therefore meaningful reality exists as such apart from the operation of any consciousness" (Crotty 1998: 8). It might appear, then, that these approaches are fundamentally incompatible, as the former involves an epistemology that is grounded in emergent, non-summative interaction and a social constructionist ontology, while the latter encompasses an epistemology grounded in (the minds of) the individual, and a positivist ontology. However, the question of compatibility is ultimately dependent on how findings are presented in the various approaches to theorizing meaning. If semantic analyses are presented as "objective truths, claiming validity, perhaps generalisability, on their behalf" and thus call on "people to accept our findings as established fact" (Crotty 1998: 41), then interactional data and semantic analyses are arguably incompatible. However, if semantic analyses and theories are offered as interpretations where we invite "people to weigh our interpretation, judge whether it has been soundly arrived at and is plausible (convincing even?), and decide whether it has application to their interests and concerns" (Crotty 1998: 41), then this incompatibility may not in fact be substantive at all. In other words, the potential usefulness of interactional data and analyses for investigating the semantics–pragmatics interface depends largely on the epistemological and ontological commitments of those theorizing meaning.

A second potential stumbling block is that it is often very time-consuming to identify phenomena of interest in natural data (Jucker 2009: 1616). This, in turn, results in the use of fairly small datasets in most interactional analyses. As Jucker (2009) points out, small datasets lack generalizability as they cannot generally yield statistically convincing results. In the present analysis of co-constructions, for instance, while a strong trend emerged for participants to orient to co-constructions as what the first speaker has said, the relatively small set of examples examined means no generalizable conclusions can yet be reached.

It is thus suggested here that interactional data and analysis, if used judiciously, provide a complementary perspective on the semantics–pragmatics interface. However, there is no claim being made here that such data or analyses are inherently better or in some way supersede intuited or experimental data. If one wishes to understand how semantic and pragmatic information contribute to the co-construction of utterances by two or more speakers, interactional data is clearly of some value. However, there are clearly limits to all forms of data and analysis, and the approach advocated in this chapter is no exception.

4. Concluding remarks

The aim of this chapter has not been to resolve current debates surrounding the semantics–pragmatics interface. Rather, its aim has been somewhat more modest, in essence, to propose that interactional data can provide complementary perspectives on the analysis of a phenomenon that lies at the semantics–syntax–pragmatics interface, namely, co-construction. The complex interweaving of syntactic, semantic and pragmatic information underlying co-constructions discussed here suggests that the semantics–pragmatics interface is unlikely to ever constitute a clear boundary. As

Jaszczolt (2005, 2009a) argues, meanings are perhaps best conceptualised as merger representations drawing from syntactic, semantic and pragmatic sources of information. According to this view, semantics ought to be about all forms of meaning, both the said and the unsaid, while logical forms come under the purview of syntax, and the study of actions and relationships (or relating) remain the primary responsibility of pragmatics. The distinction between the said and the unsaid (or implied) is important for analysing actions and relationships in some instances (Haugh 2007, 2008b), but it does not constitute a valid means of distinguishing between semantics and pragmatics, as Carston (2008) and Jaszczolt (2009b) have both argued. It appears, then, that placing less importance on the traditional Gricean distinction between what is said and what is implicated may prove the most fruitful way forward in better understanding the semantics–pragmatics interface.

Acknowledgements

I would like to thank both the editors and the anonymous reviewer for their very helpful comments on this chapter. All errors or omissions, however, remain my own.

Transcription symbols

[ ]	overlapping speech
=	latching
-	indicates a cut off of the prior word or sound
<u>underlining</u>	speaker emphasis
::	elongation
CAPITALS	markedly louder speech
°	markedly softer speech
↓	marked falling intonation
↑	marked rising intonation
(.)	micropause
( )	unclear or unintelligible speech
(( ))	extra description of paralinguistic/non-verbal features

References

Bach, Kent
2002 Seemingly semantic intuitions. In *Meaning and Truth: Investigations in Philosophical Semantics*, Joseph Campbell, Michael O'Rourke and David Shier (eds.), 21–33. New York: Seven Bridges Press.

Bach, Kent
2004 Minding the gap. In *The Semantics/Pragmatics Distinction*, Claudia Bianchi (ed.), 27–43. Stanford, CA: CSLI Publications.

Berg, Jonathan
2002 Is semantics still possible? *Journal of Pragmatics* 34: 349–359.

Bolden, Galina B.
2003 Multiple modalities in collaborative turn sequences. *Gesture* 3: 187–212.

Borg, Emma
2004 *Minimal Semantics*. Oxford: Clarendon Press.

Burridge, Kate and Margaret Florey
2002 'Yeah-no he's a good kid': a discourse analysis of *yeah-no* in Australian English. *Australian Journal of Linguistics* 22: 149–171.

Cappelen, Herman and Ernie Lepore
2005 *Insensitive Semantics: A Defense of Semantic Minimalism and Speech Act Pluralism*. Oxford: Blackwell.

Carston, Robyn
1988 Implicature, explicature, and truth-theoretic semantics. In *Mental Representations: The Interface between Language and Reality*, Ruth Kempson (ed.), 155–181. Cambridge: Cambridge University Press.

Carston, Robyn
2002 *Thoughts and Utterances. The Pragmatics of Explicit Communication*. Oxford: Blackwell.

Carston, Robyn
2007 How many pragmatic systems are there? In *Saying, Meaning, Referring. Essays on the Philosophy of François Recanati*, Maria Jose Frapolli (ed.), 18–48. Basingstoke: Palgrave Macmillan.

Carston, Robyn
2008 Linguistic communication and the semantics/pragmatics distinctions. *Synthese* 165: 321–345.

Clark, Herbert H. and Adrian Bangerter
2004 Changing ideas about reference. In *Experimental Pragmatics*, Ira A. Noveck and Dan Sperber (eds.), 25–49. Basingstoke: Palgrave Macmillan.

Cole, Peter (ed.)
1981 *Radical Pragmatics*. New York: Academic Press.

Crotty, Michael
1998 *The Foundations of Social Research.* Crows Nest, NSW: Allen & Unwin.

Ferrara, Kathleen
1992 The interactive achievement of a sentence: joint productions in therapeutic discourse. *Discourse Processes* 15: 207–228.

Ford, Cecilia and Sandra A. Thompson
1996 Interactional units in conversation: syntactic, intonational, and pragmatic resources for the management of turns. In *Grammar and Interaction*, Elinor Ochs, Emanuel Schegloff and Sandra Thompson (eds.), 134–184. Cambridge: Cambridge University Press.

Fox, Barbara A. and Sandra A. Thompson
1990 A discourse explanation of the grammar of relative clauses in English conversation. *Language* 66: 297–316.

Geluykens, Ronald
1992 *From Discourse Process to Grammatical Construction: On Left-Dislocation in English.* Amsterdam: John Benjamins.

Gibbs Jr., Raymond and Jessica Moise
1997 Pragmatics in understanding what is said. *Cognition* 62: 51–74.

Goddard, Cliff
2006 Ethnopragmatics: a new paradigm. In *Ethnopragmatics: Understanding Discourse in Cultural Context*, Cliff Goddard (ed.), 1–30. Berlin/New York: Mouton de Gruyter.

Goodwin, Charles
1979 The interactive construction of a sentence in natural conversation. In *Everyday Language: Studies in Ethnomethodology*, Georg Psathas (ed.), 97–121. NY: Irvington.

Goodwin, Charles
1995 Co-constructing meaning in conversations with an aphasic man. *Research on Language and Social Interaction* 28: 233–260.

Grice, H. Paul
1957 Meaning. *Philosophical Review* 66: 377–388.

Grice, H. Paul
1969 Utterer's meaning and intention. *Philosophical Review* 78: 147–177.

Grice, H. Paul
1975 Logic and conversation. In *Syntax and Semantics, Volume 3. Speech Acts*, Peter Cole and Jerry Morgan (eds.), 41–58. New York: Academic Press.

Grice, H. Paul
1989 *Studies in the Way of Words.* Cambridge, MA: Harvard University Press.

Haugh, Michael
2007 The co-constitution of politeness implicature in conversation. *Journal of Pragmatics* 39: 84–110.

Haugh, Michael
2008a The place of intention in the interactional achievement of implicature. In *Intention, Common Ground and the Egocentric Speaker-Hearer*, Istvan Kecskes and Jacob Mey (eds.), 45–85. Berlin/New York: Mouton de Gruyter.

Haugh, Michael
2008b Utterance-final conjunctive particles and implicature in Japanese conversation. *Pragmatics* 18: 425–451.

Haugh, Michael
2009 Intention(ality) and the conceptualisation of communication in pragmatics. *Australian Journal of Linguistics* 29: 91–113.

Haugh, Michael
2010 Jocular mockery, (dis)affiliation and face. *Journal of Pragmatics* 42: 2106–2119.

Hayashi, Makoto
1999 Where grammar and interaction meet: a study of co-participant completion in Japanese conversation. *Human Studies* 22: 475–499.

Hayashi, Makoto
2003 *Joint Utterance Construction in Japanese Conversation.* Amsterdam: John Benjamins.

Hayashi, Makoto and Junko Mori
1998 Co-construction in Japanese revisited: we *do* "finish each other's sentences". In *Japanese/Korean Linguistics, Vol. 7*, Noriko Akatsuka, Hajime Hoji, Shoichi Iwasaki, Sung-Ock Sohn and Susan Strauss (eds.), 77–93. Stanford, CA: CSLI.

Helasvuo, Marja-Liisa
2004 Shared syntax: the grammar of co-constructions. *Journal of Pragmatics* 36: 1315–1336.

Heritage, John
2007 Intersubjectivity and progressivity in person (and place) reference. In *Person Reference in Interaction*, Nick Enfield and Tanya Stivers (eds.), 255–280. Cambridge: Cambridge University Press.

Horn, Laurence
2004 Implicature. In *Handbook of Pragmatics*, Laurence Horn and Gregory Ward (eds.), 3–28. Oxford: Blackwell.

Hutchby, Ian and Robin Woofitt
2008 *Conversation Analysis* (2nd edn). Cambridge: Polity Press.

Jacoby, Sally and Elinor Ochs
1995 Co-construction: an introduction. *Research on Language and Social Interaction* 28: 171–183.

Jaszczolt, Katarzyna M.
2005 *Default Semantics. Foundations of a Compositional Theory of Acts of Communication.* Oxford: Oxford University Press.

Jaszczolt, Katarzyna M.
2008 Psychological explanations in Gricean pragmatics and Frege's legacy. In *Intention, Common Ground and the Egocentric Speaker-Hearer*, Istvan Kecskes and Jacob Mey (eds.), 9–44. Berlin / New York: Mouton de Gruyter.

Jaszczolt, Katarzyna M.
2009a *Representing Time: An Eassy on Temporality as Modality*. Oxford: Oxford University Press.

Jaszczolt, Katarzyna M.
2009b Cancellability and the primary/secondary meaning distinction. *Intercultural Pragmatics* 6: 259–289.

Jaszczolt, Katarzyna M.
2009c Semantics–pragmatics interface. In *The Routledge Pragmatics Encyclopedia*, Louise Cummings (ed.), 458–462. London: Routledge.

Jaszczolt, Katarzyna M.
in press Semantics and pragmatics: the boundary issue. In *Semantics: An International Handbook of Natural Language Meaning*, Claudia Maienborn, Klaus von Heusinger and Paul Portner (eds.), Berlin/ New York: Mouton de Gruyter.

Jefferson, Gail
2004 Glossary of transcript symbols with an introduction. In *Conversation Analysis: Studies from the First Generation*, Gene Lerner (ed.), 13–23. Amsterdam: John Benjamins.

Jucker, Andreas
2009 Speech act research between armchair, field and laboratory. The case of compliments. *Journal of Pragmatics* 41: 1611–1635.

Keinpointner, Manfred
2008 The case for core meaning. In *Meaning, Intentions and Argumentation*, Kepa Korta and Joana Garmendia (eds.), 77–112. Stanford, CA: CSLI Publications.

Kim, Haeyeon
2004 Collaborative turn completion in Korean conversation. *Language Research* 38: 1281–1316.

Lerner, Gene
1989 Notes on overlap management in conversation: The case of delayed completion. *Western Journal of Communication* 53: 167–177.

Lerner, Gene
1991 On the syntax of sentences-in-progress. *Language in Society* 20: 441–458.

Lerner, Gene
1996 On the 'semi-permeable' character of grammatical units in conversation: conditional entry into the turn space of another speaker. In *Interaction and Grammar*, Elinor Ochs, Emanuel Schegloff and

Sandra Thompson (eds.), 238–276. Cambridge: Cambridge University Press.

Lerner, Gene
2004 Collaborative turn sequences. In *Conversation Analysis: Studies from the First Generation*, Gene Lerner (ed.), 225–256. Amsterdam: John Benjamins.

Lerner, Gene and Tomoko Takagi
1999 On the place of linguistic resources in the organization of talk-in-interaction: a co-investigation of English and Japanese grammatical practices. *Journal of Pragmatics* 31: 49–75.

Local, John
2004 On the interactional and phonetic design of collaborative completions. In *A Figure of Speech. A Festschrift for John Laver*, William Hardcastle and Janet Beck (eds.), 263–282. Mahwah, NJ: Lawrence Erlbaum.

Lyons, John
1968 *Introduction to Theoretical Linguistics*. Cambridge: Cambridge University Press.

Lyons, John
1995 *Linguistic Semantics. An Introduction*. Cambridge: Cambridge University Press.

Maynard, Senko K.
1989 *Japanese Conversation: Self-Contextualisation through Structure and Interactional Management*. Norwood, NJ: Ablex.

Ono, Tsuyoshi and Sandra A. Thompson
1996 Interaction and syntax in the structure of conversational discourse: collaboration, overlap, and syntactic dissociation. In *Computational and Conversational Discourse: Burning Issues – An Interdisciplinary Account*, Eduard H. Hovy and Donia R. Scott (eds.), 67–96. Berlin: Springer-Verlag.

Ono, Tsuyoshi and Eri Yoshida
1996 A study of co-construction in Japanese: we don't finish each other's sentences. In *Japanese/Korean Linguistics, Vol. 5*, Noriko Akatsuka, Shoichi Iwasaki and Susan Strauss (eds.), 115–130. Stanford, CA: CSLI.

Recanati, François
1989 The pragmatics of what is said. *Mind and Language* 4: 295–329.

Recanati, François
2001 What is said. *Synthese* 128: 75–91.

Recanati, François
2004 *Literal Meaning*. Cambridge: Cambridge University Press.

Rühlemann, Christoph
2007 *Conversation in Context. A Corpus-Driven Approach*. London: Continuum.

Sacks, Harvey
1992 *Lectures on Conversation.* Oxford: Blackwell.

Sacks, Harvey, Emanuel Schegloff and Gail Jefferson
1974 A simplest systematics for the organisation of turn-taking for conversation. *Language* 50: 696–735.

Schegloff, Emanuel
1993 Reflections on quantification in the study of conversation. *Research on Language and Social Interaction* 26: 99–128.

Sperber, Dan and Deirdre Wilson
1995 *Relevance. Communication and Cognition* (2nd edition). Oxford: Blackwell.

Suzuki, Takashi and Mayumi Usami
2006 Co-constructions in English and Japanese revisited: A quantitative approach to cross-linguistic comparison. In *Gengojoohoogaku Kenkyuu Hookoku 13. Shizen Kaiwa Bunseki e no Gengoshakaishinringaku apuroochi* [Working Papers Linguistic Informatics 13. A Social Psychological Approach to Natural Conversation Analysis], Mayumi Usami (ed.), 263–276. Tokyo: The 21st Century COE Program, Tokyo University of Foreign Studies.

Szabó, Zoltán Gendler
2005 Introduction. In *Semantics versus Pragmatics*, Zoltán Gendler Szabó (ed.), 1–14. Oxford: Clarendon Press.

Szczepek, Beatrice
2000a Formal aspects of collaborative productions in English conversation. *InLiSt (Interaction and Linguistic Structures)* 17.

Szczepek, Beatrice
2000b Functional aspects of collaborative productions in English conversations. *InLiSt (Interaction and Linguistic Structures)* 21.

Thompson, Sandra and Anthony Mulac
1991 The discourse conditions for the use of complementizer *that* in conversational English. *Journal of Pragmatics* 15: 237–251.

Data-gathering methods in research on hyperbole production and interpretation

Attila L. Nemesi

1. Introduction

1.1. Background: Definitional problems

The notion *hyperbole* inherited from classical rhetoric goes back to the Greek compound *ὑπερβολή* ('excess', 'immoderateness'). Its first component (*ὑπερ-*) means 'over, beyond', while the second is a derivative of the verb *βαλλειν* ('to throw', 'to cast'). Traditionally, it is classified as a trope *in verbis singulis* (in a single word) like metaphor, metonymy, synecdoche, emphasis, irony, litotes, and some other peculiar devices of *ornatus* (part of *elocution* in rhetoric), but, at the same time, as a figure of thought created by immutation such as allegory and, again, irony, emphasis, and synecdoche (Lausberg 1998: §§ 552–598, §§ 893–910). Aristotle (1926) observed that Attic orators were especially fond of exaggerations, and notes that hyperboles include some sort of youthfulness and vehemence, so he does not suggest for elderly people to use them (*The "Art" of Rhetoric*, 1413a). On Quintilian's (1921) view, hyperbole can be conceived as *decens veri superiectio*, an elegant straining of verity (*Institutio Oratoria*, 8.6.67). Though in its literal sense a hyperbolic utterance counts as a lie or distortion, the end of exaggeration is not to mislead, but just to lead to the truth: by saying something unbelievable it fixes what should be believed (Fontanier 1968: 123). Hyperbole, thus, must keep credibility: it should not distort the truth too much while it crosses the boundaries of reality. Quintilian reminds the speakers of the danger of becoming extravagantly affected and ridiculous, since exaggeration is a virtue only when the subject we have to speak on is uncommon. "For we are allowed to amplify, when the magnitude of the facts passes all words, and in such circumstances our language will be more effective if it goes beyond the truth than if it falls short of it" (8.6.76), as he writes after stating that even peasants and uneducated persons use hyperboles regularly. "Everybody has an innate passion for exaggeration or attenuation of actual facts, and no one is ever contended with the simple truth",[1] which is pardonable, unless in case of a logical proof. In sum, the trope or figure of speech could be considered a "partial lie" with "reduced truth value" (Fónagy 2001: 218).

In English, hyperbole is also referred to as *exaggeration* and *overstatement.* British and American manuals of rhetoric and poetics often define hyperbole by one of the two synonyms (if they really are), such as *The New Princeton Encyclopedia of Poetry and Poetics* (Preminger and Brogan 1993) puts it: "HYPERBOLE. A figure or trope [...] consisting of bold exaggeration", which may seem to be somewhat tautological. Researchers attempt to make subtle differences between these terms. Norrick (2004: 1728), for example, agrees with the Princeton Encyclopedia (hyperboles are "bold exaggerations"), but adds that the notion of overstatement is more general: it "includes any extravagant statement of amplification or attenuation used to express emotion and not to be taken literally". Gibbs (1993: 266, 1994: 391), too, insists on that hyperbole should be contrasted with "simple" overstatement, because by an overstatement "a person *unconsciously* or *unintentionally* expresses a proposition that is stronger than the evidence warrants" (my emphases). To illustrate this contrast, he explains: "The same proposition can be overstatement in one person's mouth and hyperbole in another's. A person who states *All Americans can attain their dreams of success* without realizing that the circumstances of nature and society prevent some people from achieving their full potential has simply overstated the truth. However, a person who realizes the truth might intend the listener to understand the same proposition as hyperbole for rhetorical effect". Fónagy (2001: 218), taking a stylistic perspective, claims that hyperboles are the stylized literal forms of colloquial exaggeration. Naturally, all of these considerations are interesting, but the boundaries of boldness, consciousness, and literariness seem to me quite vague. It is for this reason that I will use here the terms hyperbole, understatement, and exaggeration interchangeably like McCarthy and Carter (2004), Nemesi (2004), and Cano Mora (2006, 2009) do.

---

1 This passage quoted from *Institutio Oratoria* unequivocally refutes the widespread charge of cognitive linguists against classical rhetoric that as a "decorative" view of figurative language it assumes that metaphors and other tropes would be only devices "of the poetic imagination and the rhetorical flourish – a matter of extraordinary rather than ordinary language" (Lakoff and Johnson 1980: 3), thus, as ornaments they would play a peripheral role in language (see also Sperber and Wilson 1990).

As is indicated above by Quintilian (1921) and Norrick (2004), hyperbole has two forms of appearance: amplifications (positive hyperboles) and attenuations (negative hyperboles) are both belong to the concept. In contrast to positive hyperboles tending toward the infinite on some semantic scale, negative hyperboles converge on zero (Fónagy 1975, 2001; Norrick 1982). At the far end of any continuum of comparison we find extreme case formulations built around extreme expressions such as *absolutely, all, always, never, best, least, every, none, as good as it gets, perfectly,* and *brand new.* Thus, extreme case formulations can be found at the end points on scales, while exaggerations occur any time a speaker makes a claim higher (or lower) on the relevant scale than warranted (Norrick 2004: 1728–1729). But, if Norrick is correct, we run into the problem of how to draw a clear distinction between negative hyperboles and understatements, for understatement (equally denominated *meiosis*, or, in its broadest sense, *litotes*[2]), the logical opposite of overstatement, also states less than objectively warranted. Consider the examples below, adapted from Colston and Keller's (1998: 512) article:

(1) a. *This fridge has tons of food in it.* (It is full of food → positive hyperbole.)
b. *This fridge has some food in it.* (It is full of food → (ironic) understatement.)
c. *This fridge has nothing in it.* (It is nearly empty → negative hyperbole.)
d. *This fridge has quite many foods in it.* (It is nearly empty → (ironic) understatement.)

In the same context (the refrigerator is full of foods), (1a) is a positive hyperbole, while (1b) downscales the actual state of affairs, so (1b) exemplifies an understatement (with an ironic tone). Similarly, when the fridge is not totally empty, but the food in it is not enough, (1c) represents a negative hyperbole (with an extreme case formulation), and (1d) will be interpreted as an ironic understatement. Hence, there exist two kinds of scale: one of amplification (or augmentation), and another of attenuation (or diminution),

[2] Litotes, in its strict sense, consists in intending the opposite of what is negated: e.g., saying "not small" for the meaning 'large'. It is closely associated with irony, but "in litotes, irony is not total but only by degrees" (Lausberg 1998: §§ 586–588). I demonstrated elsewhere that litotes, in fact, has three types: ironic, euphemistic, and emphatic (Nemesi 2009: 69, 125, 131).

along which hyperbole and understatement occupy the opposite region. In case of each over- and understatement it is supposed that the speaker could have used a more adequate linguistic expression referring to the real state of affairs, but for some reason or goal, s/he wanted to express something more (his/her expectation, impression, attitude, mood etc.). The hearer has an interpretive scheme for reconstructing the truth: s/he can apply the semantic scales, and s/he is also able to infer what other thoughts were implicated. Let us visualize in Figure 1 the scales discussed (cf. Fogelin 1988: 14):

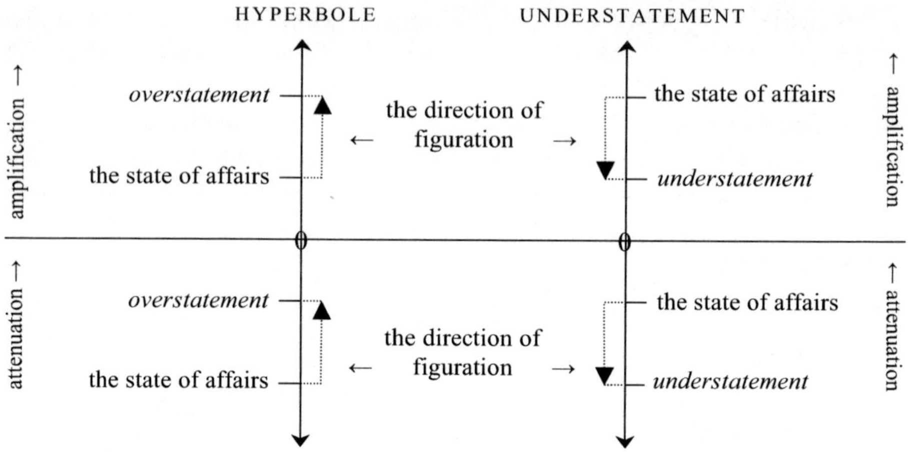

Figure 1. Hyperbole and understatement on the scale of amplification and attenuation

A further problem is raised by the fact that hyperboles, taken literally, are not always false statements but strongly subjective acts (e.g., *Your performance was frenetic* – for there is no objective scale in this respect, other judges could have different opinion of that). Given that overstatement is a powerful tool for subjective evaluation, Cano Mora (2006: 106–107, 118–123; 2009) argues that this aspect, mostly latent in classical definitions, has to be treated explicitly by revealing the semantic fields within not only the quantitative (maximizing-minimizing) but the evaluative (exalting-condemning) sphere, even if, in practice, quantification and evaluation tend to co-occur. Moreover, as far as co-occurrence in nonliteral language is concerned, the compound nature of hyperbole, well-known since antiquity, may cause additional difficulties. As Kreuz et al. (1996: 92) observed, exaggeration can interact with every trope except its logical opposite, understatement:

(2) a. *Sally is a nightmare to work with.* (hyperbole and metaphor)
b. *You came like a hurricane.* (hyperbole and simile)
c. *The whole Wall Street was in a panic.* (hyperbole and metonymy)
d. *His eyes nearly popped out of his head.* (hyperbole and idiom)
e. *Very, very funny...* (A reply to a poor joke.) (hyperbole and irony)
e. **She felt the speech was a little bit unforgettable.* (hyperbole and understatement)

Perhaps it is for their recurrence in figurative combinations that hyperboles, when examined, it has often been in relation to other tropes, most frequently to metaphor and irony, the so-called "master" tropes, or even equated to them. However, equating overstatement with metaphor or irony only serves to blur important distinctions between these tropes. In his influential handbook, Lausberg, (1998: §§ 579) for instance, claims that hyperbole "is a metaphor with vertical gradations" (in contrast with "horizontal", that is, *par excellence* metaphors), whereas Gibbs (2000: 12) regards it together with sarcasm, understatement, jocularity, and rhetorical questions as forms of verbal irony. Needless to say, such characterizations confuse the underlying conceptual differences within the realm of figures of speech, so we have to reject them.

By means of a thorough revision of the literature on the subject, Cano Mora attempts to provide an adequate formulation of exaggeration, one that enables us to clearly differentiate it from other related figures. It is summarized as follows: "hyperbole is a figure whereby the quantity or quality of an objective fact is, whether purposely or inadvertently, subjectively inflated or deflated in varying degrees but always to excess in an utterance which listeners do not normally interpret literally or perceive as a lie" (Cano Mora 2006: 108). Now let me draw the most important lessons from the above discussion and redraft a bit Cano Mora's definition: *hyperbole is a figure which disproportionately augments or reduces some element of the real state of affairs or a possible world, keeping the expression to the extreme, upper and lower end along the relevant semantic (either quantitative or evaluative) scale of amplification or attenuation, respectively.* In this vein, understatement is the logical opposite of hyperbole; a figure which moderately reduces or augments some element of the real state of affairs or a possible world, keeping away the expression from the extreme, upper and lower end along the relevant semantic scale of amplification or attenuation. While understatements invoke a mutually recognized corrective judgment toward the extreme, hyperboles work the other way round: they invite a weakening correction (Fogelin 1988: 13). Note that the evaluation of "disproportionateness" is just as subjective as deciding whether an utterance at hand is hyperbolic or literal (cf. Kreuz et al. 1996: 93–94).

1.2. Aims and the organization of the paper

This paper draws the reader's attention to the essential role of hyperbole in everyday communication. Although the use of the term, as seen above, has a long tradition from ancient rhetoric, and the pervasive frequency of hyperbole is, at least in contemporary American short stories, well documented (Kreuz et al. 1996), very little interest has been devoted to its pragmatic nature. The most extensive account of the phenomena is Cano Mora's (2006) corpus-based PhD dissertation, co-supervised by Michael McCarthy, the first author of the first systematic approach to hyperbole in interaction (McCarthy and Carter 2004). The present contribution aims to evaluate critically the developments of previous research on hyperbole production and reception with special regard to data collection and interpretation, and to offer some new insights from my own analyses of spoken Hungarian (Nemesi 2004, 2009).

Section 2 addresses the issue of semantics–pragmatics interface distinguishing between the production and comprehension process. Particular stress will be laid on terminology (literal/conventional/salient meaning). Research efforts and debates have almost exclusively concentrated on comprehension. In essence, two general ideas have been elaborated in pragmatics about understanding hyperbolic expressions. One of them is Grice's (1975) theory. Under his view, the receiver, instead of the conventional meaning, starts searching for an implicature (or, more precisely, implicatum) suitable for the context, realizing that the speaker has flouted the first maxim of Quality. The other, opposing approach is Sperber and Wilson's (1986/1995) relevance theory. In their model, exaggeration, similarly to metaphor, is a case of "loose talk": the propositional form of the statement is divergent from the form of the thought that we want to express, but the two share logical and contextual implications. Since the speaker does not find a literary paraphrase for expressing all that can be meant by a hyperbole, thus, according to relevance theory, s/he incorporates a greater contextual effect into the words in order to make it worthy for the reader to infer the intended meaning from it. I will argue in favor of Grice's account showing, however, that it needs a few refinements.

Section 3 focuses on the different data sources, comparing them on the basis of several considerations. As far as the discourse goals that hyperboles fulfill are concerned, I demonstrate that in daily conversations three main functions of exaggeration can be described according to the data: (1) expression of an attitude, (2) persuasion, and (3) self-presentation. The expression of an attitude is inseparable from hyperboles. To reveal the attitudes and the functions of persuasion and self-presentation one must know the context and the motives of the speaker thoroughly. It is suggested that feature films, for instance, are good sources for this line of research. I will illustrate the two basic strategies (the defensive and the assertive) of hyperbolic self-presentation.

Section 4 summarizes the results and yields some future directions for hyperbole research.

2. Hyperbole at the semantics–pragmatics interface

To answer the question of what aspects of figurative language (exemplified here by hyperbole) are semantically specified and which aspects come about through pragmatic processes, first it is necessary to separate the issue of production and interpretation. Then we need to adopt a tenable view on the correct division of labor between semantics and pragmatics in the explanation of the two issues. As was mentioned before, the bulk of research has extensively focused on figurative language comprehension at the expense of production. However, the production issue is at least as important as the comprehension issue, "since it may account for the existence of nonliteral forms by addressing the question of why speakers or writers should chose to express their thoughts indirectly, in a nonliteral way, when they can do it literally" (Cano Mora 2006: 190; see also Kreuz and Roberts 1993: 164). Let us start with the long neglected production processes (2.1.) and go on to the problem of interpretation (2.2.).

2.1. Production

If pragmatics is understood as the study of language use, and language use consists of the continuous making of linguistic choices (a) both in producing and interpreting utterances, (b) at every possible level of linguistic structure, (c) with various degrees of consciousness, (d) in such a way that choices evoke their non-selected alternatives (Verschueren 1999: 55–69), then the following pragmatic questions seem to emerge with regard to hyperbole production:

(1) Why do people choose exaggerations instead of their non-selected alternatives?
(2) With what degree of consciousness do they use hyperboles?
(3) How frequently is hyperbole employed in discourse compared with other forms of figurative language?
(4) How often and with which tropes do exaggerations tend to co-occur?
(5) In which text forms and genres does hyperbole predominate? Are there individual differences in preferring overstatements?

From a semantic perspective, by contrast, we have to be interested in the lexico-grammatical repertoire of exaggeration in order to classify its linguistic devices and, by doing so, to devise and analyze the quantitative and evaluative scales as cornerstones of a steady account for the notion. The most complete semantic taxonomy of hyperbolic items[3], concerning English language, is worked out by Cano Mora (2006: 108–131, 2009) according to four parameters, namely semantic field, grammatical category, interactivity with other figures of speech, and extreme of the continuum. She revealed that by far the tendency is to upscale rather than to downscale reality. Hyperbole can be realized in any word class or lexico-grammatical configuration (Norrick 1982: 170) such as in adjectives, adverbs, nouns, verbs, numerical expressions, quantifiers (*everything*, *nobody*), superlative degree, polysyndeton[4], whole clauses, etc. Cano Mora emphasizes the dual nature of exaggeration: it falls into a quantitative and evaluative realm, and these realms also fall into two categories depending on the extreme of the scale the hyperbolic item points to: overstated amplification and diminution, and overstated praise or criticism for the quantitative and evaluative dimension, respectively. The main semantic subfields of the quantitative realm are purity (completeness, absoluteness, universality, non-existence,

---

[3] "By hyperbolic item I mean the minimal unit of sense or meaning, whether a word, phrase or expression, which per se, given the appropriate context, conveys an idea of excess or extremity. In turn, different hyperbolic items may co-occur within a single utterance and form hyperbolic clusters (e.g. *lots of* people have got *nothing* to do; *everybody*'s *asleep* in *a minute*, etc.)" (Cano Mora 2006: 113, 2009: 28).

[4] Polysyndeton is defined in rhetoric as the use of several conjunctions in close succession, typically involving repetition of the same conjunction to connect a number of co-ordinated words, phrases, or clauses (e.g., *It costs millions and millions and billions of pounds to do this*; see McCarthy and Carter 2004: 163, 167).

etc.), number, quantity, measure (numerical expressions, quantity words), and magnitude (greatness, smallness). The evaluative realm includes positive evaluation (perfection, magnificence, splendor, beauty), impact, singularity, and negative evaluation (shrillness, pungency, frightfulness, violence, sorrow, etc.). As for Hungarian, Fónagy (1975) and Nemesi (2009: 155–162), without claiming comprehensiveness, offer an overview on the wide range of hyperbolic linguistic forms.

Turning to the pragmatics of exaggeration, the first question is: Why should speakers or writers elect to express their thoughts hyperbolically? The answer may be that the use of this kind of figurative language allows a person to accomplish particular discourse goals, perhaps multiple discourse goals simultaneously. Classical rhetoric considers all subtle functions of tropes subordinate to its true object: persuasion and ornamentation. Some argumentative (intimately related to political speeches) and aesthetic approaches to the usage of hyperbole are discussed in Cano Mora (2006: 21–25). What is worth knowing about the literary application of this figure is summarized briefly in Fónagy (1975: 482–484). First, as he writes, hyperbole is one of the characteristics of excited mental state: it can reflect anxiety or strong emotion resulting from losing self-control.[5] Second, similarly to such an excitement, the long-lasting thrill of love (which deserves separate mention) makes the speaker distort the perspective of reality. Third, the consistently used hyperbole renders speech dramatic, solemn, and thus idealizing, making the style too lofty for everyday use. Fourth, the overuse of dramatic hyperbole and the contrast of a petty topic with a solemn form can turn the emphatic effect backwards (see the genre of comic epic). Fifth, the desire to faithfully present the original event and to be expressive can stimulate the speaker to augment the intensity of words. Sixth, rhetorical hyperbole serves, as mentioned in general above, to fulfill the goal of persuading the audience: the orator, on the one hand, can impede the potential objections by exaggerating the phenomena, and, on the other, hyperbolic polite forms help to get positive feedback by dispraising the speaker and praising the hearer. Seventh, the demonstrative overstatement of politeness and homage verges upon irony: it can express sarcasm, antipathy, or scorn just like dramatic style. Finally, as a feature of style, hyperbole can characterize dramatic persons. For instance, Molière wittily parodies the female speech of the 17th century, especially the language of French

[5] Social psychologist Leary (1993: 140) mentions that people sometimes exaggerate their emotional expressions simply to assure that others accurately decipher what they are feeling.

salons in his *Learned Ladies* with giddy hyperboles spoken by his characters (*Pleasure will kill me*, *You can feel a thousand sweet thrills while listening*, etc.). Finally, Fónagy (1975: 484, 2001: 219) does not fail to note that some performances of hyperbole are genre-specific: it is a compulsory stylistic means of naive epic and folk-tale among literary genres, and it is also common in popular speech. Other examples from contemporary media culture can be easily added to the list (e.g., the language of advertisements, sports broadcasts, or talk shows). On the basis of her corpus, Cano Mora (2006: 250–286) identifies six different spoken genres in which exaggerations appear: decision making, debate-argument, language-in-action, comment-elaboration, service and learning encounters, plus the narrative and identifying sections embedded within some of these genres. She concludes that two genres attract mostly hyperboles: the so-called language-in-action and comment-elaboration interaction (the former encompasses cooking, packing, moving furniture, and so on, where the language is generated directly by the actions being carried out, while the latter occurs when people give casual opinions and make comments on things, other people, events, etc.), and overstatements rather respond to argumentative or explanatory purposes, not to aesthetic ones. Her list of hyperbolic functions, otherwise, contains the following: emphasis, evaluation, expression of surprise, simplification, interest intensification, contrast of differences, humor, clarification, and polite de-emphasis (Cano Mora 2006: 199–222).

Leech (1983: 135, 145–147), who adds politeness maxims and further principles to Grice's model, pondering over the role of hyperbole in "interpersonal rhetoric", remarks, on the one hand, the function of enhancing politeness (e.g., *What a marvelous meal you cooked!* – attributed to his Approbation maxim, favored in praising others), and, on the other hand, he introduces the Interest Principle ("Say what is unpredictable, and hence interesting"), assuming that idiomatic hyperboles that occur frequently in ordinary conversation and the preference of extremities on a scale of news value should be derived from it. Brown and Levinson's (1978: 222–225, 1987: 217–220) politeness theory focuses on the face-saving activity of the participants who engage in conversations, thus, under this view, a hyperbolic utterance can be an excuse offered as an explanation for being late (*There were a million people in the Co-op tonight!*), or could function as an apology or decline of responsibility for not getting in touch, indicating that the speaker tried hard not to hurt the partner (*I tried to call a hundred times, but there was never any answer*). According to Brown and Levinson, as we see, overstatement is a strategy of politeness which tends to manifest itself when the risk of losing face is relatively high; that is, what is to be said is opposed to the public self-image of the partners and their expectations originating from their face-wants, therefore it is worth leaving an 'out' (a defensible interpretation) for mitigating the offence. But, in their quite complex network of politeness strategies there is a branch which ends in the exaggerative presentation of interest, approval, or sympathy, fulfilling the partner's desire that his/her favored thoughts, acts, possessions should be admitted by the others (*What a fantastic garden you have!*; Brown and Levinson 1978: 109–111, 1987: 104–106; cf. Leech's above example). No doubt, hyperbole is such a flexible figure of speech that it is not easy to give a clear-cut account for its functions even within the umbrella of politeness.

Psycholinguistic research has also been conducted to examine the discourse goals or goal taxonomies that underlie the usage of figuration. Roberts and Kreuz (1994) asked American college students to provide reasons why they would employ a particular figure of speech on the basis of a definition and 10 examples. Based on the 134 acceptable responses, the hypothetical goals were classified according to 19 categories, out of which hyperbole was mapped mainly to "clarifying", "emphasizing", "being humorous", and "adding interest" (of course, other figures of speech were associated with other constellations of communicative goals). The most frequently mentioned goal "to clarify" is somewhat surprising given the "reduced truth value" of hyperbole (see in section 1). Unfortunately, Roberts and Kreuz do not provide us with the list of their examples, so we are left to rely on the comments of Kreuz et al. (1998: 94): the feelings or attitudes of the speaker and his/her relation to the communicated information may be clarified by using exaggeration. The utterance in (3), for example, informs us about a certain event (the national team lost a match), but the speaker's emotional reaction to the event (disgust or disillusionment) is also made clear enough, owing to the hyperbole:

(3) *I've just watched the Hungarian football team lose for the thousandth time!*

Hyperbolic speech may have, of course, other functions in specific contexts. Sell et al. (1997) videotaped conversations between preschool children and their parents in free-play situations. They found that the parents used dozens of hyperboles (more than metaphors but less than rhetorical questions or idioms). As it was expected, adults tended to use this linguistic means to encourage children in their play activities (e.g., *We can fix anything, can't we?*) and to express positive evaluation (*Wow, that was perfect!*, *The tallest bunny I've ever seen*, etc.).

My own analyses of Hungarian feature film conversations and some other speech genres (Nemesi 2004: 359–374, 2009: 141–149, 168–173), trying to reduce the proliferating functions in such a way that the resulting goals would be able to encompass what were eliminated, demonstrate that hyperbolic utterances inherently convey attitudes, either real or only presented, towards the topic of conversation. Further, according to the social psychological principles of public behavior, the expression of an attitude is often subordinated to the speaker's attempt to construct an intended impression on his/her conversational partners. And, finally, the third main goal of the use of hyperboles is to win acceptance for the speaker's attitude, that is, to persuade the hearer of the attitude suggested.

Kreuz et al. (1996) assessed the relative frequency of eight forms of nonliteral language (metaphor, simile, irony, idiom, hyperbole, litotes, rhetorical question, and indirect request) in a randomly selected, 96-page corpus of contemporary American short stories, containing about 38,000 words. They found that hyperbole (accounted for 27% of the forms of figurative language in the corpus) was a close second after the first ranked metaphor (29%), highly surpassing the rate of its logical opposite, litotes (3%), for example. Although this result is obviously genre-specific, my Hungarian data show that if we were to establish a genre-independent frequency hierarchy, it would look like as follows: metaphor (including simile, allegory, metaphoric idioms, etc.) > hyperbole > irony > metonymy (including synecdoche) > litotes > tautology > oxymora, and the majority of hyperboles are not creative but conventional expressions (Nemesi 2009: 112–121). Cano Mora (2006, 2009) has identified 343 "apparently hyperbolic item" in her sample sub-corpus (18 conversations, around 52.000 words) extracted from the British National Corpus, but this number was not compared to the frequency of metaphor, irony, litotes, etc. She indicates that exaggeration mostly occurs simple: co-occurrence of hyperbole with other figurative language forms only stands for 22.4% of the whole overstated items in her data (2006: 126–129). Metaphor is by far the trope with which hyperbole most regularly interacts, but hyperbolic idioms, similes, ironies, metonymies also exist (Kreuz et al. 1996: 92–93; Nemesi 2009: 126–129).

Individual differences in preferring one or more figures of speech are often mentioned, though never attested. Cano Mora (2006: 286) claims that "exaggeration is not a matter of personal style only. Contextual factors such as purpose, language functions or participant relations and roles determine hyperbole frequency and use". Examining the nonliteral language use of three well-known Hungarian football commentators, I pointed out that they differed in employing litotes, but the occurrences of hyperbole and metaphor were very similar altogether (Nemesi 2009: 121–126). Another understudied problem is the degree of consciousness in figurative language application. Social psychologists separate at least four levels of self-monitoring (impression oblivion, preattentive impression scanning, impression awareness, and impression focus; see Leary 1995: 47–51). Yet, it is difficult to judge the speaker's psychological state from outside. Pragmatics seeks and examines, instead, the indicators of metapragmatic awareness. As Vershueren (1999: 188) puts it, there is no language use without a constant calibration between pragmatic and metapragmatic functioning. McCarthy and Carter (2004: 174) touch upon the reflexive marking of hyperbole, as their example illustrates through the use of the lemma *overstate*, reciprocated by the listener:

(4) [Speaker 1 is extolling the delights of eating Stilton cheese to accompany port wine]

Speaker 1: Are you not a port man?
Speaker 2: Not really. But I don't really drink the stuff.
Speaker 1: Well that's what I meant by being a port man.
Speaker 2: Mm.
Speaker 1: Well have you ever tried it with stilton and digestive biscuits? Well then you haven't lived. *Well no that's a little bit an overstatement* but it's good.
Speaker 2: *Overstatements are good. I don't mind overstatements.*

2.2. Interpretation

Figurative language is of interest not only to pragmaticists but psycholinguists as well because its existence poses considerable difficulties for simple models of language comprehension. The phenomenon raises a fundamental question which has been in the limelight of pragmatic and psycholinguistic research since the 70s, namely: How to distinguish the semantic layer(s) of meaning from the pragmatic content, or, in other words, how to conceive the stratification and relationship of literal and nonliteral meanings? According to the widely accepted "standard view", pragmatic meaning entails semantic meaning; the former is dependent upon the context of the utterance, whereas the latter is predictable on the grounds of lexical meaning, sentential context, and the syntactic structure of the utterance (see, e.g., Kiefer 2004: 325–326). Searlian (1979) speech act theory and Grice's (1975) perspective on cooperative communication and conversational implicatures represent the standard way of pragmatic thinking. It takes literal (or conventional) meaning as the basis from which the intended figurative meaning can be deduced. In the past three decades the number of scholars who became skeptical about this idea has increased as several experiments conducted in psycholinguistics suggested that the mental processing of indirect speech acts, idioms, metaphors, and other types of figurative language does not take more time than understanding literal usage. Moreover, the literal meaning of the tropes and figures was recurrently not activated at all, only the figurative meanings were recalled. These findings challenge the psychological reality of the standard model (cf. Gibbs 1984, 1993, 1994, 2002; Dascal 1987; Giora 1997, 2003).

In my recent book I reviewed in detail the standard model and its rivals (the direct access approach advocated by Gibbs, Giora's graded salience hypothesis, and relevance theory), trying to outline a plausible compromise as a conclusion from the vigorous debate (Nemesi 2009: 43–109). Written the book in Hungarian, I recapitulate below my position on the semantics–pragmatics interface in figurative language understanding as briefly as possible.

The process of interpretation should be divided into two parts: (1) recognition (or triggering) and (2) the identification of the proper figurative meaning. The discovery of the principle(s) of triggering is the task of pragmatics in the first place with the few exceptions of those instances when there is an explicit linguistic marker (e.g., the conjunction *like* in case of similes or, as for hyperbole, extreme case formulations and the excessive in Hungarian[6] and in other languages). The rock-bottom of the offered explanation is the principle of the conventional use of language, which is analogous with Bach and Harnish's (1979: 12, 61) "presumption of literalness":

(5) *Presumption of literalness:*
the mutual belief in the linguistic community C_L that whenever any member *S* utters any *u* in *L* to any other member *H*, if *S* could (under the circumstances) be speaking literally, then *S* is speaking literally.

The presumption of literalness, however, is a too strict expectation due to its conceptual inaccuracy. From Searle's theory via Grice's model to Giora's hypothesis, we can observe a terminological development of the two-stage pragmatic model of figurative language interpretation (literal meaning →

[6] Let me cite two examples of the excessive from Kiefer's (2004: 328) article: "Mondhat bárki bármit, a szerelem a világon a *legesleg*jobb dolog" ('No matter what anybody says, love is absolutely the best thing in the world'); „A *legesleg*nagyobb öröm félelem nélkül élni" ('To live without fear is absolutely the greatest pleasure').

conventional meaning → the most salient meaning). As Dascal (1987: 259) looks back, the notion of literal meaning was once so unproblematic that it presumed to belong to the clearest and simplest linguistic concepts. But towards the second half of the 20th century it has come under attack in successive waves: first by philosophers, then by linguist and, more recently, by psychologists. The psychological argument purports to provide empirical evidence (mainly from reading-time and phrase classification studies) to the effect that given sufficient context people understand nonliteral meanings without analyzing before the complete literal meaning of an expression. However, several experimental findings demonstrate that listeners still process the literal meanings of figurative utterances. Gibbs (2002), critically evaluating these lines of research, continues to defend his direct access view. He argues that the direct access approach only claims that we *need not automatically* analyze the *complete* literal meanings of utterances before accessing pragmatic knowledge to figure out what speakers mean to communicate. But, putting in this way, the direct access view is quite a weak hypothesis, for it says nothing about under which circumstances people do analyze literal meanings first, and in which cases they do not. Gibbs admits that listeners may access something about what the individual words literally mean during processing of what speakers imply, and it may take longer to process a figurative meaning (e.g., a novel metaphor) than to understand a literal one. This is, he holds, "because of the difficulty in integrating the figurative meaning with the context and not because listeners are first analyzing and then rejecting the expression's literal meaning" (Gibbs 2002: 460). Nonetheless, I suspect that Gibbs commits here the error of *circulus vitiosus*: if the interpretation of figurative meanings is determined by the right context in advance, how could be difficult to integrate the *figurative* meaning with the context? Instead, I would say that figurative language understanding may take longer because of the difficulty of integrating the *conventional* meaning with the context.

As is seen, I prefer the term *conventional* to *literal* meaning, for the former is (more) dynamic in nature: the figurative meaning of an expression may become conventionalized; so, under my view, in the process of interpretation conventional meanings have priority over non-conventional (figurative or even literal) meanings.[7] Conventional meaning is analyzed

---

7 Recall that Grice (1975), too, prefers the notion of *conventional meaning*, whereas Searle (1979) adheres to literal meaning. See also Dascal's (1987) "moderate literalism" which, arguing against Gibbs's direct access approach, tries to incorporate the feature of conventionality into the concept of literal meaning.

first, and, when recognized that it is contextually inappropriate, listeners infer some implicated meaning consistent with the context. This is why I proposed "the principle of the conventional use of language" as a starting-point to account for the processing of figurative language (Nemesi 2009: 101–102), instead of the presumption of literalness formulated by Bach and Harnish (1979):

(6) *The principle of the conventional use of language:*
the general tendency of communication and the mutual belief in the linguistic community C_L that whenever any member *S* utters any *u* in *L* to any other member *H*, if *S* could (under the circumstances) be speaking conventionally, then *S* is speaking conventionally.

Note that I use the terms *conventional meaning* and *the most salient meaning* (introduced by Giora 1997, 2003) interchangeably, since Giora's four factors of the most salient meaning (frequency, familiarity, conventionality, and prototypicality/stereotypicality) can be reduced to one of them: to conventionality (which meaning is frequent, familiar, and prototypical is at the same time conventional). According to this terminology, the fact that a meaning is stored in the mental lexicon does not guarantee that it is the conventional – I mean, the most salient – meaning of the lexical unit. Stored information is superior to unstored information such as novel figures of speech inferable from the context. Besides, conventional (salient) information is highly accessible, while stored but non-conventional (non-salient) information requires contextual support to become as accessible as conventional (salient) information. When more than one meaning is conventional (e.g., both the figurative and the literal meaning of a word are equally salient), parallel processing is induced. Conventionality (salience), however, is not an either-or notion; rather, it admits degrees (Giora 1997: 183, 2003: 15).

The principle of the conventional use of language, from the speaker's point of view, is a fundamental bias; a natural tendency (norm) of expression in linguistic behavior, which is automatically followed by in the lack of special (e.g., emotional) motivation or perlocutionary goal, whereas, from the point of view of the listener, the presumption of the speaker's above bias in conversation. The default case is the form of language use that chimes in with the principle of the conventional use of language: this has the least production expense and risk of comprehension failure (albeit it is not sure, of course, that it has the greatest cognitive effect). The generation of non-conventional meanings is, in contrast, the marked case, which urges the listener to start the active inferential process.

A set of heuristics in reasoning helps the recognition of the divergence from the principle of the conventional use of language, including figurative language detection as well. In fact, this is the right status of Grice's "maxims", when we look at them from the aspect of understanding (cf. Levinson 2000: 27–42). After changing Grice's formulations only as much as required, we should concern the following heuristics: (1) Quantity heuristic: Is the conventional meaning of the utterance informative enough?; (2) Quality heuristic: Does conventional meaning of the utterance refer truly and adequately to the real state of affairs?; (3) Relation heuristic: Is the conventional meaning of the utterance relevant to the context?; (4) Manner heuristic: Is not the utterance obscure, ambiguous, or prolix in its conventional meaning? The Quantity heuristic triggers the figure of tautology, the Quality heuristic triggers metaphor, metonymy, hyperbole, litotes, and irony, whereas the Manner heuristic triggers oxymora (but it can collaborate secondarily in the recognition of metaphor, metonymy, irony, and litotes as well). The Relation heuristic is indispensable when the figurative utterance is true in its conventional meaning (e.g., *Anchorage is a cold city*; see Leezenberg 2001). Heuristics are not necessary and sufficient conditions; instead, they are cognitive aids to the machinery of understanding. The first, recognition phase is not built only on these heuristics. There are paralinguistic and nonverbal cues, such as the ironic tone of the speaker's voice, the corresponding punctuation mark (…) in written texts, the ostensive mimic, gesture. Furthermore, people have genre-specific (in connection with poetry, the ironic-bantering colloquial conversation, etc.) and person-specific expectations, too (e.g., we know that our colleague likes to exaggerate, to joke, or to use metaphors). Though these additional cues and expectations can all play a part in discovering the figurative meaning, the four heuristics mentioned above are the primary tools of triggering.

The conventional forms of figurative language are left out of the sketched framework, since their meaning is tapped in the mental lexicon, so they do not have to be noticed and interpreted again and again.[8] I suggest a distinction between the concept of *pragmatic* and *semantic figure*, to avoid the confusion caused by the restricted use of the term *figure*. Every general and productive meaning-transforming pattern or scheme based on the exploitation (using the word in accordance with Grice) of the principle of the

8 "Many metaphors and other figures of speech (including hyperboles) have become so conventionalised or even 'dead' that they may not be perceived as hyperbole in the sense of purposeful exaggeration in a specific context with a specific evaluative goal" (McCarthy and Carter 2004: 151).

conventional use of language is a pragmatic figure. Not only the meaning-transforming patterns, but, metonymically, their concrete linguistic realizations are said to be pragmatic figures as well – as long as their meanings transformed by the scheme are not conventionalized (lexicalized). Every systematic relation between the own conventional meanings of the polysemous lexical units which corresponds to the meaning-transforming scheme of a pragmatic figure is a semantic figure, and semantic figure is every linguistic expression that once was – according to the metonymic sense – a pragmatic figure, but its figurative meaning became conventionalized (lexicalized) in time. Thus, pragmatic figures are meaning-transforming schemes and linguistic expressions produced by those. They may change, through conventionalization (lexicalization), into semantic figures. Since conventionality is not a static, absolute category but a continuum, it is not always easy to draw the borderline between pragmatic and semantic figures.

But, as the lighting up of an indicator is not the process itself the start of which it indicates, the understanding of the pragmatic figures is also not only about the triggering phase. The second, more complex operation is the inferential recovery of the intended meaning – that is, the selection of the proper meaning-transforming pattern and its adaptation to the expression that violates the principle of the conventional use of language. This selection is guided by the heuristic that gives a clue to non-conventionality, but it will not solve the problem alone in every case (the Quality heuristic, for instance, can trigger several figures). If so, all the potential schemes are checked and the receiver prefers the one that makes the expression meaningful for the most part.

In general less can be said about this second phase of the interpretation as if concentrating to one particular figure. Nevertheless, the more exactly we are able to define a meaning-transforming scheme without referring to pragmatic considerations, the more semantic process of the identification of the figurative meaning will be. Concerning metaphor, the essence of the scheme is an analogy between the expression's conventional meaning (or, cognitively speaking, the concept coded by it) and its communicative context. However, almost anything can be compared to anything in some aspect. This aspect is exactly what the receiver has to discover, to which his/her pragmatic abilities are needed as well. The complex scheme of metonymy makes the transmission possible within one semantic field (or conceptual sphere). But, for example, how do we know the reason why British military surgeon and scientist Denis Burkitt (1911–1993) received the nickname "fiberman" from his colleagues and that it is a metaphor or a metonymy? Here also pragmatic inferences are needed. The case of irony would be easier if we had to think always to the opposite of the conventional meaning (for obvious counterexamples, see Wilson and Sperber 1992). Hyperbole and litotes, as showed in section 1, contrast the conventional meaning with the real state of affairs on some semantic scale, thus their schemes are relatively exact. Not so the schemes of oxymora and tautology, that were dealt with little by both semantics and pragmatics. Idiom should not be considered as an independent figure, since it is either metaphoric or metonymic; moreover, its meaning is highly conventional. Finally, rhetorical questions (often listed among the figures of speech) are, in fact, indirect speech acts: they do not transform the conventional meaning of the question but complete it with an indirect intention.

To be more precise about hyperbole, let me present in detail my (neo-) Gricean account for the steps followed by the hearer in understanding exaggerations (cf. Grice 1975: 49–50; Nemesi 2004: 364–367, 2009: 162–168):

(7) (i) The speaker has said that *p*;

(ii) according to the linguistic, metacognitive, and world knowledge of every competent language user, *p* is a hyperbolic utterance: the Quality heuristic indicates that the speaker flouted the principle of the conventional use of language;

(iii) there is no reason to suppose that the speaker is not observing the Gricean maxims, or at least the Cooperative Principle, thus s/he does not want to mislead but rather to exploit the Quality maxim;

(iv) hence, first, supposition *q* is needed, which is the adequate transformation of *p* on the relevant semantic scale of amplification or attenuation, concerning its relation to the real state of affairs (in a diachronic perspective, *q* may become lexicalized – but even so, the original semantic contrast between *p* and *q* more or less remains);

second, supposition *r* as a "weak" implicatum is needed for recovering the speaker's attitude (his/her emotion, evaluation) towards the topic of conversation on the basis of the hyperbole expressed (*r* can also be conventionalized, at least partly; however, the stylistic value of the expression holds the subjective overtones);

and third, insofar as the context and supposition *r* jointly support such an additive inference, supposition *s* as another weak implicatum is needed as well, which reveals the self-presentational role of *p* manifested through *r*;

(v) the speaker knows (and knows that the participants know that s/he knows) that it is within their competence to work out, or grasp intuitively, that *q* and *r* (and *s*) are required, surpassing the literal meaning of *p*;

(vi) the speaker has done nothing to stop his/her partners thinking *q* and *r* (and *s*);

(vii) that is, s/he intends the hearers to think, or is at least willing to allow them to think that *q* and *r* (and *s*); so s/he has implicated *q* and *r* (and *s*).

The idea of "weak" implicatures emerges in relevance theory; it is claimed that implicatures of an utterance may have different strength, and what was traditionally called "poetic effect" is, in fact, a cluster of weak implicatures (Sperber and Wilson 1990, 1995: 197–202, 217–224). As can be seen, two types of weak implicatums are distinguished in (7): an attitude-implicatum *r* and a self-implicatum *s*. By the notion weak implicatum I refer to those implicated meanings of the utterance whose cognitive representation is not a proposition but some sort of an analogue form, as reflected in everyday language by the word "impression". Examples of hyperbolic attitude- and self-implicatures will be shown in 3.1.

But further remarks are needed to make the above picture more complete. First, the Quality heuristic is not the only (however, it is undoubtedly the most common) trigger of exaggeration. McCarthy and Carter (2004: 172–174) call our attention to the fact that hyperboles are often introduced by "footing-shift markers" such as *almost*, *nearly*, and *literally* (e.g., *It was literally a prison cell, wasn't it* – talking about a student room that was prison-like). Footing-shift markers offer a new frame of interpretation, overruling literality (or, as I would say, the principle of the conventional use of language). The conversational frame offered in this way is a kind of joint pretense between the speaker and the listener, in order to create a new layer of joint activity (Clark 1996: 143). Second, I debate the view which relates hyperbole (and litotes) not to the category of Quality but Quantity, arguing that the two figures deform the real state of affairs quantitatively.[9] This

[9] "By saying less (that is, *providing less information*) than is required or by saying more than is required, S invites H to consider why" (my emphasis; Brown and Levinson 1978: 222, 1987: 217; cf. Leech 1983: 145; Gibbs 1993: 267, 1994: 392). Norrick (2004) states that extreme case formulations and non-extreme hyperbole are comprehended differently: while extreme case formulations violate the first maxim of Quality, non-extreme hyperboles violate "only the Quantity maxim". But it does not seem true to the facts; the authors quoted here seem to misunderstand the point of Grice's categories. Gibbs (1993: 267–268, 1994: 392–394),

suggests that instead of giving just as much information as required, more or less is said. I believe that Grice is right here: the exaggerated meaning is *qualitatively different* from its adequate correspondent; it is not more (or less) informative than is necessary but false or inaccurate information. Third, remember that conventional hyperboles such as *számtalan* ('countless'), *kőszívű* ('stony-hearted'), *hajmeresztő* ('hair-raising'), and the like in Hungarian are semantic figures, their figurative meaning has been coded in the mental lexicon. Conversational implicatures, by definition, are non-conventional (Grice 1975: 58; Levinson 2000: 15), thus only novel (creative, non-conventional, therefore pragmatic) overstatements are understood as described in (7).

Sperber and Wilson's (1990, 1995) relevance theory takes a different view, according to which human information processing aims at maximal relevance: the greatest cognitive effect for the smallest processing effort. It supposes that hyperbolic utterances "resemble" the speakers' beliefs in the sense of sharing some logical and contextual implications with what the speakers believe. Consider the example (8a–b) cited from Sperber and Wilson's (1995: 235) influential book:

(8) a. *Bill is the nicest person there is.*
b. *Bill is a very nice person.*

As commented on, (8a) strongly implicates (8b), but if this were all what the speaker had wanted to convey, s/he could have saved the hearer some processing effort by expressing (8b) directly. By saying (8a), the speaker encourages the hearer to look for a range of further contextual implications not shared by (8b); for instance, a suggestion that the speaker has a positive attitude to Bill (if the utterance is not ironic, of course), a certain vision of Bill and his niceness, perhaps an incentive to the hearer to agree with him/her to some extent about Bill's niceness, etc. The wider the range of possible implications, the weaker the implicatures, and the more the hearer must share the responsibility for deriving them. In this way, (8a) is consis-

---

suggesting that irony, hyperbole, and understatement do not necessarily violate the "Truthfulness maxims", attempts to weaken them in two ways: when making some statement, speakers (a) want to attribute a belief in the proposition they express not always to themselves but to someone or some cultural norm, and (b) speakers' statement need not be identical to their own beliefs but need only resemble their beliefs (cf. relevance theory). It is simply not in line with the Gricean flouting account, and I cannot see any particular reason to pursue this track of weakening the maxims; they are powerful heuristics in understanding.

tent with the principle of relevance: it conveys more contextual effects at the expense of more processing work.

Sperber and Wilson claim that there is a continuity between the phenomenon of "loose talk" (e.g., saying that *I earn £800 a month*, instead of *I earn 797.32 pence a month*) and the phenomenon of figurative language, since in both cases, (1) the propositional form of the utterance differs from that of the thought interpreted; (2) the hearer can proceed on the assumption that these two propositional forms have some identifiable logical and contextual implications in common; and (3) the same interpretive abilities and procedures are involved. Apart from the objections that Sperber and Wilson not satisfactorily define some of their central notions like context and "processing effort", and the crucial concepts of relevance and context seem to be defined in terms of each other, and thus face the threat of circularity (Leezenberg 2001: 113), the alleged continuity between loose talk and figurative language is questionable: loose talk can be explained by a *clash* of the second maxim of Quantity and the first maxim of both Quantity and Quality, whereas (non-conventional) hyperbole, litotes, metaphor, metonymy, and irony *flout* the first Quality maxim (see Grice 1975: 49). Thus, the understanding of the two phenomena hardly involves exactly the same interpretive procedures. And, although relevance theory denies the distinction between literal and figurative language, it introduces, as was mentioned, a parallel distinction between full and partial resemblance between the utterances and the speakers' thoughts in order to deal with loose talk and figurative language. But, while no one knows what thoughts in the speaker's head are, the Gricean apparatus is able to yield concrete empirical predictions. Let me repeat that we should make a difference between conventional and non-conventional (not between literal and nonliteral) meanings as far as the process of interpretation is concerned. This is what relevance theory fails to notice.

3. Data-gathering methods and their consequences

No matter what aspects of hyperbolic language one intends to study, data need to be gathered, which may happen by several techniques. In his methodological foundation for metaphor identification in grammar and usage, Steen (2007: 103–129) provides a threefold division of data: verbal, nonverbal, and meta. Verbal data are concrete manifestations of language or its use, nonverbal data cover pausing, gesture, reading times, eye movements, and brain activities collected from participants' behavior in different experimental conditions, whereas meta data are characterized as intuitions of language users (including linguists) about grammaticality, acceptability, conventionality, and discourse goals accomplished by, for instance, a figurative utterance, not displaying but reflecting upon linguistic performance, its means, cognitive processes, and products. Methods by which the three classes of data can be collected are grouped into introspection (observing the behavior of oneself), observation (observing the behavior of other people in natural situations), and manipulation (observing other people who are instructed to produce a particular language or thought behavior). Applying Steen's taxonomy (with a little correction: I will replace the term manipulation by experiment), let us first consider the collection of data pertaining to hyperbole production, with special attention to the data themselves, and then linguistic examples used in research on hyperbole understanding will be discussed.

3.1. Production

Kreuz and Roberts (1993) argued that researchers must look beyond the initial processing of tropes in decontextualized situations if we are to understand how figurative language operates in literary texts: the influence of factors like authorial intent, genre, and discourse goal satisfaction need to be involved in any comprehensive theory of discourse production. The article they published with two co-authors three years later (Kreuz et al. 1996) had been in preparation at that time, the purpose of which was, as I mentioned in 2.1., to estimate the frequency of occurrence of eight types of figures in American short stories, that is, in a written corpus. Two kinds of data can be recognized in this project: linguistic data taken from the volumes of two annual collections (*Best American Short Stories* and *O. Henry Awards*) said to be representative of current fiction, and meta data generated by the four researchers concerning the (co-)occurrence and identification of figurative segments. The corpus (linguistic data) meets the criteria of random sampling: 3–3 pages of stories were yielded by 32 different authors from 24 different sources for a total of 96 pages. However, a number of problems arose during the course of producing the meta data. Although the four authors aimed to fine-tune their figurative language taxonomy and coding criteria beforehand, they found it very easy to miss marking nonliteral elements, and the cases of perfect agreement for the labeling of a segment differed greatly from another count consisted of agreement on labeling by at least two of the three judges (each story was analyzed by three of the four researchers; see the description of the whole procedure in Kreuz et al. 1996: 88–90), suggesting a fairly big degree of subjectivity in identifying figurative expressions. But as good research should report its limitations which give the reader a chance to evaluate the quality of the measurements, Kreuz and his colleagues do not conceal their dilemmas. Beyond interanalyst disagreement and individual bias, sometimes it was hard, for example, to tell from the context what a character really meant by his/her utterance, so the judges had to make a rather arbitrary assumption about the state of the segment. The taxonomy of figurative language created by the authors is also questionable (metonymy and synecdoche categorized as a kind of metaphor, how to differentiate between dead metaphors and idioms, etc.). Despite these clear limitations, I conducted a very similar procedure, could not improving on it, but using a different taxonomy (metaphor, metonymy, irony, hyperbole, litotes, tautology, oximora) with my university students (Nemesi 2009: 115–121).

Aiming to derive empirically the specific discourse goals of the eight types of figurative language they favor, Roberts and Kreuz (1994) collect meta data from subjects (158 Memphis State University undergraduate students, cf. 2.1.), who were assigned randomly to one of eight conditions: hyperbole, idiom, indirect request, irony, understatement, metaphor, rhetorical question, and simile (19 to 21 subjects participated in each conditions). Students received a booklet containing instructions, a definition, and 10 examples of one particular figure (linguistic data), space to write 3 additional examples of that figure (elicited verbal data, ensuring that they had an adequate understanding of their figure), and a page on which to provide reasons why an individual might use that figure of speech. Subjects were encouraged to list as many reasons as possible. By examining the responses for all the figures, a discourse goal taxonomy was created. Two judges independently classified each response into a taxonomy. An acceptable level of interjudge agreement was set at 75%, averaged across all conditions. Once acceptable agreement was achieved, the two judges attempted to resolve any discrepancies that remained. Only 134 (84%) of the participants demonstrated sufficient understanding of their figure producing at least two acceptable examples of it (another kind of meta data at the intermediate phase of the procedure: the two researchers made decisions on the acceptability of the elicited data); only these subjects were included into the final data analyses. What we know about the linguistic data used in this study is that they "were drawn from a variety of published sources" (Roberts and Kreuz 1994: 163). But care has to be taken in interpreting what such data, without their context, can tell the subjects about the possible functions of a figure. Based on these decontextualized examples, what will guarantee that the taxonomy of discourse goals provided by the undergraduate students as meta data can give us an accurate description about the communicative functions that underlie the use of one or another figure of speech? People, I think, have no deep insight into the role of figurative language in usage; their responses, hence, may not be indicative of why the figures are employed in general.

Corpus linguistic approaches to hyperbole production (McCarthy and Carter 2004; Norrick 2004; Cano Mora 2006, 2009) highlight that a large corpus offers many different contexts and speech genres brought together under one body of data. Lexico-grammatical items and configurations commonly used and certain semantic fields regularly exploited for exaggeration are automatically retrievable. Corpora allow researchers to obtain great amounts of real (verbal, observed) data instead of having to rely on intuitions and invented examples. Another advantage of corpus-based studies is that, if hyperbole is viewed interactively, recurring items such as footing-shift markers, listeners' acceptance tokens and other verbal reactions can rapidly be collected. But quantitative and qualitative data gatherings and analyses should complement each other: overstatement as a figure of thought may have no linguistic marker at all (see, e.g., Fónagy's (2001: 219) example *The man who will make me gobble up mushrooms is not yet born* from the film *Buffet froid* by Bertrand Blier, 1979). McCarthy and Carter examine the occurrence of hyperbole in the 5-million-word Cambridge and Nottingham Corpus of Discourse in English, developed at the University of Nottingham, to "begin to build a framework for the description and understanding of hyperbole in interaction" (2004: 150). Conversations it contains were recorded in a wide variety of mostly informal settings across the islands of Britain and Ireland, and then transcribed and stored in computer-readable form. Norrick's (2004) data come from several sources, representing the speakers' social and regional diversity, but primarily from the Saarbrücken Corpus of Spoken English, an extensive collection of audio and video recordings of free conversations and interviews from the Midwestern United States and Britain. He also cites examples from two other generally available electronic corpora: the Santa Barbara Corpus of Spoken American English (interactions between undergraduates from the western United States) and the London-Lund Corpus (from British English speakers, many of them academics). Kiefer (2004: 328–332), who discusses the pragmatics of the excessive, resorts to the Hungarian National Text Corpus, but takes into consideration only a roughly ten-word context in each case. As I noted in 2.1., Cano Mora (2006, 2009) uses 18 conversations from the British National Corpus, a collection of over 4000 samples, both spoken and written, totaling over 1000 million words, of contemporary British English. Her appendix includes the entirety of the data examined:

all the exaggerations she have found can be scrutinized by the reader. To attach the whole corpus to a journal article or a book chapter is impossible, but as an appendix in an electronic document like Cano Mora's dissertation allows the reader to control how precisely data have been elected, identified, and analyzed.

As far as discourse goals fulfilled by hyperbole are concerned, I investigated some classic Hungarian feature films as an appropriate corpus for qualitative research (Nemesi 2004).[10] The reason why film conversations were selected was that the knowledge of their story and the transparency of the characters' intentions make the understanding of communicative functions easy. Besides, the situations in feature films, though fictitious, of course, are very similar to spontaneous everyday interactions. Let me show in (9) one excerpt from the comedy *Az én lányom nem olyan* ('My daughter is different', 1937) to illustrate my method of discourse analysis (Nemesi 2004: 371–373, 2009: 172–173).

The story of the film, in brief, is the following. Gitta Hubay is 20 years old, a girl with modern attitudes, who is courted by Feri Fekete. Not particularly liked by Gitta's parents, especially her old-fashioned father, Fekete dates Gitta in secret. When he calls her to his flat pretending to be ill, Gitta becomes disappointed in him and breaks with him. The highly respected aunt Annie, who wants to marry Gitta off, would like to introduce the girl to her husband's nephew, Sándor Kalocsay, not suspecting that they know each other through Feri, and they like each other, too. After aunt Annie tells Kalocsay who she would like to introduce to him, he goes to Gitta's house. He asks to leave the rich old lady in her belief that they would meet for the first time at the party. At this time, Kalocsay does not know whether Gitta really loves Feri, he tries, therefore, to find out about the girl's feelings by behaving in an arrogant and scornful way. Gitta's hyperbolic utterance in (9) is a reply to Kalocsay's egoistic, almost disrespectful manner: she does not know whether the handsome young man is joking or speaking seriously; however, she expresses the offendedness of a young lady in a symbolic way and refuses the impudence. Kalocsay's joke at the end of the conversation convinces her that he is teasing her because he actually wants to court her.

---

[10] Sorea (2009) studies the communicative mechanisms triggered by ironical and hyperbolic utterances as face-threatening acts (see Brown and Levinson 1978, 1987) in the dynamics of sitcom interactions ('*Married ... with Children*').

(9) Kalocsay: Ide figyeljen, én segíteni fogok magának. Maga viszont segítségemre lesz nekem. Rendben van?
'Look, I will help you. But you will also help me. All right?'

Gitta: Milyen ügyben?
'In what kind of case?'

Kalocsay: Annie tante ugyanis megígérte, hogy kifizeti az összes adósságaimat, ha szakítok a lump élettel, és megházasodom. (.4) Magát szemelte ki erre a célra…
'Aunt Annie promised that she will pay back all my debts if I break with reveler life and get married. (.4) She has chosen you for this purpose.'

Gitta: ((laughing)) S maga megígérte, hogy elvesz?
'And have you promised that you will marry me?'

Kalocsay: Meg. (.6) Neki. ((impudently)) Magának viszont ünnepélyesen megígérem az ellenkezőjét.
'I did. (.6) To her. To you, I solemnly promise the opposite.'

Gitta: ((offended)) Nagyon kedves…
'Very kind of you…'

Kalocsay: Én ugyanis megmagyaráztam Annie néninek, hogy a maga meghódításához nekem másfél évre van szükségem… Hát, őszintén szólva, ezt most már nem hiszem…
'You see, I explained to aunt Annie that I will need one and a half year to conquer you… But now, to tell you the truth, I don't think so…'

Gitta: Pedig nyugodtan elhiheti.
'But you can safely assume that.'

Kalocsay: ((courting)) Igazán? Gondolja, hogy ennyi idő alatt sikerülne?
'Really? Do you think I would succeed within this time?'

Gitta: Nem, nem sikerülne. *Magának ehhez ezer esztendő se lenne elég.*
'No, you wouldn't. You would not succeed *even within a thousand years*.'

Kalocsay: ((looks at his watch, joking)) Hát, annyi időm nincs…
'Well, I don't have that much time…'

According to the symbols introduced in (7), *p* (the conventional meaning of the hyperbolic utterance): Gitta says that Kalocsay would not conquer her even within a thousand years; *p* contains an extreme attribute of quantity, hence *q* (a strong implicatum, the adequate transformation of *p* on the relevant semantic scale of amplification or attenuation, concerning its relation to the real state of affairs): Kalocsay could not or would not conquer Gitta; *r* (an apparent weak attitude implicatum): she categorically refuses the idea of Kalocsay's courting; *s* (a weak self-implicatum): Gitta is a moral young lady, who is not so easy to conquer as Kalocsay thinks. The message of self-implicature *s* can be traced back to Gitta's self-concept, her positive and negative identity images, and the social expectations towards an ideal woman (Leary 1993, 1995; Leary and Kowalski 1990). Thus, the discourse goals of Gitta's hyperbole in (9) are (i) to express a negative attitude toward Kalocsay, (ii) to save her face from Kalocsay's symbolic attack, and (iii) to convince Kalocsay that she does not want to be courted by him.

In my (2009) book, the corpus of feature films was completed by both monologic (sports broadcastings, popular science lectures) and dialogic (formal/informal TV studio talks) genres. The verbal exchange quoted in (9) illustrates defensive self-presentation (see also Brown and Levinson's examples in 2.1.). Some kinds of assertive use of hyperbole can be observed in (10) below with different degrees of positive impression management:

(10) a. *What a fantastic garden you have!*
(Flattery from Brown and Levinson 1978: 109, 1987: 104)

b. *„A Világ Repülőgépei" sorozat nem hasonlítható össze egyetlen repüléssel foglalkozó könyvvel sem.*
'*The World's Airplanes* series is incomparable to any other books on aircrafts.'
(From a written advertisement; Árvay 2004: 251)

c. *Ilyen szép kislány nincs a világon, mint Carolina!*
'There is no such a nice little girl like Carolina all over the world!'
(Compliment from a popular song of Hungarian singer Pál Szécsi; Nemesi 2009: 8)

d. *Gól! Fölrobban a stadion nyugati része, mert 1:0 a Milan javára.*
'Goal! The western part of the stadium is blowing up because one-nil to Milan.'
(Interest intensification from a football commentator's speech; Nemesi 2009: 156)

3.2. Interpretation

There is a group of verbal data, as Steen (2007: 112) notes, that are neither elicited nor observed, but imagined. These verbal data are made up by researchers themselves, so might be related to introspection in a sense. The advantage of exploiting such imagined data is that less frequent language phenomena or even allegedly impossible expressions can be studied easily, which may be useful for particular theoretical purposes. Made-up data are widespread in the pragmatic analyses of hyperbole interpretation. However, exaggeration is not a rare phenomenon in usage, and collecting natural and elicited data has experienced recently a considerable status rise in the study of figurative language. I cite Grice's (1975: 53) own example in (11) to demonstrate imagined verbal data and the problem they pose:

(11) *Every nice girl loves a sailor.*

Since we do not know the context in which utterance (11) is or can be said, the implicatum is not obvious at all (it may not be by chance that Grice, unusually, failed to detail it). For instance, one might argue that *every* should be simply replaced by *many*, and the implicature is worked out. But let us conceive a realistic context: if the speaker is a sailor and the hearer is a nice girl, then (11) can also implicate that the girl should like the speaker, and this is the indirect message that seems to be the intended one.

Remember that Sperber and Wilson's (8a) example is imagined, too. Psycholinguist Gibbs (1984, 1993, 1994, 2000, 2002) also refers to made-up data in discussing figurative language (e.g., *All Americans can attain their dreams of success*; see in section 1). This kind of intuitive data generated by a native speaker may be illustrative and, hence, important to collect at a preparatory stage in processing research, to form hypotheses and calibrate the experimental materials as representing, for instance, groups of hyperboles with particular properties, after which the experimental material can then be used. But corpus-based experimental materials are much more reliable than those compiled from intuitive examples.

Cano Mora (2006: 48–60) offers a good survey of psycholinguistic research on hyperbole comprehension. As far as data are concerned, in the experiment of Winner et al. (1987), for instance, children viewed videotapes of characters interacting, each ending with an understatement, a sarcastic, or a hyperbolic remark. After each episode, children were asked questions about the truth, literalness, and intent of the final statement. Overall, children had more trouble understanding hyperbole and understatement than sarcasm; hyperbole, when misunderstood, was seen as either deception or error. (Of course, older children's interpretations were more accurate than were younger children's.) Researchers, thus, used in this experiment linguistic data observed by children to elicit meta data on the reception of hyperbole. Kreuz, Kassler, and Coppenrath (1998) raise that when speakers choose to express themselves in an exaggerated way, they have a great deal of latitude in specifying the form of their statement, and this factor makes hyperbole different from other types of figurative language:

(12) a. *To get the tickets, I had to wait in line for hours!*
b. *To get the tickets, I had to wait in line for days!*
c. *To get the tickets, I had to wait in line for weeks!*
d. *To get the tickets, I had to wait in line for months!*
e. *To get the tickets, I had to wait in line for years!*

The authors attempt to answer the following questions: Are there psychological consequences for specifying varying degrees of impossible quantities? Why might a speaker choose one level of exaggeration over another? How are such statements perceived by their hearers? Eight experiments were conducted with undergraduate students to quantify the relationship between exaggeration and listener judgments, and to determine the importance of physical possibility as a cue for nonliteral intent. Researchers wrote 20 experimental scenarios, all with the same form: 7 sentences that introduced two (or more) characters and a particular situation (e.g., moving a piano). The last sentence of each scenario contained a (potentially) hyperbolic remark uttered by one of the characters. The scenarios were given to the subjects recruited from the psychology department participant pool. They were asked to read each scenario and make ratings on scales with endpoints labeled, for example, "not at all exaggerated" and "very exaggerated", "not at all likely" and "very likely", and so on. Hyperbolic statements, contrary to the authors' hypotheses, were perceived as making less sense, as being less likely to be used, and as less appropriate then nonexaggerated statements. In addition, slight exaggerations were remembered better then highly exaggerated utterances. The results seem to be at odds with intuitive ideas about hyperbole, but provide some support for the idea that physical possibility is psychologically significant. Data of this research, in sum, can be characterized as follows: imagined verbal scenarios were observed by undergraduate students to provide completions (verbal data) or meta data on the invented verbal data (experiment). This methodological scheme is true of other psycholinguistic studies regarding the reception of hyperbole,

Table 1. A comparison of data-gathering techniques in research on hyperbole

studies	Type of data	Data-gathering method	Source of verbal data	Variety of realistic contexts	Transparency of discourse goals
Grice (1975); Sperber and Wilson (1995)	verbal	invention (introspection?) (observation?)	researcher's own linguistic competence	–	–
Winner et al. (1987) / Kreuz et al. (1998); Colston (1997), etc.	verbal + meta	experiment	videotaped interactions / written scenarios	?	?
Kreuz et al. (1996)	verbal	observation	random sample of literary texts	+	+
Roberts and Kreuz (1994)	verbal + meta	experiment	unknown (published sources)	–	–
Sell et al. (1997)	verbal	observation	videotaped parent-child conversations	–	+
McCarthy and Carter (2004); Norrick (2004); Cano Mora (2006)	verbal	observation	a large corpus / corpora of various spoken genres	+	+
Kiefer (2004)	verbal	observation	a large corpus of written texts	+	–
Nemesi (2004) / Sorea (2009)	verbal	observation	feature films / sitcoms	+ / –	+

too (see, e.g., Colston 1997; Colston and Keller 1998; Colston and O'Brien 2000; Stewart and Kreuz 2003).

Table 1 on page 411 summarizes the main differences of the most important studies in hyperbole production and interpretation concerning their data collection methods.

4. Conclusion and future directions

The interest in figurative language, although it has always been among the key issues of pragmatics, seems to have witnessed considerable growth in the last two decades. Both experimental psycholinguistic research and corpus linguistics continue to provide pragmatics with new empirical evidence and improving methodology. The bulk of research concentrates on metaphor and irony, but the present contribution has aimed to push hyperbole to the forefront, one of the most common but long neglected trope or figure of speech. In section 1, I have examined the definitional problems posed by the many faces of overstatement in language use and its relation to meiosis or understatement. I have concluded that hyperbole disproportionately augments or reduces some element of the real state of affairs, emphasizing the role of the semantic (quantitative and evaluative) scales along which reality is distorted by the exaggeration. In section 2, production and interpretation processes have been divided and extensively discussed, keeping the division of labor between semantics and pragmatics in view. As for hyperbole production, the in-depth analysis of its lexico-grammatical repertoire and the relevant quantitative/evaluative scales has been delegated to semantics, while I have outlined the job of pragmatics as involving the study of its occurrence, interaction with other forms of figurative language, discourse goals, reflexive markers, typical genres, and so on. I have defended the "conventional meaning first" approach in a Gricean (1975) spirit against Gibbs's (1984, 1993, 1994, 2002) direct access hypothesis and relevance theory, but I have borrowed the idea of weak implicatures from Sperber and Wilson (1990, 1995).

The validity of data depends on the aim of the research. Building upon Steen's (2007) categorization, I have estimated the data collection methods of several scholars who addressed the question of hyperbole production or reception. Though I prefer observable verbal data taken from spoken corpora, there is no reason, in my opinion, to question the usefulness of imagined and meta data for particular purposes. But it should be kept in mind that human beings are not good enough at describing certain aspects of their own language production and cognitive processes, and written scenarios prepared for eliciting verbal or meta data might be too artificial to evoke reliable answers from the subjects. Corpus-based studies have fine prospects within pragmatics not only in research on hyperbole production (individual, cross-cultural, cross-gender differences, overstatement-prone genres such as stand-up comedy, talk show, and everyday storytelling, metapragmatic awareness, etc.) but in research on its interpretation (children's understanding of hyperbole, style attribution and other perlocutionary effects, listeners' responses to overstatement, etc.) as well. I am sure that by the end of the next decade pragmaticists will have noted with satisfaction that "there's hundreds of them" (see the title of McCarthy and Carter 2004), and this will not sound as a high exaggeration.

Acknowledgement

This paper was supported by the János Bolyai Research Scholarship of the Hungarian Academy of Sciences.

References

Aristotle
1926 *The "Art" of Rhetoric.* Cambridge, MA / London: Harvard University Press / William Heinemann Ltd.

Árvay, Anett
2004 Pragmatic aspects of persuasion and manipulation in written advertisements. *Acta Linguistica Hungarica* 51: 231–263.

Bach, Kent and Robert M. Harnish
1979 *Linguistic Communication and Speech Acts.* Cambridge, MA: MIT Press.

Brown, Penelope and Stephen Levinson
1978 Universals in language usage: Politeness phenomena. In *Questions and Politeness: Strategies in Social Interaction*, Esther N. Goody (ed.), 56–289. Cambridge: Cambridge University Press.

Brown, Penelope and Stephen C. Levinson
1987 *Politeness: Some Universals in Language Usage.* Cambridge: Cambridge University Press.

Cano Mora, Laura
2006 *"How to Make a Mountain out of a Molehill": A Corpus-based Pragmatic and Conversational Analysis of Hyperbole in Interaction.* Universitat de Valencia: Servei de Publicacions. http://www.tdx.cesca.es/TESIS_UV/AVAILABLE/TDX-0521107-115306//cano.pdf

Cano Mora, Laura
2009 All or nothing: A semantic analysis of hyperbole. *Revista de Lingüística y Lenguas Aplicadas* 4: 25–35. http://www.upv.es/dla_revista/docs/art2009/02_Cano_Mora_L.pdf

Clark, Herbert
1996 *Psychology of Language.* Cambridge: Cambridge University Press.

Colston, Herbert L.
1997 "I've never seen anything like it": Overstatement, understatement, and irony. *Metaphor and Symbol* 12: 43–58.

Colston, Herbert L. and Shauna B. Keller
1998 You'll never believe this: Irony and hyperbole in expressing surprise. *Journal of Psycholinguistic Research* 27: 499–513.

Colston, Herbert L. and Jennifer O'Brien
2000 Contrast of kind versus contrast of magnitude: The pragmatic accomplishments of irony and hyperbole. *Discourse Processes* 30: 179–1999.

Dascal, Marcelo
1987 Defending literal meaning. *Cognitive Science* 11: 259–281.

Fogelin, Robert J.
1988 *Figuratively Speaking.* New Haven, CT: Yale University Press.

Fónagy, Iván
1975 Hiperbola [Hyperbole]. In *Világirodalmi lexikon*, Volume 8, István Király (ed.), 480–486. Budapest: Akadémiai Kiadó.

Fónagy, Iván
2001 *Languages within Language: An Evolutive Approach.* Amsterdam: John Benjamins.

Fontanier, Paul
1968 *Les Figures du Discours.* Paris: Flammarion.

Gibbs Jr., Raymond W.
1984 Literal meaning and psychological theory. *Cognitive Science* 8: 275–304.

Gibbs Jr., Raymond W.
1993 Process and products in making sense of tropes. In *Metaphor and Thought*, Andrew Ortony (ed.), 252–276. 2nd edition. Cambridge: Cambridge University Press.

Gibbs Jr., Raymond W.
1994 *The Poetics of Mind: Figurative Thought, Language, and Understanding.* Cambridge: Cambridge University Press.

Gibbs Jr., Raymond W.
2000 Irony in talk among friends. *Metaphor and Symbolic Activity* 15: 5–27.

Gibbs Jr., Raymond W.
2002 A new look at literal meaning in understanding what is said and implicated. *Journal of Pragmatics* 34: 457–486.

Giora, Rachel
1997 Understanding figurative and literal language: The graded salience hypothesis. *Cognitive Linguistics* 8: 183–206.
Giora, Rachel
2003 *On Our Mind: Salience, Context, and Figurative Language*. Oxford: Oxford University Press.
Grice, H. Paul
1975 Logic and conversation. In *Syntax and Semantics, Vol. 3: Speech Acts*, Peter Cole and Jerry L. Morgan (eds.), 41–58. New York: Academic Press.
Kiefer, Ferenc
2004 Morphopragmatic phenomena in Hungarian. *Acta Linguistica Hungarica* 51 (3–4): 325–349.
Kreuz, Roger J. and Richard M. Roberts
1993 The empirical study of figurative language in literature. *Poetics* 22: 151–169.
Kreuz, Roger J., Richard M. Roberts, Brenda K. Johnson and Eugenie L. Bertus
1996 Figurative language occurrence and co-occurrence in contemporary literature. In *Empirical Approaches to Literature and Aesthetics*, Roger J. Kreuz and Mary Sue MacNealy (eds.), 83–97. Norwood, NJ: Ablex.
Kreuz, Roger J., Max A. Kassler and Lori Coppenrath
1998 The use of exaggeration in discourse: Cognitive and social facets. In *Social and Cognitive Approaches to Interpersonal Communication*, Susan R. Fussell and Roger J. Kreuz (eds.), 91–111. Mahwah, NJ: Lawrence Erlbaum.
Lakoff, George and Mark Johnson
1980 *Metaphors We Live By*. Chicago, IL: University of Chicago Press.
Lausberg, Heinrich
1998 *Handbook of Literary Rhetoric: A Foundation for Literary Study*. Leiden: Brill.
Leary, Mark R.
1993 The interplay of private self-processes and interpersonal factors in self-presentation. In *Psychological Perspectives on the Self*, Vol. 4, Jerry Suls (ed.), 127–155. Hillsdale, NJ: Lawrence Erlbaum.
Leary, Mark R.
1995 *Self-presentation: Impression Management and Interpersonal Behavior*. Boulder, CO: Westview Press.
Leary, Mark R. and Robin M. Kowalski
1990 Impression management: A literature review and two-component model. *Psychological Bulletin* 107: 34–47.
Leech, Geoffrey N.
1983 *Principles of Pragmatics*. London: Longman.

Leezenberg, Michiel
2001 *Contexts of Metaphor*. Amsterdam: Elsevier.
Levinson, Stephen C.
2000 *Presumptive Meanings: The Theory of Generalized Conversational Implicature*. Cambridge, MA: MIT Press.
McCarthy, Michael and Ronald Carter
2004 "There's millions of them": Hyperbole in everyday conversation. *Journal of Pragmatics* 36: 149–184.
Nemesi, Attila L.
2004 What discourse goals can be accomplished by the use of hyperbole? *Acta Linguistica Hungarica* 51 (3–4): 351–378.
Nemesi, Attila L.
2009 *Az alakzatok kérdése a pragmatikában* [The issue of figurative language in pragmatics]. Budapest: Loisir.
Norrick, Neal R.
1982 On the semantics of overstatement. In *Sprache erkennen und verstehen*, Klaus Detering, Jürgen Schmidt-Radefeldt and Wolfgang Sucharowski (eds.), 168–176. Tübingen: Niemeyer.
Norrick, Neal R.
2004 Hyperbole, extreme case formulation. *Journal of Pragmatics* 36: 1727–1739.
Preminger, Alex and T. V. F. Brogan (eds.)
1993 *The New Princeton Encyclopedia of Poetry and Poetics*. Princeton, NJ: Princeton University Press.
Quintilian
1921 *Institutio Oratoria*. Cambridge, MA / London: Harvard University Press / William Heinemann Ltd.
Roberts, Richard M. and Roger J. Kreuz
1994 Why do people use figurative language? *Psychological Science* 5: 159–163.
Searle, John R.
1979 *Expression and Meaning: Studies in the Theory of Speech Acts*. Cambridge: Cambridge University Press.
Sell, Marie A., Roger J. Kreuz and Lori Coppenrath
1997 Parents' use of nonliteral language with preschool children. *Discourse Processes* 23: 99–118.
Sorea, Daniela
2009 Hyperbole and irony as sitcom props. In *Semantyka a konfrontacja językowa*, Vol. 4, Violetta Koseska-Toszewa and Roman Roszko (eds.). http://www.scribd.com/doc/12536990/DANIELA-SOREAHyperbole-and-Irony-as-Sitcom-Props.

Sperber, Dan and Deirdre Wilson
1990 Rhetoric and relevance. In *The Ends of Rhetoric: History, Theory, Practice*, John Bender and David Wellbery (eds.), 140–156. Stanford, CA: Stanford University Press.

Sperber, Dan and Deirdre Wilson
1995 *Relevance: Communication and Cognition.* 2nd edition. Oxford: Blackwell. Original edition: 1986.

Steen, Gerard J.
2007 *Finding Metaphor in Grammar and Usage: A Methodological Analysis of Theory and Research.* Amsterdam: John Benjamins.

Stewart, Craig O. and Roger J. Kreuz
2003 On the communicative function of exaggeration: How to be a million times clearer. *Communication Research Reports* 20: 331–340.

Verschueren, Jef
1999 *Understanding Pragmatics.* London: Arnold.

Wilson, Deirdre and Dan Sperber
1992 On verbal irony. *Lingua* 87: 53–76.

Winner, Ellen, Gail Windmueller, Elizabeth Rosenblatt, Laurie Bosco, Edella Best and Howard Gardner
1987 Making sense of literal and nonliteral falsehood. *Metaphor and Symbolic Activity* 2: 13–32.

Index